Preventing Chaos in a Crisis

Preventing Chaos in a Crisis

Strategies for prevention, control and damage limitation

Patrick Lagadec

**Translated by
Jocelyn M. Phelps**

McGRAW-HILL BOOK COMPANY
London · New York · St Louis · San Francisco · Auckland ·
Bogotá · Caracas · Hamburg · Lisbon · Madrid · Mexico ·
Milan · Montreal · New Delhi · Panama · Paris · San Juan ·
São Paulo · Singapore · Sydney · Tokyo · Toronto

Published by
McGRAW-HILL Book Company Europe
Shoppenhangers Road, Maidenhead, Berkshire, SL6 2QL, England
Telephone 0628 23432
Fax 0628 770224

British Library Cataloguing in Publication Data
Lagadec, Patrick
  Preventing Chaos in a Crisis: Strategies
  for Prevention, Control and Damage
  Limitation
  I. Title
  658.4

  ISBN 0-07-707774-1

Library of Congress Cataloging-in-Publication Data
Lagadec, Patrick.
  Preventing chaos in a crisis: strategies for prevention, control,
  and damage limitation / Patrick Lagadec.
    p. cm.
  Includes bibliographical references and index.
  ISBN 0-07-707774-1
  1. Crisis management. I. Title.
HD49.L33 1993
658.4—dc20   92-33415
                                                                  CIP

1234 CUP 9543

Typeset by BookEns Limited, Baldock, Herts.
Printed and bound in Great Britain at the University Press, Cambridge.

Contents

Part 3 Learning about crisis

Preface: tools for thinking about, preventing, and managing crisis

Crises and their contexts

Crisis has many faces: Bhopal, Chernobyl, Seveso, waste dumps, the *Exxon-Valdez*; evacuations of a Toronto suburb, flooding in southern France, threats to the drinking water supply in London, structural flaws in the design of a whole public housing project or a school building; major public health crises, ranging from a sudden jump in air pollution levels that threatens to bring urban life to a standstill, to flu outbreaks, the AIDS epidemic, or widespread food poisoning.

More generally, we live surrounded by installations or vehicles that generate major risks (Lagadec, 1981*a*, *b*). Vast energy, information, and supply networks are vital for many systems that have no alternative means of survival should a somewhat serious failure occur. We are confronted with economic and social tensions that avoid degenerating into chaos because they are propped up daily by impressive balancing acts; but at any moment, for a random or even minor reason, they can explode into crises that overwhelm everyone involved. To this must be added the real or perceived changes in our broader environment, such as global warming or urban decay. These, too, have the means to trigger seriously destabilizing crises. Throw in the risks of criminal or terrorist acts, and the picture begins to emerge in all its complexity. Furthermore, any event occurring today becomes part of a highly sensitive context: the public is terribly aware of safety issues, and it senses vaguely that our systems hang by a thread; the media project the slightest information or rumour immediately, on an unprecedented scale.

Not a week goes by that is not marked by the violent eruption of this type of often explosive and always awkward situation. It calls for specific responses, yet it occurs in a disturbingly complex context in which every move seems to backfire. What do you do in the middle of the cyclone, when your compass is broken and the media whirlwind is blowing a confusing situation into a huge drama? This is the urgent question facing many decision makers and organizations. Today our societies seem to be, if not more dangerous, at least more vulnerable and unstable than ever before.

No effort will be made here to convince those who are most sceptical about the gravity of the situation, but we have clearly entered an era of strong turbulence and crisis on a previously unknown scale— even though every age of human existence has had its hardships.

Goals of this book

In *States of Emergency* (Lagadec, 1988), we presented a series of ideas collected from key actors involved in recent major post-accident crises. This was probably the first time that so many European and North American managers—as well as participants and direct observers representing victims, experts, journalists, leading political figures, union leaders, organizational and communications consultants, specialized researchers, and militant social critics—agreed to talk openly and in detail about what were often painful experiences. Their testimony has not, however, stemmed the quest for understanding, or for know-how.

The publication of that book triggered numerous requests urging us to focus resolutely on the operational aspects, and to provide key guidelines for managing a crisis, whether caused by a technological incident or, more generally, any disruptive episode that poses a threat to an organization. Many top managers suffer from a cruel lack of decision-making tools adapted to such exceptional circumstances. Yet these are precisely the situations that are most difficult and most dangerous for all the investments made in the past, and the most determining for the future.

This book seeks to satisfy these requests. Though it continues the work of attaining an in-depth understanding of the crisis phenomenon, which is indispensable for building a strategy, its vital focus is on taking action. It tackles the question of what a manager facing a crisis needs to know, and how to react to this type of situation.

The research undertaken across the world on this subject has begun to lay some useful groundwork. The efforts made by some major organizations to prevent or prepare for crisis situations comprise a first database of experience that can be used to move towards a diagnosis and proposed solutions.

This point actually serves to highlight a different type of emerging threat: those who stay on the sidelines of these efforts may not survive very long in a rough situation, faced with competition from actors who are better prepared. In both Europe and North America, it has been observed that the leading organizations in this field are getting a considerable head start. This gives them a decisive strategic advantage in the event of a crisis: they understand the subject intellectually and have made the fundamental adaptations (in terms of technical and organizational tools, and especially business culture). This grants them an immediate and enduring supremacy.

As a result, the requests become more insistent: *What do we do, then, to prevent and manage crisis?*

Immediately a clear choice had to be made between two alternatives. The first approach would have been to write a guide, similar to others that already exist (see, for example, ten Berge, 1990; Fink, 1986; Meyers and Holusha, 1986; Regester, 1989; Kharbanda and Stallworthy, 1987), which would offer the decision maker some basic answers. For many reasons, which will become clear in the next chapter, we abandoned this approach.

The other option was to portray as closely as possible the complexity and ambiguity of crisis situations, and to suggest tools for thinking about them and offer means to ask questions—and, of course, to provide the answers that have already been tested, with all their limitations, on the best-known aspects of the issue. This is the approach adopted here.

The target of this book is the decision maker who is faced with a difficult situation: the first requirement is not a first-aid kit, but the means of sharpening the decision maker's judgment. This requires not only providing answers, but also broadening horizons and focusing thoughts in order to go beyond simply becoming aware of the problems involved. Then and only then is it possible to think about strategic responses to the outbreak of a crisis.

The task is not to provide some sort of multi-risk insurance; instead, it is to work simultaneously to reassure those involved by establishing some fundamental guidelines, and to encourage both individuals and the group to start innovating with courage and creativity.

Preventing Chaos in a Crisis simultaneously pursues three goals which are hard to separate: identifying the fundamental problems that characterize the crisis landscape and crisis management; developing a basic tool for strategic orientation in order to respond to a crisis situation; and formulating proposals to help managers design, undertake, and organize the learning process that cannot be circumvented in such a new field, marked as it is by continuous events calling for ongoing efforts to adapt.

How this book is organized

This book is logically organized around these three goals. It comprises three main parts.

1 *What is a crisis?* This first section describes the essential elements of crisis dynamics and the major issues that confront managers. Naming these difficulties and situating the general theatre of operations provides an indispensable starting point that is directly applicable to the situation.

2 *How do you manage a crisis?* This is the heart of the book. The discussion focuses on three critical moments in responding to a crisis: the *initial phase*, in which the danger is that you will be immediately discredited; the *thinking and mobilizing phase*, which should give you a foothold on the slippery surface of the crisis and should shape your response until the end of the challenge; and the *strategic action phase*, which corresponds to managing the crisis, at least in the narrowest sense of the term.

3 *How do you develop a learning process for the individuals, teams, and organizations involved, in order to prevent crises?* This section sets some guidelines for undertaking and developing the learning process in this field, as a growing number of institutions are seeking to do today.

A preliminary chapter sets the stage for this ensemble. It serves to situate more clearly the tasks and the approach used. In this work, we have simply applied the rule that is essential in handling any crisis situation: *always take the time to define both the problems and their context, and always force yourself to ask questions first and to take some critical distance before plunging into action.*

Three things remain to be specified in order better to outline the task at hand.

First: the ground to be covered. On the one hand, the phenomena discussed here are clearly situated in time: the typical case involves a sudden breakdown, even if its effects are felt over the long run.

Much less attention is paid to so-called crises lasting an indefinite period of time, e.g. the agricultural crisis or the economic crisis. On the other hand, this book starts from the field in which we have the greatest experience, i.e. crises related to technological breakdowns, but it opens to analyse a much broader area. The approach taken here does, however, focus primarily on non-conflictual crises rather than on crises involving issues like terrorism, war, takeover attempts, massive lay-offs, or factory closures. Nevertheless, the diagnosis and the proposals made here may be largely useful, if not directly applicable, to managing such conflictual crises. In fact, many references and proposals employed here have been drawn from these areas.

Second: how to use this book. It seeks to provide both a tool for preparation and a support for thinking about a present situation. It is important to emphasize, however, that *the thought process during critical moments cannot be validly developed unless the people and systems involved have been prepared in depth*. The first task of this book, then, is to contribute to this prior effort to adapt to the foreign environment created by crisis. This should not prevent users from finding a tool here for immediate management assistance. In situation, users can turn to the first part of the book to remind themselves, if need be, of the many difficulties they may see arise in the course of events; the second part may then be used not so much to find solutions, as has been indicated, but to enhance a thought process that always runs the risk of being oversimplified in troubled periods.

Third: to whom is this book addressed? Clearly, the book's primary public are the decision makers. (In this text, the term 'decision maker' does not refer to a specific individual, but rather to the person(s) who must make decisions during a crisis situation.) Whether they are from the public or private sector, with regional or national responsibilities, working in public administration or municipal government, they are the people on whom everyone counts to handle these crisis situations. If they start to look weak, everyone else suffers that much more.

Preventing Chaos in a Crisis was also written for all the other actors concerned by these difficult situations: victims, journalists, experts, consultants, employees, union leaders, political leaders, associations, and the person on the street. Anyone who may be implicated in one way or another by a crisis should be legitimately interested in the guidelines and techniques that exist for handling these situations as well as possible. Also, being well informed on all sides—even on opposing sides—is a vital necessity in order to avoid the extremist attitudes and the slip-ups caused by misunderstanding. It is important that everyone recognizes the ordinary difficulties inherent in this type of situation and how they can be approached and dealt with. Equally important is realizing how we may be perceived by others, since everyone is a player in the crisis game. For these purely tactical reasons, the learning process cannot stop with the decision makers. Everyone will have personal decisions to make, personal organizations to direct, and relations to establish and maintain with the authority in charge. Crisis management is not merely management at the top, or a monopoly of some commander-in-chief.

At a deeper level, this approach is part of a perspective that does not involve management alone. It raises a flurry of fundamental questions that cannot be excluded from the debate.

At the heart of any crisis lie questions about power and how it is used. Handling a crisis is first and foremost a matter of making judgements, redefining standards, establishing options, defining strategies, remodelling power relationships, and sticking with a position—all this when the conventional framework has become completely obsolete.

In a crisis situation, we approach the future gravely and with a necessarily more narrow point of view than is normally the case. To give an extreme analogy, if an airplane pilot, when approaching the critical lift-off speed (which is actually called the 'decision speed'), notices that one of the engines is out, he or she will not take that opportunity to start wide-ranging discussions before deciding whether to lift off or hit the emergency brakes. What happens in those moments does not represent solely the momentary whims of one person: for the most part, the reflexes that come into play are based on prior preparation. This explains precisely why much more open reflexes must be developed. Of course, there are many other, less extreme situations that are not concentrated in a single pair of hands—and there, in contrast, it is vital to open up the thought process.

Clearly, it is impossible to ignore these issues of power sharing and democratic process when discussing crisis management.

As we have already seen, there are no short cuts in handling this subject. But patient individuals can take solace in the fact that there is simply no other way to tackle a crisis. Worse yet, crises exploit those miracle solutions that are supposed to deflate them—indeed, they feed off them with an application matched only by their perverseness.

Reader's guide

If you wish to know more about the general research being done in this field and to understand better the underlying difficulties involved in crisis management, turn to the Introduction which explains the methodology used here.

If you want to focus on the operational results derived from research, go directly to the beginning of Part 1. You may also skip the beginning of Chapter 4, which discusses the meaning of the concept of crisis.

Acknowledgements for the French edition

This book owes a great deal to a great many people, teams and organizations in France, Europe and throughout the world. Unfortunately, I cannot cite them all here.

Gérar Renon (French Secretary of State for Defence, previously in charge of major technological and natural risks) and Claude Frantzen (Director of the Aeronautical Training and Technical Control of Department at the General Direction of Civil Aviation) encouraged me to write a practical guide for managers facing crises. Without their friendly insistence, I probably would not have undertaken this venture. In this decision, I am also indebted to Alain Nadaud (specialist in audio-visual adaptations) for his encouragement.

William Dab (doctor, Professor at France's Ecole Nationale de Santé Publique, and a specialist in emergency epidemiology), Claude Henry (Professor of Public Economics at Ecole Polytechnique), Claude Gilbert (researcher at CNRS, the French National Centre for Scientific Research, where I have recently assumed responsibility for co-leading GDR–Crise, the CNRS research group on crisis and major risk which will be occasionally referred to in this book), Bernard Magnon (engineer at Electricité de France), and Maurice Sadoulet all gave me their support and their wise advice from the first outline to the final phase of this project.

Joseph Scanlon (Professor of Journalism at Carleton University in Ottawa, Director of a Research Centre on Crisis Communications, and Professor at the Canadian Police College), and later Enrico Quarantelli (founder of Disaster Research Center, the world's largest study centre on catastrophe issues) agreed to work on the first versions of the manuscript in France.

Philippe Vesseron (Deputy Director of the French Institute for Nuclear Protection and Security and former technical advisor to Michel Crépeau and Huguette Bouchardeau at the French Ministry of the Environment), Péter-J. Hargitay (Chairman of Hargitay & Partners, Zurich) and Rolf Kaiser (an OECD expert who has spent recent years working in Paris) were of invaluable help to me.

I was also able to count on Philippe Dessaint (journalist and consultant) with whom I have led numerous training and simulation seminars on crisis situations and how to handle them.

To discuss the issue of victims, I benefited from the efficient assistance of Karine Robak (President of the Association for the Defence of Victims of Dioxins and Furans) and Françoise Rudetzki (President of SOS–Attentats), as well as that of Claude Peyrat and Colette Bonnivard (victims of a 1986 terrorist attack in Paris).

Daniel Verpeaux (General Manager) and Bertrand Robert (Manager of the Crisis Division) at the Francom Group included me in numerous business consulting projects wihch have left their mark on this work.

Nor can I forget the following persons who, among others, lent me their support: Lucien Abenhaim (Professor at McGill University in Montreal); Robert Andurand (aide to the Director of Security at the Institute for Nuclear Protection and Security); Marie-Catherine Bovis (philosopher); Micheline Colin (army medical officer, head physician, and deputy to the Firefighting and Rescue Department of the Rhône district, France); Jean-François David (consultant at Euréquip); Geneviève Decrop (associate with GDR–Crise); Jean-Luc Delpeuch (civil engineer, formerly Manager of the Environment Division of DRIR for the PACA region); Thierry Dubuis (engineer at DRIR for Nord-Pas-de-Calais); Nicole Fabre (psychoanalyst); Jean Fabre (former General Controller at Electricité de France and founding Director of CEPRIG, the centre for the Study and Advancement of Industrial Research and Management); Jacques Fournier (CFDT union representative to the High Council of Classified Industrial Installations); Roger Grollier-Baron ('safety-reliability' consultant to the Director of the Institut français du pétrole); Philippe Legorjus (former Commander of French SWAT forces and the author of *La Morale et l'Action*); Joseph Moingt (theologian); Henri Ollagnon (French Minister of Agriculture); Kim Ottavi (interpreter); François Régnault (consultant at Alentour); Philippe Rocard (Head of the Industrial Environment Department at the French Ministry of the Environment); Philippe Roqueplo (Research Director at CNRS); Monique and Raymond Sené (French group of scientists for information on nuclear energy); Marie-Pierre Touron (associate with

GDR–Crise); Lars Weisaeth (Catastrophe Psychiatry Division at the Medical School of the University of Oslo).

Françoise Ballanger and Pascale Robert-Diard contributed all their skill to re-reading the manuscript.

I would also like to thank Florence Fabre, Eliane Nitiga and Lucie Soquet for their material assistance, and I will never forget the hospitality of Max and Fernande Dutillieux, who surrounded me with the calm essential for the first drafts.

Of course, I alone am responsible for this book and its contents, and for its inadequacies and any errors in it.

This work received financial support from the Industrial Environment Department of the French Ministry of the Environment.

It was based at the Econometrics Laboratory of Ecole Polytechnique, Paris, France, which is now directed by Michel Balinski, and where Claude Henry took me in 1977 in order to carry out interdisciplinary research on the subject of major contemporary risks.

Acknowledgements for the English-language edition

Jocelyn Phelps is to be thanked for her competence in translating this book.

I would especially like to thank Rhône-Poulenc for the financial support it has provided, making the translation of this book possible.

This contribution to the dissemination of knowledge is a sign of the importance that this international group attributes to the emerging issue of crisis prevention and crisis management.

Rhône-Poulenc's interest and support are yet another example of the spirit that has characterized the many fruitful contacts I have had with its management in recent years. They also reflect the efforts Rhône-Poulenc has made in the field of risk prevention and crisis preparedness. As is demonstrated by several of the case studies in this book, Rhône-Poulenc has been a major innovator in developing procedures for rapid mobilization in the event of incidents or accidents—innovations including technical responses as well as communications.

From the beginning, Pascale Flambry took charge of this project, managing to re-read and correct the manuscript without ever losing her temper. Many thanks to her.

Extracts from:

Charles F. Hermann (editor), *International Crises: Insights From Behavioral Research*. Copyright © 1972 reprinted with permission of The Free Press, a Division of Macmillan, Inc.

Theodore C. Sorensen, *Decision Making In the White House*. Copyright © 1963 Columbia University Press: New York. Used by permission of the publisher.

Michihiko Hachiya (edited and translated by Warner Wells). *Hiroshima*

Introduction: prior questions— the demand and the goal

An acute need and scattered knowledge

The 1960s were characterized by the problem of change: stability was less and less an appropriate reference in a world in which the pace of technological innovation kept accelerating. The 1990s seem to offer up a new challenge: crisis. Major accidents, worldwide threats, organizational breakdowns, collapsing systems, and cultural diversity are no longer the exceptions they once were. With increasingly troublesome regularity, they are harshly trying for everyone concerned, and especially for those in positions of responsibility. Of course, managing large systems has always been something of a balancing act. Of course, major crises have occurred in the past, and the study of crisis is not a brand new discipline—the Cuban Missile crisis of 1962 is often considered to be a critical date in the history of the field. Yet the way the First World War was triggered, and even the plague that decimated Europe in the Middle Ages and shook the world are also important examples of crisis.

Today, however, the organization of human societies seems to have reached a degree of complexity such that even strategic management no longer appears to be possible.

In a world of uncertainty and vulnerability, all it takes is one detail, one threat, one rumour, and everything seems to crumble into unmanageable chaos.

Igor Ansoff, one of the fathers of strategic management, has recently emphasized the need to rethink the basic concepts behind the way organizations are managed. Large systems, he argues, are increasingly dependent on their overall environment, which in turn is going through ever more complex and radical changes. A few decades ago it was enough to carry out after-the-fact controls because the pace of change was sufficiently slow. As the pace picked up, it became necessary to operate by extrapolation, and then by anticipation as discontinuities became too sharp. But the situation has become more difficult: today, flexible and rapid answers are required, and they must often be activated in response to weak signals that are difficult to interpret. Managers must follow not only the general trends, but also the specific events that can change the course of these trends. It is no longer enough to have contingency plans in order to take up the slack in long-range planning; it has become necessary to deal with complexity and discontinuity both as general laws and as challenges concentrated in a specific event (Ansoff and McDonnell, 1990, pp. 3–25, 467–85).

It is easy to understand why decision makers are increasingly interested in finding new ways to respond to these challenges. What is to be done? How can new guidelines be established?

The first step in finding useful references for action is to look at those decision makers who have successfully taken charge of this type of phenomenon. Their experience can be an incomparably rich source of information—which we have often used, especially in this work. The accounts of these decision makers are also useful because they are constant reminders of the complexity of these matters and of how carefully any model must be evaluated. But simply drawing on experience is not enough. In fact, in this area several problems frequently arise, and it is important to be aware of them. In an interview (Lagadec, 1990, pp. 222ff) Enrico Quarantelli explains that an actor generally has only a limited amount of experience, from which he or she may well try to make generalizations. In fact, he or she may actually draw the wrong conclusions from this 'battle experience', yet will cling to them with irrational fervour. To use a metaphor developed by Enrico Quarantelli, 'military strategy is based not on war memories but on systematic analysis of the situations. The same applies to crisis: everybody can think of interesting anecdotes, but that is not the way you learn to win wars'. Such actors can only speak for one point of view—their own, which is not even necessarily representative of their organization as a whole. This heightens the danger of one ever-present risk: that of reasoning in terms of the past, when a crisis is most often a confrontation with a new set of givens.

Another approach is to turn to the wealth of scientific knowledge available on the subject. The purpose of research is, after all, to give shape to a more general understanding by taking into account observations of a wide variety of situations.

This second tack also has its limits: it again involves a degree of compartmentalization, between disciplines in this case. But above all, it highlights two diverging perspectives: the studies available tend to be oriented more towards describing and outlining a field than towards providing operational guidelines. And thinking, even in detail, about just one (carefully delimited) aspect of the many facets of the crisis phenomenon is simply not what the decision maker is looking for. Unlike the analyst, the decision maker must be able to grasp all the elements of a system and assume responsibility over the long run for the multiple consequences and potential side effects of the actions taken. This points up the difference between an expert and a decision maker: the former can be satisfied with making very specific, limited diagnoses, while the latter must integrate many elements—the most difficult thing to do in a crisis situation.

What are the various trends in scientific research that a decision maker can turn to? It is worth taking a moment to consider this field of scientific expertise, in which this book and its ideas have their place.

The field of technological risk is a good starting point. The broader current of risk analysis provided the first basis for a discussion of the social issues of risk, and more specifically, major technological risks (Lagadec, 1979a, b), a concept which we introduced in the late 1970s. The purpose of this concept is both to describe the necessity for a fundamental reconsideration of the issue of industrial safety and, more specifically, to anticipate the challenge of post-accident crises (Lagadec, 1981a, b). The references in this field are constantly increasing.

Outside of this specific field, the primary resource is the immense wealth of knowledge accumulated over the past 30 years by sociologists working on group and organizational behaviour in post-catastrophe situations. In particular, Enrico Quarantelli, Russel Dynes and their colleagues at the Disaster Research Center in the United States have been working for more than 30 years in the world's largest research centre devoted to this topic. They have studied more than 500 disasters and accidents of all types, on every continent, and they are the focal point of a network of correspondents ranging from Europe to Japan and from China to South America (Lagadec, 1990, pp. 222–31).

In this same tradition, numerous other sociological studies focus on communication in crisis situations, and especially the work done by

Joseph Scanlon at the journalism school of Carleton University in Ottawa.

In a closely related field, and one which is actually tending to draw closer to this sociological line, the geographers' approach was introduced by Gilbert White at the University of Chicago in the early 1950s and has now been adopted by the University of Colorado at Boulder. Originally, these geographers were interested in the physical aspects of phenomena such as floods (the subject of White's thesis). They gradually turned to the problems upline from these natural disasters: prevention and damage control efforts. Their work focuses less on the paroxysmal moment of the crisis than on the pre-crisis period—a phase that deserves a place in any comprehensive planning done on crisis issues.

Another deep-rooted tradition, though in a very different register, is that of specialists in international relations. Most notably, they produced the first attempts to develop theories on the crisis concept (including the article published in 1968 by James Robinson in the *International Encyclopedia for Social Sciences*) and developed models of the decision-making process in crisis situations. The best-known research was done by Graham Allison of Harvard University on the Cuban Missile crisis (Allison, 1971) and by the Mershon Center group at Ohio State University (Hermann, Robinson, Milburn and others, whose work will be examined later). These studies are being pursued today in a range of venues, from universities to governmental or private-sector analytical centres such as the Rand Corporation, and the work is often carried out in close collaboration with the United States Department of Defense (Perez, 1988). This provides for a stimulating examination of decision making in very high-stake crisis situations of the type that large, complex systems can encounter.

Another deep-rooted and very specific source is that of psychologists interested in problems of mental health in general, and more particularly in therapeutic treatment of individuals in stressful situations. This research has been supplemented by psycho-sociological studies on small groups. This work done on both individuals and small groups cannot be neglected; it plays a central role in crisis management, as will be seen later.

More recently, administrative and management science have become interested in this field, as indicated by the remarks of Igor Ansoff. (See also such works as Peters, 1989; Drucker, 1980; Ansoff and McDonnell, 1990.) Other scholars working more directly in the area of crisis management include Alexander Kouzmin (Kouzmin and Jarman, 1989), a professor of management in Canberra, Australia, Ian Mitroff, director of the Center for Crisis Management and professor of management at the University of Southern California, and Thierry Pauchant, a professor at HEC in Montreal (Mitroff and Kilmann, 1984; Mitroff *et al.*, 1988).

This is, of course, only a rapid overview. In many disciplines today, efforts to tackle the issue of extreme situations are emerging and taking shape. In the longer run, much can be hoped for as some of these fields, jealous of their specificity, nevertheless draw closer together. The geographers are moving closer and closer to the sociologists. Administrative science is discovering the variety of work that has been done by organizational behaviour specialists on catastrophe situations. In the past, various efforts were made to bring together researchers from related disciplines around this field—Charles Hermann (1972) provided such a focus in international relations, as did Edgar Morin (1976) in the area of social sciences. Today bridges have been built between different disciplines. In the past few years, teams and individuals have begun to acknowledge each other and to develop connections and structures. This has enabled the development of 'melting pots' of knowledge, experience, and expertise. Such is the purpose of the international conferences organized by the Industrial Crisis Institute in New York under the impetus of Paul Shrivastava, a professor of management and author of an in-depth study of the Bhopal case (1987*a*). These conferences bring together scholars, consultants, and managers from government and the private sector. Uriel Rosenthal and his team in the Netherlands also have the merit today of working to weave together the many fields of knowledge by breaking down barriers between disciplines. In the recent past, they demonstrated to scientific researchers how the issue of crisis could provide a means to bridge two sorts of gaps: between disciplines which have individual theoretical outlooks and research backgrounds, and between real life and laboratory experience (Rosenthal *et al.*, 1989, p. 6).

Great strides remain to be made before all those who work on one aspect or another of crisis can begin combining their efforts. Among the groups that could be brought into the circle are physicians in the field of disaster medicine and emergency epidemiology, who often have excellent references to share.

This book fits into this general trend. It draws from the experience of researchers as well as managers, from consultants and journalists, from specialists and victims. Our purpose was to delve into this multi-form wealth of knowledge while holding fast to two ideals: constantly to deepen the fundamental understanding of these phenomena, and to assume the comprehensive point of view of decision makers. As was indicated above, these are people who need not so much to dissect reality as to be able to act on it and shape it.

A demand to be handled with caution

But before undertaking to provide a response for decision makers, it is only honest to point out several reasons to be prudent about this exercise.

From the very beginning of our work in this field, we found one striking metaphor for it: a crisis situation is like a kaleidoscope. If you touch the smallest element in it, the entire structure is altered. Consequently, the crisis resists attempts to simplify it. It requires strategic judgement more than predefined tactical responses. How, then, is it possible to produce a management guide built around finger-tip references developed for emergency specialists? These people need above all to make specific, quick, and clearly defined gestures. This tool could even prove dangerous for anyone in a difficult situation who was simply looking for a rule book.

Yet another reservation arises because the atmosphere of crises is never transparent. How is it possible, then, to discuss them when to a large extent we stand outside the corridors of power where these issues are being wrestled with directly?

Does this demand for answers not sometimes hide a secret desire to find an easy way around a serious obstacle which deserves more than a rapid-reference user's guide? There is a degree of hubris in wanting to find simple, clear, comprehensive responses to these questions that destabilize both decision makers and academics. Before anyone can deduce a brilliant universal law, large-scale investments in theory are called for. The real task is to comb through a range of disciplines or theoretical approaches (e.g. political science, decision-making science, administrative science, organizational theory, psychology, sociology, social psychology, law, ergonomics, cognitive sciences), and to see what they can tell us about borderline situations, how they can work together on a terrain that defies any partial approach, and how they can function, taken separately or together, in an emergency setting. Only then is it even vaguely possible to begin making recommendations.

Is there not also good reason to fear the consequences of overly effective crisis management tools? The already insufficient efforts at risk prevention, anticipation, and control of vulnerability would be reduced even further. Is there not a further danger that these tools would serve first and foremost to bury and repress the real issues, of which crisis is sometimes a helpful symptom? And no one can underestimate the risk that some will use these arms to their own ends, in order to reinforce the status quo.

These are not imaginary concerns. The individuals who bear responsibility are so eager for solutions that any response whose limits are not clearly understood can become a recipe for disaster. Take the case of terrorism, for instance: if the theory is incomplete, it can spell death for numerous victims. Even if the theory is good, it may still lead to failure if the terrorists learn it faster than the decision makers.

Clearly, these reservations are not only of an intellectual order. In fact, those with whom we have worked for years in corporate settings admit that they are less and less confident about the actions they take. Some managers have discovered, much to their chagrin, that they could furnish very good communications about, say, a food contamination problem that proved to be a false alert—and that within the week, they would have to deal with dozens of malevolent and very real acts of the same type. Yet another example is the broadcasting of the spectacular images created by forest fires— fascinating images that have pointed numerous latent arsonists towards their vocation.

This is actually nothing more than a well-known principle in another field full of surprises: warfare. As Li Ch'uang wrote in a commentary on Sun Tzu's *The Art of War*, 'There are no set rules. The rules can only be established according to the circumstances' (1972). This explains why many experts remain non-committal. Nevertheless, the reasons for forging ahead are stronger than those for lingering in doubt.

The tool offered to decision makers need not take the form of a user's guide. In this way, it avoids the risk of fostering dangerous simplifications.

There is no reason why the leaders wrestling directly with an event should be the only ones capable of formulating proposals to handle the issue. In fact, they often lack the time, objectivity, and motivation to do so. Research-consultants can be the ideal people to tackle this challenge, provided, of course, that they draw more from their practical experience than from their theoretical background, and that they call on their networks of hands-on actors as much as on their scientific colleagues. They are then in a position to work from a much larger base than could any decision maker, even one who knows 'everything' about a clearly delimited sector.

On subjects whose importance can be so vital, it is difficult for ethical reasons (if for no other) to keep putting off the issue until tomorrow and waiting for a good general theory, an almost perfect method for risk and vulnerability prevention, or a society so in harmony that new tools may be introduced without threatening any of the actors. There comes a point when this wait-and-see attitude becomes suspicious: it actually satisfies the temptation to hold onto models so cut off from reality that they do not force anyone to take risks, or raise any ethical issues.

There are risks involved in establishing any diagnosis, and even more so in making any recommendations. But these should not paralyse us. The sole guideline should be to practise moderation and always be aware of one's limits.

It is also important to recognize clearly that not all the difficulties can be eliminated. Crisis is by nature an ambiguous landscape. There is no such thing as a final answer. The closest we can come is by remaining constantly vigilant about new discoveries and how they may be used.

An intellectual challenge

When facing the crisis phenomenon—a situation which seems to pose urgent and virtually insurmountable, or at least very difficult, problems—your most immediate reaction will be a feeling of unease, which quickly turns to giddiness.

The uneasiness arises before a situation that first emerges as a cascade of negatives, which Uriel Rosenthal summarizes as 'un-ness': 'unexpected, unscheduled, unprecedented, and almost unmanageable' (Rosenthal *et al.*, 1989, p. 5). As Rosenthal further notes, the victims of 'un-ness' find themselves suddenly yanked out of their daily routine and thrown into a world in which the line between opportunities for brilliant success and crushing defeat is very thin.

The uneasy feeling is also caused by a reality that always seems to escape human comprehension as well as action. Analysts must begin by acknowledging that they are incapable of mentally circumscribing such an extreme, out-of-scale, aberrant set of facts. When they think they have a grip on one part of the crisis, it slithers off in another direction. Why? The theoretical understanding is insufficient; and perhaps more fundamentally, one of the constitutional features of crisis is that it refuses to be pinned down.

Where can you turn? To science? As was indicated above, the situation in this field is changing, and scientific knowledge is now of greater help. But outside specialized circles, doubts and barriers remain, and they are a source of hesitation and distress, as our Dutch colleague wisely states: 'Scientists do not feel at ease with those events and developments which seem to be at odds with the neat and tidy theories they have based on "normal" circumstances and environments. Crises seem to be in perfect contrast with the very assets of modern social science' (Rosenthal et al., 1989). Edgar Morin made the same point as early as 1972: 'There is no science of the exception, there is no science of unusual events' (p. 6). As a result, there is no solid scientific tradition to lean on (progress has been made in some areas, such as René Thom's catastrophe theory, or chaos theory, but the practical applications are still very uncertain).

Furthermore, analysts do not hesitate to proclaim their limitations. It is interesting here to consider the precious experience acquired in the field of international crisis, and in particular to listen to one of the specialists in this arena, Coral Bell (1978, pp. 50–2) of the University of Sussex. Her message is far-reaching and worth dwelling on for a moment:

> International crises are normally confluences of decisions which flow from many disparate sources, some of them as remote and obscure as underground rivers, only reaching the surface of historical visibility at the moment of crisis. To theorize about them, even to ask questions about them, is therefore always to a certain extent to risk comparing like with unlike. There is no symmetry about the events with which we shall be concerned from which we might say with any certainty, or even plausibility, that all crisis decision making by governments tends to take this or that form. Even the notions of 'a decision' and 'the decision maker' often look like mirages as we approach the actual event. [. . .]
>
> [Various examples] provide a useful caution against any supposition that crisis management could be reduced to a set of rules or theorems, which could be taught to policy makers. Such

successes as one may historically discern in crisis management derive from historical imagination, intellectual creativity, and a capacity for perceptive response to the signals of the other side. I doubt that these qualities can be taught, and indeed I would argue that the effort to base response on a system of rules and precedents may have effects of a very counter-productive sort. [. . .]

Crisis management must certainly be thought of as an art or craft, not a science, and as in other arts, success may depend on the imaginative capacity to disregard rules and precedents. I would therefore be doubtful of any ambitious effort to attain a high level of abstraction in the analysis of crisis. Abstraction requires simplification: to simplify realities that are in fact very complex is to falsify them. Dr. Kissinger once wrote 'History is more complicated than systems analysis', and it might well serve as a motto for the crisis manager.

Even the term 'crisis management' is rather worrying, for the overtones of the word 'management' imply a rational, dispassionate, calculating, well considered activity, conducted with judgement and perhaps even at a leisurely pace with a view to long term as against short term interests. Actual crisis decision making is not usually at all like that: it is improvised at great pressure of time and events by men working in a fog of ambiguity. Perhaps it might better have been called 'crisis bargaining' or crisis diplomacy, since those terms do not carry such a freight of implication that everything is under control.

Despite all these warnings, Bell offers a clear message: it remains 'necessary that the dynamics of a car in a skid should be analyzed, and practical rules devised for its management'.

Can you turn to experience instead? Then the uneasiness becomes even greater. The only patterns that produced 'good' results in another situation threaten to exact a terrific cost in the apparently similar case at hand. Or you may choose to adopt an approach opposite to one that produced unpleasant consequences elsewhere—only to find that these contrasting guidelines are equally unsuccessful.

Besides, how is it possible to take into account the infinite variety of crises—post-accident crisis, labour crisis, financial crisis, and others? Even within the sole field of technological accidents, the difficulties are legion. It is humbling to see how inevitably we become victims of the tricks and traps of crisis: expert chemists predicted that a given type of situation had the potential to produce at most a serious accident (a few dozen victims), and then Bhopal occurred, with thousands of dead and tens of thousands of victims in critical condition.

Attitudes and safety measures had barely been reviewed in the light of Three Mile Island (1979) when along came Chernobyl (1986), an event that overwhelmed all the hypotheses imagined. Yet, on the other hand, consider a case like the false cloud of toxic gas in Nantes, France (1987): the incident took place at a facility that was not classified as exceptionally dangerous, and it led to a very real evacuation—the biggest ever carried out in France in peace time (Gilbert, 1988, 1991). And while planners worry over the idea of large-scale accidents, a case like the askarel contamination of a building in Reims, France (1985) is allowed to turn into a quagmire.

What about handling crises in the field of consumer safety? There was the imaginary problem with Perrier (1990), which figured in a real economic battle with tremendous business issues at stake. The battle simply shifted onto the public health terrain for the space of a few weeks—usually a minefield, but in this case unusually safe, as the health risk was, most exceptionally, non-existent. Very shortly thereafter came the Katellroc affair in Brittany (1990), in which a laboratory was accused of unjustly attacking a small mineral water business in the region. The facts revealed that the laboratory's results were accurate, but in any case the company was on the verge of bankruptcy. The real crisis here was not the more visible one, and the apparent crisis may actually have been merely a clever ruse.

And if we wish to create an even greater disturbance we can consider the case of the announcement made in the United States that a French pharmaceutical laboratory had discovered a miracle drug against AIDS. This false good news quickly became a real crisis for the laboratory. Then there was the grapefruit crisis in Italy in April 1988:

The case of the blue grapefruit (April 1988): the fear of malevolent food poisoning
A call to boycott Israeli products was launched at the doors of a supermarket in the Rome area by young people distributing pamphlets that read, 'Don't buy Jaffa grapefruit. Boycott Israel.' Shortly thereafter, six stained grapefruit were found: was the colouring methylene blue? Cyanide? Everyone supposed the fruits were harmless . . . until they killed five laboratory rats. To make matters worse, the results of the analysis were withheld for six days before being released. The city of Rome quarantined all grapefruit from Jaffa. Its example was followed by the Piedmont region, then Lombardy. The Italian minister of health extended the measure to the entire country: 7 000 000 kg of

grapefruit were impounded. The alert reached the European level.

With hindsight, there was no need to sound the alarm throughout Europe. There had been no massive poisoning, and though it is true that five unfortunate rats had died, one particular property of the fruit had been neglected: grapefruit, even when perfectly edible, kills these animals in any case when they consume the fruit in a fasting state (Vermont, 1988 and additional interview with author). The *Corriere della Sera* concluded, 'The tale of the grapefruit lost a great deal of its dramatic appeal along the way: there is no longer any question of an international conspiracy, and probably none of poisoning. At most, experts today go so far as to say there may have been a moderately toxic substance involved. Little more than a stupid joke inflicted on everybody by four extremists from the suburbs. But since everyone has delicate nerves, these six grapefruit in Casalbrucciato were the talk of a good part of the planet, from Tokyo to New York' (Gallo, 1988, p. 7). In case anyone should rush to conclude that the case was closed, the newspaper reported two terrible pieces of news on the same page: 'In Florence, a woman drinks a fruit juice and falls ill' (she was hospitalized), and 'A suspicious fruit impounded in Modena' (it was sent with all due ceremony to the regional analytical laboratory).

If the facts waltz dizzily, so do the roles people play. Consider the communications officials who had been trained all their professional lives to give suitably filtered information to the press according to careful timing. At the worst moment in the history of their company, in the midst of the Bhopal crisis, they were alerted to events by the press and found themselves totally dependent on the journalists— suddenly they were the ones asking for information, a position they had never been in (Irvine, 1987).

Uneasiness, dizziness, and worry crowd around questions whose answers always come too late. Seveso was a sort of 'foundation' technological crisis, and officials like to note that it was a victimless crisis. But this is what they say ten years after the facts. Those in charge at the time would have been happy to feel so self-assured.

Things can become even more disturbing. The idea of pessimism or optimism assumes that some sort of accurate appraisal can be made, and from it can be determined an ideal line of action to strive for. But crises are often far from such a model. They are volatile and unpredictable, and they shatter this underlying idea that there is an optimum to be found or a balance to be struck. Once again, the field of international crisis, with the much studied Cuban Missile crisis its central reference, is a rich source of instruction. Numerous authors and witnesses had reached the conclusion, after years of work, that this case was an over-exaggerated episode of White House pessimism—until the Soviet Union opened its archives and witness reports and it was revealed that the two sides had brushed very closely with a third world war. The best and the brightest of America, enlightened by the Bay of Pigs fiasco one year earlier, were applying all their know-how in Washington to handling the crisis, yet a more recent look at the case (Garthoff, 1988, p. 77) has reached a gloomy conclusion: 'Several aspects of the search for an end to the crisis were unpredictable and subject to the hazards of chance and subjective error.' The publication of the correspondence exchanged by Khruschev and Fidel Castro simply reinforces this uneasy and conservative re-evaluation. As Jacques Amalric (1990) wrote in the French daily *Le Monde*, 'M.K. had integrated the concept of dissuasion according to which nuclear arms were only effective if they were not used. The ideological ranting and the visceral anti-Americanism of Castro [. . .] prohibited him from proceeding according to common sense and forced him to accept "heroically" the prospect of the Apocalypse, for his people and for many others.'

This could suggest another fearful verdict: that no theory is possible; that at best we must reason empirically, case by case; we must be satisfied with a historical approach, developed long after the facts. This is of no use for immediate action, and yet it, too, is unreliable, since there is room for massive error even in the best-documented cases.

Finally, no study of crisis takes place without some unexpected upsets. The very field of analysis is full of deep and solid apprehension. If you look at crises and try to understand them, you may often stumble across unwritten rules, murky balances of power, or even buried secrets. There may not even be any deplorable intention to cover up the truth. The simple fact seems to be that people and institutions need a certain degree of secrecy in order to function. Consequently, collecting data is always an adventure, and often a discouraging one.

But if those involved in the process remain clear about the outlook— that is, if they acknowledge the complexity of the issue—then it is possible to make both pertinent and useful progress.

Meeting the challenge: learning to reason strategically

The clever observer will note that the above panorama is simply a list of all the difficulties inherent in any type of crisis management, viewed here from an intellectual point of view: the actors involved find themselves on unknown territory, there is high ambiguity, the potential outcome is unknown and seems likely to be largely a matter of chance.

As it will become progressively clear, when handling any crisis it is important to take one's distance and to ask questions before taking action—and to work to maintain this critical distance throughout the episode.

To this end, we found that the thoughts of Clausewitz (1965) in his attempts to develop a theory of war and warfare were of great help. His ideas provide a clearer theoretical framework for the present work. His methodological commentary is of central importance to this work on crisis management. After all, this field, too, is certainly 'an unexplored sea, full of rocks,' characterized by 'an infinity of petty circumstances,' 'chance,' 'uncertainty of all data,' and 'friction [. . .] which makes that which appears easy in War difficult in reality'. Most crucial for this work is Clausewitz' distinction between theory and method, judgement and doctrine:

> Theory must be of the nature of observation, not of doctrine. [. . .] It does not necessarily require to be a direction for action. [. . .] It should educate the mind of the future leader in War, or rather guide him in his self-instruction, but not accompany him to the field of battle; [. . .]

> Method will therefore be the more generally used, become the more indispensable, the farther down the scale of rank the position of the active agent; and on the other hand, its use will diminish upwards, until in the highest position it quite disappears. For this reason it is more in its place in tactics than in strategy. [. . .]

> On the other hand, any method by which definite plans for wars or campaigns are to be given out all ready made as if from a machine [is] absolutely worthless.

> All principles, rules, and methods, [. . .] exist to offer them-selves as required, and it must always be left for judgement to decide whether they are suitable or not. Such results of theory must never be used in criticism as rules or norms for a standard, but in the same way as the person acting should use them, that is, merely as aids to judgement.

An aid for judgement; this is the fundamental perspective in which this book is written.

Another great classic author on the art of war, Sun Tzu, suggests adopting the same point of view:

> So a military force has no constant formation, so water has no shape
>
> (Sun Tzu, 1972, p. 49)

> [. . .] A general must know how to evaluate opportune changes in circumstances.
>
> (Sun Tzu, 1972, p. 155)

The goal here is to formulate aids for strategic reasoning which will help decision makers to develop patterns for response and specific action. At the same time, and despite the reservations stated here (which apply to the book as a whole), we have tried to provide the reader with the most up-to-date knowledge and practices currently employed. Other discussions of the issue are available in the work done by the research group on crisis and major risks at CNRS, the French national scientific research centre, and especially in Claude Gilbert (1991).

It seems important to adopt a humble posture from the very outset: this book presents a set of proposals which remain to be confirmed and detailed. As a result, the reader must constantly rely on his or her own good judgement. Because of the nature of the subject, those attempting to deal with crisis feel an irrepressible need to be reassured. For this reason, we do not hesitate to repeat what will become a leitmotif in this book: in a crisis, the solution is not to be found in magical formulae that decision makers can apply with their eyes closed, and with as little reflection as possible.

In a crisis, more than anything else it is urgent to begin by thinking. The sole ambition of this book is to help everyone, individually and as members of teams and networks, to cultivate their critical intelligence.

Part 1

Crisis dynamics: an overview of the problems managers face

Normal patterns of unusual situations

The first part of this book attempts to paint an overall picture of the crisis phenomenon and the many difficulties that it tends to generate in the normal course of events.

To help the actors involved to find their marks, it is vital to survey the terrain systematically before a problem arises: in a crisis situation, these reference frameworks are so easily lost. Understanding the problems that crisis poses as a matter of course is a way of reducing its surprise effect and the resulting stress it causes. This also makes it possible to anticipate difficulties that will probably or plausibly appear. Last but not least, it provides the means for preparing ahead of time, when things are calm.

Chapter 1
Normalcy, disturbance, and crisis

This chapter outlines the characteristics of a 'classic' accident, in order to illustrate what a crisis is by comparison and to make decision makers aware of how they normally think, by demonstrating how this thinking is not adapted to dealing with crisis situations.

What is a crisis? It will take several chapters to answer this question. We shall propose many definitions for the term, but they are clearly not the most useful tools to describe the concept. Crisis is too complex a term to be rigidly defined like a concise dictionary definition.

We shall take a first look at the problem of crisis management by describing three states in which that system operates: normal conditions, disturbed situations, and crisis dynamics.

Under normal conditions, a system functions without dramatic fluctuations. A set number of regulations helps the system remain in balance and maintains its everyday pace. Naturally this frame of reference itself may be 'disturbed' to a greater or lesser degree, calm, or close to the breaking point, but on the whole, the system holds together within its established framework.

An incident upsets normal conditions and creates a disturbance. In this case, specialized functions are put into effect to bring about a return to normalcy. This strategy, however, only applies to the 'classic accident': one that can be handled by existing emergency regulations. Once an accident has passed a certain limit then we enter the world of crisis. This occurs when the trigger event is a 'major accident'.[1] This may also occur when an accident happens in a system that was already unstable or close to the breaking point *before* the event took place. At this third level, the crisis dynamic, specialized emergency functions are no longer enough to bring the situation back to either of the previous stages.

The key features of the classic accident are presented in the summary at the end of this chapter. It is a single problem occurring within the normal functioning of the system that, in a larger context, is not threatening. Appropriate specialists are capable of solving or diminishing the problem fairly quickly and without great difficulty. When called upon, they arrive quickly at the site of the problem and know exactly what to do: they can immediately start working on the problem. Even if the specialists come from different organizations they are generally few in number and either know each other personally or know their respective organizations. These professionals respond to the classic accident with speed, dexterity, and experience. Should the problem broaden in scope, increased resources and special approaches exist which can be brought into play. This makes it possible to maintain necessary efficiency and vigilance.

A very good example of this approach (taken from the field of the protection of resources and property) is the regulations and practices of firefighters in Paris[2] or the practices and guidelines used in catastrophe medicine. These two kinds of guidelines are designed to deal with large-scale events that go beyond the mere incident. In the case of a classic accident, these agencies shift their focus from the individual to the collective need. For example, they go from taking care of individual patients to 'triage',[3] and from immediately helping the injured to the nearest hospital to applying medical regulations that allow for the emergency re-allocation of a hospital's resources.

The role of each organization is clear. Each one knows its responsibility and there are few conflicts of authority (problems with the command structure were foreseen and resolved beforehand). If any conflicts remain, they are small enough not to affect the situation at hand.

All the actors involved, both inside and outside, perceive the situation as 'manageable.' If problems do arise among the actors, the impression remains—at least on the outside—that the organizations involved can handle the situation.

It is important to note that most accidents are 'classic.' It would be wrong to confuse a fleeting incident with a crisis. It is equally important to bear in mind that the main objective of the work being done in systems management is to push back the threshold at which an accident breaks out of its frame of reference. An accident will either be well controlled or will lead to destabilization, depending on the decision makers' degree of preparation and competence. Of course, a crisis for one person may be a simple problem for another. The concept of crisis is relative.

In other words, there is no point in complicating the issue of ordinary incident management with a discussion of crisis techniques. As a leader in the rescue field told us when we raised the issue of border-line problems, 'We are not here to create problems, we're here to solve them' (Noto *et al.*, 1987).

Nonetheless, decision makers may find themselves in situations they believe to be truly exceptional. It is, therefore, useful to study the reference framework for ordinary accidents for two reasons. The first is clear: this list will allow decision makers to distinguish between the classic accident and the major risk or major menace that they will have to confront. The second reason is less clear, but experience has shown that when suddenly faced with a crisis, crisis managers have a tendency, from the outset, to try to follow familiar references. The more disturbing the situation, the stronger the urge to take refuge in familiar procedures. In other words, to understand a situation, many managers automatically try to apply guidelines from the ordinary world of the classic accident. Therefore, we shall describe the essential characteristics of the 'classic' world not only because they are needed to treat commonly faced problems but also to show why these guidelines should not be applied when facing a major accident and crisis dynamics.

The decision maker suddenly discovers a brave new world. The guidelines that are remembered during the first stage of the crisis—the usual references—will no longer function. This incident is not just an ordinary problem: welcome to the world of the major accident.

Summary

Conventional incidents

- A well-understood event, of limited scale
- Clearly defined emergency procedures
- A limited number of actors
- The organizations involved know one another
- Clear-cut roles and responsibilities
- A well-acknowledged authority structure
- A situation that is perceived to be manageable
- A breakdown that is quickly brought under control.

A hole in the dyke that is rapidly patched over

Notes

1. This term is taken from industrial security; however, it remains that 'major accidents' may encompass all destabilizing forces in a system regardless of the frame of reference.
2. Brigade of Firemen, Paris, 1983: *Règlement sur l'organisation et le fonctionnement du service d'incendie et de secours.*
3. Triage consists of sorting out, on the accident site, the wounded persons according to the seriousness of their wounds, in order to dispatch them to the most appropriate hospital.

Chapter 2

The major event: a world out of scale

The decision maker is faced with something that no longer looks like an ordinary incident, and is overwhelmed. None of the regular landmarks suits the scale of things; everything seems uncertain. This chapter presents an overview of the major factors that usually characterize this type of situation.

There 'it' is, big as life, or possibly worse, hovering like a threatening ghost. Immediately, shock and gnawing anxiety set in: just what is going on? You do not understand, you cannot put a name on the difficulty or outline the problem. From all sides come threats, calls to retreat, failures, bad news, aggravating turns of events. Nothing works; everything is falling apart. The feelings of all the actors on the front line can be summed up in a single question: 'What's going to happen to us *next*?'

Obviously this is not an ordinary breakdown; it is no longer a simple hole in the dyke. The usual mental control panel seems to have stopped working: all the dials are in the red zone, the data are misleading, and the measurements mean nothing.

Very quickly, it is realized that everyone is turning to the manager: What should be done? Or rather, what does it all mean? What new guidelines can be found so that people can act? How does the manager get a reading on the situation?

Before looking for answers, it is better to start by identifying the characteristics that may appear in these events which destabilize us so severely. This chapter draws up a first overview of the factors that structure a crisis situation.

A large-scale breakdown

This is the most obvious parameter: the problem and its consequences are enormous. The quantitative difficulties faced are greater than anything that had been imagined before.

Examples include the *Amoco-Cadiz* tanker spilling 230 000 tons of oil on 16 March 1978; the *Exxon-Valdez*, that polluted 1600 kilometres of coastline on 24 March 1989; Bhopal (3 December 1984) with thousands of dead and tens of thousands of seriously injured; or the fear of contamination in a whole network of products, as in the Johnson & Johnson Tylenol case in 1982, necessitating the recall of 31 million tablets; or Chernobyl on 28 April 1986 and the radioactive cloud that circled the earth.

A very destabilizing *type* of breakdown

The type of problem is a second parameter that may fall into any of several categories:

- The type of breakdown had not been imagined.

  A pharmaceutical product (enterovioform) apparently caused 1000 deaths and created 30 000 invalids in Japan, yet it had given satisfactory results everywhere else it had been used (Négrier, 1979). Other typical cases would be a forest fire in the middle of winter, a flood during a drought;[1] a company suddenly losing its top executives, or the destruction of its headquarters; the discovery that some electric fields may not be as innocuous as was once thought; or a rumour suggesting that radiation from some video display terminals could endanger users' health.
  (Lagadec, 1988, pp. 262–3.)

- The breakdown strikes a vital nerve centre.

  A simple fire may begin by destroying the telephone exchange used by the alarm system (as was the case in a major Montreal hospital[2]); a flood may strike the crisis management centre first (which happened in Darwin, Australia—see Scanlon, 1979); a bridge collapses, bringing automobile traffic to a halt, but it also breaks off the electricity and telephone networks that ran across the bridge (as a result, the firemen will be delayed in receiving the alarm).

- The breakdown strikes one or more vital networks.

  Hinsdale, May 1988
  A fire in a telephone switching centre in the Chicago area caused an outage of part of the Illinois Bell network. Half a million residents and business customers were deprived of both voice and data communications. The cost of the outage, which lasted

from two days to three weeks depending on the area, was estimated at $200–300 million.

The loss of this vital network triggered a chain of events: banks could not cash checks or transfer funds; travel agencies and mail order companies headquartered in Chicago were paralysed; cellular phones and paging systems in the area were hindered; businesses located in the affected areas were cut off from each other and the rest of the country. Many businesses, especially banks, discovered that they could be affected by a major crisis whose cause was totally foreign to them, and the impact is even heavier when both telephones and computers go down. Similar cases have already occurred in New York (1975), Lyon, France (1981), Tokyo (1984), Brooklyn, NY (1987), and Sydney, Australia (1987).

(See Pauchant et al., 1989.)

- Instead of a single problem, the breakdown combines several failures.

A fire may occur when the computer inventory system is not yet operational (Sandoz); an accident happens during a strike; a product must be recalled because of a manufacturing defect and a computer failure, making it impossible to know what was delivered to whom.

- The problems to be dealt with are immediately massive.

This was the subject of a recent simulation game in Washington, DC: a powerful earthquake in Missouri had consequences for the rest of the country.[3] In the quake zone, hundreds of thousands are left homeless. Essential infrastructure including roads, bridges, railroads, and airports is destroyed. Regional electric power, water systems, sewer systems, and telecommunications are knocked out. In addition, several transcontinental gas pipelines and delivery of oil to the north are disrupted, affecting tens of millions of citizens outside the quake area. A major earthquake in Missouri means Chicago, Boston, and New York may be deprived of vital supply lines for as long as two months. This immediately creates vast economic problems that could throw the country into a general economic crisis.

As Enrico Quarantelli points out, efforts to analyse a crisis must be open to problems that are still incubating. For example, all our technological systems are increasingly vulnerable because they are based on computers, which are prone to failure. But the new characteristics here are the risk of total breakdowns and the impossibility for individuals to get around the problem, as the systems are highly interdependent. The systems are so complex that repairs are long and difficult, and sabotage is always a danger (Forester and Morrison, 1990).

Very grave situations, degrading exponentially

Some specific situations must be handled with extreme urgency. There are also chains of events that tend to snowball. Time is on the side of the crisis, working against those in charge. The rule of thumb given by firefighters applies even more harshly to crisis: after one minute, you need a glass of water; in ten minutes, one truck; in one hour, the whole station. This is even more true when a major event hits—in whatever field. Every delay causes things to get worse, and this exacerbates the immediate issue, as the following example shows:

> *French Prime Minister Michel Rocard and the collapse of*
> *agricultural prices*
> I remember that the market price of pork suddenly collapsed,
> falling so low that thousands of farmers demonstrated angrily. I
> had twenty-four hours to find a means of raising prices (e.g. by
> filling the freezers, financing advance purchases by collective
> agencies, or setting up a minimum guaranteed payment), find
> financing for it (by negotiating firmly with the Ministry of
> Finances), get the European Community to accept it (through
> two-pronged negotiations with Brussels, directly with the Com-
> mission and indirectly through our Ministry of Foreign Affairs),
> maintain law and order while ensuring that when it was necessary
> to repress violent actions, this didn't turn public opinion among
> farmers against the public authorities. I did not have control
> over the law enforcement agencies, and I knew that they were
> more interested in 'cleaning' the streets than in keeping every-
> body calm. This was only a minor crisis. But it taught me that in
> those cases, you have to be ready to learn fast.
> (Michel Rocard, 1987, pp. 89–90.)

Emergencies that do not play by the rules

Against this type of event, the available means for reaction are inadequate. There is a lack of basic resources, especially in terms of specialist advice and communications. No one knows how to co-ordinate the different emergency plans that must be implemented by very diverse organizations. In the worst case, the defence systems in place or the conscientious application of the usual emergency action plans can backfire.

> *Pemberton, British Columbia*
> This is a Canadian city well protected from floods by the dyke
> constructed along the river flowing through the city. In 1982, this
> protective system was virtually turned inside out. Instead of rising
> from the river, the flood waters came down from the mountains
> overlooking the town, and flowed perpendicular to the river.

The dyke would not let the water escape, making it the major
factor for disaster.

(See Scanlon *et al.*, 1984.)

Stock Market Crash, October 1987
To a large extent, the snowball effect that set in was caused by
the computerized program trading systems that usually served
to regulate trade.

(See Arbel and Kaff, 1989.)

*Contradictions during the Mississauga Rail Accident near
Toronto in 1979*
For some authorities, it was vital to hose down the railcars to
prevent the propane from exploding; for others, it was vital not
to, as this could crack the layer of ice inside the overturned
chlorine car which was preventing this liquid gas from evaporating.

(See Lagadec, 1983.)

Hurricane in southwestern France, 1982
The weather services published a special weather bulletin
announcing high winds, which meant wind speeds greater than
90 km/h. Fire departments and paramedics were warned, so that
they could be ready to respond rapidly to a great many calls.
But the winds that hit reached speeds of 172 km/h. Under those
conditions, it is important *not* to send out the equipment. These
are cyclone conditions, and if you send out equipment during
the storm, you lose it. Fortunately, the colonel commanding the
fire department in the Hérault region had also worked overseas
in the former French colonies, and he intuited the situation. He
did not send out his equipment, thereby protecting it—and it
was available for action as soon as the hurricane had passed.[4]

Even more important is thinking ahead to the risks that are still incubating. It is worth wondering, for example, about the trend towards
decentralizing vital functions,[5] which may perturb the possibilities
for action when a problem strikes. More and more today, major
management functions are being spread across entire continents,
which creates new windows of vulnerability: the headquarters is in
one region, the incidents tracking system in another, the crisis centre
in a third—and each region has its specific local organization, which
makes running the crisis from the outside that much more difficult.[6]

San Francisco Earthquake, 17 October 1989: one big surprise
Many fire alarms and smoke detectors used by major San
Francisco institutions were monitored from Chicago. Under normal
conditions, this seemed to be a satisfactory and rational solution.
In a generalized emergency, the remote monitoring centre could
not reach the fire station in the affected area. The whole basis
for the system collapsed because of one detail: the telephone
network was overloaded, and no one could call in from outside.

(See Scott and Freibaum, 1990, p. 4.)

The unknowns: a step beyond uncertainty

In every problem situation, those involved discover they lack sufficient information and knowledge. But here, once again, things go far beyond the usual boundaries. There are no estimates, no measuring devices, and no basis (whether physical, toxicological, epidemiological, or other) to interpret what is known, whether the issue is causes or immediate or long-term effects. And no one knows how to find out. Beyond uncertainty, we enter the world of unknowns. Unknowns are tolerable if they do not last longer than the first moments of the crisis. They become seriously disturbing if they go on much longer. Unknowns can be compensated for by a general knowledge database if references are available on the subject in question (e.g. an airplane crash involving a model with years of flight time). The issue is much more sensitive if there is no such experience in the field (e.g. an unexplained crash involving a new type of plane).

> *Fire at Saint-Basile-le-Grand near Montreal, Canada, 23 August 1988*
> A warehouse believed to contain PCBs was destroyed by fire. The plume of smoke created spread over three municipalities. More than 6000 persons were evacuated urgently to avoid potential contamination. Uncertainty reigned about the contents of the warehouse, whose owner had apparently fled to Florida; and about the best way to fight the fire, i.e. using foam or water. The weather was uncertain. It was also uncertain who should take responsibility for managing the crisis. Nor were the risks clear: it took the specialists 17 days, until 10 September, to determine how toxic the products involved were. People were evacuated for 18 days.
>
> (See Denis, 1989.)

Beyond the emergency: the broader issue of time

Time—a crucial dimension in a crisis—immediately becomes a disconcerting parameter, for several reasons:

The duration How long do the triggering event, the acute critical phase, or the after-effects last? People, mechanisms, and organizations are worn down by long duration. The menace of lasting effects, and even worse, delayed effects, hangs over the post-accident landscape. This has been the problem, for example, with the inevitable need to expand the contamination zones around Chernobyl.

The threat or problem can evolve It ceases to be a problem to be solved once and for all. Instead, the manager is faced with a real dynamic process.

> *Airplane Crash in Gander, Newfoundland, 12 December 1985*
> At first, the problem was handling a conventional air disaster. The next day, it had become handling the contamination of water supplies for the city nearby, as a result of the firefighting efforts.[7]

The problem of responding A crisis is generally a patchwork of successive problems. Any one of these is largely sufficient to throw the actors into general confusion.

Time's erratic pace 'Inert' periods may be followed by sharply accelerating events that call for lightning reactions—after the previous period has strained people by forcing them to use restraint. It is difficult both to anticipate and to keep up with these irregular and apparently random ups and downs.

A growing number of authorities involved

This may be one of the most striking parameters. In a conventional breakdown, only a few specialized services are required to become involved. Here, a vast number of agencies must be called in: the Gander crisis involved 65 agencies, all vital. The same number was required during the fire at a tyre storage site in Canada in 1990.

> *Hagersville, Ontario, 12 February 1990*[8]
> A fire broke out in a gigantic tyre warehouse, storing twelve million tyres. It burned for 18 days. More than 60 agencies were eventually mobilized around the site, including:
> - 26 units of firefighters
> - the Ministry of Health, because of the public health issues (air and water pollution) raised
> - the Ministry of Agriculture, because of the problems with crops and livestock
> - the Ministry of the Environment, because of the pollution and the threat to water tables (500 000 litres of toxic oils were produced by the burning tyres)
> - the police, because of possible criminal causes of the fire
> - the municipality
> - the regional authorities
> - provincial authorities (four leaders of central government)
> - the forest fire services, needed if water bomber planes were called for

- social services to take care of evacuated persons (1000 people from a 15-kilometre radius)
- ambulances to take care of wounded firefighters
- members of the construction industry, who provided vital equipment such as tanker trucks to remove the contaminated water
- the telephone company, to lay new lines
- the electric company
- the weather services, which had a very hard time forecasting the weather on such a small scale (it was important to know whether the water bombers could be used, since this became very risky when temperatures approached freezing)
- the roads and highways department, as it was necessary to build a new road to handle the problem, as well as a pipeline to which fire hydrants could be attached[9]
- the hospitals in the area, which were placed on alert in case the great quantities of smoke released should necessitate their evacuation
- the Army (a federal agency) could have become involved, but the province refused; this in turn brought the province's political authorities into the picture.

To complicate things even further, despite the involvement of so many people, the question that often arises is: 'Aren't all these agencies really secondary?' Everyone begins to wonder if anyone is really in charge of the situation. Does anyone really know what is on that boat, or in that warehouse, or why or how?

At the same time, an incalculable number of consultants selling their services, self-designated experts, volunteers, and observers suddenly appear on the scene. And the media are never far behind. For example, Sandoz and the polluting of the Rhine saw 17 television teams arrive; the Gare de Lyon train crash in Paris, 14; Three Mile Island, some 1400 to 1500 journalists. After the San Francisco earthquake, there were traffic jams in the air space because of the number of press helicopters flying around.

Of course when an event like Three Mile Island occurs, the networks of actors involved become that much more complex.

Critical communication problems

A crisis presents four immediate challenges: communicating within each organization, among the actors involved, with the media, and with the concerned public. Communicating does not simply mean being able to send messages: it also means being able to receive them.

Voids are often created, which inevitably hinder understanding and foster conflict and rumours. The following case demonstrates the terrible problems that may exist from a purely technical point of view, even in the best-equipped regions of the world.

San Francisco Earthquake, 17 October 1989
The AT&T telephone system functioned poorly during the first hours of the crisis, mainly because the network was saturated. Long-distance communication was particularly difficult. The 911 emergency number for the entire United States was temporarily out of service and remained so for several days in some areas. People turned to cellular telephones, but here again, the system proved vulnerable as soon as the relays were damaged. This network also became saturated, especially at the crisis centre. When the telephone lines worked, peopled turned to faxing. But the massive and often inappropriate use of this means of communication (e.g. sending ten- or fifteen-page documents) caused it to become saturated as well. Mobile-to-mobile communication also encountered difficulties, so that some units simply resorted to transmitting messages face to face.
(see Scott and Freibaum, 1990.)

Huge stakes

The issue in a crisis is not whether to reimburse buyers for a given product, or to redesign a given subsidiary or plant. The stakes are incredibly high for a great many individuals and numerous organizations, and potentially for the economy of an entire country. As a result, the obvious radical solutions are usually the least acceptable: it is difficult, for instance, simply to stop everything, have a look, or take everything apart in order to solve the problem.

An event defined by how it is perceived

This section has described the intrinsic features of a major event. In the next chapter, we shall examine the importance of context to the event. But the issue of context, though vital for the clarity of this discussion, can be misleading. In practice, a major event goes hand in hand with the image people have of it. It needs only touch on an area of particularly sensitive images (e.g. nuclear power, biotechnologies) to make the borders between fact and perception blur completely.

This last point is very important: to trigger a crisis, it is not necessary to have an immediate, tangible, and indisputable problem. The situation needs only to be perceived as such by internal or external actors. A simple rumour or hypothesis can be devastating, especially if the manager does not really know whether the threat is real. Even if the manager is convinced that the risk is minimal, it is impossible to demonstrate that a problem does *not* exist. Indeed, this is much more difficult than proving that one *does* exist. It is not uncommon to see situations in which the people in charge are convinced that the allegations made are unfounded, but cannot disprove them. In fact, as the technical world becomes increasingly complex, this type of situation is increasingly common. Furthermore, a 'purely' subjective problem can quickly become an objective reality—the computer may create a snowball effect based on false information, but the snowball effect is very real, as is the crisis it creates.

The differences between these major events and the simple accidents described at the outset are clear. The problems of a major event cannot be circumscribed; this is no longer a single hole in the dyke. Each question interreacts with the others, and each organization becomes totally caught up in the event; the whole system begins to resonate.

Whether all these difficulties or only some are present, whether they strike immediately or hover menacingly, they are highly disturbing. Quickly or inexorably, the foundations on which organizations stand begin to crumble. At first, the person in the driver's seat feels overwhelmed, or worse: that person, usually the manager, is gnawed by anxiety at seeing all familiar frames of reference disappear; the situation seems slippery, and reality becomes a crumbling puzzle whose pieces may suddenly fall together again in a new pattern according to rules no one understands.

Depending on the type of crisis, the personal shock may be severe if, in addition to financial and technological issues, there are also important effects on public health, raising questions of life and death or massive casualties.

Until now, for purposes of clarity we have examined the various dials on our control panel individually. Now, we shall examine a case that involved several simultaneous challenges.

Tornado in Edmonton, Alberta, 31 July 1987
Tornadoes are not an unusual phenomenon in this region. This one hit the city from the south, then moved north along the east side, passing through in about an hour. The casualties totalled 27 dead and hundreds of injured. This case clearly illustrates the

points mentioned above. Notably, the essential services, though highly competent, collapsed bit by bit. Catastrophe medicine, which had already proved its utility, was taken by surprise. (The principles of this strategy are: control of the affected site or sites; triage on site to determine priorities for treating victims; distribution by medical personnel of the injured throughout the various available hospitals in order to prevent the slightly wounded from overwhelming the nearest hospitals; and putting hospitals on alert about the number of injured to expect, and their condition.)

Even before the tornado struck, the media, on which the population relies heavily for information, were paralysed by an electricity outage. The alert reached the hospitals 14 minutes after the tornado struck, often by unexpected means. For example, one employee called home and was told of the disaster by her daughter. Ambulances were dispatched immediately. It took them 22 minutes more to arrive on site. By then, the many of the victims had already been taken to the various hospitals. This dealt a serious blow to the two strategic tenets of catastrophe medicine, as there was no control over the affected area or over the distribution of injured to the hospitals. Contrary to the general theory, triage had to take place at the hospital and not on site. Yet the medical personnel who should have handled this function were out in the ambulances, often stuck where they were because of storm damage. Sorting did, of course, take place at the doors of the hospitals, but for the security personnel doing this work, the main task was directing traffic. Priority was given to letting in official vehicles (e.g. ambulances, police cars). Sorting was based on the type of vehicle transporting an injured person, and not on the state of the person's injuries.

During this time, things continued to develop. The worst part of the tornado was not what happened in the south and got people mobilized. The storm then moved north and hit an industrial zone. High winds overturned a 36-ton truck. The storm left the city, returned, and hit a mobile-home park. The results included 14 chemical leaks, panic over a natural gas tank truck blown over by the storm, damage to the railway line that ran from east to west across the city, obstacles blocking roads and forcing emergency personnel to circulate on foot, and flooding of the underground passages normally used to cross under the railroad tracks. The city was effectively cut in two.

The telephone network was saturated. To the north, the exchange had been destroyed. The police radio system was also saturated. Most police cars were trapped in traffic jams. The fire department's radios were saturated. The radio system used by the ambulance services, which was supposed to handle general coordination, was destroyed by lightning which brought its computer down. There were electricity outages. A sewer system imploded. And paradoxically, a large part of the city was unharmed: people went to see what the tornado was like.

The central hospital lost its electricity. One hospital thought it would have to evacuate because of flooding, which was blocking the ambulance entrance in particular. The six hospitals in the area were taken completely by surprise. They had emergency plans, but not for tornadoes, and these plans did not allow for potential combinations of problems, i.e. flooding *and* electricity outages *and* communications breakdowns, while the injured came rushing in. Some of the hospitals saw the erratic pacing discussed above: things were totally calm just after the alert, then the injured began arriving massively by non-conventional means. The busiest hospital was the one closest to the site. It was a psychiatric hospital whose only emergency plan dealt with the problem of dangerous patients. Yet this hospital sent its own firefighting service to put out gas fires and help the injured in the mobile-home park. Some hospitals began to feel slighted because no one was sending victims to them—they were unaware of the fact that no one was in charge of distribution.

(See Scanlon and Hiscott, 1990.)

Summary

The major event

A matter of real problems or perceptions

- Enormous quantitative difficulties
- Qualitative difficulties
  - Unusual problems
  - Vital resources affected
  - Combined breakdowns
- An emergency
  - Conventional emergency plus snowball effect
- Emergencies that do not play by the rules
  - Insufficient, inadequate, or counterproductive procedures
  - Totally obsolete procedures
- Beyond uncertainty, the unknowns
- The issue of time
  - A long duration
  - An evolving threat; how to respond?
  - Violently contrasting paces
- Growing numbers of authorities and officials involved

- Critical communication problems
  - Within and among the organizations in charge
  - With the media and the concerned public
- Huge stakes
- Subjective perceptions become objective realities

These problems and threats cannot be circumscribed

Notes

1. Joseph Scanlon has created the concept of 'unseasonal disasters' for such cases.
2. Interview with Joseph Scanlon.
3. Crisis simulation organized in Washington, DC on 8 December 1990 by the Center for Strategic & International Studies.
4. Patrick Lagadec, joint expert advisory group on major risks, Ministry of the Interior, following the hurricane that struck fourteen departments of southwestern France and the Principality of Andorra in November 1982.
5. There are obvious problems with the traditional practice of centralizing vital functions. Yet uncoordinated decentralization, done solely in the name of technical or economic efficiency and planned only on the basis of 'normal' conditions, creates serious risks that must be weighed. This is especially true when the systems in question are used for safety purposes and must, by definition, operate in troubled and exceptional circumstances.
6. Interview with Enrico Quarantelli.
7. Interview with Joseph Scanlon.
8. We are grateful to Joseph Scanlon for providing this example. His Ottawa research group studied the case (J. Scanlon and Angela Prawzick, to be published, Protection Civile Canada). We also examined the excellent press file collected by the press service at the French general consulate in Quebec and Montreal (Pierre Henri Guignard, who had already helped us a few years earlier in Mexico in studying the San Juan Ixhuatepec disaster in 1984, and Hervé Mignot, who also helped us several years ago when investigating a case in Venezuela).
9. *Le Journal de Montréal*, 20 February 1990.

Chapter 3

When the event finds an echo in its context

We have just seen a series of crisis factors linked to the essential nature of an event. Now another front opens in the battle: the event begins to find an echo in its context. Like a cyclone that draws its life force from the waters it disturbs, the major event feeds upon all the problems and instabilities already present in the context where it exists.

The major event is not a simple accident that is well defined or clearly delineated. What is even more disturbing is that the event with all of its aspects and ramifications constantly interacts with its environment. This context in which the event takes place will determine its ultimate nature and its overall force for destabilization.

A certain number of contextual parameters must be taken into account in order to understand or anticipate how the shock wave of a major failure will spread. Geographic, cognitive, historical, political, cultural and symbolic factors all shape the event. They provide the fertile ground for the the seeds of chaos.

Notably, breakdowns are much more damaging if they occur after decades of discussion and reassurance that a failure was impossible. This is especially true if the responsible organizations or authorities admit that they are impotent, powerless, or ignorant. The explosive impact also increases if the incident comes in the wake of a report discussing the existence of unacceptable risks. In another field, if major labour unrest breaks out during a period of high social tension it will have the effect of a spark in a tinderbox.

The list of points that call for particular vigilance goes on and on. What counts is to emphasize the importance of everything, above and beyond the intrinsic nature of the failure (real or imagined), that can contribute to a crisis. This is especially important when failures take on symbolic value or when a situation was inherently vulnerable. What starts as a snowball turns into an avalanche of interacting phenomena. A small byproduct of a crisis can develop into a grave problem for what was already a weak point in the entire system. The crisis gets a second wind; it changes direction and rebounds like a cyclone that defies all predictions. Those involved are surprised to realize that an infinitely more serious accident that occurred in the recent past did not create a crisis of this kind. It is this last manifestation of this type of event, ignored until it was too late, that triggers a crisis.

The full dimension of a major breakdown derives from the breadth and the depth of the forces brought into play. So closely linked are the complicated forces involved that it becomes impossible to tell which result from the event and which come from its context. The initial destabilization produced by the shock of the event sharpens existing problems within the system. In effect, the initial accident may provide an outlet for problems that are ordinarily kept in check or suppressed. This is especially true when the confusion produced affects the systems of regulation and social constraint. In addition, perceptions change and the value of news depends on when it is 'made'. This, too, makes it hard to predict the turn a crisis will take. For example, if a technical failure took place on the day the Berlin Wall opened, it would have very little impact; the situation is completely different when a very small accident takes place on a quiet weekend with no other events.

This is the profound duality of the crisis phenomenon. It has an internal energy and yet its reality is created by outside forces. The event is both the culmination of a long process and the primal cause of the rupture.

To this effect, the social-psychologist René Kaës makes interesting remarks that go well beyond the field of psychology:

> The crisis: in the serenity of the aftermath, we imagine that the problem appeared out of nowhere, all at once, and surprised us. It is characteristic of all crises to appear this way—unexpected and unique. It is only after a crisis breaks out that we realize the causes, origins and even solutions were already foreshadowed. That is when we remember the crevasses that broke open what we imagined to be the smooth, faultless surface of the world, history and incidents, and we realize that we suffer from manifold scars.
>
> (Kaës, 1979, p. 1)

At the very least, this lesson teaches that we must always examine each event as a truly specific problem. At the same time, we must examine the deepest roots of the crisis and the interaction between the facts of the event and its context.

This illustrates why otherwise disturbing situations do not develop into crises. Gas explosions in Mexico (San Juan Ixhuatepec, 19 November 1984) that caused over a thousand victims did not lead to any significant outcry. A sudden rise in pollution at a chemical site in Cubatao, Brazil—a site that already suffers from various types of pollution—would probably remain unnoticed (until the fateful day . . .). The scenario would be very different in a suburb of Manchester or Frankfurt. One death in a nuclear power plant would undoubtedly have more impact than ten deaths in a chemical plant. It would even cause more outrage than the 10 000 people killed every year on French roads and highways.

This leads us to a more general focus on the historical context of an event. As Julien Freund (1976, p. 101) writes, 'During the twenty years preceding World War One, there were many assassinations of high-ranking politicians and heads of state; however, only the assassination at Sarajevo plunged the world into chaos.'

By examining crises from this more general perspective, two options become clear. A crisis may be caused by a sudden, single event; however, it may also be the result of a general trend that itself leads to a break. Again, Julien Freund (1976, p. 102) explains this clearly:

> In general, crises follow a sudden and unexpected modification that disturbs the ordinary course of events. This leads to a state of instability and uncertainty. The critical juncture may be of two types. Either the crisis is the result of factors outside of normal development or it is the result of the development itself, occurring as the result of an internal build-up. Once this development passes a certain point, it creates a state of chaos.

In this book, we shall focus on crises caused by powerful trigger events rather than on gradual historical trends that lead to chaos, even though these, too, may be labelled crises.

Summary

Fertile ground for crisis

- Symbolic or strategic locations
- Explosive issues (e.g. nuclear power, dioxin)
- Vulnerable targets threatened (e.g. children, pregnant women)

- A range of uncontrollable factors (space, time)
- Repeated failures (a string of misfortune)
- Previous official assurances are discredited
- Warnings not taken into account
- Science and technology remain ineffective
- An institutional vacuum
- A fragile context

The event feeds on its surroundings

Chapter 4

Crisis, or the loss of the reference framework

We have just analysed several experiences in order to illustrate a few preliminary guidelines. Before proceeding, it is important to pause for a moment to reinforce these foundations. Several essential observations should be made, which involve:

- examining the idea of 'crisis,' a term that will be used throughout this book
- presenting the fundamental characteristics of the crisis experience as confronted by the decision maker.

The concept of crisis: resisting it and discovering its depth

All studies of crises must eventually confront the basic problem of defining terms and seeking to understand, 'What is a crisis?' The question is certainly a scholarly one; however, decision makers, too, must be concerned with the issue, otherwise, they will severely limit their capacity to think about crisis and, consequently, to act. Whenever a crisis occurs, the decision maker's reflexes in a dynamic situation become a determining strategic factor.

A broad new field for the scholar

Confronted with the difficulties that we have described, the decision maker's first response is to turn directly to the scholar. Surely the scholar's theories can provide definitive answers? However, the analysts, too, are in some distress: because the concepts are so vague, there is no clearly stated theory. On the subject of international crises, for instance, Wolf–Dieter Eberwein of the University of Bielefeld in Germany has called for a more disciplined use of the term *crisis*: 'Concept formation in theory construction is basic because we thus fix, with the necessary precision, the meaning of the terms we wish to designate the phenomena we want to explain' (1978, pp. 126–7).

The scholar must admit to the decision maker that he or she is struggling with the omnipresent yet ephemeral idea of crisis, a concept that seems more like a mirage than a scientific tool. Indeed, in the opening sentence of his article 'Crisis' in the *International Encyclopedia for Social Sciences*, James A. Robinson states, ' "Crisis" is a lay term in search of a scholarly meaning' (1968, p. 510).

This explains why analysts shy away from the word 'crisis'. Do we really know what we are talking about when we use this term? Isn't there a tendency to exaggerate situations or events? Each new attempt at definition seems to prove the validity of such criticisms.

Edgar Morin, who has worked to develop a science of crisis, notes that the meaning of the word has undergone complete transfiguration. The term that originally meant 'decision, or the decisive moment in an uncertain process' has been transformed to the point where 'crisis now signifies indecision: it is the moment when uncertainty exists at the same time as a problem' (Morin, 1976, p. 149). This change in definition has led to a real loss of meaning of the word:

> The concept of crisis has spread in the twentieth century, making a place for itself in every aspect of contemporary life. There is no realm that is not haunted by the threat of a crisis. (. . .) Yet because of these generalizations, the term 'crisis' has virtually been gutted from within.
>
> (Morin, 1976, p. 149)

> The term 'crisis' is becoming an empty shell. It is a ready-to-use catch-phrase that is merely a final resort in the face of the distress we feel when we can neither diagnose a situation nor predict where it is heading.
>
> (Béjin and Morin, 1976, p. 1)

In the medical field, A. Bolzinger recognizes the same trend (1982, p. 475):

> If we label every period of conflict and change a crisis, with its implications of resistance to change and tension, then life as a whole is a crisis . . . The press and television have made us accustomed to the use and abuse of crisis as a diagnosis. What event can escape this definition if it creates a stir in the news or engenders fears of what tomorrow will bring?

As a medical specialist, Bolzinger (1982, p. 476) comments, 'We do not speak of every pathological condition as a crisis; not every serious or dangerous condition deserves to be called a crisis.'

The historian Randolf Starn (1976, p. 13) is just as critical:

> The term crisis has a long history, and considering its many
> varied uses, no one can expect its meaning to be unequivocal.
> As all journalists and politicians know, crisis is a very useful
> term in the age of mass media. It suggests drama and the need
> for decisions, creates emotion without requiring sober reflection,
> and magnifies the importance of both non-events and events,
> coup d'états and minor incidents (. . .). For the historian, the
> word 'crisis' has often been used as a convenient cliché to
> describe critical junctures and processes in history. In fact, a
> sceptic would say that the mere convenience of the word
> explains its popularity. It is hard to resist using ready-made for-
> mulas. How many times has the word 'crisis' been used by his-
> torians? How many authors have included it gratuitously in the
> titles of their books, even when it was unnecessary?

It should not take the decision maker long to realize that for scholars
and analysts, too, this is a wide open field in which serious efforts
remain to be made.

In concluding his article 'Crisis' in the *International Encyclopedia for
Social Sciences*, James Robinson explains that the word cannot
become a useful concept unless it finds its place within a theoretical
framework. Edgar Morin (1976, p. 163) is equally demanding:

> It seems strange that although the idea of crisis has become
> more and more intuitively evident and the term is used ever
> more widely, it remains a vulgar and hollow little word. Instead
> of waking people up to a problem, the term puts them to sleep.
> As a diagnostic explanation, it has lost all value. Our task today
> is to reveal this crisis in our awareness in order to forge an
> awareness of what crisis is. The crisis affecting the concept of
> crisis is the start of a theory of crisis.

The decision maker may leave this fundamental research to the
scholars, but will soon realize that they are no better prepared to
understand or explain this complex domain. Is it even possible to
come up with a sufficiently solid, clear, and comprehensive crisis
theory? Perhaps one of the most basic characteristics of crisis is that
the analyst or the decision maker can never get a firm grip on it. As
early as the 1860s, Randolf Starn points out, an Italian lexicographer
decried the abuse of the medical term 'crisis' (Starn, 1976, p. 7).

Although it has not furnished any definitive keys to our problems,
this look at the scholarly approach does teach us humility. The concept of crisis, as Starn concludes, is rich because of its malleability, its
facility for capturing unusual movements in history, and its ability to

build bridges between different disciplines (Starn, 1976, p. 18). The decision maker must bear in mind the same need to remain modest. A crisis demands immediate local solutions, and it does allow for action in a number of different fields. But there is no time to wait until all the broader social contradictions which the crisis reveals have been resolved. As Edgar Morin (1976, p. 149) rightly says,

> The word now serves to name the unnameable. It refers to a two-fold gap—a gap in our knowledge (at the very heart of the term crisis), and a gap in the social reality in which the crisis appears.

Shedding light on the problem

Instead of asking the scholar to provide a definitive crisis theory, the decision maker can more judiciously request a practical overview of what existing field experience already provides. The decision maker must ask for practical information that sheds light on the problem, not comprehensive theoretical answers.

Even if this method forces the decision maker to use a variety of approaches, it can provide a range of information.

It is useful to begin by retracing the development of the concept of crisis. André Béjin and Edgar Morin have proposed the following overview of the term:

> In the religious language of Ancient Greece, Krisis signified interpretation (of the flight of birds or of dreams) and choice (of sacrificial victims). In legal terms, Krisis expressed the idea of judgment based on decision rather than on mechanical evaluation of evidence. For authors of Greek tragedy, the term meant a critical event which required that a decision be made. The 'krisis' involved the past, the future and the action whose course it determined. In Hippocratic medicine, the word denoted a sudden change in the condition of a patient, described in terms of time ('critical days') and space (the way 'morbid humours' travelled through and were excreted by the body).

> During the seventeenth and eighteenth centuries, the medical concept of crisis was adopted to describe and analyze society. This shift was accompanied by the loss of a host of concrete observations on diseases of an organism. Instead, 'crisis' acquired an imprecise meaning so that it could be used as an analogy for the ills of 'social organisms'. It now merely stood for a state of uncertainty or a serious problem, and it could there- fore be used in a wide variety of nineteenth century political theories. The sole common ground shared by these theories

was their evolutionary perspective and their emphasis on the cyclical nature of markets, which they were used to quantify.

From the nineteenth century, the word was used in ambitious studies of cultural change which included 'crisis of values,' 'crisis of civilization,' and 'spiritual crisis'. In addition, the term became a useful theoretical instrument for new and growing disciplines such as developmental psychology and even ethology. This transformation took place at the same time that some of the disciplines in which 'crisis' had its origins, such as medicine and economics, were changing. All these factors contributed to alter the meaning of crisis considerably.

(Béjin and Morin, 1976, pp. 1–2)

This rapid history is enough to suggest a sense of the richness and diversity of meaning behind crisis.

Legal language led to the first definition of 'crisis': examining, deciding, judging, and discerning. It was 'the moment of judgment, when decisions are made, and the critical juncture that determined with more or less urgency the road to be followed' (Guillaumin, 1979, p. 222).

To this idea of discernment or judgement is added the second definition of crisis as a turning point or fork in the road, which comes from ancient Greek physicians. Bolzinger further explains:

In Hippocratic medicine, the clinical term 'crisis' describes the crucial instant when the disease approaches a conclusion or a resolution—for better or for worse. It signals the aggravation of symptoms and foreshadows the denouement. (. . .) A 'crisis' is a paroxysm of uncertainty and anguish—a period when everything is in suspense (. . .) while awaiting the coming resolution of the illness. In fact, the resolution of a disease is not always clear-cut. Sometimes, an illness disappears slowly and invisibly. Hippocratic vocabulary distinguishes between two types of conclusions: crisis (a sudden return to health) and lysis (a gradual return to health). We must not forget the third type of possibility which is neither a crisis nor a lysis—death. The specialist's job is to predict the 'critical days' in the evolution of the disease. These days determine the balance between the pathological process and the organism's defenses. At the same time, the doctor must watch for critical symptoms that mark the end of the pathological episode and lead to the start of convalescence. In this regard, the crisis is not the sign of an illness, but a sign of resistance against the disease. It is a rebound rather than a decline. The organism is not incapable of regulating itself, but it opts momentarily for an extraordinary means of protecting and defending itself. There is neither anarchy nor chaos in such crises.

Rather, a new equilibrium is established related to the degree of emergency and mortal danger.

(Bolzinger, 1982, pp. 475-80)

Also in this medical vein, another concept of crisis emerges—one that is much closer to our own time. This is the crisis as *pathology*—a crucial concept for decision makers:

Eighteenth century medical thought added a new dimension to the Hippocratic concept of crisis. There are of course crises that mark the peak and conclusion of an illness, but there are also initiating crises. Such crises do not announce a return to health—they are pathological. The defense mechanisms of the organism are often poorly adapted and excessive. While some fevers are beneficial, others are debilitating. The swelling of an ankle after a sprain is just one example of an uncontrolled crisis in which harmful reactions proliferate wildly. In modern medicine, therefore, crisis signifies an initial trauma. This last definition of crisis is at the origin of the modern medical terms 'stress,' 'incident' and 'attack'. This modern definition of crisis has been stripped of its curative connotations. 'Crisis' is no longer a resolving, salutary, terminal event. It has become an initiating factor and a mere reaction without any any potential for healing. Sometimes it even becomes pathogenic when it causes excessive defensive responses.

Today, we seem to use two concepts, either simultaneously or interchangeably, that medical thought has developed—the curative crisis and the crisis as illness.

(Bolzinger, 1982, p. 476)

To add a fourth sense of the word, Starn (1976, p. 5) indicates that crisis situations at the heart of Greek tragedies 'are not only key points in the process of change. They became moments of truth in which light is shed upon characters and events.' In tragedy, the crisis is the moment when the past, whose significance had escaped the actors, suddenly re-emerges clearly. As Starn observes, this meaning of the moment of truth appears later in the writings of Thomas Paine, expressed in a way that all those who have confronted difficult crises can appreciate: '. . . their peculiar advantage is, that they are touch-stones of sincerity and bring things and men to light which might otherwise have lain forever undiscovered. . . . They sift out the hidden thoughts of men, and hold them up in public to the world.'[1]

Finally, a fifth sense of crisis is opportunity:

Crises wipe the slate clean. In the first place, they rid us of an infinite number of lifeless conventions that could never be touched because of their historical rights. In addition, they do away with a number of pseudo-organisms that should never have existed at all. These organisms burrow their way into almost every walk of life, and they are the main reason for our love of mediocrity and our hatred for anything that is extraordinary.[2]

This is reminiscent of the well-known Chinese definition of crisis, depicted by the double ideogram representing both danger and opportunity.

The notions of decision, turning point, pathology, moment of truth when the past collects its due, or opportunity all come together to comprise the diverse and malleable term 'crisis'.

Interesting attempts at definition

The issue of definitions probably creates the greatest discomfort in the face of the wealth of proposals. These cover a wide spectrum (Eberwein, 1978, p. 129):

- extremely abstract definitions used in specific disciplines, such as this proposed method of analysing a system: 'A crisis is a situation that creates an abrupt or sudden change in one or more of the basic systematic variables' (Hermann, 1972, p. 10)
- definitions which simply list a series of characteristics, in a more or less systematic fashion
- classifications that provide a preliminary organizational structure— for example, these may include dichotomies such as natural vs technological, conventional vs nuclear, or crisis with conflict vs within a context of consensus
- simple descriptions of the crisis as a process that evolves through different stages
- constructs taken from secondary elements that contribute to crisis dynamics, e.g. stress, conflict, or tension.

James Robinson (1968, p. 510) wisely facilitates this approach by proposing a number of categories. We have followed his suggestions and have listed a few guidelines that will broaden the decision maker's basis for assessment.

Approaches focusing on crisis content

In the field of international crises, for example, Herman Kahn has identified 44 levels in political-military escalation, from minor provocations to full-scale nuclear holocaust.[3] The decision makers in the business world will find similar approaches to their own fields. Gerald Meyers, for instance, suggests that:

There are today nine distinct types of business crises. [. . .] public perception, sudden market shift, product failure, top management succession, cash, industrial relations, hostile takeover, adverse international events, and regulation and deregulation. Each has its own symptoms and treatment and though each is different from the others, all have some common characteristics.

(Meyers and Holusha, 1968, p. 9)

Less simplistically, Ian Mitroff and Thierry Pauchant have proposed the framework shown in Figure 4.1. One of the axes measures the internal or external degree of various crisis factors, and the other, the extent to which the factors involve technical or human aspects (Mitroff *et al.*, 1988, pp. 85–6; see also Pauchant, 1989, pp. 4–13).

TECHNICAL/ECONOMIC

Cell 1	**Cell 2**
Product/service defects Plant defects/industrial accidents Computer breakdown Defective, undisclosed information Bankruptcy	Widespread environmental destruction/industrial accidents Large scale systems failure Natural disasters Hostile takeovers Governmental crises International crises
INTERNAL	EXTERNAL
Cell 3	**Cell 4**

Failure to adapt/change
Organizational breakdown
Miscommunication
Sabotage
On-site product tampering
Counterfeiting
Rumours, sick jokes, malicious
  slander
Illegal activities
Sexual harassment
Occupational health diseases
	Symbolic projection
	Sabotage
	Terrorism
	Executive kidnapping
	Off-site product tampering
	Counterfeiting
	False rumours, sick jokes,
	  malicious slander
	Labour strikes
	Boycotts

PEOPLE/SOCIAL/ORGANIZATIONAL

Figure 4.1 Different types of corporate crises

Approaches focusing on characteristic signs of crisis
To illustrate crises and their manifestations, various authors have collected series of items that are representative of the situations in question.

Take, for example, the twelve general crisis attributes identified by Wiener and Kahn[4]:

1 Crisis is often a turning point in an unfolding sequence of events and actions.
2 Crisis is a situation where the requirement for action is high in the minds and planning of participants.
3 Crisis is a threat to the goals and objectives of those involved.
4 Crisis is followed by an important outcome whose consequences and effects will shape the future of the parties to the crisis.
5 Crisis is a convergence of events whose combination produces a new set of circumstances.
6 Crisis is a period in which uncertainties about the assessment of the situation and alternatives for dealing with it increase.
7 Crisis is a period or situation in which control over events and their effects decreases.
8 Crisis is characterized by a sense of urgency, which often produces stress and anxiety among the actors.
9 Crisis is a circumstance or set of circumstances in which information available to participants is unusually inadequate.
10 Crisis is characterized by increased time pressure for those involved.
11 Crisis is marked by changes in the relations among participants.
12 Crisis raises tensions among participants.

Along the same lines, another type of list of crisis characteristics may be drawn from the fields of psychology and sociology[5]:

1 A crisis situation is acute rather than chronic, although its length is usually unspecified.
2 Crisis results in behaviour that is frequently 'pathological' such as inefficiency or scapegoating.
3 Crisis threatens the goals of persons involved.
4 Crisis is relative: what is a crisis for one party or participant may not be for another.
5 Crisis causes tension in the organism, including physical tension and anxiety.

Thomas Milburn, an expert on international crises, has made several additional observations on what constitutes a crisis and the reactions it generates (cf. Milburn, 1972, p. 262):

• Values identified by the policy makers as significant are threatened.
• Pressure exists to decide relatively quickly.
• There is a relatively short time in which to decide to act.
• The crisis is unexpected so that there is no set of plans or any existing program to handle it.
• Pressure to innovate in problem solving since no programmed decision, or relevant contingency plan exists.
• Information overload.
• Ambiguity.
• Increased number and importance of demands.
• Conflicts with others within the group or organization.
• Considerable fatigue.

Uriel Rosenthal and his team have more recently attempted to nuance some of these classic guidelines which they viewed as too limited, or even inaccurate. According to Rosenthal, what is a threat for some may be an opportunity for others. Uncertainty may be purposely maintained by some of the actors. In fact, the emergency is sometimes caused by the actors themselves through their own impatience. The dichotomy between natural and technological is also too simplistic. Similarly, it is often difficult to distinguish frankly between crises based on conflict and other crises. And there are always conflicts of interest. Rosenthal *et al.* (1989, pp. 445–7) suggest other guidelines instead:

• the *unimaginable crisis* requires that we think about what is truly unthinkable (these are actually very rare).
• the *neglected crisis*.
• the *quasi-unavoidable crisis* occurs despite attempts at prevention.
• the *compulsive crisis* results from a sort of innate ineptitude on the part of the relevant actors to manage the crisis (instead, through their actions these actors help create a crisis situation).
• the *wanted crisis*, desired by certain actors (such actors are not limited to terrorists; they may even include managers themselves).
• the *wilful crisis* is apparently secretly desired by all involved.

Clearly, to comprehend the crisis phenomenon, it is constantly necessary to make allowances for the simplistic aspects of any approach.

Attempts at comprehensive definitions

Certain authors have nonetheless tried to develop more concise definitions of crisis. The one proposed by Charles Hermann, an expert on international crises, has been a reference in the field (Herman, 1972, p. 13):

> . . . a crisis is a situation that (1) threatens high priority goals of the decision making unit, (2) restricts the amount of time available for response before the decision is transformed, and (3) surprises the members of the decision making unit by its occurrence.

Other authors, notably Uriel Rosenthal, have since sought a definition that could be applied more generally. According to Rosenthal, it is not only goals that are at risk. The crisis is not necessarily a question of survival, but rather one of 'critical choices'. The element of surprise, in contrast, should be placed in the larger context of factors that can lead to a great degree of uncertainty. This uncertainty, finally, is a key element in any crisis. Rosenthal consequently suggests the following definition:

> . . . a serious threat to the basic structures or the fundamental values and norms of a social system, which—under time pressure and highly uncertain circumstances—necessitates making critical decisions.[6]

In a sociological rather than organizational study, Julien Freund (1976, p. 103) sheds light on the subject by providing the following definition:

> From a sociological standpoint, a crisis is a group situation characterized by contradictions and breakdowns, full of tension and discord. This tension causes groups and individuals to hesitate as to which path they should follow. Ordinary rules and institutions are of little use or are even out of phase with the new possibilities created by the interests and ideas that arise from this change. At the same time, the group cannot clearly determine how accurate or effective any new approach is.

As useful as these definitions and approaches are, they are not enough for the decision maker. It therefore becomes necessary to look for criteria more directly related to operations requirements.

The crisis experience: a few keys for decision makers

Given the objective of this book—to help managers in large organizations—it seems useful at this point to abandon the general perspective and focus on a few essential keys for decision makers.

The crisis, its universe, and its phases

As organizational consultant Steven Fink has indicated (Fink, 1986, pp. 15–16), a certain number of problems traditionally go hand in hand with a crisis:

> From a practical, business-oriented point of view, a crisis (. . .) is any prodomal situation that runs the risk of:
> 1 Escalating in intensity.
> 2 Falling under close media or government scrutiny.
> 3 Interfering with the normal operations of business.
> 4 Jeopardizing the positive public image presently enjoyed by a company or its officers.
> 5 Damaging a company's bottom line in any way.

In an equally comprehensive fashion, Dieudonnée ten Berge, a communications crisis consultant, proposes the following table for decision makers attempting to describe a crisis (ten Berge, 1990, p. 8):

- the need for quick decisions
- inaction is likely to produce undesirable consequences
- a limited number of options
- inappropriate decisions may have far-reaching implications
- groups with conflicting objectives have to be dealt with
- the chief executive becomes directly involved.

Guidelines for handling the time factor are equally important, since, as we have already seen, a crisis is a dynamic event. As a result, any action taken must not be based on a static interpretation of the phenomenon. Steven Fink, among others, proposes the following sequence of events (Fink, 1986, pp. 20–5):

> - A crisis can consist of as many as four different and distinct phases. (...)
> - The prodomal crisis stage is the warning stage. (...)
> - The acute crisis phase tells you that [the crisis] has erupted. (...)
> - The chronic crisis stage (...) the clean-up phase, or the postmortem (...) With good crisis management skills, it also may become a time for congratulations (...) The chronic stage can linger indefinitely. But crisis management plans can, and do, shorten this phase.
> - The crisis resolution stage.

In order to take into account the immediate problems a decision maker faces when trying to come to grips with this type of disturbance, the following definition was proposed (Lagadec, 1984, pp. 41–2):

> Crisis: A situation in which a range of organizations, struggling
> with critical problems and subjected to strong external pressure
> and bitter internal tension, find themselves thrust into the lime-
> light, abruptly and for an extended period; they are also brought
> into conflict with one another . . . this occurs in the context of a
> mass media society, i.e. 'live', and the event is sure to make
> headlines on the radio and television and in the written press for
> a long time.

Living through a crisis

It is tempting to stick to a purely functional approach to crisis. Yet
doing so would seriously contradict all our efforts. And indeed, anyone
who has been in the eye of the storm places the greatest emphasis
on how incredibly difficult it is to *live through* a crisis. The testimony
of various managers agrees remarkably on this point: 'It couldn't
happen, not to us! We did what we liked, everyone did what they
liked, and we got caught in our own trap. We created our own crisis'
(cf. Lagadec, 1990, ch. 3).

It is indispensable here to introduce a few psychological considerations. Bolzinger (1982, p. 478) provides the necessary key words:

> Sudden: The crisis is perceived as a stunning event that bursts
> violently into the subject's life, even when it develops pro-
> gressively and takes a few days to settle in.

> Irrepressible: The crisis makes itself felt even in the most private
> spheres of the lives of those involved with pressing and un-
> avoidable currency, allowing neither respite nor rest.

> Incomprehensible: The crisis seems to be a curious series of
> coincidences; even if the subject undergoing the crisis fully
> accepts the logic of the situation in which he finds himself, he
> continues at some level to be surprised and strangely perturbed.

> Artificial: For the subject, the crisis is like a set of parentheses
> abruptly opened in the ordinary rhythm of his existence; it is a
> momentary paroxysm that is perceived as an objective reality
> that is distinct from the individual's objective reality.

Bolzinger (1982, p. 478) further emphasizes, 'Without this feeling of
being in crisis, there is no crisis; the mere clinical perception of the
symptom is enough to make the diagnosis.' The fact that the event
disturbs the subject may even be the primary source of the crisis.
And it is worth noting that what is true for individuals is equally true
for an entire organization. This evokes echoes of the general statements
often heard when diagnosing a crisis: 'An organization is in a crisis

when it recognizes the fact,' or 'You know the crisis has hit when you implement the crisis plan'.

Yet Bolzinger (1982, pp. 478–9) goes even further:

> The subjective experience consequently comprises the necessary and sufficient condition for understanding the concept of crisis. It relegates any objective comprehension and any observations made outside the crisis framework to a secondary role. The concept of crisis is inseparable from its subjective foundation.

In other words, the subjective dimension must be unconditionally included in any analysis and any attempt to manage a crisis. It will never be possible to face a crisis—from within or from without—merely by applying a series of purely rational technical measures.

A three-fold blow to the organizations involved

The explanations provided above form a useful basis for reflection. But experience has shown that the first thing a crisis manager needs is to create some order in the difficulties with which he or she is faced. We have already seen the importance of the way the crisis is experienced. What needs to be clarified now are the major types of more strategic challenges that must be dealt with. Edgar Morin's fundamental contribution, mentioned earlier, will be an important source here (Morin, 1976).

From the manager's point of view, crisis dynamics are driven by three principal problems, which can be summarized in three images:

A tidal wave
A crisis is first of all a sudden avalanche of an impressive number of problems. The most frequently reported sign of this tidal wave is that communication networks are saturated, telephone switchboards are blocked, and extreme tactical contradictions appear that are absent from ordinary incidents. In short, a crisis can be considered here as an emergency situation that overwhelms the usual problem-solving resources.

Disruption
At a time when remarkable levels of performance are required, the crisis strikes a critical target: the general regulatory system. Confronted with such excessive disturbance (from inside or outside), the organization discovers that its ordinary operating methods are insufficient for the task at hand. Paradox and unexpected side effects counteract the steps taken to stabilize the situation; the

response mechanisms freeze up; any deviation tends to become more extreme rather than bringing the usual corrective phenomena into play. Underlying antagonisms become explicit, while clearly complementary resources become dissociated. Alliances tend to be fragile and fleeting, while conflicts are exacerbated; an increasing number of contradictory needs demand to be satisfied simultaneously. Some of the figures involved wave magic wands, while others take refuge in a dream world. The search begins for a miracle worker or a secret formula, but all it produces are scapegoats. Those involved try to unearth a conspiracy or frame-up (the likelihood of which may not be zero; but it is certainly less than that of the simple incapacity of the systems involved to deal appropriately with the situation[7]).

> *Richard Thornburgh, Governor of Pennsylvania during the Three Mile Island accident*
> As the combined result of a mix-up between the various agencies involved, poor internal information sharing among municipal, federal, and regional authorities, and bad relations with the media, Richard Thornburgh learned from the press that he had given orders for a general evacuation—which was news to him.[8]

Breakdown
The difficulties create absolute barriers. Minor tendencies become irreversible choices of direction. Because information receptors are rapidly saturated, perceptions and images turn into snapshots presenting a one-sided, all-or-nothing point of view. The situation quickly begins to develop along distressingly simplistic binary lines. An echo begins to arise from the context: the entire past is re-examined, all the old wounds are re-opened. Problems are lumped together in a block, and the contradictions grow and multiply. The margin for manoeuvre shrinks to zero: this is a no-win situation. Every choice seems to lead to a complete failure, in the short or long run.

This is an extremely ambiguous situation, because the vital road to recovery runs, or appears to run, closely parallel to the path to ruin. At least in theory, the crisis offers simultaneous opportunities for both failure and renewal. In the heat of the action, however, nothing can be determined with certainty. All the landmarks, both internal and external, have vanished. The tidal wave and resulting disruption make the actors involved fragile and impotent. Once the system has been shaken this way, the fundamental questioning and probing destabilize it even further. These three processes combine to produce crisis dynamics.

The combination of these three phenomena threaten to bring about a general collapse. The situation is very difficult to control, especially if the organizations involved have neither the psychological nor the practical prior preparation necessary to confront this type of powerful disturbance. 'All these things overlap, criss-cross, conflict and combine with each other,' writes Edgar Morin, who notes, 'The development and the outcome of a crisis are uncertain, not only because disorder progresses, but because all these extremely rich forces, processes, and phenomena influence and destroy each other within the disorder' (Morin, 1976, p. 160).

The system seems at this point not only to be caught in an emergency, but to be collapsing. Key values and guidelines, both internal and external, are cast into doubt. This is a dubious and in many ways arbitrary battle between the forces of regression and the forces of renewal, and it generates high anxiety. Here is the core of the crisis phenomenon: the familiar world threatens to fall apart. The feeling that results is expressed in the most common reactions: 'Nobody understands anything any more; people keep struggling, but they no longer know why.'

As things fall to pieces, the crisis dynamics become endowed with a new independence. In the worst cases, the trigger event becomes a mere accessory factor which is soon forgotten. Dealing with it fails to cause a return to normal: the crisis begins to feed on its environment, drawing sufficient strength to continue on its own. Like a satellite in orbit, it is carried by its own inertia, and the launch rocket is only a memory. The crisis takes on a life of its own. On the basis of the various elements available at this stage in our reflection, two obvious traps, described by Rainer Muller (1985, pp. 38–9), are clearly lying in wait for crisis managers:

- Crises represent complex realities, bound up with both issues from the past and the present social context, which is rarely cut and dried. It is, of course, tempting to limit any action taken to remedying the surface problems, and to take immediate steps without thinking about the underlying issues that connect all these problems. This type of improvisation is usually doomed to failure.
- It is also tempting to consider crisis management as a purely technical affair, which it is not. How can the political aspects of crisis

management be safely neglected? All too often, a crisis serves to reveal profound conflicts which do not lend themselves to 'technical' solutions.

What is to be done? Executives and organizational leaders are threatened with the loss of their credibility, their legitimacy, and even their dignity, if they remain sufficiently inflexible.

At this stage, the point of view adopted in this book is becoming clear. Managing a crisis is not a frantic rescue operation to be undertaken when there is virtually nothing else to be done. Rather, it is a way of acting on a threatening process as that process unfolds. The goal is to avoid slipping into a vicious circle and losing all control. This is why much of crisis management has to do with prevention.

Summary

Crisis: a three-fold challenge

1. The tidal wave

- Difficulties pile up and combine
- Normal logistics are ineffective, and defences prove to be illusory
- The situation becomes overwhelmingly complex and uncertain
- Contradictory tactical demands accumulate.

Crisis = An emergency that overwhelms problem-solving resources

2. Disruption

- Many support structures fail to function
- The wheels of the system seize up
- Self-regulating mechanisms are not triggered (deviations become exaggerated)
- Underlying antagonisms become explicit
- Alliances become fragile or fleeting
- Those involved take refuge in dream worlds or magic solutions.

Crisis = The system threatens to crumble

3. Breakdown

- Difficulties create absolute barriers
- Minor tendencies turn into irreversible choices of direction
- Concepts are transformed into immutable snapshots
- The crisis finds an echo in its context

- All the thorny cases, past and present, are re-opened
- Problems are lumped together
- Strategic requirements contradict each other (a no-win situation)
- Fundamental choices and values are discredited
- The situation is overshadowed by ambiguity
- The crisis takes on a life of its own.

Crisis = The familiar world threatens to collapse

Notes

1. *The Complete Works of Thomas Paine* (P.S. Foner, ed.), New York, 1945, vol. 1, pp. 50–1, cited in Starn, 1976, p. 6.
2. J. Burckhardt, 1971, pp. 216–17, quoted in Starn, 1976, p. 9.
3. Herman Kahn, 1965, cited in Robinson, 1968, p. 510.
4. Antony J. Wiener and Herman Kahn, 1962, cited in Hermann, 1972, p. 21.
5. Kent Miller and Ira Iscoe, 1963, 'The concept of crisis: current status and mental health implications', *Human Organization*, 22, p. 195–201, cited in Robinson, 1968, p. 511.
6. Uriel Rosenthal, 1986, cited in Rosenthal *et al.* (eds), 1989, p. 10.
7. This does not mean that such possibilities must be automatically ruled out. It is easy to imagine that an attack made against one organization could be carefully exploited, or even encouraged, by another, more powerful actor. A company involved in a trade war with another firm could 'take advantage' of the presence of certain elements within that firm who could be used to trigger a crisis. The important thing is not to let this type of consideration overshadow all other analyses of the event.
8. Richard Thornburgh in Lagadec, 1990.

Chapter 5

Crisis dynamics: recognizing the general difficulties

The previous chapters have outlined the basic structures of the crisis phenomenon. But the managers who must actually deal with a crisis need a less theoretical description.

In this chapter we propose to give a detailed reconnaissance of a number of conventional yet very disturbing difficulties that crisis managers are sure to encounter.

Now that we have begun to comprehend what crisis is, the central question returns: What should we do? To begin with, we should follow one of the key rules for managing chaos: before answering, start by patiently analysing the problem. This is why we shall attempt to look more closely at the problems in which actors and decision makers will be involved. A manager's first step into a crisis is often a slippery one. Then, almost immediately, shadows from the past reappear like creditors with an account to settle—and the price is that of poor preparation. Very quickly, the many hurdles and complications that comprise any crisis start to appear on the horizon.

Of course, in this chapter and throughout the book, ideas will necessarily be presented sequentially. In reality, the points that will be raised here successively would very likely arise simultaneously, or in a different order from that adopted here. And, of course, this book does not pretend to be exhaustive: its main goal is to provide tools for evaluating and adapting to situations.

The crisis begins: initial destabilization and defeat

The shock

The world seems to be collapsing around you; word comes that there are victims, or that there could be massive casualties; information pours in from all sides—or the silence is deafening. Events move too fast for human comprehension. The facts are immediate, over-whelming, and unbearable. The battle promises to be a long one, and it threatens to bring a series of crises in its wake once you have lost the position that seemed so secure, or that represented the bulwark of your defences.

The Amoco-Cadiz oil slick
'You have to call the prefect right away, there's a problem.' . . . A big problem. What could I do at one in the morning? My first concern was for the people on board. (...)

'Mr. Becam, you have to go on-site. I am delegating all my powers to you. You have the same powers as the Prime Minister. You must take charge of the clean-up battle.'

'Listen—all right, but how? I don't have any training in this. I was trained as an agricultural engineer—well, all right.'

'Coordinating meeting in an hour and a half at [the Prime Minister's] offices.'[1]

Henry Kissinger on Watergate
What he told me shattered everything (. . .) I was stunned, and now through acts that made no sense, discord would descend once again on a society already weakened by ten years of upheaval. I felt like a swimmer who had survived dangerous currents only to be plucked from apparent safety by unexpected and even more violent riptides toward uncharted seas. As I con-sidered what this portended for foreign policy, my heart sank.
(Kissinger, 1982, vol. 2, pp. 73, 76)

A late or poorly processed warning

It is a common—and misguided—idea that crises are preceded by warning signals which are received early enough that the protection and action systems can be triggered and brought into operation. Very often, the crisis begins in a completely different manner: there is no warning, or the first signals are misunderstood or rejected because they cannot possibly mean what they seem to be saying. When the crisis hits, it is already under way, catching people and defence systems off guard. The manager who starts to tackle the event already suffers from a severe handicap: the media were the first to sound the alarm, or it was a consumer protection organization, in conjunction with a major foreign laboratory, that revealed how much more alarming the situation was than the authorities wanted to admit. Often, by the time an organization and its executives have been alerted, and by the time people have become aware and have begun to mobilize, a lot of time has been lost.

Two scenarios can lead quickly to defeat: failing to respond appropriately to a clear and specific set of events, and failing to recognize the burgeoning crisis for what it is, especially if it does not coincide with a clearly identifiable trigger.

Especially when the crisis emerges slowly or insidiously, the danger is that none of the warning lights will be triggered: since nothing gives the alert, it takes so long for awareness to set in that the crisis is already well under way before the need and the urgency of reacting become apparent. No one moves to act; no one takes charge of the problem. Quietly, the crisis seizes the high ground, only to emerge when virtually all its elements are already in place.

Naturally, there are variations on this theme of crisis dynamics: a slow-burning, serious crisis may be hidden behind a clear-cut event that seems to be a simple, ordinary incident.

> Take the case of a traffic accident during rush hour in the fog on a highway skirting a major city. It may be some time before the firefighters realize that in the resulting pile up, there is a tanker truck full of ammonia that is leaking toxic gas. This explains why the waiting drivers are so strangely calm, and why radio contact has been lost with the patrol car located somewhere nearby.

No matter what the actual scenario may be, a number of factors come into play to levy a heavy price for this lag between event and response.

A massive and shattering challenge
The crisis hits without the slightest warning. A hospital is 'forewarned' that something has surely happened when masses of injured people begin spontaneously filling its waiting room.

> *The flooding of the Loire river, 21 September 1980*
> A woman living near the Loire: 'At 11.30 am, everything was normal. At noon, I ran to the window and saw a vision of the Apocalypse: camping trailers were floating along, one after another, on the foaming black water. They bobbed up and down. It was like a diabolic merry-go-round.'
>
> Another witness stated that at noon, he was watching TV with his family. At 12.15, the mayor came to warn him that the flood waters were coming. At 12.30, he was on the roof of his house, where he remained stuck until six in the evening, watching trucks float down the river.
>
> (See Bouquin *et al.*, 1990, p. 43.)

A completely unfamiliar event

The phenomena may be so new that no one knows how to interpret them correctly.

Explosion of the Mont-Blanc in Halifax on 7 December 1917[2]
The ship had been burning for twenty minutes when it exploded. No one suspected that the situation was dangerous: people were at their windows to see the show. And it was the explosion that caused some 2000 deaths and thousands of injuries from shattering glass. No one knew that the boat was transporting large quantities of explosives.

Hiroshima: what do we have to fear from a single bomb?
. . . when the bomb exploded—I don't know how many bombs were really dropped—I clearly saw two parachutes coming down. There were some twenty or thirty soldiers watching, too, and they were clapping their hands in glee because they thought the B-29 had been shot down and the pilots were trying to escape.

(Hachiya, 1955, p. 162)

Insufficient or faulty warning systems

Surprise is the rule of the game here. There is an endless supply of anecdotes, which are often worthy of a comedy of errors:

Telexes or fax messages are 'lost' in the office; phone messages don't get through; the offices are closed all weekend; the only specialists who could help can't get past the police barricade a few hundred yards from the burning factory; without his secretary, the executive is paralysed because he cannot work the telex or the fax; it is impossible to reach a manager, though the person is definitely somewhere in the building; the list of emergency phone numbers does not include direct lines, and the switchboard is closed after 6.00 pm. Other, more sophisticated problems also come into play: to call the fire department on his car telephone, an executive automatically dials 999, but because of where the car is located, the call goes to a fire department with which he has never worked and that doesn't know the specific nature of his plant.

Individual inertia and inexplicable gaps in organizational operations

The warning comes through, but it fails to 'ring a bell' in people's minds. The individuals in charge blank out, and no one reacts.

Exceptional flooding of the Loire, 21 September 1980
The mayor of a small town near the river was alerted that a flood was coming. The message arrived four hours before the high waters, but no one reacted. The municipal officer continued to follow the day's agenda. The second warning was a siren: he didn't hear it.[3]

(See Bouquin et al., 1990, p. 43.)

The case of the EC-121, an American military plane shot down by North Korea in 1969
At 2.17 A.M. Radio Pyongyang announced that North Korea had shot down a United States reconnaissance plane (. . .). But for reasons unfathomable to me at this remove, everybody decided to ignore the broadcast. On the ground that we had no independent confirmation, the shootdown was still classified as 'unconfirmed' as late as 7.20 A.M., when I briefed Nixon (. . .). It was as if someone had pushed a button labeled 'crisis management' and the answer that came up was 'nonchalance'.

(Kissinger, 1979, Vol. 1, p. 316)

The sluggishness of all administrative operations

An event occurs: it is confusing and fuzzy and is not really covered by the job description of this or that department. It could involve everyone, or no one, or some of the above, depending on how you look at it.

Nothing is more difficult for an organization to handle. Someone has to decide who is in charge, and in what pigeonhole this new event can be classified. This approach is vital to keep the enterprise running smoothly—without order, chaos would soon take over.

But this logical behaviour can become a sort of caricature of itself: some bureaucracies seem more concerned with who is running a given territory than with what is happening there.

In this context, organizations simply become paralysed when they are suddenly faced with an event that does not fit into any existing category. It would be so much easier if the crisis would plainly define its type, in accordance with bureaucratic classifications. Then it could be assessed, classified, and attributed (as if Earthlings would require a Martian to state whether it would speak English, French, or Chinese before its presence could be acknowledged).

In addition, an organization develops its operating systems to handle its problems as a whole, not to deal in a hurry with a few, sudden exceptions. If an extraordinary situation is not recognized as such, it will be treated according to the book. Consequently, the vital information will be somewhere in the system, but will not reach the decision maker. This has been clearly analysed in such cases as the Cuban Missile Crisis. John F. Kennedy was informed late of the state of events. It took more than ten days for the information to be processed, checked, compared, and forwarded to the highest level (Roberts, 1988, pp. 40–1). But this is virtually standard practice.

Henry Kissinger
It is a common myth that high officials are informed immediately
about significant events. Unfortunately, official information must
almost invariably run the obstacle of bureaucratic review or the
need for a cover memorandum to put the event into somebody's
perspective. It happens not infrequently—much too frequently
for the security adviser's emotional stability—that even the
President learns of a significant occurrence from the newspapers.
(Kissinger, 1979, Vol. 1, p. 185)

Saturated operators

A manager and the manager's team are already normally overwhelmed by information and problems to be solved. Under these
conditions, even the most strident warning cries are not always
heard. Systems are actually calibrated to digest a certain amount of
information. Beyond that threshold, the circuit breakers switch on.
Jean-Claude Wanner, a specialist in systems security and man–
machine interfaces, has highlighted this type of problem, and his
comments about technical operators are equally applicable to top
management teams.

Jean-Claude Wanner: Airplane accident
An operator is already saturated by the number of ordinary
operations to be performed . . . it is difficult to ask him to
absorb any further information, even if it is presented, say, as a
sound signal, on the grounds that his eyes are already busy. An
overwhelmed operator can ignore even a very loud noise, as the
following real-life anecdote shows. This happened to an experienced pilot a few years ago. If the landing gear fails to come
down during the landing phase, the warning takes the form of a
piercing siren. This was the dialogue between the pilot and the
control tower:

'Charley Bravo, you are authorized for landing.'
'This is Charley Bravo, final approach, landing gear and wing
flaps down, locked and checked.'
'Charley Bravo, hit the gas, your landing gear is not down.'
'This is Charley Bravo, please repeat, I'm not receiving you
clearly, there's a siren blowing in my ears.'
And the plane landed!
(See Nicolet *et al.*, 1989, p. 59)

Relatively weak warning signals

Some crises, it should be noted, are more insidious and slow-moving.
Their warning signals are very close to the normal background noise
from the system, until they explode. The trap here is that nothing
triggers the warning systems, as they are not wired to capture such
weak signals or to detect the threat in question. Draped in a fuzzy

ambiguity, the crisis silently infiltrates the territory and only unveils itself when its work is virtually accomplished. The classic example here is what the specialists call the non-event—though they alone regard it as such.

> *Philippe Vesseron: Disposing of the Seveso dioxin drums*[4]
> Strangely enough, the matter began by a very serene period.
> [. . .] The whole thing appeared in French and foreign press
> agency dispatches without raising any of the questions that
> common sense should have dictated in such shadowy circum-
> stances. The Minister of the Environment undertook to clarify the
> mystery before anyone asked him to [. . .] No one was asking us
> the questions we wanted to be ready for. The only interrogation
> at the Assemblée Nationale was regarding the old project to
> make a sea dump. [. . .] All that made us feel satisfied. That
> Hoffmann-La-Roche provided us with the most detailed response
> fit in with the idea that each industrial leader had to be able to
> account personally for the conditions in which waste from his
> plants is eliminated. [. . .] In fact, this was a period in which the
> matter was dissipated in the wheels of the administrative works.
> [. . .] as soon as an issue is no longer urgent and doesn't pre-
> cisely fit anyone's job description, the information may very well
> not be used fast enough. [. . .]
>
> At the end of December, Senator Noè [. . .] gave us a copy of an
> affidavit drawn up on December 13 by a Milan notary, certifying
> that [the disposal] had gone as planned. What surprised us was
> that the language was almost identical to that used by Hoffmann-
> La-Roche in October. [. . .] That was when we began to ask the
> troubling question of who really knew what.[4]

Preconceived notions, set ideas, and great mental stumbling blocks
There are two phenomena at work here: the intellectual briar patch and the psychological one. This is what Wanner calls 'perceptional errors'. They prevent the situation from being correctly analysed. All the facts are available, but no one understands anything, or rather, everyone misunderstands. This is an extremely powerful psychological process. Prisoners of habit, operators and organizations fail to evaluate correctly the signals they are receiving. What is the reflex reaction when an air-raid siren sounds? 'Oh, that must be the first-Wednesday-of-the-month test.' No one stops to think that it isn't Wednesday. And the issue is even thornier when the danger is caused by the pro-tection systems themselves. This was the problem with the dyke dis-cussed earlier, which provided protection from river flooding but became the primary cause of disaster by retaining water flowing from the mountains. Or in the city of Minamata, where the local pop-ulation had always considered eating fish as the remedy for bad

health—even when the fish became contaminated. The sicker people got, the more they felt they should eat fish, and the greater the dose of poison they absorbed.

The same mechanisms go to work even in the largest organizations:

> *Henry Kissinger: Blindness of all observers prior to the 1973*
> *Yom Kippur War*
> The day before the war the CIA reiterated its judgment: Egypt did not appear to be preparing for war with Israel. Clearly, there was an intelligence failure, but misjudgment was not confined to the agencies. Every policymaker knew all the facts. (. . .) The general plan of attack, especially of the Syrians, was fairly well understood. What no one believed. (. . .) was that the Arabs would act on it. Our definition of rationality did not take seriously the notion of starting an unwinnable war to restore self-respect. There was no defense against our own preconceptions or those of our allies.
>
> Our mind-set was dramatized by events on October 5, when we woke up to the astonishing news that for twenty-four hours the Soviet Union had been airlifting all its dependents out of Egypt and Syria. Technical and military advisers seemed to be staying, however. It is now inexplicable how that development was misinterpreted.(. . .)
>
> The breakdown was not administrative but intellectual.
> (Kissinger, 1982, Vol. 2, pp. 464, 466)

Struggling desperately not to admit something could be wrong

When incoming information is disturbing, we have an intuitive and as yet vague feeling that something is seriously wrong. The natural response is often to hide or to refuse the facts. We simply put the troubling data out of our minds. Granted, a quick though voluntarily hazy glance tells us that things are certainly no longer the way they should be. Yet the idea persists: 'This is nothing, everything is under control, business as usual.' There is also a vague realization that if ever it were necessary to take action, something would have to change—if nothing else, the daily schedule—and that alone is annoying and unsettling.

So the vicious circle continues to turn around the two poles of increasing evidence and reinforced refusal of the facts. On the one hand, the data that keep piling up will eventually have to be interpreted as a warning signal. On the other hand, everyone secretly realizes just how disruptive it would be if the alarm were real. That would mean admitting there could be a danger, and running the risk of being accused of having panicked for nothing.

The combat becomes more bitter. If anyone acknowledges the reality of the situation, the steps that must be taken will necessarily be more and more drastic. This explains why the actors most directly involved are often the last ones to fathom what is happening. (Take the example of a Canadian hospital in which every storey was evacuated because of a fire—except the floor that was burning.) Often the alarm must be sounded on the outside, by actors who are less closely involved. After all, there are none so blind as those who will not see, until the veil is ripped from their eyes, until the framework that has been forced around the data suddenly bursts. This is when the crisis comes to collect its due, with astounding brutality.

Everyone can think of examples, even ordinary ones, from personal experience. Think of those high winds whose violence was far greater than predicted by the weather service. The brain reacts immediately: 'Come, come, there are no cyclones in this region! How can I cancel all my important appointments, especially for such a silly reason? No, this is nothing, let's not be ridiculous.' Yet the signs remain, and the winds blow even harder. The mind begins to work on two tracks: on the one hand, it seeks to reassure itself: 'This is nothing special, let's not panic.' On the other hand, vague worry sets in: 'What if I'm wrong?' The battle is on between these two lines of analysis, though a careful effort is made to avoid actually evaluating the available evidence. This goes on until the warning signal gives way to a solid event that is undeniably unusual: for example, the roof blows off. Suddenly, all the illusions dissolve as a sort of putsch occurs in the world of perceptions, and the message finally gets through. The next reaction is to run for cover, but it's too late—the storm is already there, in full force.

> Albert Camus: He knew very well that this was the plague, but . . .
> Next day, by dint of a persistence which many thought ill-advised, Rieux persuaded the authorities to convene a 'health committee' at the Prefect's office.
>
> 'People in town are getting nervous, that's a fact,' Dr. Richard admitted. 'And of course all sorts of wild rumors are going round. The Prefect said to me, "Take prompt action if you like, but don't attract attention." He personally is convinced that it's a false alarm.' [. . .]
>
> The Prefect greeted them amiably enough, but one could see his nerves were on edge. 'Let's make a start, gentlemen,' he said. 'Need I review the situation?'
> Richard thought that wasn't necessary. He and his colleagues

were acquainted with the facts. The only question was what measures should be adopted.

'The question,' old Castel cut in almost rudely, 'is to know whether it's plague or not.'

Two or three of the doctors present protested. The others seemed to hesitate. The Prefect gave a start and hurriedly glanced towards the door to make sure it had prevented this outrageous remark from being overheard in the passage. Richard said that in his opinion the great thing was not to take an alarmist view. All that could be said at present was that we had to deal with a special type of fever, with inguinal complications; in medical science, as in daily life, it was unwise to jump to conclusions. Old Castel [. . .] said that he knew quite well that it was plague and, needless to say, he also knew that, were this to be officially admitted, the authorities would be compelled to take very drastic steps. This was, of course, the explanation of his colleagues' reluctance to face the facts and, if it would ease their minds, he was quite prepared to say it wasn't plague. The Prefect seemed ruffled and remarked that, in any case, this line of argument seemed to him unsound.

'The important thing,' Castel replied, 'isn't the soundness or otherwise of the argument—but for it to make you think.'

Rieux, who had said nothing so far, was asked for his opinion. 'We are dealing,' he said, 'with a fever of a typhoidal nature, accompanied by vomiting and buboes. I have incised these buboes and had the pus analyzed; our laboratory analyst believes he has identified the plague bacillus. But I am bound to add that there are specific modifications which don't quite tally with the classical description of the plague bacillus.' Richard pointed out that this justified a policy of wait-and-see; anyhow, it would be wise to await the statistical report on the series of analyses that had been going on for several days.

'When a microbe,' Rieux said, 'after a short intermission can quadruple in three days' time the volume of the spleen, can swell the mesenteric glands to the size of an orange and give them the consistency of gruel, a policy of wait-and-see is, to say the least of it, unwise. [. . .] It has small importance whether you call it plague or some rare kind of fever. The important thing is to prevent its killing off half the population of this town.'

Richard said it was a mistake to paint too gloomy a picture, and, moreover, the disease hadn't been proved to be contagious; indeed, relatives of his patients, living under the same roof, had escaped it.

'But others have died,' Rieux observed. 'And obviously contagion is never absolute; otherwise you'd have a constant mathematical progression and the death-rate would rocket up catastrophically. It's not a question of painting too black a picture. It's a question of taking precautions.'

Richard, however, summing up the situation as he saw it, pointed out that, if the epidemic did not cease spontaneously, it would be necessary to apply the rigorous prophylactic measures laid down in the Code. And, to do this, it would be necessary to admit officially that plague had broken out. But of this there was no absolute certainty; therefore any hasty action was to be deprecated.

Rieux stuck to his guns. 'The point isn't whether the measures provided for in the Code are rigorous, but whether they are needful to prevent the death of half the population. All the rest is a matter of administrative action, and I needn't remind you that our constitution has provided for such emergencies by empowering Prefects to issue the necessary orders.'

'Quite true,' the Prefect assented. 'But I shall need your professional declaration that the epidemic is one of plague.'

'If we don't make that declaration,' Rieux said, 'there's a risk that half the population may be wiped out.'

Richard cut in with some impatience. 'The truth is that our colleague is convinced it's plague; his description of the syndrome proved it.'

Rieux replied that he had not described a 'syndrome'—but merely what he'd seen with his own eyes. And what he'd seen was buboes, and high fever accompanied by delirium, ending fatally within forty-eight hours. Could Dr. Richard take the responsibility of declaring that the epidemic would die out without the imposition of rigorous prophylactic measures?

Richard hesitated, then fixed his eyes on Rieux. 'Please answer me quite frankly. Are you absolutely convinced it's plague?'

'You're stating the problem wrongly. It's not a question of the term I use; it's a question of time.'

'Your view, I take it,' the Prefect put in, 'is this. Even if it isn't plague, the prophylactic measures enjoined by law for coping with a state of plague should be put into force immediately?'

'If you insist on my having a "view", that conveys it accurately enough.' The doctors confabulated. Richard was their spokesman. 'It comes to this. We are to take the responsibility of acting as though the epidemic were plague?'

This way of putting it met with general approval.

'It doesn't matter to me,' Rieux said, 'how you phrase it. My point is that we should not act as if there were no likelihood that half the population wouldn't be wiped out; for then it would be.'

Followed by scowls and protestations, Rieux left the committee-room.

(Camus, 1948, pp. 43–6)

Slowly getting mobilized

For one or another (or perhaps even several) of the reasons identified here, the crisis progresses without encountering a defensive reaction from the system under attack; the crisis progresses in an (unjustified) atmosphere of nonchalance that seems astonishing with hindsight. Consequently, the initial phase of the crisis may well arouse nothing more than a wait-and-see attitude.

This tendency is reinforced by the solid organizational motivations that underlie it. Organizations are able to function because they are capable of sorting out real warnings from the background noise. If the emergency system were triggered at the drop of a hat, nothing would ever get done. The name of the game is 'never cry wolf'. But this line of argument tends to remain in use long after it is no longer valid. And this organizational behaviour seems all the more reasonable when no thoughtful questions are asked and no prior planning has been done. No one has described the significant phenomena to be monitored or the subtle, potentially threatening symptoms, so there are no *ad hoc* receptors ready to operate.

The dynamics of this prudent approach, virtually taking two steps back for every one forward, also characterizes the internal information process. Very often, a vacuum develops as soon as a crisis is suspected. Information does rise through the hierarchy, but only slowly. Everyone is bothered at having to pass on such muddled, disturbing data, and no one seems to have clear and definite responsibility for it. The more confused and anxiety-producing the situation becomes, the more marked is this tendency towards foot-dragging. In such cases, every parcel of information must be analysed with special care.

By the same token, a certain number of key decision makers seem to disappear, or it becomes difficult to contact the decision-making centres. Here again, several feelings—that of treading on dangerous ground, of not being implicated, that of preferring to understand better before attempting anything, and of being afraid—all combine to foster further delays and 'disappearances'.

These two tendencies foster each other mutually: the person who sends a message up the line is satisfied with having done so and does not bother to check whether it was actually received, whether it was read, or whether the person who received it is in a position to do something about it. As a result, those in charge are often informed late in the action, when the crisis has already gained significant amplitude. It is commonplace to observe that, at every level, a problem is not tackled until individuals at that level have no longer the means to deal with it. The crisis begins to undermine by attrition: bit by bit, the organization loses its various means of resisting and responding.

In short, a crisis inspires those involved to reject responsibility up and down the line more often than it encourages anyone resolutely to take charge. This is, at least, the most natural backdrop that tends to fall into place if individuals, teams, and organizations have not been specifically prepared for such eventualities.

This is how the development of the situation escapes the organization's control. Outside players, such as the media, take over. But they, too, may be one step behind the event. At this stage, grassroots associations or victims may well become the driving force. Quite understandably, they bring into play all their perspicacity and energy when their interests—and especially their health—are or appear to be threatened.

The crisis finds reinforcements: the past settles its accounts

This is a leitmotiv: the ability to deal with a crisis situation is largely dependent on the structures that have been developed before chaos arrives. The event can in some ways be considered as an abrupt and brutal audit: at a moment's notice, everything that was left unprepared becomes a complex problem, and every weakness comes rushing to the forefront. The breech in the defences opened by crisis creates a sort of vacuum.

A cascade of technical problems that aggravate the actual breakdown

Many latent weak points are unveiled in times of trial. A structure that was supposed to provide a fire block for at least 30 minutes burns down in less than five, because the blueprints were not followed and the necessary checks were not run. A concrete containment wall proves to be porous, when its main purpose is to insulate and prevent leaks. In short, all the difficulties that can arise from underestimating or ignoring preparations or failing to oversee a subcontractor, come to fan the fires of the crisis.

Organizational problems that hamper emergency action

The shock of the event is all the greater because no one has prepared for such problems or thought ahead of time about them. Consequently, several problems soon become apparent.

The absence of prior reflection
Basically, the actors are caught off guard. They simply do not have the mental reflexes or framework to think about the problem. And the midst of the crisis is hardly the ideal time or place to develop the fundamental references that they need.

Stupefying organizational gaps
Faced with the situation, no one seems to feel qualified to take charge of the problem.

> *Henry Kissinger and the Opening of China (1971): A country off the State Department's maps*
> The problem [the Executive's battle against its bureaucratic inertia] was accentuated by the anomaly that some long-forgotten State Department reorganization had placed the subcontinent in the Near East Bureau, whose jurisdiction ended at the subcontinent's eastern boundary; it excluded East Asia and any consideration of China. Senior officials who might have been conscious of China's concerns had been excluded from the opening to Peking. Hence, there was no one at State who felt fully responsible for the 'China account' or even fully understood its rationale— this was one of the prices paid for our unorthodox method of administration.
> (Kissinger, 1979, Vol. 1, p. 865)

No emergency plans
Emergency plans should outline the resources, operating procedures, responsibilities, and chains of command. When no such plans exist, a strategic vacuum develops and a myriad of little tactical problems accumulate that wear down the heartiest actors. A plan is an indispensable tool, because it lays out the rules for action and considerably facilitates the 'footwork' required during a crisis (especially gathering basic data). This frees those involved to think about the specific problems posed by the event. When there is no emergency plan, a

desperate treasure hunt begins which quickly saps people's energy and consumes both time and internal communications resources—and the situation is aggravated by the fact that what should be basic logistical reflexes are also missing.

Paper plans and imaginary capacities

Often, when an emergency plan does exist, it has never been tested: these are paper plans, and their thickness and the 'confidential' stamp do not ensure that they are relevant. A plan should be a truly operational tool, and not just a reference whose only purpose is to reassure everyone when things are calm. It must be a continuous process, of which the document marked 'plan' is simply a written presentation. This goes for the technical aspects of the plan, but even more particularly for its relational aspects: one of its basic requirements is making a prior effort to identify and develop relations among the various organizations that could be implicated. Unless this actual prior planning effort is made, the plan quickly proves to be nothing more than a mythical reference.

The consequences are well known. It quickly becomes clear that the resources or the specialists that were foreseen or the procedures that were set down cannot be counted on. The guidelines prove very difficult to use, and communication between organizations functions poorly—yet this is hardly the time, as the pace of events accelerates, to sit down and become better acquainted. Another frequent stumbling block arises even when various in-house teams or contacts in different organizations think they know each other: all they have shared is mutual assurances about their respective capacities. When it comes time to manage a crisis, however, it is important to understand each other's vulnerability, doubts, and the unthinkable situations feared by each team or organization involved. A crisis quickly makes a mockery of earlier meetings when everyone showed how infallible they were and sought above all to mark out their territory. Consequently, a new basis for these relations must be forged in the midst of the chaos, in an atmosphere of suspicion and fear, when the actors absolutely must be able to trust one another and interact effectively. Generally, the test is so harsh that individuals tend instead to become closed and resistant.

> *Maurice Grimaud and France's emergency plans in May 1968*
> In our morning meetings at the Prime Minister's offices, I was surprised to learn how all the major government services had been caught off guard by events and found themselves helpless in the face of accumulating difficulties. Not that we hadn't made

very lovely plans long before to guarantee that these services would go on functioning in case of trouble or a general strike. Rather, none of these plans worked, primarily because no one had ever tested them.

There was a plan to guarantee a minimal train service, and one for civil aviation, and another for transporting fuel and supplying the cities, and for maintaining radio and television broadcasts. All of them, to be effective, presupposed that electric power plants and the grid would be in working order, because without electricity and telephones, all the others would grind to a halt. These plans had been studied down to the last detail by administrative units combining civil servants and military men. They were based on assistance from the army and on requisitioning certain categories of public service agents. But once signed and stamped with 'Secret' seals, they were apparently all locked carefully in the safes full of confidential documents located in each ministry, and they had gathered dust there until today. It wasn't just by coincidence that they generally bore names inspired by mythology—rarely was an organization more mythical than that one.

(Grimaud, 1977, pp. 206-7)

Typical mistakes and behaviour deserving criticism

A crisis becomes even more complex to handle when it reveals not only imprudent behaviour, but uncooperative and even hostile attitudes in the pre-accident phase.

Thirteen million burning tyres in Hagersville, Ontario (February 1990)
The newspaper *La Presse*[5] reviewed a number of facts that were certain to complicate the way an industrial leader would manage the crisis. 'Tyre King Recycling had been enjoined three years earlier by the government of Ontario to proceed with significant modifications in order to avoid a major disaster, and Jim Bradley, the Minister of the Environment, criticized the company harshly yesterday for having preferred to fight the directive in the courts rather than take the measures required to limit the danger. In January 1987, the government requested Edward Straza, the owner, to install a reservoir on the site for use in case of fire, and to store the tires in piles of a hundred each, separated by fire breaks. "We were worried about the fire danger represented by this yard, and we asked the owner to make the changes necessary to protect the environment," stated Mike Lewis, spokesman for the Ministry.

'Straza, however, took the ministerial injunction before the environmental board of appeals, which ruled in favor of the government last April. "Tyre King represents a serious danger for the environment," declared the board, "and it could cause a major ecological disaster. Even if the risk is slight, the probable consequences of a fire, namely the release of contaminants in the environment, would be very serious." Straza appealed this decision, but the case had not yet been heard when the fire broke out.'

Le Devoir[6] took a broader point of view: 'For years, various governments have known that the mountains of tyres like the one that is burning in Hagersville, Ontario [. . .] were ecological time bombs simply waiting to explode. But they have preferred to prepare regulations—which regulate nothing, and which the polluters make a sport of contesting in court, while they wait for a fire to start.'

A wealth of defiance

The same reserve that marks relations with the other organizations involved emerges even more strongly in contacts with the public and the media. Levels of prior information, confidence, credibility, and legitimacy are often very low. No prior relationships may have been established, or worse, the atmosphere may be heavy with mutual suspicion. This creates a very negative basis for the next phases of the crisis.

This is the so-called inheritance: What was said in the past? What was done in terms of safety, especially in the case of a project for which acceptance was hard won? What type of relations have been cultivated over the years? How much information has been kept under wraps to avoid provoking 'unnecessary anxiety'?

> *Problems of confidence surrounding high-risk sites about which insufficient information is distributed*
> Anne Lalo, professor at the University of Grenoble, has shown in a study of the southern French district of Bouches-du-Rhône that public confidence is sometimes very low. In fact, the actors who receive the lowest confidence rating before an information campaign were, in decreasing order, the industrial leaders themselves, local elected officials, and journalists.
>
> *Concerns raised about nuclear power*
> When a problem arises, all the shadows from the past resurface. These include the following types of elements (which would certainly have less impact at present, in light of recent efforts to provide better information).
>
> • Revelations like those made around the Windscale affair in Great Britain; the matter was kept secret by order from the British Prime Minister, and the emissions were only acknowledged some 30 years after the fact.

- The handling of the Chernobyl accident in France highlighted
  an immediate vulnerability of public authority. (The early official
  line suggested that the radioactive cloud had stopped at the
  Franco-German border.) The extent of the communications
  failure could be measured in the headlines in the press following revelations made on 10 May 1986 on French television.
  These ran the gamut from 'Radioactive lies' to 'Radioactive
  contamination in France: the Truth' to 'Nuclear energy: What
  the experts aren't telling you' or 'The Day France was radiated'.
  In a Gallup poll published on 24 October 1986, the damage
  proved to be considerable: when asked, 'Have you been told
  the truth?', 79 per cent answered 'no'. 'Are the technicians
  telling the truth?' Answer: 64 per cent 'no'.
- If further examples were needed, there is the case of the
  Mont-Louis, which sank in August 1985 while transporting
  drums of uranium hexafluoride. This, too, produced a communications failure that remained entrenched in people's
  minds. All the French newspapers ran headlines on the cover-
  up, from 'Uranium: Hush, we're sinking' to 'Silence of the
  Deep' to 'The cargo was more dangerous than they said'.

(See Lalo, 1988, p. 43)

The past comprises a collection of assets or liabilities, and these
quickly determine the path taken by crisis dynamics. (This path may
be different at the local, national, and international level.) This is an
important point: in some cases, the prior groundwork may be so bad
that no crisis management tools are of any utility.

All the failures of the prevention phase come to light

Anything that can be interpreted as a sign of pre-accident negligence
will immediately be brought into the limelight and subjected to very
critical examination.

Three Mile Island
A senior engineer of the Babcock & Wilcox Company (suppliers
of the nuclear steam system) noted in an earlier accident, bearing
strong similarities to the one at Three Mile Island, that operators
had mistakenly turned off the emergency cooling system. He
pointed out that we were lucky that the circumstances under
which this error was committed did not lead to a serious accident
and warned that under other circumstances (like those that
would later exist at Three Mile Island), a very serious accident
could result. He urged, in the strongest terms, that clear
instructions be passed on to the operators. This memorandum
was written 13 months before the accident at Three Mile Island,
but no new instructions resulted from it.

(Kemeny, 1979, p. 10)

Challenger (January 28, 1986)
The engineers at Thiokol, manufacturers of the ring that was to cause the tragedy, expressed serious reserves on the eve of the launch about the prevailing temperature conditions on 27 January 1986. This information quickly overshadowed the post-catastrophe debate.

(See Nicolet *et al.*, 1989, p. 139)

The DC-10 crash in Ermenonville, France in 1974: 346 dead[7]
A search was undertaken for any precedents that should have set warning lights blinking about the potential for an incident involving the cargo compartment doors, and one case—Detroit, 12 June 1972—was found.

Efforts were made to identify any warnings that might have been given that should have attracted the attention of those in charge, and examples came to light. Following the close call in Detroit, the engineering director working on the design of the cargo door (at Convair) circulated a very explicit memo:

'The airplane demonstrated an inherent susceptibility to catastrophic failure when exposed to explosive decompression of the cargo compartment in 1970 ground tests [. . .]. Murphy's law being what it is, cargo doors will come open sometime during the twenty years of use ahead for the DC-10. [. . .] It is recommended that overtures be made at the highest management level to persuade Douglas to immediately make a decision to incorporate changes in the DC-10 which will correct the fundamental cabin floor catastrophic failure mode.'

Nothing was done.

Then came the hunt for who was at fault. The obvious targets were the FAA and the NSTB, the administrations in charge of air traffic security. Eventually blame was placed not only on the laxity of these agencies, but more seriously, on the way in which their executives were appointed:

In 1969 the President nominated—and Congress approved—John Hixon Shaffer, then fifty, an ex-Air Force officer with rock-solid Republican loyalties, but with very little experience of commercial aircraft to qualify him to head the most powerful and influential aviation-regulating body in the world.

In March 1971, the chief administrator of the NTSB, Ernest Weiss, was retired and replaced, on the recommendation of the White House, by Richard L. Spears. Mr. Spears's qualifications for the $36,000-a-year job of running an agency that is exclusively concerned with public safety were minimal: He had worked for an aviation company, Aerojet General Corporation, but had no technical qualifications, and more recently he had been a Republican political aide.

The road into the impasse may also pass via complaints about the lack of prior information and communication, along the lines of, 'if you had done a better job of informing us, we could have found a way out of this situation much more easily'.

> *Catastrophe on the Piper Alpha offshore North Sea drilling platform, 7 July 1988: 166 dead*[8]
> A British union condemned a Department of Energy decision to withhold information about the compatibility of different types of survival clothing. A report had been prepared evaluating the different combinations of immersion suits and lifejackets, but the union had to fight to obtain a copy. In it, they learned that of the 24 combinations available, only six provided satisfactory protection. The information had been unavailable before the accident.
>
> *The Times* announced on its second page: 'The Department of Energy yesterday confirmed it had withheld information—which a union says could have helped save the lives of offshore workers [. . .]. The Department of Energy said last night that the report on lifejackets and immersion suits would "soon" be made available to the industry.'

This is a common trap for management: when an issue is deemed to be too outrageous, the tendency is to ignore it. And yet, a wild hypothesis or an incredible 'revelation' will quickly come to be considered as well-founded, especially if no one addresses it—this silence turns into virtual official acknowledgement of the truth.

It is also important to recognize that, generally speaking, critical investigators almost always find something when they begin digging into the past. After all, no system functions perfectly. The most awkward situation is when a warning was issued on a given point, and not taken into consideration—until it reappears at the heart of a breakdown. It may have been quite reasonable not to listen to the doomsayers, but it is very difficult to build a convincing defence when the arguments pointing to the guilt and negligence of those in charge is so apparently flagrant.

Forgotten documents rise to the surface

As is so often the case in the field of crisis, a number of obscure processes are set in motion, and they are strengthened by the degree of difficulty caused by the problems discussed above.

Inevitably, reports will come to light or be 'leaked'. These may be intelligent, premonitory documents, alarmist reports, or memos simply intended to provide cover for the author. (Some actors may very well have attempted to cover themselves in anticipation of a crisis event by pointing out trouble spots, while at the same time signing other documents which give the system a clean bill of health.) The reports which declared that everything was fine will be kept in the archives. In addition, all this information will be removed from its context: gross negligence will of course appear as such, but the decision to ignore a minor risk will also become an act of unpardonable negligence.

> *Henry Kissinger*
> After every crisis there surfaces in the press some obscure intelligence report or analyst purporting to have predicted it, only to have been foolishly ignored by the policymakers. What these claims omit to mention is that when warnings become too routine they lose all significance; when reports are not called specifically to the attention of the leadership they are lost in bureaucratic background noise, particularly since for every admonitory report one can probably find also its opposite in the files.
>
> (Kissinger, 1979, Vol. 1, p. 38)

Individuals pushed to the brink

To face a crisis effectively, the individuals involved must be in excellent physical condition, with solid mental stability, and their intellectual ability must be at its height. This is the only way they will be able to reflect, anticipate, rethink the steps they need to take, and find new approaches to situations that seem insoluble. At the same time, a major event severely curtails all these aptitudes.

A difficult ordeal

In general, each individual receives the initial shock like a body blow, with feelings of impotence, urgency, uncertainty, and guilt combined with a sense of all that is at stake and the feeling of having lost the reference framework. This is one of the most difficult moments in a manager's life. Here again, the past casts a long shadow, and the pathos of the moment revives old memories of earlier traumas.

> *Robert Kennedy at the brink with his brother, the President, during the Cuban Missile Crisis (1962)*
> It was now a few minutes after 10:00 o'clock. Secretary McNamara announced that two Russian ships, the Gagarin and

the Komiles, were within a few miles of our quarantine barrier. [. . .] Then came the disturbing Navy report that a Russian submarine had moved into position between the two ships. [. . .] I think that these few minutes were the time of gravest concern for the President. Was the world on the brink of a holocaust? Was it our error? A mistake? Was there something further that should have been done? Or not done? His hand went up to his face and covered his mouth. He opened and closed his fist. His face seemed drawn, his eyes pained, almost gray. [. . .] For a few fleeting seconds, it was almost as though no one else was there and he was no longer the President.

Inexplicably, I thought of when he was ill and almost died; when he lost his child; when we learned that our oldest brother had been killed; of personal times of strain and hurt. The voices droned on, but I didn't seem to hear anything until I heard the President say: 'Isn't there some way we can avoid having our first exchange with a Russian submarine—almost anything but that?' 'No, there's too much danger to our ships. There is no alternative,' said McNamara. [. . .]

We had come to the time of final decision. [. . .] I felt we were on the edge of a precipice with no way off. This time, the moment was now—not next week—not tomorrow, 'so we can have another meeting and decide'; not in eight hours, 'so we can send another message to Khrushchev and perhaps he will finally understand.' No, none of that was possible. One thousand miles away in the vast expanse of the Atlantic Ocean the final decisions were going to be made in the next few minutes. President Kennedy had initiated the course of events, but he no longer had control over them. He would have to wait—we would have to wait. The minutes in the Cabinet Room ticked slowly by. What could we say now—what could we do?

(Kennedy, 1971, pp. 47–9)

It is worth examining and identifying in greater detail the problems with the most direct organizational impact which afflict each participant.[9]

- The event will necessitate long hours of work.
- The key figures will almost certainly be absent or unavailable.
- It will suddenly be necessary to coordinate work with a large number of people; everyone and anyone will come knocking at your door.
- Often, these will be high-ranking figures, although you will be scarcely acquainted, if at all; you will not know the codes and requirements of these foreign worlds. It therefore becomes difficult to interpret the messages that arrive or to formulate the answers requested.

- The pressure is extraordinary. For example, requests may come down directly from the company's CEO, instead of through the normal hierarchical channels. Consequently, it is hard to know how to regard the normal hierarchy. Short-circuiting the usual chains of command raises at least two difficulties: first, it creates strains within the structure and, second, it puts individuals in an awkward position, for the post-crisis period if not immediately.
- And all these requests may be contradictory. You may receive three phone calls: one from a top executive you have never met; one from another executive you hardly know, and a third from your immediate hierarchical superior. How do you deal with these demands, each of which poses its own problems?
- The pressure from events naturally produces conflicts between private and professional life. An employee may be worried about family members who could be affected by the crisis. And a family-related problem completely independent of the crisis, and which in normal times would not have created any problem, can provoke a wrenching conflict of interest (in the absence of a crisis, a manager would not hesitate, for example, to leave work in order to take a spouse or child to the hospital).[10]
- The crisis keeps everyone absorbed with specific tasks, thereby preventing them from tackling other work which is also urgent—indeed, if those other tasks are ignored long enough, they may engender new crises. Of course these questions may retreat into the background, but they continue to be a burden.

Very quickly, the decision maker becomes aware, as Steven Fink (1986, p. 144) relates, that the whole situation is 'overdetermined': 'For any one effect there may be five causes, and for any one cause there may be five effects'. Not to mention fear that 'you—the decision maker—are in a lose/lose situation', which includes the fear of losing self-esteem. Fink suggests a striking metaphor for the psychological overload to which such decision makers are subjected: 'Walking through a maze backward, wearing a blindfold, and juggling lighted sticks of dynamite'.

If those in charge try to adhere to confirmed decision-making techniques, the techniques no longer work. It becomes impossible to isolate problems from one another; everything has an impact on everything else. It is equally impossible to wait and decide 'once we know', because by then, it will be too late. Firm decisions must be made in the midst of uncertainty, and efforts to optimize must give way to attempts to find the least daring solution. In short, the usual decision-making methods, and indeed the entire decision-making culture, suddenly prove to be inappropriate for dealing with this shattered environment. Also, there is no respite in which to undertake some basic research on the implications of what is happening. The emergency is often very pressing, even if, as we shall see, it is just as often less drastic than it seems.

All this engenders a high level of stress. With regard to the issue discussed above, the degree of preparation has a direct effect on stress levels: when there is no prior experience, no tools, and no training, the organization has no repertoires of answers available, and this heightens the stress. The more unfamiliar the event, the greater the adaptation required (Smart and Vertinsky, 1977). A complex of circumstances falls on an individual's shoulders, and that person cannot help but become more anxious. This in turn impinges upon any capacity to act.

Stress and its consequences

Psychologists have clearly demonstrated that stress produces physical fatigue, insomnia, irritability, feelings of guilt and shame, paranoid reactions, and a tendency towards suspiciousness, hostility, and accentuated defensive behaviour. The subjects' features become tense, they are less flexible, their ability to focus is narrowed, and their conceptual frameworks become very rigid (see, for example, Parry, 1990; Rivolier, 1989).

All these responses only contribute to disturb further the ability to reflect and to act, as has been equally well documented (Milburn, 1972, pp. 264–6; Parry, 1990, pp. 18–31):

- While mild stress often improves performance, especially when the responses are uncomplicated or well learned, increased stress tends to reduce performance. Very intense stress can cause complete disintegration of performance. The more complex the task at hand, the greater the disruptive impact of stress on performance.
- An individual who is already under stress may be severely affected if the stress intensifies. Yet a crisis, as has already been shown, never hits with just one blow. To the contrary, by its very nature, it consists of a series of shocks, that cause continually escalating aggravation.
- An avoidance mechanism may come into play: the decision maker refuses to discuss or think about the problem. The victim of a

severe shock may also feel disconnected from reality, under a sort of mental anaesthesia.

- Learning under stress seems to be difficult, except for simple defensive conditioning, which is usually facilitated by stress. Yet the ability to learn quickly is precisely what is called for in a crisis situation.
- Stress provokes a certain regression, in which complex behaviour disappears and simpler, more basic behaviour re-emerges. This leads to a simplification of perceptual processes: the subjects usually display reduced spatial and temporal focus and a decreased ability to make fine discriminations. Thinking processes become more rigid, and individuals tend to fall back on models they used successfully in the past, even if the current situation is not at all comparable.
- High anxiety levels affect judgement: there is a tendency to lend credency to ideas that would normally be dismissed. This can create a vicious circle.
- Individuals' personality traits become exaggerated: an anxious person becomes very anxious, repressive personalities become even more repressive. Some individuals feel so uncomfortable with the situation that they begin to panic and seek to withdraw as quickly as possible.
- The way people interact is also affected. Leaders who are more task-oriented than human-relations oriented reach the point where they neglect human relations altogether (and vice versa).
- Those involved in the crisis also tend to cut themselves off from social contacts, just at a time when it is vital to establish new relations with the environment.
- Some individuals become depressed and are overwhelmed by a range of negative thoughts.

The following traps, which have a more direct impact on operations, are also lying in wait for decision makers (see, among others, Fink, 1986, pp. 145–6; Smart and Vertinsky, 1977; ten Berge, 1990, pp. 13–16).

- The existence of the danger, the threats, and the crisis are simply denied.
- The siege mentality sets in: those in charge withdraw, do nothing, say nothing, and become inert.
- Panic strikes: it emerges as the overriding emotion, leaving no room for calm reflection.

- The search begins for a scapegoat: everyone wants to fix the blame on someone or some organization.
- Data are deformed by the prisms through which they are filtered: in particular, too much weight is given to historical analogies. The past does have its lessons, but it can turn into a prison. The present is what must be dealt with immediately. This point was already raised above: decision makers tend to shut out any information or warnings on the risks they are running, to the point of becoming deaf and blind.
- Instability sets in: the decision makers adopt the latest opinions they have heard.
- Management turns defensive: the declaration 'everything is under control' is issued as a reflex.
- The decision maker becomes 'hypervigilant', searching frantically for a solution and jumping from one idea to another without being able to concentrate on a given possibility, or latching on to any idea with a lack of critical judgement.
- The focus becomes narrow-minded: those involved tend to limit the range of options drastically. They focus on the short term, and everything becomes an absolute emergency.
- Reasoning becomes rigid: this is when everything becomes black or white, good or bad, and the ability to adapt is diminished.
- Decisions are made arbitrarily, without considering their consequences.
- Stress also reduces an individual's capacity for abstract reasoning and tolerance for ambiguity. This can in turn make the individual unable to identify the consequences of the options selected.
- Those in charge begin to reason egocentrically: the decision maker retreats into isolation and can no longer understand or think about others.
- If the crisis persists, people fall into the rut of rumination and indecision.

In other words, 'increasingly severe crisis tends to make creative policy making both more important and less likely'.[11] And this process becomes self-reinforcing:

> Creative decision making in part depends on an input of ideas from a wide variety of individuals reflecting different experiences and expertise. During a crisis, there is a tendency, however, for a contraction of authority to occur in an organization. Authority for decision making shifts to higher levels and there is a reduction in the number of persons participating in the decision process.

> As the decision/authority unit contracts, the amount of stress on
> decision makers increases since each member feels a greater
> responsibility for potential failure. The greater the level of felt
> stress, the greater the perceived pressure for decisiveness.
>
> (Smart and Vertinsky, 1977, pp. 642-3)

All these factors combine to produce actions that are merely caricatures
of the behaviour that would be seen under normal conditions.

Individual worth

The individual human factor cannot be underestimated in a crisis
situation. As Robert Kennedy said on the subject of the Cuban Missile
Crisis, 'The fourteen people involved were very significant . . . If six
of them had been President of the U.S., I think that the world might
have been blown up' (Neustadt and Allison, 1971, p. 128).

A decision maker who is plunged into a crisis should realize that the
quality of the individuals involved is going to play an important role.
There are useful exercises available for preparing a team and, as we
are attempting to do here, quickly comprehending the difficulties
that are likely to be encountered. Thomas Milburn makes the following
observations:

> (. . .) people who have more than their share of anxiety should be
> avoided; so, also, should impulsive people or those who lack
> ability to imagine in some detail the consequences of choosing
> one line of action over another. Since crises may arouse
> defensiveness in those who must take risks on the basis of
> incomplete or otherwise inadequate information, it is preferable
> to work with people who ordinarily are free from defensiveness
> and are fairly open and direct.
>
> (. . .) it is better to work with people who have had broad
> experience on the social firing line and who have known a variety
> of cultures and situations, rather than with those whose lives
> have been more circumscribed and whose thinking has been in
> narrow or parochial areas.
>
> Although the obvious and optimum preference is for people who
> have intimately known several past crises—so that they do not
> over-generalize from experiences in a particular one—it may
> matter less whether they were principal actors or assistants who
> merely observed the proceedings. One significant guideline is to
> select people who are cognitively complex and who think in
> terms of fairly long time spans.
>
> Since it is sometimes difficult to find colleagues with actual crisis
> experience, the next best procedure is to train them.
>
> (Milburn, 1972, p. 267)

These ideas should be counterbalanced, however, with the following warnings:

- Avoid taking a romantic approach to crisis management. This is not a task for the lone hero or a few exceptional individuals: the situation is too complex to be resolved by a single genius. Nor can the problems be laid at the doorstep of one person who is judged incompetent.
- The person who was fantastic in one crisis situation may collapse in another. Worse yet, someone who is extraordinary one day may commit serious errors the next day, or at the end of the crisis: this is the case of the individual who manages the whole situation masterfully, only to stumble on a decisive issue and lose everything in one blow.
- Though some individuals may blossom during a crisis, it is better to be able to count on a range of well-trained managers who can tackle the situation together. The problem with revelations is that, like miracles, they cannot comprise a solid strategic line of defence.

In short, the individual human factor must be incorporated, but it must not overshadow the other aspects of the situation. This should be borne in mind from the beginning of a crisis, as well as in any evaluations: it is important not to place blame on individuals alone. This factor should also be taken into consideration in more general planning: of course, it is important to recruit competent individuals, but it is also crucial to build teams and organizations that compensate for moments of individual weakness.

Yet the fact remains that individual personalities play a crucial role in this type of situation. This is when their actual capacity to function in an environment of chaos is put to the test. The forces which an individual has acquired throughout previous experiences of deep personal crisis are tested. This is in fact what makes crisis so disturbing: it revives other, often fundamental conflicts, and threatens to let them explode.

Henry Kissinger
In a crisis only the strongest strive for responsibility; the rest are intimidated by the knowledge that failure will demand a scapegoat. Many hide behind a consensus that they will be reluctant to shape; others concentrate on registering objections that will provide alibis after the event. The few prepared to grapple with circumstances are usually undisturbed in the eye of a hurricane. All around them there is commotion; they them-

selves operate in solitude and a great stillness that yields, as the resolution nears, to exhaustion, exhilaration, or despair.

(Kissinger, 1979, Vol. 1, p. 598)

Robert Kennedy
They were men of the highest intelligence, industrious, courageous, and dedicated to their country's well-being. It is no reflection on them that none was consistent in his opinion from the very beginning to the very end. That kind of open, unfettered mind was essential. For some there were only small changes, perhaps varieties of a single idea. For others there were continuous changes of opinion each day; some, because of the pressure of events, even appeared to lose their judgment and stability. (. . .)

The strain and the hours without sleep were beginning to take their toll. However, even many years later, those human weaknesses—impatience, fits of anger—are understandable. Each one of us was being asked to make a recommendation which would affect the future of all mankind, a recommendation which, if wrong and if accepted, could mean the destruction of the human race. That kind of pressure does strange things to a human being, even to brilliant, self-confident, mature, experienced men. For some it brings out characteristics and strengths that perhaps even they never knew they had, and for others the pressure is too overwhelming.

(Kennedy, 1971, pp. 9, 22)

Theodore Sorensen, special adviser to John F. Kennedy at the White House
I saw first-hand, during the long days and nights of the Cuban crisis, how brutally physical and mental fatigue can numb the good sense as well as the senses of normally articulate men.

(Sorensen, 1963, p. 76)

Small groups: between cacophony and pathological closed-mindedness

Between the individual and the organization as a whole, there are teams, and more specifically, crisis management groups. These small groups play a critical role, which is why it is important to look here at the specific problems raised by the way they function. Obviously, this type of group approach to crisis is used because it offers certain advantages: a group brings together various skills, and it doesn't become entrapped by the perceptions of a single person. It also avoids placing all the burden on one person, who may give in to fear, euphoria, or anger. The answers provided by groups, however, are not without their own difficulties. There are actually two primary, contradictory dangers.

Confusion and conflicts

The classic danger is that of general confusion. After all, here is a group of people and teams from different worlds, with very different cultural responses to risk and emergency, having often very distinct prejudices about the threats to be dealt with and the goals to be met, and whose individual and corporate interests lend themselves poorly to broader cooperation. And they are all expected to work together under pressure.

Without prior preparation, it will take many precious hours or days initially to turn these many actors into a group. And the work of adjusting to one another will be a factor to be reckoned with throughout the crisis. A fault line is often visible between those who are accustomed to dealing with emergencies and those who have not assimilated all the requirements of this type of situation. For example, the latter group finds no reason not to wait until Monday to begin tackling the problem: 'We don't work on weekends.' This will draw howls of indignation from those who are used to taking immediate action. Yet the emergency specialists do not necessarily form a solid front either: pre-existing conflicts do not disappear simply because there is a crisis—all to the contrary.

Yet another danger tends to affect groups, notably when they are facing their first trial, and especially if it occurs while they are being trained in crisis management issues. The danger is that everyone soon begins to observe the process and to take excessive interest in what makes the situation tick, rather than effectively coming to grips with the situation. Remember, this is no longer a case study.

> *Henry Kissinger: The EC-121 case, the first crisis after Nixon's election, 14 April 1969*
> The NSC system became a device to accumulate options without supplying perspective or a sense of direction. All the principals were so fascinated by the process of decision-making that they overlooked its purpose in ordering priorities for action.
> (Kissinger, 1979, Vol. 1, p. 315)

Flight into unanimity: the dangers of groupthink

The opposite risk is that the group becomes pathologically close-minded. This phenomenon, in which the group strives for unanimity, was identified and studied by Irving Janis (1982) under the generic term 'groupthink'. This risk is well worth discussing, because it is considerably less well known. Even though it is also less frequent than the opposite response, it can be much more dangerous, as it is often too subtle to be detected.

Groupthink involves excessively strong cohesion among the members of a crisis group. This in turn leads to faulty decision making. Janis presents the central theme of his analysis as follows:

> The more amiability and esprit de corps among the members of a policy-making in-group, the greater is the danger that independent critical thinking will be replaced by groupthink, which is likely to result in irrational and dehumanizing actions directed against out-groups.
>
> (Janis, 1982, p. 13)

Janis then adds:

> I use the term 'groupthink' as a quick and easy way to refer to a mode of thinking that people engage in when they are deeply involved in a cohesive in-group, when the members' strivings for unanimity override their motivation to realistically appraise alternative courses of action. [...] 'Groupthink' refers to a deterioration of mental efficiency, reality testing, and moral judgment that results from in-group pressures.
>
> (Janis, 1982, p. 9)

At the origin of the work on groupthink was the realization that many fiascos in the realm of international crisis could only be explained by the way decision-making groups operated. 'Groupthink,' writes Janis, ' . . . can take its toll even when the decision makers are conscientious statesmen trying to make the best possible decisions for their country and for all mankind' (Janis, 1982, p. 12).

The classic situation is one involving a homogeneous group of high-ranking officials who form a cohesive unit with clearly defined leadership. In such cases, the gravity of the problems to be handled, the heightened sense of responsibility, mutual confidence, and a sort of group support all reinforce the sense of being isolated and belonging to an elite in-group. Janis suggests that this leads to the deterioration of both cognitive powers and moral sensibility. The presence of this phenomenon can be diagnosed by eight symptoms, which Janis (1982, pp. 174–5) classifies under three types:

Type I: Overestimations of the group—its power and morality
1 An illusion of invulnerability, shared by most or all the members,
   which creates excessive optimism and encourages taking
   extreme risks.
2 An unquestioned belief in the group's inherent morality, inclining
   the members to ignore the ethical or moral consequences of
   their decisions.

Type II: Closed-mindedness
3 Collective efforts to rationalize in order to discount warnings
   or other information that might lead the members to
   reconsider their assumptions before they recommit themselves to their past policy decisions.
4 Stereotyped views of enemy leaders as too evil to warrant
   genuine attempts to negotiate, or as too weak and stupid to
   counter whatever risky attempts are made to defeat their
   purposes.

Type III: Pressures towards uniformity
5 Self-censorship of deviations from the apparent group consensus, reflecting each member's inclination to minimize the
   importance of his or her doubts and counterarguments.
6 A shared illusion of unanimity concerning judgments conforming
   to the majority view (partly resulting from self-censorship of
   deviations, augmented by the false assumption that silence
   means consent).
7 Direct pressure on any member who expresses strong
   arguments against any of the group's stereotypes, illusions,
   or commitments, making clear that this type of dissent is contrary to what is expected of all loyal members.
8 The emergence of self-appointed mindguards—members who
   protect the group from adverse information that might shatter
   their shared complacency about the effectiveness and morality
   of their decisions.

When a group functions predominantly in this manner, Janis (1982,
p. 175) observes that the following flaws are often considerably
reinforced:

1 Incomplete survey of alternatives
2 Incomplete survey of objectives
3 Failure to examine risks of preferred choice
4 Failure to reappraise initially rejected alternatives
5 Poor information search
6 Selective bias in processing information at hand
7 Failure to work out contingency plans.

Janis brilliantly illustrates his theory by analysing a number of major
fiascos in American foreign policy. He naturally takes pains to

emphasize that in each case a great number of factors—political, bureaucratic, technical, and others—all intervened to produce the fiasco. Yet the 'groupthink' hypothesis is necessary to explain the often incomprehensible blindness shown by some decision-making groups throughout the episode in question. Janis' book should be required reading for anyone in a position of responsibility, as it provides an essential in-depth understanding of crisis issues. It is interesting here to take a brief look at some of the points raised by the Bay of Pigs.[12] This example (based on Janis, 1982, pp. 37–43) illustrates the outline presented above. Though analysed here using examples from American foreign policy, the phenomenon can obviously affect any organization.

Irving Janis: The Bay of Pigs (1961)

Euphoria reigned in the group united around Kennedy, sure of its lucky star in the service of a man who had enjoyed so much success. The feeling was, 'Nothing can stop us!' Athletic teams and military combat units may benefit from such enthusiasm. But policy-making committees usually do not: it creates a white noise that prevents them from hearing warning signals.

The rule was, no criticism. Stating personal reservations would have marred the apparent consensus. Besides, it was not easy to face the disapproval of the group. Against the 'viril poses' adopted by military and CIA representatives, the other members of the advisory group were afraid of passing for 'soft' idealists.

At a party, Robert Kennedy took Schlesinger, a member of the advisory group, aside and told him that even if he were right to oppose the project, it was too late to do so; the time had come to support the President. Similarly, Undersecretary of State Chester Bowles, who attended a White House meeting at which he was unable to express his views, wrote a strong memorandum dissenting against the project. He asked Secretary of State Dean Rusk's permission to present it to the President. Rusk replied that there was no need for concern, and he kept Bowles' memorandum buried in the State Department files. Rusk acted the same way with the director of intelligence and research in the State Department when asked for permission to present the project to the department's Cuba experts: Rusk refused on grounds of confidentiality. Rusk also failed to inform the President that his most trusted intelligence expert had grave misgivings about the invasion plan. The leading civilian members of the Kennedy team were virtually colluding to prevent anyone from criticizing the plan prepared by the CIA and Joint Chiefs of Staff.

The President gave such priority to CIA representatives during meetings that it was impossible for other participants to voice any objections. The President permitted the CIA to refute each tentative doubt immediately, instead of asking whether anyone else had the same reservation or wanted to pursue the discussion. Kennedy did bring Senator J. William Fulbright, an eloquent opponent of the invasion plan, to speak at the crucial 4 April meeting. Yet Kennedy did not open up discussion after Fulbright's 'sensible and strong' speech, and no one pushed him to do so. Instead, the President went around the table asking each person to state his final judgement. After hearing opinion leaders like Secretary of Defense McNamara, it was increasingly difficult to express a different point of view. Tactics like going around the table or taking open straw votes are procedures that are well known for pushing individuals to agree with the group.

Finally, Janis (1982, p. 87) makes the following complementary points:

1 The only window of lucidity may take the form of jokes which, like slips of the tongue, become one of the rare ways that doubts can be expressed. The same thing happens when simulating a crisis: the laughter, caricatures, strange comments or *non sequiturs* tossed off just at the end of a session often have much to say about the deeper feelings of the group. Laughing together or indulging in black humour or irony about a dangerous subject is a way of mentioning the problem behind a protective shield, and it is a typical signal of a potential groupthink process.

Irving Janis: Pearl Harbor, 7 December 1941
Admiral Kimmel asked Lieutenant Commander Layton about the puzzling loss of radio contact with the Japanese aircraft carriers on 1 December 1941. 'What, you don't know where the carriers are? Do you mean to say that they could be rounding Diamond Head [at Honolulu] and you wouldn't know it?' Layton replied that he hoped they would be sighted well before that. (This is reminiscent 'of the shared amusement at the Lion's Club meeting when, a few days before disaster struck, one man jokingly displayed a parachute as his answer to the town engineer's warning that the town might cave in.')

'The admiral was making it clear, though in an indirect way, that he would be inclined to laugh derisively at anyone who thought' that the Japanese could attack Pearl Harbor. This alone might not have been enough to prevent intelligence officer Layton from pursuing the issue. But the admiral's little joke 'certainly encouraged him to remain silent about any vague, lingering doubts.' As Layton later said, 'I did not at any time suggest that the Japanese carriers were under radio silence approaching Oahu. I wish I had.'

'Because this ominous inference was never drawn, not a single
reconnaissance plane was sent out to the north of the Hawaiian
Islands.' No one dared to risk the scorn of other officers.

'In the atmosphere of apparent unanimity, with no clear-cut
warning signal indicating that the Japanese were planning a
sneak attack against Pearl Harbor, even the most conscientious
military adviser would find it easier to risk what seemed to be a
very low-probability threat of an enemy attack rather than face
the high-probability threat of social censure for questioning the
validity of the group's recent reaffirmations of . . . business-as-
usual [. . .] inducing sensible men to remain unsensibly lacking
in vigilance [. . .]. The result is a shared psychological set that
involves a marked distortion in information processing . . .'

(Janis, 1982, pp. 87–8)

2 As time goes by, it becomes increasingly difficult to break through
this protective shield. What originally would merely imply a
warning against an erroneous interpretation quickly comes to
signify casting doubts on an entire policy. Consequently, any
criticism becomes intolerable. Janis' ideas can be supplemented
here by another remark: as in tragedy, every player prefers to
pursue a destiny, running headlong towards a failure which is
hazily considered to be inevitable. Why stop, even briefly, to
indulge in a painful moment of lucidity? The groupthink phenomena function flawlessly at this stage: even if the group leader
begins to have doubts, he or she will quickly be reassured, i.e.
brought back to the straight and narrow path, by the members of
the group.

Janis: Pearl Harbor, 7 December 1941
As the various warnings were received . . . it would have been
doubly difficult for any of Kimmel's advisers to voice misgivings
. . . For a member of the Navy group to become alarmed by the
last-minute signals . . . at the very least . . . would show lack of
confidence in the group's capabilities in fulfilling one of its
fundamental missions—providing adequate security at Hawaii in
order to protect the Pacific Fleet, the naval base at Pearl Harbor,
and the local population. Kimmel, as leader of the group, had
sufficient 'idiosyncrasy credit' to be able to express his last-minute
gut reaction on the afternoon of December 6, but he was quickly
reminded of the group's standard rationalization for setting
momentary qualms aside. Kimmel thereby lost his final chance
to remedy the gross state of unpreparedness of the fleet.

(Janis, 1982, pp. 77 and 78)

3 This mechanism may continue to operate over the long term, affecting a broader policy. This is what happened during the escalation of the Vietnam War from 1964 to 1967.

Janis: Escalation in Vietnam
. . . those who openly questioned the escalation policy [were made] the butt of an ominous epithet: 'I am afraid he's losing his effectiveness.' This 'effectiveness trap'—the threat of being branded a 'has been' . . . inclines its victims to suppress or tone down their criticisms. . . . it makes any member who starts to voice his misgivings ready to retreat to a seemingly acquiescent position in the presence of quizzical facial expressions and crisp retorts. . . .

. . . whenever members of the in-group began to express doubts . . . they were treated in a rather standardized way . . . The dissenter was made to feel at home, providing he lived up to two restrictions: first, that he did not voice his doubts to outsiders . . . and second, that he kept his criticisms within the bounds of acceptable deviation, not challenging any of the fundamental assumptions of the group's prior commitments. (This technique produced 'domestic dissenters'.)

. . . the subtle domestication process may work well . . . The nonconformist can feel that he is still accepted as a member in good standing. . . . he has the illusion that he is free to speak his mind. If on occasion he goes too far, he is warned about his deviation in an affectionate or joking way and is warned only indirectly of his potentially precarious status. . . . The others in the group . . . feel satisfied about giving full consideration to the opposing position and can even pat themselves on the back for being so democratic about tolerating open dissent. Nevertheless, the domesticated dissenter . . . knows that if he is not careful he will reach the boundary beyond which he risks being branded as having lost his 'effectiveness'.

(Janis, 1982, pp. 114–18)

4 Another point to be considered is the possibility of a series of groupthink phenomena simultaneously affecting all the groups involved, even outside the central decision-making unit. This is what Rolf Kaiser, who has worked on this type of crisis issue at the OECD, calls 'metagroupthink'. Each agency and each group develops the symptoms—because its attitude is reinforced by that of the others.

Irving Janis: Pearl Harbor
There were three interlocking groups in this matter:
The Navy and Army groups in Hawaii and the War Council in Washington. All three assumed that the United States fleet anchored at Pearl Harbor was safe.

In their messages to each other, the three interlocking groups mutually reinforced their lack of vigilance, often by what they did not say. They did not exchange views about specific preparations needed in Hawaii to ward off a possible surprise attack.

- The Navy group said nothing to the Army group in Hawaii about activating its radar stations or its anti-aircraft guns and allowed the local Army leaders to persist in their belief that the mere presence of the fleet guaranteed protection against any form of hostile action except sabotage.
- The Army group, in turn, neglected to communicate to the Navy group that all the radar stations and anti-aircraft installations were hardly in operation at all except for training purposes.
- The War Council in Washington did not inquire about the kind of alert that had been instituted in Hawaii, and the Navy group did not bother to inform anyone in Washington about its decision to make no changes whatsoever after receiving the war warnings. When the military members of the War Council were sent a relevant message from the Army command in Hawaii stating that only an anti-sabotage alert had been set up, they did not notice it. . . .

Thus, the three groups helped each other maintain a façade of complacency and set the stage for America's astounding unreadiness at Pearl Harbor.

(Janis, 1982, pp. 95-6)

5 It should be added that even an outsider, asked to come help the group, can be caught up in this phenomenon and lose all critical perspective.

A word of warning, however: groupthink theory should not be applied with impunity. A number of conditions must exist before it can be suggested. First of all, the group must be marked by a high level of cohesiveness. Second, there are typical organizational features: the group is very isolated; it has a strongly charismatic leader who fosters adhesion more than critical observation; there are no standards for adequate decision-making procedures (e.g. looking at the pros and cons of each option under consideration); the group members tend to have a homogenous frame of reference (e.g. social background, ideology). All these things threaten to provoke premature consensus.

Generally speaking, as Janis clearly states, only decisions in which the consensus of an in-group plays a key policy-determining role should be analysed for 'groupthink' phenomena. After all, many other causes may be responsible for the failure of a policy or decision, from faulty implementation of the decision by actors outside the decision-making unit to unforeseen accidents beyond the control of those in charge, to sheer bad luck (Janis, 1982, p. 195).

Once again, the precautions given above apply: when dealing with crisis, avoid narrow-minded analysis. Though groupthink theory is appealing, it should not be asked to provide all the answers. Janis even encourages such caution when he describes the possibility that abrupt disaffection may arise, for example when members of a group suddenly feel that they are personally at risk and that the group does not provide adequate compensatory protection. This results in an 'every man for himself' attitude of the type seen during the Watergate scandal. The veil that had masked all the group's illusions is suddenly torn from everyone's eyes. The same sort of disengagement occurs when a leader ceases to inspire sufficient confidence (see Janis, 1982, pp. 253–4).

On the other hand, groupthink as a potential diagnosis should not be eliminated too quickly. Even when, at the outset of a crisis, a group shows little cohesiveness, the members must remain vigilant: stress, fatigue, the pressure of events, and being isolated together for long days and nights can combine to generate an atmosphere of pathological cohesiveness even in a group that did not originally seem susceptible to the problem.

Groupthink progressively shuts off its victims from outside influences, making them less and less capable of resolving a crisis. Complexity and ambiguity are replaced by an increasingly inappropriate tendency towards simplification. Faced with a situation composed first and foremost of burgeoning difficulties, groups, like individuals, tend to limit the scope of their responses and to employ capacities that are largely inferior to those they would normally use to handle much simpler episodes.

Organizations operating at the limits of their capacities

Every crisis is in part an organizational crisis: this was made clear in the discussion of how organizations delay reacting to a crisis or its early-warning signs. When the context becomes unsettling, even threatening for their survival, organizations are suddenly confronted with operating difficulties. Decision makers must bear this in mind if they are to avoid being surprised when such problems arise (whether in 'concentrated' form or as derivatives in new combinations). To simplify the discussion here, these problems can be divided into issues specific to the individual organizations involved, and those which result from the interaction of multiple actors.

Each organization struggles with its own difficulties

Paralysing absences and destabilizing deficiencies

When the crisis hits, it is not at all unusual to discover that the people or resources that are missing are those on which everyone relied, explicitly or implicitly, to deal with this type of event. Perhaps the highest-ranking leader is absent—during the *coup d'état* in Trinidad, the prime minister fell into rebel hands—or a crucial specialist or vital piece of equipment is missing. The odds of encountering this type of breakdown are not slim, given that crises often break out at inconvenient moments (over the weekend, at night, at the height of the vacation season). The fact is that systems are most vulnerable at these very moments, and incidents can metamorphose into crises all the more easily.

It is always a shock to realize that you will have to tackle a crisis without all your resources. This type of scenario can be paralysing for managers. Some will persist with pathological obstinacy in attempting to recreate the reference conditions foreseen by their emergency plans. They will soon be reduced to dealing with this obsession, rather than managing the situation as it presents itself (Gilbert and Zuanon, 1990; see also Gilbert, 1991).

The trend towards instant Brownian motion

The initial passivity soon gives way to chaotic Brownian motion. This may be due to one of two underlying causes: if organization members jump into the breech, this may have the same effect as maintaining a prudent reserve. In either case, they actually avoid coming to grips with the event itself and how it should be treated—indeed, the hidden purpose of all the fuss may be to compensate for a basic inability to act. At the basic level of observing the phenomena, however, what happens? In the absence of sufficiently well-defined and well-known plans and procedures, everyone suddenly begins to strike out in all directions, and general confusion reigns. One particularly damaging result is crippling pressure on the communications system and reduced access to key decision makers.

The classic example of this type of problem is the in-house telephone network: A calls B to get some information; B doesn't have the answer and promises to call C; B calls C, but A, not convinced that B can be relied upon, also calls C; C says that D and E must first be consulted, and so on. This type of exponentially expanding activity, combined with a lack of preparation on the actors' part for working on exceptional subjects under emergency conditions, quickly congests the entire system and wears everyone out—and all in an effort to transmit data that may not even be vital. Often the lack of information drives those affected to fill the void—which is always intolerable—with inexact or irrelevant data, seized at random. Then, to make themselves feel useful, to show that they are present, to have the feeling of doing *something*, these actors dispatch their 'information' in all directions. This activity exhausts the organization, and it quickly proves to be almost useless, if not counterproductive. The result is that decision makers continue to be better informed by the media than by in-house channels. This can be seriously damaging for their morale, and morale is an essential parameter in such circumstances. They are saddened and discouraged by such a tremendous waste of energy.

Opaque, biased, and excessive information and in-house communications

Every organization naturally develops an immense filtering mechanism, but in this case it begins to misfunction. It has already been shown how an individual, especially when subject to stress, may add a bias when assimilating and transmitting information. This type of distortion is multiplied all along each channel and throughout networks of every sort. The combined effect of all these filters is significant distortion of information, both as the data go up the line and as the orders come down.

To understand the kinds of problems this raises, it is enough to look at the questions that cannot help but be asked by the public and the media: 'You failed to provide us with this information, yet it is available from one of your departments.' How can a manager make the outside world understand that in-house information does not automatically circulate perfectly, or that such a slip-up was more likely due to a normal problem than to a purposeful attempt at a cover-up? On the other hand, how can an executive be convinced that some vital information that was received late was not deliberately being hidden?

Naturally, nothing about a crisis situation is ever completely black and white, and it may well be that an attempt was made at some point to dissimulate information. This only complicates the discussion.

To bear up, decision makers have a tendency to focus their attention even further. This means they limit their number of information sources and restrict their perspectives (Smart and Vertinsky, 1977, p. 643). As a result, the problems of the organization threaten to produce decisions of poor quality.

In response to the many information-related problems they perceive, top executives will attempt to know what is 'really' going on. They start taking direct action, cutting through intermediate links in the chain. In so doing, they upset both the organization and the individuals in it. By the same token, each division and each manager tends to lean on the groups on the front line. This may not increase levels of random movement, but it rapidly strikes a death blow to smooth operations as the front line units find themselves assailed from all sides.

> **Example**: Imagine a chemical-producing branch of a large industrial group that suffers a major breakdown in a given European country. Immediately, every department in the branch will attempt to call the company's top representatives to know what has happened. At the same time, all the departments in Europe will call this same group of representatives in order to get the 'scoop'. Soon, branches of the group from all over the world are calling in. On top of that, requests for information are arriving from the outside, from national, European, and international sources. It is physically impossible to respond to such an avalanche of calls.[13]

Destabilization caused by abandoning standard procedures

Smart and Vertinsky (1977, p. 646) highlight this other source of trouble: organizations develop standard procedures for everyday events, and new situations are either ignored or forced into the mould. But crisis situations often create sharp breaks that make it necessary to realign resources, roles, and functions. To begin operating again, an organization must undertake to 'unlearn' its habits. This is very hard to do in an emergency, because the procedures are deeply rooted in the corporate culture.

More specifically, organizations are forced to act according to unusual rules. With respect to an emergency, this means in particular that it is more important to take relevant steps than to take rapid ones. This is a well-known factor in emergency medicine and catastrophe medicine, but it exists to varying extents in all fields. As Enrico Quarantelli very rightly points out (1982, p. 13): 'Appropriateness of response rather than speed of response is far more crucial.' But procedures cannot be unlearned and relearned with a snap of the fingers, especially in a highly disturbing situation.

San Francisco earthquake of 17 October 1989
According to a State of California report attitudes, habits, skills and resistance to change of field and supervisory personnel make it very difficult to introduce new communications systems or devices during a crisis. Therefore, any new equipment, satellite or terrestrial, must be simple and look like, sound like, and feel like a telephone or existing mobile radio.
(Scott and Freibaum, 1990, p. 8)

Henry Kissinger: The bureaucratic crisis created by Richard Nixon's first trip to China (1970)
The remaining technical problems solved themselves as easily as was compatible with the obsessive single-mindedness of the advance men. The communications expert came up with an ambitious plan that would have preempted every telephone line in Peking. I told Chou that by the time we got through he would surely be able to call Washington; whether he could still reach Shanghai was another matter. The head of our security detail distinguished himself by requesting a list of subversives in each locality the President was likely to visit. This raised an interesting problem, because in China conservative Republicans would undoubtedly be classed as subversives and if we asked how many Communist sympathizers there were we would get the unsettling answer of 800 million. Our security expert also fiercely resisted the proposition that the President might travel in a Chinese plane or a Chinese limousine—in his manual there were no reliable foreign machines.
(Kissinger, 1979, Vol. 1, p. 780)

The problems with implementing decisions made

Organizations also have difficulty implementing the decisions that have been made—yet this must be done quickly. Here again, the problem stems from trying to mobilize a large number of elements (Smart and Vertinsky, 1977, p. 648). These elements may feel little motivation to operate outside the norms that have always been applied (especially in terms of deadlines). Communication channels are cluttered by 'static' and by rigid procedures which may delay delivery of messages and the taking of response action; the orders given 'do not compute'.

It may be indispensable to change the normal operating procedures (for example, to agree to work on a weekend). Yet this arouses serious resistance: the fear of seeing one's territory impinged upon is one of the fundamental terrors of organizational life. Differing degrees of exposure to the crisis may exacerbate differences of perception or priorities among units, and this in turn heightens internal conflicts.

Finally, in addition to this resistance from various units, the control systems themselves, which should provide rapid signals to the central units when adjustments are necessary, may instead be too rigidly programmed. As a result, they sometimes fail to indicate when a decision has been poorly implemented.

Conflicts inside the executive suite

A crisis is a time of trial for individuals and groups. As has often been shown, it may strengthen team spirit and bring people together to form a united front against the crisis. But it may also trigger grave and destabilizing conflicts. Everyone suffers from fatigue, anxiety, the uncertainty of the situation, an unbearable lack of information, and ethical choices that may go against the individual grain. Not to mention the prospect of facing serious consequences when events return to normal (some individuals may feel that their heads will be the ones to roll, which does nothing to soothe their fears). Against this backdrop it is hardly surprising that pre-existing conflicts or wounds that had healed more or less, should be re-opened. In short, for a wide range of reasons, important internal tension is bound to exist within the crisis management groups.

The very realization of this fact can be disturbing, creating feelings of guilt. After all, the ideal in such situations is that everyone should work together.

> *Philippe Vesseron: The Seveso waste drums (1982–1983)*
> The hardest period for me was when I realized that there were serious conflicts regarding the drums within our administration. This is really nothing astonishing—it's classic to see divisions, and even parallel initiatives emerge within an organization in times of crisis. After all, if a crisis begins to sour, you have to be able to fall back on other people or other strategies. The problem is that these internal tensions can actually be causes of failure! What helped me at the time was having learned previously that the phenomenon is perfectly banal. If you've integrated this obvious idea into your personal attitude, it's almost amusing to watch the thing in action. Otherwise, discovering this type of tension in the heat of the action could have highly destabilizing effects, especially as everyone spontaneously feels heavily implicated in a crisis, where you are constantly having to act on very different fronts.[14]

Pierre Rocolle: Dien Bien Phu (1954)
This marked the beginning of a serious misunderstanding
between General Navarre and General Cogny. Navarre wanted
to speak that very night with his subordinate [. . .]. But General
Cogny didn't come to him until the next morning, and the
members of their entourage heard both the reproaches made by
General Navarre and the way General Cogny replied to them.
Navarre didn't want to create a vacancy in the command structure
at such a critical juncture, so he did not request to have Cogny
relieved of his functions. But Cogny knew he had lost the trust of
his superior, and this simply made his attitude more intransigent.
He stated his objections more frequently, or put them in writing,
and he made a point of executing orders he received literally.
                              (Rocolle, 1968, pp. 428-9)

Inter-organizational problems

The challenge of having so many organizations involved

The number of actors involved is, as was seen in Chapter 2, a source
of many difficulties.

- Organizations have very little time to establish links with a great
  number of organizations that they didn't even know existed until
  recently, and with agencies or institutions that they had never considered as possible partners (a corporation may have to deal with
  a bureaucracy in a distant country).
- They lose some of their autonomy of action. Activities that would
  be considered normal, such as entering or leaving one's own
  property, may be restricted by outside order (Quarantelli, 1982,
  pp. 5–6).
- Organizations working together have to adjust to one another, as
  they do not have the same approaches or habits. This must be
  accomplished in very little time, while touching on often sensitive
  issues, such as choosing tactics for intervention, redefining the
  borders between organizations that have become hazy, or informally
  sharing personnel, tasks, and equipment (Quarantelli, 1982, pp. 5–6).

Joseph Scanlon: two agencies, two firefighting strategies
In May 1985, New Brunswick had to cope with 50 forest fires all
in one day. Five reached residential areas . . . [leading] to conflict
between provincial and local fire authorities. . . . Municipal fire
fighters like to put out fires. Forestry personnel prefer to direct
them. There is a distinct difference in style.
                              (Scanlon, 1990*b*, p. 10).

- They lose the thread of the event and responses to it because of a
  double standard for operations that develops: on the one hand,

the channels provided for in the rules are cumbersome; on the other hand, short-cuts for circumventing them develop both internally and on the outside.

Long channels and short-cuts
A typical example was the case of a recent incident in the area of the border between Alsace and Switzerland. By the time the alert came down through official channels, the short-cut had already done its work: the people involved learned by the official siren that they should stay indoors, just at the moment when more direct information indicated that the alert was over. In that specific case, the time lag simply caused a few snide remarks. But if the problem had been more serious and the emergency more acute, it could have been a key to disaster.

- Conflicts develop between organizations. This risk is especially high, notes Scanlon (1990*b*, p. 10), when the agencies involved have not integrated their action plans and each one acts independently. Such is frequently the case when the crisis overlaps with several administrative jurisdictions: for example, when action must be taken near an airport, at an embassy, on a military base, or in a border area.

Simply avoiding hopeless tangles in this organizational quadrille during a turbulent situation is a challenge in itself. The risk of sinking into confusion is tremendous: no one knows who is in charge of what, or who is doing what. The major problem then is that different agencies begin to act on the basis of different sets of information. This sets them on the fast lane to defeat.

These difficulties are further accentuated when the prior preparations made have not been based on inter-organizational cooperation: here again, the past comes to collect its dues (see Scanlon and Prawzick, 1986).

Unfortunate reflex reactions: pulling into the shell
Confronted with so many challenges, and especially the number of people and agencies to be dealt with, organizations in crisis tend to lose the very quality that gives them strength, namely that of a corporate body functioning within a network of relations.

In the face of an all-encompassing problem that overreaches specific, individual skills, a coordinated response is required. What appears is just the opposite: each entity slips into isolation and pulls in on itself.

The crisis quickly begins to feed on the vacuum, the contradictions, and the delays created and exacerbated by the dynamics of isolation. Of course, the ability to isolate a troubled sector can be very useful in large networks: exposing the whole system uselessly is not the objective. But the reflex of withdrawing when you find yourself on the firing line simply leaves the field open to the crisis and its complications. The key here is to realize that this is an automatic, natural reflex, just like a clam closing up when it is disturbed. The isolation reflex is immediate, and it can only be overcome with wilful training.

The sector-isolating phenomenon quickly develops even within the organization: each division and each department is busy fighting its battle, isolated from others and from its partner divisions. Even small groups become scattered, and individuals encounter similar difficulties. This creates unbearable contradictions which in turn provoke new changes of events. Sometimes the people in charge can no longer tolerate the gap that develops between their personal convictions and the official line of their firm. This is very trying for the individuals involved: it generates endless rumours if they speak their minds at a 'private' function, and the result can be explosive if the conflict comes into the open, say, in a television studio.

Hard-to-grasp command structures
Organizations are accustomed by definition to assigning clear and unequivocal responsibility. Consequently they will inevitably be perturbed by two factors that must be borne in mind:

- Generally speaking, it will be unclear who is in charge of what. It may help to read the emergency plan, but only in organizations and agencies that are used to working together. For them, consulting the plan will at most provide a guideline to keep them in line with a strategy that they are well equipped to follow. But in most cases, the system suffers from a lack of leadership, or at least of clearly accepted leadership.

The Amoco Cadiz oil spill
What is at issue here is a complicated system in which information is shared among various agents who are more or less unaware of each other, and in which any bit of information is chopped up and circulates badly. Paradoxically, the information received finally results in the ignorance of the authority with competence to act. This is a system in which one administration has powers but no material means and must request the latter from another administration, which decides whether it would be advantageous to grant them, or inversely, an administration having material means does not receive the information that would stimulate it to

use them, or does not have the power to use them. In short, this is a fractured system, deprived of any synthetic function.

(Colin, 1978, p. 223)

- Because the crisis is dynamic, the response systems cannot remain static. They must evolve, and this will create further problems for organizations. In particular, over time and as the scope of the matter becomes apparent, the guidelines to be followed become more strict, and decision making tends to concentrate at ever higher levels. What constitutes vital tasks to be accomplished must also be capable of evolving throughout a crisis. The steps that are appropriate during the extreme emergency period are not necessarily advisable when the time comes to build a consensus.

For these reasons, it would be illusory to seek a clear and definitive definition of the organization's command structure.

Joseph Scanlon: Mississauga train derailed (10 November 1979)
The first decisions were made by the first responding fire and police officers. The second set of decisions were made by more senior personnel, mainly the chief of police, usually in consultation with the fire chief. For a while, at the time of the hospital [evacuation] decision, there was a slightly larger decision-making group, the two chiefs were joined by the mayor and the regional chairperson. While this was an *ad hoc* arrangement, not in the plan, it still involved persons used to working with each other, though not in crisis management. As more and more outsiders began to arrive, these *ad hoc* arrangements gave way to still more *ad hoc* arrangements, causing the structure to begin breaking down. Eventually, the provincial cabinet minister had to step in and create a new and very formal structure, one not envisaged in [. . .] any other plan.

(Scanlon, 1989a, p. 318)

Major systems: between unmanageable complexity and disintegration

As soon as a crisis breaks out, everyone naturally tends to look to the 'major actors' involved: to understand the situation, identify its causes, and anticipate future developments, it is their fundamental goals that are examined. Using this approach, the decision makers hope to establish an outline for their decisions and actions.

Bit by bit, though, this illusion fades: the complications increase, and the rational basis adopted seems to apply less and less. This is clearly, then, a key aspect of crisis dynamics and one that will pose constant problems for those in charge.

In order better to circumscribe these difficulties, the analytical models developed by Graham Allison, an analyst of international crisis at Harvard University, are especially useful. Allison's work has led to remarkable progress in this field. We shall review his concepts here briefly, though it should be noted that their applications extend far beyond the field for which they were originally developed: this becomes apparent as soon as we begin to apply them to any major crisis. With the basis provided by these concepts, it will then be possible to carry this examination further and identify new areas of difficulty.

Managers facing different levels of difficulty: three analytical models

The rational actor model and its failings

Analysing the behaviour of major systems during crisis has traditionally been part of this first type of approach: the overall framework is examined in which key actors are supposed to produce decisions and practise behaviour which stems directly from their general strategic goals. This is, of course, one aspect of organizational operations that must be taken into account during any crisis. What are the major problems to be solved, what are the primary tensions that exist and the fundamental values and references of these systems? These questions are at the heart of the strategies implemented by the major actors.

But Allison has shown that two other types of analysis must also be performed. He emphasizes that a crisis brings more into play than major systems that can be identified by their goals and their fundamental values (model 1, the 'rational actor' model). These systems are also, or even primarily, composed of a range of organizations, which are shaped by key individuals.

Bureaucracy: the organizational model

To a large extent, decisions emerge out of complex mechanisms, procedures, and programmes which are specific to the organizations involved. This is a step away from the rational actor model: a decision is no longer made by a unified group with an unequivocal perception of the problems, and which controls its options and carefully co-ordinates its initiatives. To the contrary, this model highlights bureaucratic routines rather than one central option, one logic, or one implementation. In this second approach, what takes place is more the fruit of perfectly conventional organizational performance (with all its constraints, its limited capacities, its habits, and its turnaround times) than of intelligent strategic calculations. Therefore, to understand an organization's activities, it becomes necessary to ask much more specific questions than in the previous model: What are the components of the system? Which ones traditionally deal with the type of problem at hand, and what is their degree of relative influence? What repertoires, programmes, or measures are available to these organizations in order to implement variations on their actions? What conflicts exist among the components of the system?

Individual games: the political model
Here the emphasis is placed on the interplay of many specific actors, and especially on individual actors. All these actors have their own motivations, goals, and personality traits. The leading questions for understanding crisis dynamics from this point of view are: Who are the key individuals involved? How are the decisions made by central actors affected by the pressures of the positions they hold, the stances they have adopted in the past, or personal qualities?

Systems crushed by the crisis, leaving the decision maker little leverage

Allison has applied this three-fold approach to an analysis of the Cuban Missile Crisis. In particular, he demonstrated that the optimistic conclusions that could be drawn from the rational actor model alone, namely that the world powers are rational enough to avoid entering into a nuclear exchange, does not hold up to in-depth scrutiny with the other two models.

The organizational model calls for a great deal more prudence: government leaders had only very little control over organizational programmes that could have provoked a disaster. In many cases, chance was what saved the day. The lesson Allison culls—that nuclear crises between machines as imposing as those of the American and Soviet governments unfold in an intrinsically random manner— could well be extrapolated to describe the operations of any major system grappling with a serious crisis. This is why the following points must be borne in mind when analysing any major crisis:

- The information and estimates which decision makers have available in a given situation are as much a reflection of the goals and routines of their organizational machinery as of the facts.
- There is much less diversity among the options offered to these decision makers than could be hoped.
- Attempts to carry out decisions reveal the inevitable rigidity of existing procedures and protocols.
- Organizations do not coordinate with one another as well as those in charge would like to think.

During a crisis, observers constantly wonder why decision makers react so badly, why they adopt such inefficient options, or what Machiavellian calculations drive their attitudes. Much of the time, the answers are to be found in the nature of the organization. Bureaucracies, whether public or private, are cumbersome machines, ill-suited to adapt to crisis contexts. If you accept the way they operate, your decision-making process is necessarily threatened by inertia; if, in order to keep up with the crisis, you try to change their habits, make them work at a different pace, or switch strategies in the heat of the action, you may trigger internal collapses that have even greater repercussions.

The political model further underscores this feeling of fragility: if this had not been the second 'Cuban' crisis John F. Kennedy had to face, Robert Kennedy and Sorensen might not have been members of the decision-making group, and the choice probably would have been made to attack by air—which would have been much more serious than the blockade that was implemented. If Kennedy had already earned a domestic reputation for courage, the diplomatic option alone might have prevailed. Here again, Allison's conclusions can be generalized:

- Crisis dynamics work in obscure ways and are fraught with danger.
- The course of action adopted by those in charge may well aggravate the situation.
- The interplay of internal forces within the circles of power is often poorly understood and can lead to extreme positions.

These three models are, of course, mere guidelines for understanding a process. All these levels of complexity interact with each other, and this must be kept in mind in any analysis.

In fact, these three approaches to problems are most relevant in a crisis situation. When things are calm, regulatory procedures come into play to control the influence of these various levels, at least partially. In a crisis, these distinct layers are crushed together by time pressures, the gravity of the threat to fundamental interests, the loss of the reference framework, and many individual factors. This simply exacerbates both the difficulties to be dealt with on each level and their overall impact.

Reality becomes ever more complex

Allison's approach is vital to demonstrate that the great conventional, one-dimensional lines of reasoning are overly simplistic. Once this message is received, however, the quest must go further. First of all, it should be noted that Allison is rooted in a highly structured reality, with two major superpowers (USA vs USSR), large bureaucracies (the Navy and the Air Force), and actors in clearcut roles (e.g. the President, his advisers, other cabinet members). Thinking about crisis also calls for taking into account other, less clearly defined, realities.

Highly complex systems of actors
It is particularly interesting to note the criticisms made by Coral Bell, one of Allison's colleagues. She calls for an analysis of crises based on less 'ideal' situations than the famous missile crisis.

> *Coral Bell: the danger of the Cuban Missile Crisis as a reference—the case was too simple*
> It has been rather misleading and unfortunate that the academic study of crisis management was initiated chiefly by the Cuba missile crisis of 1962, which has served as a basis for several of the most notable studies of the subject. [. . .] It appeared to approximate to the form of a 'two-person game' [. . .]. The episode really did look rather like diplomatic chess [. . .]. I am not saying that these things were the realities of the Cuba crisis, only that they were the way it was perceived in the West [. . .]. Cuba 1962 was non-typical in practically all aspects: a much more typical example of crisis would be Cyprus 1974.[15] If there is a 'game' model for that crisis, it was certainly not chess, but poker for five or six hands in the traditional Wild West saloon, with the participants all wearing guns, and quickness on the draw rather than the fall of the diplomatic cards tending to determine who eventually acquired the jackpot. [. . .]
>
> The Cyprus crisis thus offers a good illustration of the chief difficulty in constructing any plausible generalisations about crises or their management: what one might call the asymmetry of decision making. In this case there were six individuals or

collectivities chiefly involved [. . .]. First, the Archbishop, whose decision to seek the removal of the Greek officers from the island provided the starting-point of events: then the faceless, anonymous leadership of 'Eoka B', which responded by deciding to mount the attempted coup against him: then the disintegrating junta in Athens [. . .]: then the complex machinery of decision making in Washington, involving the Secretary of State, the Departmental officers, the Ambassador in Athens, the CIA stationed there, and the Pentagon, and finally the decision making in Ankara, whose complexities are less subject to inspection.

(Bell, 1978, p. 50)

Bell's thoughts can be applied equally to major civilian systems of great complexity, from the nuclear energy system to urban infrastructures to other major networks or the school system. Some of these systems seem to be dinosaurs, and no one is quite sure how they would react to a crisis situation. This impression is heightened by previous experience or intuition, which indicate to some members of the systems that one or another of the individuals or groups they must deal with inside the network has insufficient technical ability or background, especially in the field of communication with the public— and that such individuals or groups are capable of bringing the whole edifice tumbling down around their ears.

Outbreaks of severe competition: shattering power blocks
Up to this point, we have only looked at systems within their usual boundaries. In actual fact, these outlines quickly explode in a crisis situation, and the customary power blocks are truly shattered.

* The boundaries which also served as protections for authority prove to be feeble lines of defence. Even a government may no longer be completely in charge on its own territory.
* Even the most prestigious scientific laboratory does not automatically enjoy public confidence: its results will promptly be compared to other information. If no comparisons are possible, suspicion will set in immediately.
* Large private firms, concerned about their public image, may well request second opinions from other laboratories. They will publish their own findings and take decisions contradicting those made by public authorities. This generates further risks of destabilizing the situation.
* Major press groups may also take unsettling initiatives—and at the same time, they will be fighting their own serious credibility problems. (The post-Chernobyl opinion poll cited earlier[16] showed that the media were in a weak position on this issue: 61%

of those asked 'Do you trust journalists in this matter?' replied 'No'.)

How power blocks are shattered: a few examples

- After the terrorist threats made against American airlines following the Lockerbie attack (Pan Am flight 103, 21 December 1988), the official network proclaimed that special high security measures were being implemented. But how much impact could that reassuring message and the pictures of energetic searches at boarding gates have in light of the other message broadcast by the media? IBM and other major corporations were banning executive air travel on American airlines. Similar decisions along parallel lines would be conceivable in large agro-business groups in the aftermath of a nuclear incident.
- After the rioting that broke out in suburbs of some large French cities, the Leclerc group loudly announced its intention in November 1990 to close down its hypermarkets in these areas.
- After an incident involving askarel leaks in the suburbs of Lyon in 1986, a local yoghurt manufacturer announced it was destroying its production.

All these initiatives make the crisis manager's task that much more complex. But the disintegration may reach even further.

A shattered and scattered universe

In many fields, the general backdrop today is more uncertain than ever—it seems literally scattered—and references determined for clearly structured situations must be applied with caution. If no one can really say what the general goals should be, how can anyone still speak of flagship projects or primary options that would normally provide fundamental guidelines for the major actors? When no organization seems to have real control over the issues of the day, even within its own field, is it still possible to reason in terms of the complex machinery which Allison used to limit his model to a few main players? When the figures who manage to take charge seem to appear out of nowhere, is it worth focusing on players clearly rooted in a given context?

A manager who has only studied the classic cases will be like a lion tamer who walks into a swarm of angry bees: no one has trained the bees in the rules of the game.

Expert advice and the experts: briar patches and a false sense of security

The problem of experts and their advice is a touchy one that often creates a stumbling block during a crisis.[17] Common sense on this point is generally deceptive, as it takes two angles: first, it is important to obtain a good diagnosis from the experts and, second, it is impossible to get two specialists to agree with each other. These will be the decision maker's first impressions, but they deserve a closer look.

The impossibility of getting rapid, reliable results

In a crisis, both knowledge and specialists must be brought into play rapidly. This quickly leads to a series of problems.

The classic reflex is to consult the individual or agency with which the company normally works. This has its advantages—it saves time, and there is no need to get acquainted. It is also risky: the person or agency may not have the necessary skills (but will not necessarily admit this, or even be aware of it); their designation will give considerable weight to their opinions, which can be dangerous if these opinions are ill-founded.

Another possible scenario is that the event is so particular that specialists must be called in with whom the company has never worked. The first step is to find them. It is important to develop some idea of their trustworthiness and of the credibility they have *vis-à-vis* their colleagues and other publics. Once they have been found, they still don't necessarily know each other. This means the crisis group must make initial adjustments in order to be operational. And even with experts on board, sufficient knowledge may not be available on the problem at hand: this was the case with the dioxin released in Seveso, and with the PCBs and other chemicals involved in various transformer fires.

> *Pierre Manière, Prefect of the Marne district: What were the risks in the askarel case in Reims?*
> [The Prefect of the Marne underscores this problem in a case he dealt with:]
> There were a lot of meetings: no one was ever certain about the ultimate consequences of the event. The specialists were unable to give an opinion for the long term or to decide what the danger thresholds were. They would say, 'The figures we have could imply a risk, but not necessarily.'
> (Lagadec, 1986*b*, p. 163)

More specifically, the highly specific knowledge that would be required to handle the crisis is not available. For example, if a population has been exposed to a certain type of pollution, the standards developed for acceptable peak exposure levels may not be available. Very quickly, the issue becomes knowing what can be tolerated over a short period. Choosing to apply standards developed for chronic exposure could lead decision makers to take inappropriate measures.

Experts may also be unable to produce the requested information as quickly as decision makers need to have it. As the problems deepen and impatience grows, the answers fail to arrive.

> *Theodore Sorensen: Analyses are useless when they arrive too late*
> The desire for more argument or more facts is always pressing, but overly prolonged fact-finding and debate may produce answers to questions which no longer exist. [. . .] the future rapidly becomes the past, and delay is itself a decision.
> (Sorensen, 1963, p. 30)

Those who must make decisions may also receive contradictory advice.

> *Enrico Quarantelli: Two dramatically contradictory opinions on the imminent danger of a dam bursting[18]*
> About 20 years ago, an emergency services manager in a California town received two messages within a few minutes of each other. The first came from an agency announcing that the earthquake which had just occurred had weakened the dam located just above the urban agglomeration, and that the dam would soon burst. Then a second agency, which was equally official and well equipped, sent in the opposite opinion. In fact, the manager received a third report, some time after the episode, which specified that even if the dam had broken, this would not have happened abruptly and there would not have been the horrible wave of water that was feared.

The decision maker must incorporate a range of opinions, each coloured by uncertainty and rooted in its own specific environment.

> A family doctor, for example, will be most concerned about the health of a patient; the toxicologist will point out that a given chemical is highly dangerous; the epidemiologist is more concerned with whether the event affects the broader population; an economist highlights the cost of the steps being considered and notes that these may also have health consequences.

To illustrate these points, consider a case in the field of public health. This is certainly one of the most difficult areas, and it gives rise to severe tension. Professor Lucien Abenhaim makes the following important comments on the subject (Abenhaim, 1989, pp. 831, 837–8):

On deep uncertainty
We don't know what all the possibilities are, or what the probability of their occurring is, since there is not enough information on previous events.

A product's danger is evaluated by making risky extrapolations
Even for extremely well known products whose pathogenic effects are well documented and for which we have both abundant toxicological data and information from various epidemiological sources, we must make a series of extrapolations. Depending on the methods used and the expertise accepted, these lead to widely varying results. Extrapolations are made from high doses to low doses, from one population to another, from animals to human beings, or from one set of exposure conditions to another.

Laboratory analyses can produce more problems
It takes a week to obtain reliable analyses of soot (that means a week of facing the press without having this data available!). Analytical errors are always possible and even, so it would seem, frequent unless the laboratory is exceptionally well qualified. A laboratory is capable both of detecting miniscule quantities of a substance and of stating after the fact that soot which was not analyzed, or which was analyzed with a given detection limit, actually contained significant quantities of the substance being tested for.

The available statistics can often be called into doubt
Most of the persons observed were removed from exposure too quickly for any of its effects to be detected. But they form too small a group to produce statistics of any value regarding this absence of effects (even if any effects detected individually can be accounted for). With carcinogenic substances, it may take decades before chronic effects start to appear. And the 'worst-case scenario' has never actually been encountered.

In addition to the scientific hesitation which is part of the game, individual conflicts between experts may surface. In the darkest picture, each specialist will refuse to recognize the other as such, taking advantage of the crisis to pursue an earlier battle with this 'esteemed colleague' on this new ground. This conflict between well-known experts quickly threatens to become the main crisis—to the greater distress of the decision maker, who is called on to choose between radically incompatible, highly publicized positions, which he or she is not well placed to evaluate.

Delicate relations between experts and decision makers

The difficulties raised by getting experts to work together are rein-forced by their problems in working with decision makers. These problems emerge late in the day, and they are heightened when the specialists in question come from a university background.

First of all, the specialists to whom a decision maker turns may not be accustomed to the atmosphere into which they are thrown: a sense of urgency, high stakes, high visibility in the media, or direct contact with top executives. Their background has often kept them distant from this world of urgent decision making and all it implies. They may also be solitary figures lacking experience in working with large groups.[19]

The decision maker is looking for certainty when consulting an expert. But uncertainty is the life blood of science, and its findings cannot be made to say more than they mean. A group of scientists brought together will never produce a decisive statement. Rather, they will offer a range of advice on several limited aspects of the problem, and always with restricting qualifiers. Those who must make a decision are looking for a distinct statement, but all the scien-tists have to offer is, 'yes, but it depends . . .'

> *Senator Edmund Muskie's request*[20]
> Peter Sandman, an American professor, cites a very illustrative anecdote about Senator Muskie, who 'complained to an aide when the experts kept qualifying their testimony with "on the other hand": "Find me an expert with one hand." '
>
> *Monique and Raymond Sené: a prefect's question and a scientist's answer about starting up a nuclear power plant*
> The Prefect: Can I give the authorization to start up this power plant again without subjecting the population to undue risks?
> The Scientist: I can't answer the question as you have asked it. Our analysis has not provided us with elements that would allow us to say, 'Yes, you can start it up again,' or 'No, you can't'. The only thing I can tell you is, there are enough unknowns to require continued surveillance of this power plant.[21]

The people who must make decisions tend to place unbearable pres-sure on the specialist to produce findings as quickly as possible. This is understandable: they have to announce something. This pressure rises proportionately with the degree of difficulty the situation pre-sents for the decision makers (and the time and care required in making the analyses). This is a sure recipe for inducing analytical error as well as serious tension between the specialist and the decision maker (since the specialist reacts poorly to such pressure). Reciprocal misunderstandings may develop as the decision maker becomes convinced that the expert has failed to appreciate the urgency of the situation: the decision maker starts to believe that this scientist is primarily concerned with doing an interesting piece of scientific work and is unaware of the deadlines and stakes involved. Consequently, the decision maker won't be able to resist applying pressure to receive the awaited results. The tensions that accumulate in this relationship may eventually explode with a bang, in full view of the media. Better yet, the parties may even turn the media into their battlefield.

Decision makers should also know that the diagnosis supplied by experts is socially conditioned. The expert has a reputation as someone who can read the secrets written in the great book of nature and whose answers consequently can be taken at face value. The reality is not so simple. Specialists necessarily are concerned about their credibility. They are aware of the fact that their analysis will be more or less well accepted or will arouse varying degrees of protest from peers, from the public, from the media or the victims. They may want to make up for an unfortunate earlier performance which damaged their credibility. If they played down the risk during an earlier event, this time around they will increase it systematically, or vice versa.

Basically, decision makers must realize that scientific specialists can never give them what they really need. The resources of science will never provide more than a series of information nuggets from individual disciplines. By its very nature, the scientific knowledge proffered to the decision maker will be of limited use. It will comprise opinions on various individual products, institutions, or settings—whereas decision makers are faced with comprehensive problems. On the one hand lies compartmentalized information, on the other, the encompassing reality of the event; and in the middle stands the decision maker. In the worst cases, each specialist pleads that his or her diagnosis should be adopted, while the media campaign for the application of a miracle solution outlined by a completely unknown expert. There is a huge gap separating the scattered knowledge of individual disciplines and the operational know-how that is called for. As a result, those who must make decisions must never expect too much from the specialists who have something to say about several disparate elements, but never enough about the system as a whole.

There is also a rather hasty tendency to place experts and scientists in the same basket. According to the etymology of the word, an expert is someone who has been tried and tested, who has learned by experience, who has undergone trials. This term also has the root 'periculum', so it could even include the meaning of one who has come through a danger. All decision makers would hope to have better things to say about the experts chosen to work at their side than Li Ch'uan said about Chao Kua in a text by Sun Tzu: 'All Chao Kua knows how to do is read books [. . .]; he is absolutely incapable of establishing correlations between changing circumstances . . .' (Sun Tzu, 1972, p. 118—unofficial translation).

The temptation is great among people in positions of authority to shift this role onto an expert and thereby relieve themselves of their decision-making responsibilities. The transfer may be made in rather subtle ways: a manager may seem to forget momentarily that any decision must incorporate a wide range of considerations (since a single factor is rarely sufficient to determine a course of action). Turning suddenly to the expert at hand, the manager will ask, 'Well, professor, should we evacuate?'

The expert, pressured to assume the mantle of the decision maker, tries to build in a solid margin for safety. Indeed, once the total is made of all the margins for safety proposed by all the experts consulted, the outlook is so dark that it really provides nothing to the actual decision maker other than a vision of the Apocalypse. To reach that point, was it really necessary to consult such an array of fine minds? Expertise is only useful if it is employed wisely. Fundamentally, this means the decision maker cannot use it to palm off responsibility, or leave the experts with that impression. This is a point that needs to be made explicitly at the outset and reaffirmed as the event is being handled.

By the same token, the experts may be tempted to become decision makers. They could be overwhelmed by the situation, unaccustomed as they may be to having their opinions solicited to such a point, to strolling through the corridors of power, to being in the media spotlight, and all the rest. The temptation is all the greater for experts since, at least at the outset, they enjoy great credibility, greater than that of the people in charge. They may even be held up as saviours.

As a result, scientific and technical advice may quickly drift towards 'political' counsel. This leads straight towards terrific dangers, including that of role confusion, and it is important to have thought about this problem beforehand. As a first step in this direction, it is interesting to examine the thoughts of Theodore Sorensen, an adviser to John F. Kennedy.

Theodore Sorensen: Experts in politics
[Sorensen notes that Presidents are often criticized for not respecting the advice of their own advisers.]
But not all experts recognize the limits of their political sagacity, and they do not hesitate to pronounce with a great air of authority broad policy recommendations in their own field (and sometimes all fields). Any President would be properly impressed by their seeming command of the complex; but the President's own common sense, his own understanding of the Congress and the country, his own balancing of priorities, his own ability to analyze and generalize and simplify, are more essential in reaching the right decision than all the specialized jargon and institutionalized traditions of the professional elite. [. . .]

Essential to the relationship between expert and politician, therefore, is the recognition by each of the other's role, and the refusal of each to assume the other's role. The expert should neither substitute his political judgment for the policy-maker's nor resent the latter's exercising of his own; and the policy-maker should not forget which one is the expert.
(Sorensen, 1963, pp. 66–7)

Henry Kissinger and Theodore Sorensen also add a few useful warning notes on turning to outside advice:

Henry Kissinger: The academic and crisis action
A policymaker's greatest need for outside advice is in an inter-mediate realm between tactics and goals. Tactics are usually so dependent on the immediate situation that outsiders without access to cables can rarely make a significant contribution. At the other extreme, ultimate goals reflect philosophical perceptions and political necessities; while an adviser can provide some insights here, to be effective he must be conversant with the perceptions of the policymaker—changes of course require self-confidence rather more than expert knowledge. The dimension for which outside advice is more useful is the medium term, to carry the policymaker beyond the urgent but short of the ultimate—the perspective of two to five years. Unfortunately, this is normally the routine preoccupation of academicians interested in political problems and they seem to feel themselves cheated, deprived of the excitement of proximity to power, if they are called to Washington to do no more than they can accomplish at

home. So instead of focusing on the medium term they tend to flood the policymaker with minute tactical advice or elaborate recommendations as to grand strategy until, glassy-eyed, he begins to feel new and unaccustomed affection for his regular bureaucracy.

(Kissinger, 1979, Vol. 1, p. 704)

Theodore Sorensen: The expert in politics
Expert predictions are likely to be even more tenuous than expert policy judgments, particularly in an age when only the unpredictable seems to happen. [. . .] Nevertheless, each rumor [. . .] was checked out; increasing rumors brought increasing surveillance; and when, finally, the unexpected did happen, this did not diminish the President's respect for these career servants. It merely demonstrated once again that the only infallible experts are those whose forecasts have never been tested.

[. . .] a president may seek or receive advice from outside the Executive branch; [. . .] Whatever the justification, outside advice has its own limitations. As national problems become more complex and interrelated, requiring continuous, firsthand knowledge of confidential data and expert analysis, very few outsiders are sufficiently well informed. The fact that some simple recommendation [. . .] seems more striking or appealing or attention-getting than the intricate product of bureaucracy does not make it any more valid.

Moreover, once the advice of a distinguished private citizen or committee is sought and made public, rejection of that advice may add to the President's difficulties.

(Sorensen, 1963, pp. 67–8, 73)

Finally, there are the borderline situations, which are especially tricky. When experts have the feeling they are dealing with an especially troubled group of decision makers, or one without any experience in handling such matters, they may feel a sort of duty to intervene directly, a desire to come to the rescue of the whole group. But this transforms them into decision makers.

The case may also arise in which one point is so crucial that an expert's word will in fact seal the decision. After an earthquake, for instance, if an expert says there is a strong risk that a nearby dam will break within 24 hours (but not within three minutes, as in the previous example), the expert knows that his or her word outweighs any other, and an evacuation will be ordered. The decision maker, however, retains responsibility for determining how to evacuate, whom, and other questions.

The crisis management expert: an expert who doesn't exist

The term 'expert' usually conjures up an image of a scientific specialist or an expert in a specific field—Sovietologist, Sinologist and the like.

There is virtually no such thing as an expert in crisis management well acquainted with the type of overall difficulties encountered by decision makers in such cases, except in a few rare consulting firms, and there this role deals mainly with communication.

Few individuals have had sufficient experience with crises or have analysed enough case studies to be able to offer truly efficient assistance in these situations.

Furthermore, advice on crisis can only come from truly interdisciplinary teams, accustomed to working together, and with sufficient practice to offer vital but discreet help without overstepping the boundaries of their role. For each crisis an appropriate team must be composed to tackle the specific problem, and it must draw from an adaptable network that can be rapidly put into action.

Such veritable expert crisis management teams, capable of integrating scattered information, are what decision makers really need. But, for the time being at least, they simply do not exist.

Facing the media: from horror to revulsion

The points discussed above show how difficult the crisis is to handle even inside the organization. In-house communication is actually a major issue. Too often neglected, it leads organizations to fatal implosions.

But we shall stop to look here at communication with the media, which is often felt to be the most destabilizing challenge. This is certainly the most fashionable aspect of crisis management today. The field of communication is where managers feel the most helpless, and this is the front line on which the harshest collisions with the outside world have occurred.

There is nothing astonishing in this, given the outdated conceptions that still shape communications policy. One executive, who is now convinced of the importance of good communications, summarized his experience: 'When I joined the company, I was greeted by the CEO, who told me, "Here, nobody except me talks to the outside, and my rule of thumb is to say nothing." ' Then there is the famous remark by an American industry leader: 'No comment, and that's off the record' (Draper, 1986, pp. 30–8).

We shall attempt here to enter into what most managers experience as a chamber of horrors: the world of the media. Of course this is not a uniform world: there is no comparison between a specialized journalist—who knows something about the field, who is used to turning to a whole network of experts to check out technical details, who has worked hard to become credible and does not want to squander that reputation—and the two-bit reporter who tries to turn a scoop into a career springboard. There is no comparison between the newsreader for a major TV channel, who cannot announce just any information, and the host of a splashy special broadcast that features the crisis the way a vaudeville show features a new star. But these ideas all run together in the minds of executives when they think about the media, and quickly become a muddle. As we shall see by adopting their point of view, this is perfectly understandable.

A landscape that looks like the apocalypse

Here come the media, adding to the pressure on systems already strained to the breaking point. And what pressure they apply![22]

The barbarians attack
In this section we have carefully avoided organizing the ideas presented. Instead, we shall observe the whirlwind that sweeps up unexpecting managers who suddenly see the media charge through the door and invade their frame of reference.

The first incredible aspect lies in the way events unfold: managers begin watching the media to know what is happening in their own companies.

> *Bhopal, 1984*
> The telephone rings at Union Carbide Headquarters in Danbury, Connecticut at 4.30 am. CBS News is on the phone wanting to talk to somebody about an accident in Bhopal. The media relations manager is suddenly plunged into the media event: 'They had a wire service report out of India that said there was a gas leak and a few people had been killed,' he recalled. 'At the time the guy said 30 to 35. He started giving me all of the details, including the cows that were lying dead in the streets. As I talked to him, he kept getting more reports. By the time I got off the phone the death count he had was up to 200 to 300 people.'
>
> (Irvine, 1987, p. vii)

Three Mile Island (TMI), 1979
[A Harrisburg radiostation's] traffic reporter . . . uses a CB radio
to gather his information. About 8.00 am he heard police and fire
fighters were mobilizing in Middletown . . . [The radio's] news
director called TMI . . . He was connected with the control room
to a man who told him: 'I can't talk now, we've got a problem.'
WKBO broke the story . . . on its 8.25 am newscast . . . At 9.06
am, the Associated Press filed its first story.
(Kemeny et al., 1979, p. 104)

Gander, Newfoundland, 1984
The Pentagon learned of the airplane crash and the deaths of
248 military personnel via Radio Canada.[23]

A factory in eastern France
The general manager of this plant left his office, did a few
errands, went home, and turned on the TV set. The first thing he
saw was his plant, in flames.[24]

This obviously creates quite a shock for the people in charge. They
always suppose that nothing really serious will ever happen; if there
were a problem, they would decide together with the executive team
what should be said, when, and how. But the world suddenly stands
on its head: it is the media who know what is happening, and the
manager is reduced to asking them for information. The first stage in
this declaration of war is a humiliating act of surrender.

Not that this first shock leaves behind any breathing room. The second blow hits, and promises to be followed by a chain of unbearable
challenges.

Immediately—in the space of a few minutes, or at most a period ten
times shorter than the decision maker ever expected—the media
descend. The first shock is their numbers and the enormity of the
decision maker's task:

Challenger, 1986
As NASA's director of public affairs recalls, 'I don't know how
that many people could have appeared from almost nowhere in
so short a time (. . .). We had 400 to 500 newspeople
credentialed for the launch, and most of those were
photographers. By nightfall 800 more had come. By the next day
we had 1400 to 1500 members of the press. It was wall-to-wall
people.
(Irvine, 1987, p. ix)

Tylenol, 1982
Calls from the press came in bunches of 50 and 100 . . . When
we had 26 calls stacked up waiting, we'd just take the next one
on top . . . Over a period of three months after the incident, we
handled a total of 2,500 media calls.[25]

Then comes the feeling of intrusion: there are journalists everywhere. The organization involved has the feeling that it has become the prey of unspeakably rude invading hordes who act like victors in a conquered land.

> *Three Mile Island*
> The media continued to show their prowess by gathering license plate numbers of cars parked at the plant. Journalists then hunted down employees and tried to glean information from them. Better yet, one patient reporter managed to find the radio frequency being used by officials: 'Parked directly across the Susquehanna from the plant, Nordland tooled with his fancy scanner radio searching for TMI transmissions. Nothing on the utility band, nor the police band. He switched to a frequency the instruction booklet said was reserved for "federal interagency cooperation during nuclear war". And they were there.'[26]

These encroachments may take the form of a photographer discovered inside a factory, perched above a damaged storage tank and preparing to take flash photos in a highly volatile environment—or a helicopter hovering over a leaking tanker truck in order to get a great bird's-eye view.

> *Accident on the highway near Lyon, France, 10 April 1985*
> A propane truck flipped over, creating a cloud of gas that spread to the parking lot of a supermarket downwind. Luckily, a team of firefighters saw the scene on its way back from a call. They were able to stop traffic immediately, alert the authorities, and go to work. The supermarket was evacuated (a drill of this type had been run a few days earlier). A ban on flights over the area was requested and obtained. But that didn't stop a press helicopter from coming in directly over the site, at very low altitude. This of course threatened the lives of rescue workers on the ground (as well as the helicopter).

The media pressure reaches its peak immediately. Answers must be given about everything, to everyone, at a time when there happens to be other work to be done—such as saving lives and preventing an accident from turning into a major catastrophe.

Nothing to be done: the outside world demands 'good' communication and total transparency, at a time when the organization is going through the most trying period in its history. Its leaders are summoned to tell all, and fast: give an exact, certain, and final diagnosis of what is happening; state how things will evolve, without uncertainty or errors; explain the entire strategy that will be applied; provide firm decisions about liability, guilt, and indemnification; and make solemn commitments to cease operating or to transform radically the systems involved. Of course, the most fundamental demand is to give the media total access to all information and all sites.

The press also wants to deal with no one but the chief executive or the specialist. It rejects the official spokespersons. Anyone who is not ready for this reaction will be brutally swept aside. Yet the key figures scarcely have the time, and rarely are prepared, for the media adventure. The press also does not care about the responsibilities assigned by job descriptions: it knows who it wants to see, and it seeks out that person. Another surprise is the disappearance of the journalists with whom the organization is familiar—the ones with whom it has worked to build a relationship over the years.

The traditions and habits of this media world are also deeply disturbing. This is a partner whose capacities are astonishing: its 'where there's a will there's a way' attitude contrasts with the corporate sluggishness encountered by any manager during a crisis. The exceptional event is the fundamental stock in trade of the journalist, who is most at home in out-of-scale situations. Thanks to high-performance, highly mobile technical resources, the media can overcome time and space; and they have access to experts who feed them technical information and opinions—effectively robbing the managers of their control in this area.

Then there are the questions. Managers and specialists are suddenly confronted by a potent journalistic mixture of ignorance and specific knowledge culled who knows where. How can they respond to these demands for information, certitudes, firm positions, and definitive commitments, which are always inversely proportionate to the uncertainty, fragility, and explosiveness of the situation?

There are the answers provided—and how they are transcribed. The battle proves to be an uneven one: a journalist always has the right to make mistakes, but any error on the manager's part is firmly denounced (on the double grounds of incompetence and a will to misinform). Offering to re-read an article in order to correct technical errors is of course the most provocative gesture a manager can make—it threatens the journalist's freedom. What is fundamental for the manager, i.e. giving accurate data to the public, comes much lower in the journalist's scale of values. What counts there are speed and the writer's absolute freedom.

If by chance the reporter does agree to verify the technical points, there is still room for surprises. Remember, the journalistic world is often a world of 'generalists'.[27]

The danger of not fully checking a transcription
Raymond Sené, researcher at the Collège de France and
member of GSIEN, had a misadventure when he was contacted
with a question on nuclear power. The journalist called back to
check his article. The scientist had no problems with what he
heard over the phone: 'The effect of gravity [*la pesanteur* in
French] makes the control rods fall.' Imagine his surprise the
next day when he saw himself quoted as saying, 'The absence of
gravity [*l'apesanteur*] makes the control rods fall.' In this case,
the error was so blatant that the specialists simply laughed.[28]
But the result can be more twisted, and above all more
dangerous, if the data given immediately saturates the
audience's ability to absorb information, thereby making it
impossible to correct the mistake.

The social stature of television reporters also comes into play:
because of their apparently intimate relationship with the public, it is
hard to compete with them on their own turf.

This is enough to unbalance the best-prepared organizations.
Imagine the situation of the vast numbers who are ill-prepared. The
natural reflex is to stonewall, to refuse to leave oneself open or
become an exhibit in what feels like a media sideshow, to reject this
vacuous activity. Besides, it could be extremely dangerous.

This goes both for the organization as a whole and for the individual
who is personally exposed, especially in television interviews, as we
shall see below.

Organizational failure
Two examples should suffice to paint a generally applicable picture.
NASA's media management of the crisis around the Challenger
catastrophe, first of all, shows that the world's best organization for
responding to journalists can have serious difficulties during a crisis.
The case of Three Mile Island remains a reference for traumatic
experiences. (We shall use some of the key points made in the study
by Sharon Friedman, a consultant for the Presidential commission
that investigated the accident.)

Challenger
The spaceship blew up at 11.40 am. More than an hour later,
NASA announced it would hold a press conference at 3.00 pm. It
was twice rescheduled, and finally at 4.40 pm spokesman Jesse
Moore had little to say other than to confirm what millions of
people had seen on television five hours earlier. He could have
made this statement—all but the fact that a search showed no
signs of survivors—well within the 20 minutes directed in

NASA's disaster contingency plan. Because of its delay, NASA demonstrated it had lost control of the crisis.

(Irvine, 1987, p. 347)

Shirley Green, NASA's newly appointed director of public affairs, sits in stunned silence with everyone else in the control room. As emergency procedures go into effect, she carries out her first duty by calling the administrator's office in Washington and then starts thinking about the statement that has to be made to the public. (. . .) NASA's management is out of town or tied up in implementing its contingency plan for accidents. The top executive for the Office of Space Flight at the Kennedy Space Center that day says he'll talk with reporters, but he keeps being pulled into meetings and saying it will be a few more minutes. Meanwhile, every phone in the NASA press center is ringing, and reporters are milling around wanting details, pictures, information, interviews—anything.

A press briefing is scheduled and then repeatedly postponed. White House Press Secretary Larry Speakes is calling, wanting to know when NASA is going to say something. He keeps getting the same answer—in a few more minutes. More hours pass. By the time a briefing is held, the die has been cast. What went on in those four and a half hours so tainted NASA's relations with the news media that neither Shirley Green nor anyone else would reverse the situation in the following months.

(Dilenschneider and Forrestal, 1987, p. viii)

Three Mile Island
Metropolitan Edison [the operator] and the NRC [the government authority] were the prime information sources for the media about what was happening during the accident, but they provided very little useful information during the first few days. Because neither had emergency public information plans, their responses to media queries were confusing, conflicting, and disorganized. On the first day of the accident, no one even knew who was in charge of informing the public. MetEd issued statements from three different places, all saying something different about off-site radiation. (. . .)

One mistake [by MetEd] was an attempt to play down the amount of radiation being released into the air. This resulted in Lt Governor William Scranton stating in a press conference that the utility was not telling everyone all that it should. Such mistakes continued for several days, culminating in a disastrous blunder. Right in the middle of the nation's most serious nuclear accident, the vice president for generation told the press that he did not know why he had to tell reporters each and every thing MetEd did. This lost the utility whatever credibility it had managed to retain at that time. (. . .) The NRC spoke with multiple voices . . . the Region I information officer, . . . NRC national headquarters . . . NRC engineers at TMI, and . . . the NRC Commissioners themselves.

For the accident's first two days, MetEd and the NRC gave almost no organized help to reporters. (. . .) Not until the third day of the accident . . . did MetEd set up a press center, and then it was in Hershey about 20 miles from TMI and only for phone calls. The NRC did not set up a press center until the following Monday, six days into the accident. The lack of a press center meant no central place for reporters to gather information, few public relations aides, and even fewer technical personnel to explain the complex technological aspects of the accident.

Confusion mounted. It became very bad on that Friday, after a 1,200 millirem radiation release from the plant led to a discussion of a possible meltdown. This confusion was not the media's alone. Pennsylvania's governor was getting confusing reports from the NRC about the danger and whether to evacuate the populace. (. . .)

Throughout the accident, the clash of the different worlds of the engineer and the reporter took its toll. Reporters were confronted with complex explanations in which engineers made various distinctions based on technical information reporters could not understand. (. . .) Engineers found press ignorance frustrating. They were particularly concerned about having to give short, simple answers to complicated questions and about having to deal with 'what if' questions that led to meltdown scenarios.

Yet media needs proved as baffling to engineers as reactor technology did to reporters. The engineers did not realize that the media needed to have information on a regular basis because newspapers do not print blank pages and television news programs cannot run 30 minutes of recorded music. They also could not understand the media's tight deadlines and reporters' need for something new. The engineers wanted time to solve reactor problems, while the media and citizens were concerned about potential health hazards and possibilities of evacuation.

(Friedman, 1989)

Also (Fink, 1986, p. 110):

The chairman of the board of GPU [MetEd and TMI's parent corporation] recommended that newspapers located near nuclear power plants should hire reporters who are familiar with nuclear energy and physics. [The] editor of the Harrisburg *Patriot* and *Evening News* shot back: 'All nuclear plants should hire people who are familiar with the truth!'

Facing the camera: a personal descent into hell

Here again, Mr X, the person in charge, discovers problems sufficient to make him lose what remains of his composure in times of crisis. The pattern is typical:

He will be contacted by a journalistic world that is as strange to him as his own universe is to the members of the press (indeed, everything of which the executive stands accused seems strangely applicable to the media as well). The person who contacts the executive is not the one hosting the broadcast; any questions the future guest asks receive carefully vague answers. But the promise is made that he will meet the interviewer before the show.

If this manager attempts to contact the journalist again, he realizes how annoying it is to try to reach someone who is always unavailable.

Having failed to rough out the interview before arriving at the studio, he asks upon arriving to see the journalist, as had been promised. Ah, but this is impossible: that person is busy putting the final touches on the show. The executive becomes convinced that the journalist has actually sought to avoid him. While he is being made up, he runs into the interviewer, who is all smiles. But behind this apparent friendliness, he senses a veiled threat: 'Don't worry, I'm gonna chop you to bits.' Having been stripped of all external signs of power, the executive feels that the elementary rules of protocol have been reversed. He senses that he is going to be a plaything, and the newsreader will be making all the rules.

Then comes the studio, as pleasant as an operating room. The bright lights, the heat, and the absence of any shadows or relief, emphasize that everything here is simple and direct. There is no room for reserve, nuance, prudent thought, or complex and intricate ideas—which all form the basis for the entire response to the crisis. The decision maker suddenly feels very much alone, an unhappy guest: What am I doing here? Why me? The tension is similar to what he may have felt going into a big job interview. But with a difference: here, every question must be answered in 10- to 30-second sound bites. Another imperative: the whole statement must be built around images and clichés that describe a clear approach, yet they must be comprehensible for the person-on-the-street, i.e. verging on oversimplification. Despite all appearances, this is not a dialogue: the executive is really speaking to millions of viewers. Even more upsetting is the role of the image. Radio requires a primarily intellectual effort; here, the guest's personality is what fills the screen. Half the message has already been sent by the first image, before he even opens his mouth, and much of the rest comes through in the silences and hesitations. In fact, the unhappy guest must never hesitate (unless he has mastered the art, but this is not for beginners). One dead second and the message is clear: he is uneasy, therefore incompetent and a liar. Any break in the sound on television is loaded with meaning: the image, which generates constant messages, then becomes extraordinarily forceful, and the visible discomfort that goes with this hesitation is devastating. Furthermore, the sudden absence of sound in a world of noise leaves the viewers with a disturbing sense of impending collapse. The gladiator has been wounded, and the viewers in their armchairs are torn between turning their thumbs down or feeling pity, which perturbs their comfort as image consumers.

Going through such an ordeal is hard enough when you are invited to boast about an accomplishment; meeting the challenge in a crisis situation seems impossible, especially in the face of an accumulation of objective difficulties:

- In a crisis, there is a cruel lack of information. This means the data needed to answer most of the questions are not available. By the same token, it is impossible to deny the allegations put forward, no matter how outrageous they may be.
- In front of the cameras, the guest can never be as comfortable as a newsreader who does this every day. Generally speaking, people have little experience with this tool. Treating the experience like a normal conversation is a trap: if you do not correct an inexact statement or pick up on a dangerous overtone immediately, the interview will be over before you can go back to the subject. On European television, air time is incredibly short and hard to manage well. In fact, within the time given for the allotted interview, each sentence pronounced is the equivalent of a chapter or set of chapters in a book. In the United States, where interviews last no more than 20 seconds, and sometimes just 10, there is barely time to state the title and three-quarters of one of its major themes.
- Any error is immediately broadcast to millions of viewers and taken up by all of the press, especially if it is serious.
- The stakes are, of course, very high: there is no way of casting off the public's worries lightly.
- Subtle issues of roles and legitimacy come into play: one manager cannot answer for another. Yet it is equally unacceptable to

respond too systematically that a given issue is not part of your responsibilities; and in a crisis, responsibilities tend to overlap.

- Yet another challenge: How do you speak simultaneously to all the groups behind the camera, including the victims if any, the company's personnel, customers, the general public, your competitors, the authorities, the lawyers and judges, the politicians, and concerned foreigners?

You may be faced with impossible contradictions. For example, if a huge and obvious human error has been committed, how can you manage not to acknowledge the fact—since that would trigger an uncontrollable crisis in-house—yet not lose your public reputation and your dignity with regard to the victims, who care little about the atmosphere inside the company that has made them so miserable?

Against this backdrop, the executive must confront the journalist's questions. These are sound-bite questions, with rapid-fire follow-up, traps, questions too emotional to be answered, or so turned, in extreme cases, that they could actually endanger people's lives. Behind them all, one obvious assumption on the interviewer's part: the executive must be hiding something, making the executive guilty of both incompetence and deceit.

The interviewer may even ask a question that is perceived as being perfectly abominable. Imagine the reaction of the representative of a major pharmaceutical firm during a crisis caused by the discovery that blood transfusion techniques used until then could be a source of AIDS contamination. The journalist asked, 'So how many people have you bumped off?'[29]

The interviewer is, of course, faced with personal difficulties. The newsreader for a newscast must juggle with the available time, the technical problems, and 20 different topics. Each newscast is a technical feat that generates high tension. This may surprise the interviewee, who is accustomed to seeing the calm and suave atmosphere that is projected into the homes of viewers. How do you keep your concentration in such moments—especially if the control room suddenly encounters an insoluble problem, or a teleprompter[30] breaks down, or the order of the topics changes? How can you remain calm when confusion reigns and you are surrounded by conflicts in the studio among journalists or among technicians? The newsreader may also be on edge after a series of gaffes in the broadcast.

Another possible scenario may also emerge, once again at the last minute: the manager is left virtually alone in the studio, peering into the camera, with a single technician. After preparing for a dialogue with a journalist and learning the basic rule, i.e. never look into the camera, the interviewee discovers that the interview is to be done in duplex. The new rule is, always look at the camera, and above all, do not 'talk' to the journalist's image on the control monitor.

At a deeper level, the interviewee is hounded throughout the experience by the feeling that there is a double standard: 'The journalist can attack me, I can't talk back.' And above all, 'I'm the only one who has anything to answer for; if I make a mistake, the press reports fan the fires and I make the crisis worse. If the journalist makes a mistake, everyone will conveniently ignore the slip—not only the station, but the rest of the press, out of solidarity.'

Pre-recorded broadcasts can also offer surprises. Here, the bone of contention is the cuts. Those interviewed regularly denounce the propensity for dramatizing. And they are basically right. The journalist has to produce a short product, since that person, too, is pressured by media time, and the result must be striking enough to prevent viewers from zapping, since that hurts the Nielsen ratings. If the tension in the message drops the slightest bit, if the pause for thought is a little too long, hundreds of thousands of viewers lose interest. The montage can leave no room for nuance.

The chorus of complaints against the press
As the trials go on, people reach the limits of their tolerance. This is when the violent complaints against the press begin, describing journalists' behaviour and their 'feats' during crises. The themes are well known:

- *Sensationalism* On this point, those who have handled crises cite a collection of examples including '3000 deaths in Bhopal caused by dioxin', or a case of 'radioactive dioxin', or the headline 'Terror on the Tarn River' following a minor incident.
- *Superficiality* 'No time to read your press release, give me two knock-out ideas for my article, quick'; 'I don't know anything about nuclear power, and I have two days to write my script; the out-of-state filming is already done, so what do we come out against?'
- *Falsehoods* 'Authorities are on the track of the 41 waste drums from Seveso, filled with *pure dioxin.*'
- *The slippery eel* As soon as the damage is done, the journalist can no longer be reached.
- *Randomness* One matter is splashed across the front page, while

another—much more serious from the manager's point of view—
gets no attention.

- *Ethical issues* Company officials often perceive journalists' demands
  as consisting of: 'You must tell me everything, or else you are mor-
  ally finished; you can't ask me anything, or else you infringe upon
  the freedom of the press.'
- *Irresponsibility* The articles are published, the sound tracks played,
  the images shown, no matter what the consequences, even for the
  victims. (We shall return to this issue later.)

The standoff

In the absence of a regulatory device, a *perverse relationship* develops:
'I can't stand them, but I have to keep being nice, or else they'll tear
me apart.' This mask of forced amiability hides deep rage rooted in
the conviction that professional ethics is just a fancy excuse for journalists to do as they please, and that their virulence is actually a way
of compensating their lack of real power. For a short period, the crisis
seems to grant them remarkable opportunities based on the troubles
of those in charge.

Once the floodgates of such criticisms have opened, everything
comes rushing out. One manager quotes a journalist who revealed a
disturbing lack of esteem for his trade (he wrote for a nationally
known specialized review): 'If I make a mistake, it really isn't important. Readers know we're just journalists. We have no credibility,
and anyway, all our articles end up in the garbage.' Another highlights the ambiguity of the press, especially during a crisis: 'No matter
what you call them, these are wars—organizations face off via the
media, and many articles are simply dictated to the press. In the
realm of pure information, we are nothing.'

From all this arises a violent feeling of repulsion on the part of the
organizations: 'We fail to understand how they can behave this way
when so much is at stake in a crisis.'

Of course, our focus here is on the difficulties encountered by
unprepared managers and executives suddenly forced to confront
the media world, and we have adopted their point of view. The journalists are also tense, and justifiably so. Is it not their basic responsibility to reveal the truth about an event, despite all the risks? (If they
do not do so, the effect on the situation could be even worse—after
all, we live in a media society.) Are journalists supposed to resolve
all of society's contradictions? Reporters may be criticized for being
ill informed, but what about the companies' practices of refusing or

hiding information? If those in charge made the work easier, journalists might make fewer errors. These issues are worth looking at in depth, though this is rarely done. Instead, each side remains tense from fear, weakness, and its unwillingness to call itself into question.

But let us stay with the picture we are developing. The decision maker caught up in these situations is hardly in a position to wonder about the fundamental questions of the media society.

Reacting: what not to do

When faced with so many difficulties, the most natural reaction for the person in charge is to tense up, especially if, as is often the case, this is his or her baptism by fire into the media world.

Facing the journalistic investigation

Tensing up leads individuals to do everything on the 'What Not To Do' list (see Dessaint, 1988, pp. 4–8):

- Stay silent until it is no longer possible to do so.
- Be closed and evasive as long as possible; those in charge are 'not available for comment'.
- Reply 'no comment', which can be interpreted in any number of ways.
- Issue denials that do not fool anyone.
- Make uncertain statements in which the primary message is how unsettled and unprepared the organization is; give the impression that the top executives refuse to come to the front line; do not coordinate statements and actions. This is the world of double-talk, which is the way a generally hazy attitude appears in speech.
- Then begin making firm declarations that try to sound reassuring; they should be obsessed with avoiding panic. The two stock leit-motivs here are 'everything is under control', which is interpreted as 'every man for himself', and 'we don't know what's happening but it's nothing major'.
- Add a few inopportune remarks along the lines of 'we're the best, our record is spotless', or 'the ones who criticize our position aren't experts'; or simply try to save your own skin: 'I did my job'.

All of this hides an actual incapacity to provide information about the event, the context, any precedents, and so forth. The picture can become much darker when people start dissimulating information or making diversionary manoeuvres intended to draw attention to one problem in order to hide another. As soon as evidence to this effect is produced, all credibility is lost. All the decision makers have to do now is to cast aspersions on the newsmakers' abilities, or show their impatience with or anger at the media, and their fate is sealed. The communications battle will be lost.

Other information sources will be heard first, and their views will take precedence. A pattern of revelations and confessions will set in as the organization, unable to communicate, finds itself with its back to the wall, forced to acknowledge the facts one after another. Very quickly, sometimes immediately, it becomes discredited. As we saw in the case of Three Mile Island, the first press conference given by the plant operator was so disastrous that the government authorities themselves silenced it. Anyone who makes these kinds of communication errors becomes the ideal sacrificial lamb who is so useful in crisis situations to counterbalance their unbearable complexity and uncertainty. These attitudes of rejection may also bring out the avenging angel in people, always a prompt phenomenon to appear in moments of doubt and soul-searching.

The risk then is a slide into a general rout affecting a much broader area than just the communication aspect. It is important to remember the guidelines given by Joseph Scanlon (1982a and b, 1975):

- An emergency is an information crisis.
- Information gaps must be filled.
- Whoever controls the access to information becomes the centre of operations and control.

Facing the victims in a media situation
A debate in which an official representative is confronted with the victims raises the difficulty another notch. Nothing in the representative's background offers a preparation for this type of test. The organization has made no preparations for such an adventure.

The 'guest' gets the feeling of being drafted by the organization. There is little if any support from the firm he or she works for. The legal department warns about everything that could go wrong, generally concluding that it would be better not to go. Other employees who managed to turn down the invitation all point out the risks this creates for the company, not to mention for the representative's own career. There is no room for manoeuvre, no human preparation. When confronted with the victims, the representative may be overwhelmed by feelings of unbearable danger. The classic reaction is to hide behind the technical explanations and the numbers. This puts across a message that can be summed up in one word—indecency—and it quickly completes the destruction of what is left of the organization's reputation.

Here a real example can be helpful: the preparations for a major TV show that was to bring together an organization and a group of victims after a serious accident.

Philippe Dessaint: Preparing for a major TV show
I was asked for my opinion. What should they do about this invitation to take part in a television debate that would surely be awkward because of the presence of victims? I said nothing and watched the group.

The first question was, should we agree to participate or not, knowing that there will be victims present and that we will most likely be torn apart?

The first reaction was, we won't go.

I asked, 'Do you think this is the best way to respond?'

The group then brought out all the excuses, all the statistics possible. All the legal advice. All the technical arguments they had to show that the company was beyond reproach. Not a weak point in their armor. Above all, no emotion; if that got started, where would it end?

Then came the dreaded question: Who will go?

A volunteer had been found. What message had he been given? 'Careful, this is terribly dangerous: the company is risking everything. Whatever you do, don't say that. Here are the notes on the victims. Here is the technical data you can give. Don't let them get you down. And look out for the journalists. Look out for the victims' lawyers.' The poor man admitted he hadn't slept for three days, and the filming was for the next day. He was frozen with fear. As an individual, he no longer existed—he was simply the sacrificial representative being sent to slaughter by his firm. His mission was impossible; he was to show no emotion, to be as technical and exact as possible. The others, relieved that they would not be sent, began to bombard him with facts and figures he was to dish out—when in fact he was going to meet with human beings who had suffered and were suffering still. Nothing in the background of the volunteer or the company, nothing in this preparation would let him show that he was human, and that he too had suffered, terribly. He was supposed to behave like a real leader, hard as a rock and serious from head to toe.

The trap was obvious. It is psychologically impossible to go into a television studio with that mindset. The only possible escape on camera is to keep an even stiffer upper lip. The individual must be even more self-assured, even more technical, even more arrogant. He will top off the technical breakdown with social condemnation.

The group was vaguely aware of this. After an hour and a half, back to square one: 'What if no one went?' This time they tried to get me to approve their strategy.[31]

I said nothing. They got angry. I pointed out that they were taking the wrong approach to the problem.

The appointed volunteer exploded. After all, why should he be the one? Being a martyr wasn't part of his job.

We kept going in circles.

The only way to unblock the situation was for the person who would go to be himself and not a mere mouthpiece for the organization. But this is a skill that cannot be improvised overnight.

The group seemed to wonder whether it could help the volunteer by doing a filmed rehearsal. The volunteer could learn to give the impression that he cared about the victims and their suffering. I immediately let them know that I would not play this kind of game (something only an outside consultant can say). If they did not know for themselves what respect meant, I would not help them make a mockery of it. Not only for ethical reasons, but because it wouldn't work. There is nothing worse or more obvious than false solicitude along the lines of, 'And I would just like to let all the victims know . . .'.

The meeting ended in an atmosphere of fear and confusion.[32]

Beyond the immediate experience, a few guidelines to how the media work

The points discussed above should enlighten crisis managers about a number of immediate difficulties and traps. But in order to react and develop strategies for action—which will be the focus of Part 2—it helps to have a long-range view of how the media operate in crisis situations and the problems they may cause.

Before undertaking this examination, however, it should be noted that in some exceptional cases the media may vanish from the scene for several reasons. On the receiving end, the crisis may damage the media's physical resources or limit their access to the affected site. On the distribution end, they may no longer be able to receive or broadcast, e.g. if an electrical outage cuts off television. Given all that has been said above, decision makers could be thrilled by this. But they would be wrong. The media's absence can have negative consequences. Those in charge can no longer issue warnings, send messages, or learn the needs and expectations of the public. They have lost their primary communications tool. They may also have lost a good early warning system. It may be unpleasant to learn bad news from the press, but it is better to know.

Now back to the standard situation, with the media fully functional. How do they work, how do they react? The purpose of the argumentation that follows is to provide a series of points which may help those in charge to think, to plan, and to be aware of their behaviour.[33]

The media will hear of an event

The conventional reflex is to believe that problems can be concealed, 'the way they always are'. This is a dangerous assumption, as the media are everywhere now. Furthermore, in a truly menacing situation, this gives formidable leverage to those who are already in the know—and they are rarely a small group. It should be clear that if the cover-up does not work, the crisis will be tainted from the start with dissimulation, a cardinal sin in our age. This is what happened with Chernobyl. The news came from Sweden, so that any later message issued by the Soviet Union was immediately disregarded. This is what happened, for instance, when the first death toll of two was announced. A figure thousands of times higher, announced by an uncertain American source, was attributed just as much credibility.

A crisis is a good deal for the media, which will try to obtain further information

In this business, bad news is good news. A crisis provides an excellent opportunity to forget about vital and infinitely less interesting major problems, such as interest rates, EC agricultural policy, or GATT negotiations. None of these creates a spectacular image. A crisis generates episodes that are made for television, with drama, action, and a real story including a beginning, a middle, and an end.[34] So the media set to work.

They make use of all the sources and means imaginable, and they do so with incredible speed and ingenuity.

They will use their files to add to the story. Consequently, if errors were made in the past, there is every chance they will find their way into the new media coverage. If the organization involved chooses to remain silent, these past errors may become even more predominant in the stories.

The media will dispatch reporters to the scene. Here again, they use all available means, leaving reporters a greater degree of freedom than they usually enjoy. (A reporter was once parachuted into the middle of the Atlantic ocean to be picked up by the boat transporting a group of kidnappers.)[35]

The media may make demands about communication tools, transportation, and other resources. This may place a strain on the means available for treating the event, e.g. by saturating the telephone system or even, as was the case during the San Francisco earthquake, saturating the air space with helicopter flights. The media may attract attention to the detriment of the victims.

The media assume that those in charge know exactly what is going on, which is not necessarily the case. These actors may then be tempted to pretend they do understand everything. But they should realize that as they attempt to put the pieces together, the media will become acrimonious over the difficulty they have in getting information, even if no one is concealing anything from them.

Information will be reported as it is received
The normal checking procedures regarding the quality of information and sources are generally loosened. This is especially true of media like radio and television that produce continuous information. Unlike the written press, which must only publish a limited number of editions, these media must fill hours of air time.

Information will spread from one medium to another.

The media operate in cycles. They first focus on the key points, seeking out less dramatic data later on in order to fill in the gaps in calm periods.

Even if an event proves to be of little significance, the journalists must supply information to justify being there. The important thing is to find something to fill the bill. This is when the people handling a crisis may come in for a surprise.

The media will attempt to fit the news into a framework
Journalists want news in terms of how many victims, how many homeless, the cost of damages, and who was responsible. They will push hard for this type of information and will not realize that in the immediate aftermath of a disaster, it may not be available. Those in positions of authority should be aware that this is not the type of information they normally collect. As a result, they may not be able to catch the media's interest.

The media may demand official press conferences
Such conferences are useful to them because the information they provide helps to flesh out other data. Also, they present an opportunity to record official statements. Press briefings are also precious to the media because they ensure that different journalists all have the same information. (According to Joseph Scanlon, the key is not so much to obtain a scoop, but to avoid being scooped by a competitor.)

The various media—radio, television, and print—will act differently
Different media will behave differently. Each medium has its own requirements and logistical problems. The written press must supply more information and greater background. Television needs images, and radio wants sound pictures. There are other differences between the local, national, and international press, between big agencies, television, radio, and print journalism; between specialized journalists, the general press, and yellow-rag journalism. Each of these elements must be answered differently.

In a truly major event, journalists cooperate with one another on the scene. But competition remains the rule in terms of finding images, or between journalists working for the same organization but in different departments.

Foreign correspondents often form a group of acquaintances who travel together from one event to another. They are virtually associates, though they remain rivals. They will exert pressure together to obtain an information focus that satisfies their expectations. This may put them into conflict with the local press, especially if officials are awed by the presence of big names from the national and international press.

For many journalists, especially the beginners, a crisis is one of the biggest opportunities in their careers. This highlights the extraordinary difference in attitude between journalists and officials in charge of the crisis.

Naturally, a distinction must be made between sensation-seeking media and everyone else. What the scandalmongers want are scandals, whether real or fabricated (and preferably in serial form). Generally speaking, however, all media do have to sell.

The reality created by the media quickly becomes the accepted reality, even at the highest levels
This is especially true of stories made-on-television.

The media are not above persuading people to act in a specific way to ensure that the images produced conform to the media's conceptions of how a given type of event should look.

Three Mile Island
TV crews asked people to move indoors so that they could show deserted streets.[36]

The media also release images that spread information over which they have no control.

Report on a 'Gulf Crisis' with the Indians near Montreal, summer 1990[37]
Television images showed that French Canadian and English-speaking regiments behaved differently. This was only obvious to well-informed viewers (especially with regard to uniforms). This detail escaped the media, but it could create conflict among the organizations directly involved.

Whether the report is exact, false, or biased, what it shows becomes the target for the reactions of public opinion, politicians, and even officials in the crisis.

San Francisco earthquake, 17 October 1989
The fires attracted the most attention. This is what television filmed, because it had the means to do so, and the images were good, even at night. The more severely affected areas got much less attention. Animosity was created because of the perception that the media were more interested in selling news than in providing assistance. (. . .)

Inaccurate information or excessive inter-network competitive pressures are counter-productive and can result, for example, in sending the wrong relief supplies to the wrong location at the wrong time.
(Scott and Freibaum, 1990, p. 7)

This will to a large extent determine what is requested of those in charge. In the age of non-stop reporting, this type of factor can change the way crises are handled. One example is the impact made by a network like CNN during the Gulf Crisis in the Middle East. The dynamics can reach the crazy stage at which people respond only to representations of reality, which take on lives of their own. Joseph Scanlon cites the example of a police officer directing operations during a catastrophe. He gave a telephone interview to one journalist based on the images from another station he was watching on television.

Conversely, the information the media choose not to release may not get any consideration, or will not receive the attention it deserves. Today, an actual event that does not become a media event may not be treated as a problem to be dealt with.

> *Tornado in Brittany, France, October 1987: Media absence and underreactions*
> This disaster failed to capture the attention of the national media—'not enough people killed' was the explanation given to those who tried to get reporters to the scene. The lack of media coverage resulted in a 'national emotional deficit', according to Louis Le Pensec, a politician from Britanny. His comments made the headlines in *Ouest-France* (24 October 1987).

Television now has the technical means for immediate information
In recent years, television's tools have changed substantially. Events are now immediately accessible, wherever they happen.

> *Philippe Dessaint*
> We've come a long way from film that had to be developed, and even from video cassettes that had to be brought back to the studio. Lightweight, live cameras with satellite connections are becoming widespread. Changing these tools has caused a revolution. Television is getting further and further away from classic reporting, where someone went out to investigate, came back, wrote the script and read it. Now the camera captures the whole story live—but with no distance and no analysis. The implicit idea, which is false, is that images do not lie. So we see major crises brought into people's living rooms, while the journalists and specialists in the studio do not know what to say about this material being thrown at their viewers.[38]

In a world in which the media influence everything, television ends up filming its own creations
At this stage the urgent need to think about how the eye of the beholder affects what it sees, becomes clear.

> *Philippe Dessaint*
> History is now coming to be shaped by the media. The actors are careful to produce messages that will pass through the filter of the cool medium; events are programmed as a function of when they can be shown on TV. For example, farmers demonstrating in northern France a few years ago were planning a spectacular nighttime operation. They called the local television station: 'We're planning a surprise operation at the prefecture tonight.' Prudently, we told them, 'We don't have any equipment available tonight.' They answered, 'No problem, we'll do it tomorrow night.'[39]

In general, there comes a point at which the media slant on a situation largely overshadows any other reality.

Predicted earthquake in New Madrid, Missouri, 2 December 1990
CBS News cameras filmed people filming other people who were filming the rescue equipment being set up in the event something actually happened.

There were even suggestions that the actual forecast might have been a media coup started by a scientist known for his radical positions. The media were criticized by NEPEC (the National Earthquake Prediction Evaluation Council) for their lack of discernment in publicizing the prediction. News reports attributed accurate predictions in numerous previous disasters to the person who forecast the quake, including the 1989 San Francisco tremour. Emotion ran so high in Missouri that NEPEC was forced to take seriously a case which had no scientific value; the issue was delicate because the probability of tremours in that region is high. To ensure their objectivity, the media turned to scientific experts, one arguing for and one against the likelihood of the quake. The proponent had in the past used procedures based on paranormal means to refine his predictions.[40]

The media may or may not publish vital information
In some cases, the media will agree to withhold information. This is common practice with kidnappings. It lasts as long as all media outlets honour the request.

But no one should expect too much reserve in presenting images. We shall examine the victims' point of view later. Here is the view of a journalist.

Tour bus accident and its unbearable images in Beaune, France, 1982[41]
I remember the Beaune catastrophe, that bus accident that killed more than fifty children from a single village. At the time I was a journalist with FR3's local Picardie station. That day an official came with a list. As if he were announcing the results of a contest, he read the families the names of the dead. (Sometimes a single family had lost several children.) The cameramen filmed. The scene was unbearable, and we refused to air the images. But Paris wanted visuals. As a young journalist, I couldn't say no. Today, I would have refused. The television stations showed those images, and the little burnt bodies being pulled out of the bus.

This same penchant re-emerges with each catastrophe: showing bits of corpses, scattered members, pools of blood. This is unbearable audio-visual material that provides no information whatsoever, but above all, it is cruelly taunting in a broadcast for the general public. It's just plain voyeurism. You can imagine a voice off-camera cackling, 'Sorry, sweets, that's what good images are all about!' Probably what it would take would be the guests, if any, daring to say on camera how revolted they were by a station's showing such indecent and pointless images.

But I don't have any illusions. Hot images are the primary information we have. When we have nothing else, this is what we present. We scarcely take the time to think about it. Simply getting the images back to the studio and on the air is a real feat, without stopping to think about it. This process takes on a life of its own, at least in the first hours. There's no room for ethical questions. We ask those later—if we ask them at all.

And we bring out the same emotional images each time the subject or the issue comes up again—and especially on anniversaries of the event.

The media can also be stupifyingly irresponsible. In the Tylenol case, one television station stood out by demonstrating on camera just how to go about contaminating a batch of medication (ten Berge, 1990, p. 29). In extreme cases, the coverage of terrorist actions[42] can be full of surprises.

Unless otherwise indicated, the following illustrations are taken from Kelly (1989, pp. 122–3):

On 22 November 1974, four hijackers took over a British Airways DC-10 in Dubai scheduled to fly to Libya. They demanded an exchange of terrorists for hostages. A plane that supposedly contained the terrorists arrived in Cairo. At that moment, a local journalist revealed live that there were no terrorists aboard the plane. It is believed that one of the hostages, a German banker, was executed as a direct consequence of that broadcast.

In the 1979 Mogadishu case, an Israeli amateur radio operator intercepted messages between the plane transporting German anti-terrorist forces and its home base, and passed them on to a French news agency. Although the Germans asked that the information be withheld, Israeli television broadcast the news. Two British newspapers, *The Times* and *The Daily Telegraph*, also decided after consultations at the senior level to ignore the German request and publish the story.

In 1974, terrorists took hostages in a courthouse in Washington, D.C. They were holding the hostages in a room separated from another room by a two-way mirror, which meant that if the lives of the hostages were endangered, police officials could have shot the terrorists through the glass. This feature, which protected the hostages' safety, was lost when the media revealed the ruse. The terrorists ordered the hostages to place a cover over the mirror.

The British television station ITN defied police instructions by hiding a camera behind the Iranian Embassy in London during a hostage crisis. The camera betrayed the presence of SAS troops and showed their minute-by-minute preparations to storm the embassy and free the hostages. The terrorists had access to a television set. Fortunately, there was a four-minute lag in the retransmission, which probably saved the lives of the hostages as well as several SAS members.

In June 1985, hijackers took over a TWA flight to Beirut. US Secretary of State George Schultz severely criticized the media for having reported on the movement of Delta Force troops from their base in the United States and the sailing of Navy ships from Haifa and other ports to the Lebanese coastline.

In April 1982, hostages were taken in Edmonton, Canada. One of the radio stations covering the event stated, 'The police have requested that we not provide so many details on its tactics, but we do know that members of a SWAT team are posted at various points around the house'.

(Scanlon, 1984, pp. 169–94)

In another hostage crisis in Canada, the following dialogue took place between a journalist and a hostage taker:

'Why are you asking for so little? Wouldn't it be just as easy to request $25 000 or $30 000?' (The hostage taker had requested $10 000.)
'You're right. Maybe I should ask for more. You gave me an idea.'
'That isn't what I meant.'
'Things will work out fine. Why don't we ask for the jackpot, while we're at it? Something like $150 000? That sounds more serious. What a great idea!'.

(Scanlon, 1981, p. 143)

It is interesting to look in greater detail at the coverage of a hostage crisis at the Turkish Embassy in Ottawa in May 1985 (Kelly, 1989, pp. 124–7).

At 7.15 am on 12 March 1985, a Canadian press agency received a phone call from a man announcing that he had taken hostages to make Turkey pay for the Armenian Genocide. The attack had been carefully organized to capture media attention.

The terrorists had come into the embassy with a list of telephone numbers of the major press agencies. The incident was over in five hours, once they had obtained the publicity they sought. The media posed a certain number of characteristic problems.

Blocking police access
One key problem was the inability of police to establish

telephone contact with the terrorists for more than two hours. The lines were constantly kept busy by journalists.

Complicating negotiations

Some journalists engaged in questionable interview practices. One reporter asked the terrorists what their demands were, whether they would negotiate, and what would happen if the Turkish government did not give in to their demands. A journalist from CBC asked a similar question, and upon hearing the list of demands, responded to the effect that 'Those are long-term demands. Do you have any short-term demands to resolve the situation right now?' This elicited a long silence as the hostage taker apparently weighed the merits of having some short-term demands.

Disclosing tactical information

Several instances of this type occurred. Journalists speculated on camera about what the police were going to do. One reporter announced that SWAT units were taking up positions. Throughout the morning, live film coverage showed movements on the balconies of sharpshooters and SWAT team members as they deployed around the embassy. There was a television turned on inside the embassy. Fortunately, the terrorists were probably too preoccupied with their hostages to watch it.

At one point, a police officer, apparently unaware his remarks were being transmitted live, disclosed that the Turkish ambassador was lying wounded beneath a window outside the embassy and could not be moved. This clearly placed the ambassador's life in danger. The officer later acknowledged his error, but stated he had acted under the pressure of the moment and did not know his comments were being carried live.

Worse yet, one CBC reporter announced on camera that the police were hoping to use a truck as cover to remove the ambassador; at another point, he announced that the police had wired the back of the embassy with explosives and were planning to blast a hole in the wall and enter the building. This same journalist later received a national media award for his coverage of the incident.

Pressuring crisis managers

The conventional strategy used by authorities is to avoid abrupt actions, to play things down, and to draw out discussions in order to reach an acceptable denouement. By focusing on highly charged images and sharp individual emotions, the media hinder this strategy. They ask the burning question: Why are the authorities so indecisive, so slow to react? In this episode, this was certainly part of the problem.

It is troubling to make such observations. Some journalists also have their doubts:

Journalists won't let presidents or members of Congress control what the media broadcast or write; they won't let the millionaires control them; they certainly won't let terrorists control or manipulate them. We don't want our government to tell us how to cover an event. But there are circumstances in which we actually do let terrorists do just that.[43]

When facing such risks, it is tempting, here again, to try to simplify things by handing down strict decisions, like censoring the press. But in a crisis situation, being simplistic never solves anything. A major figure in the field states:

Frank Boltz, New York Police Department
If you don't give media coverage to what terrorists are doing— let's say you impose a blackout on all information—they'll do something so spectacular that you will be forced to lift the censorship.[44]

Contradiction: the heart of media–crisis manager relations

It should now be obvious that beyond the various problems or the positive examples it generates, the media world produces contradictions that can have a serious impact on how post-accident crises dynamics are managed.

Contradictory operational approaches
In a turbulent situation, the officials in charge try to counteract confusion and the push for radical solutions or abusive simplification. They try to reduce levels of anguish, explain how the systems work, start the healing process, provide a sense of consistency, distinguish between the essential and the secondary, between what is current and what is past, break the grip of fantasy and imagination, and find means by which the systems can right themselves and start functioning again.

On each of these points, the media take an approach that fosters problems.

- The media system in and of itself is like a giant sounding board on a national or international level. It can even create logistical problems by organizing aid that is particularly inopportune if it cannot be channelled before reaching the scene. Dealing with floods of useless donations can handicap the efforts of the actors involved.
- Some features specific to the media raise serious questions when the phenomena to be dealt with are complex, which is inevitable in any technological crisis. For example, just how 'short and sweet'

can a message be? What is the minimum time needed to make a complex statement? The same goes for the rule 'keep it simple'—spots and sound bites are the great media models. These means are not suited, however, to dealing with a subject that cannot be simplified. Yet it must be simplified—but at what price?

- In a crisis situation, communication follows patterns that are hardly conducive to bringing the fever down. A shocking image, for example, promptly saturates the viewers' capacity to absorb other information. Once this information is released, it becomes virtually impossible to correct it. Any attempts to do so merely make the situation worse. What is the consequence, then, of an error which is so easily made in these fuzzy situations?
- Error is precisely the pitfall awaiting the media. Officials often remain silent, the experts cannot yet render a verdict, and the journalists are usually generalists. Yet everyone is functioning in a situation that requires instant declarations.
- The press creates many other difficulties. By producing an information glut, it keeps citizens in a state of high tension. With a range of data, it demonstrates that systems are poorly controlled. By revealing contradictions, the ultimate investigative tool, it exaggerates interpersonal and inter-organizational rivalries. While officials do everything they can to prove that systems are organized to withstand crises, the press churns out masses of contradictory statements, frightening images, outrage, and declarations that scarcely flatter the person quoted. It digs out old stories and revives discussions that had already created strain, both in-house and with the outside.

Different principles, different backgrounds
In case the picture still seems to have some bright spots, it is important to realize the great divide that separates these two worlds.

The media usually operate, in practice if not from its deepest convictions, on two hypotheses:

- A fact is a fact.
- Any fact should be reported if the reporter finds it worth while.

Both of these points conflict with the approach taken by executives and managers. The conflict becomes all the more strident in a crisis situation.

For the journalist, the facts in a crisis are even more blatantly true than in normal circumstances; it is therefore even more vital to report them.

For the executive or manager, the facts in a crisis become even harder to define, and it is extremely dangerous to take them at face value and project them post haste on the little black box.

Scientific attitude can never coincide with journalistic principles on the issue of what is fact. For scientists, a fact is not something blatantly true because a valiant journalist braved dangers and dissimulation to reveal it. A fact is by definition something constructed.

The same is true for news stories. According to Paul Ricoeur, reporting does not mean telling the truth; it means building a story based on facts which have also been constructed. Producing an account means transforming the events into a story; it means organizing a list of occurrences into an intelligible whole. Ricoeur continues, 'Creating an intrigue is the process that derives a configuration from a simple succession of ideas, composes an ensemble out of such heterogeneous factors as actors, goals, means, interaction, circumstances, and unexpected results; out of this ensemble, it builds a temporal whole' (Ricoeur, 1983, pp. 103, 105). In short, an account makes a significant whole out of a simple chain of events.

A journalist is a builder of stories rather than a simple channel for direct transmission between 'the' reality and the public.[45] Consequently, the journalist's trade is a subject worth thinking about, and such reflections do not automatically violate journalistic ethics. The basis for conflict remains, however, on every occasion.

How many journalists, accustomed to high-speed, high-impact television reporting on the most complex crises, would agree unflinchingly with the words of magazine editor Jean-François Kahn (1989, p. 22): 'Common sense readily suggests that the facts speak for themselves. (. . .) In reality, the facts are generally mute or tongue-tied. They aren't the ones that speak; the information giver makes them speak'? In any case, an official would pay dearly for quoting these lines to the MC of a major documentary-cum-sideshow presented during a crisis.

These thoughts are somewhat superfluous when a given incident is simply covered briefly, in passing. They become terribly important when the event turns into a crisis. Consider the case discussed earlier of a Californian dam that threatened to burst following an earthquake. The police chief learned that, within two minutes, the city could be covered by water. He had no time to undertake any action whatsoever. He did, however, make one decision: he radioed the five patrol cars in the threatened area and told them to flee as fast as possible. From his point of view, this was the only humanitarian gesture he could make, and he had to make it. It was also an important tactical move. If the disaster took place, he still had to be ready to act in the post-accident phase. Yet when the media learned of his action, it produced headlines of the type 'Police: Heartless Abandon', '80,000 people left to die by the police', or 'Police: Hit and Run'. The information on this tactical decision had not been given by those directly involved in it, precisely because of the construction they knew the media would place on it.[46]

This tendency becomes inevitable if the crisis turns into an affair, i.e. a quagmire maintained by leaks from unknown sources. Reality then becomes something almost entirely constructed, though no one really knows by whom.

> *The Watergate quagmire, as seen by Henry Kissinger*
> The journalists play a double role [in the area of leaks]: they are simultaneously the neutral instruments for their retransmission and the judges who evaluate them; they cover their informants on the pretext of respecting professional secrecy, and they often determine the final verdict by emphasizing now one, now another available version. They are both spectators and actors. The people have a right to know—but only what the press decides to tell it. When struggles are going on between different departments, keeping secret the identity of the sources of some leaks frequently deprives the reader of the most important part of the story. The journalist may attempt to remain objective, his competitors may have every reason for demolishing his article, but the sources of the leaks can always stage a dramatic action whose impact feeds on the reactions observed around the victim as well as around those waiting in the wings of power. Rarely, it would seem, does anyone worry about the informant's motives; yet serious ethical questions could be raised when the journalist's interest in obtaining a scoop coincides with the personal interests of the informant, which is the case in some investigative journalism. It then becomes difficult to know who is using whom.
>
> (Based on Kissinger, 1982, vol. 2)

With Enrico Quarantelli, we can expand on these first guidelines concerning the differences between these two worlds. In a recent article,[47] the former director of the Disaster Research Center paints a more complete picture of the differing cultural references that separate scientists and members of the media. In examining his analysis below, it should be borne in mind that decision makers basically belong to the scientific framework, although they diverge from it on certain points (Quarantelli, 1990).

- The world of mass communication puts an accent on things that are unusual or different. As the old cliché says, 'Dog bites man' is not news, but 'Man bites dog' is. Only the latter situation is interesting from a media point of view. In contrast, scientists build on patterns, even in what is abnormal.
- Scientists try to attach their findings to the context of established knowledge. The mass communication world highlights what is new.
- Science is a world of specialists who hesitate to venture outside their areas of expertise. Journalists, to the contrary, start with the idea that a generalist can discuss any subject.
- Media people do not look for feedback from their public; they are the sole judges of their work. In contrast, scientists are constantly involved in evaluating the work of other scientists, and this is a very important process for all concerned.
- The two worlds have different ideas about objectivity. Mass communication believes that a balance must be respected between opposing points of view. The basic hypothesis is that on any question, there are at least two points of view, and both must be aired. Scientists value accuracy and validity more than impartiality or neutrality. Science is seeking the truth, while journalism is seeking a balanced presentation of different points of view.[48]
- Journalists value timeliness. Scientists, to the contrary, focus on the relevance of information. In their world, information is never final, and there can be no definitive proof—whereas journalists present all data with conclusive certitude.
- Mass communication seeks to personalize events as much as possible. In science, depersonalization is the rule. Journalists do not want to know, for example, whether the epidemiologist's study shows that given hypothesis A, there is a risk of degree B for category C of the population. They want to know if the scientist would go live on the site with his or her family. The key point in journalism is bringing a dead story to life and making abstract ideas concrete.
- The central hypothesis of the media is, 'the facts speak for themselves'. Scientists do not believe this. So according to the media, scientists produce theories instead of facts.

From these observations, Quarantelli draws the following fundamental conclusions:

- It is not easy to change the way journalists work. What they do is deeply engrained in their subculture. Journalists will only behave differently if this subculture changes—for instance, at journalism school.
- It is probably easier to change behaviour in the other camp, especially by encouraging research organizations to communicate better with the media. For example, weather services can look at the way their storm warnings are perceived, rather than clinging to the idea that the populace fails to respond to them because it is too stupid. Working with the media on this point has proved very effective in the United States. Each department can establish closer contacts with its 'own' media, especially the specialized press.

Nevertheless, Quarantelli calls for continued questioning. In this field as elsewhere, it is not enough to solve yesterday's problems. What will happen as new communication tools develop? These raise serious issues. As Alvin Toffler notes, 'The basic direction of change in the media since at least 1970 has been toward the break-up of mass audiences into segments and subgroups, each receiving a different configuration of programs and messages via traditional TV, cable, satellite, VCR, and, soon, interactive hybrids of video and computer.'[49]

Jobs so contradictory that the riddles overwhelm all certitudes

At a fundamental level, the contrasts outlined above are based on the contradictory social roles of decision makers and journalists. As Soren Elmquist, the information director for Danish television, writes:

> The authorities' functions are to analyse the situations, lay out a strategy for tackling the whole scheme, make decisions and try to get the people involved or the population to react in specific ways.

> The media have two functions: to inform the population in clear respect of the 'right to know' and to cover journalistically what is going on—including exercising what is often called the fourth estate—the controlling one, being the citizens' representative.

> That does create a schism or even a conflict almost automatically between the authorities and the media people. The two parts can't just go together in handling the situation, because the authorities must all the time feel themselves controlled by the media, and the media must all the time—along with informing the population—watch the authorities carefully and critically, as is also their task.

Whether we like it or not there is an antagonism built into the relationship which often leads directly to mistrust. Many civil servants—civil as well as military—feel that the journalists are spying on them and consequently dare not rely on them, and many journalists are convinced that even the smallest piece of cooperation with authorities is a threat to their journalistic integrity.

(Elmquist, 1989, pp. 6–7)

The frequent accusations made by officials run up against these underlying oppositions. Certainly the media have always asked this question. The very presence of an outside observer and the check and balance it represents creates a problem, despite the fact that the principle of critical observation is a basic requirement for any democratic society.

But the situation is exacerbated in a crisis: at a time when it is even more necessary for these critical observations, these checks and balances to operate, the difficulties inherent in the practice of journalism make themselves even more sharply felt. This is especially true in the age of radio and television, notably because, for those in charge, the many problems posed by the media have little to do with defending fundamental values.

Officials, like journalists, should pause over the words of Hubert Beuve-Méry and Jean Lacouture, who summarize the heart of the issue of crisis communications. In these few words, they touch on the essential difficulties faced by parties on both sides.

Hubert Beuve-Méry
In a world in which the profusion of information media merely seems to foster the multiplication of errors and lies, it becomes a little harder every day to determine and show forth the truth.[50]

In reality, there are truths that should not be told, at least not right away, or not without precautions about the way they are told, because of the consequences this could have. Here again, there are many examples. Some information could endanger the life of a kidnapped child (. . .) especially when the information is instantaneous and is delivered to the general public, as is the case with radio and television in particular.[51]

(. . .) it seems to me that journalists should always demonstrate a certain prudence—I would almost go so far as to say a certain timidity. Except when something essential is at stake, and then, on the contrary, it is better to risk everything and to fight against the stream. The contradiction and the nobility of our trade is that these two rules seem equally true! Reserve in everyday life, and the fundamental, overriding obligation to become totally committed when something essential is at stake.[52]

Jean Lacouture
No one has the right to draw a line for his own personal use between publishable truths and unspeakable ones. Yet these lines exist when the issue is the survival of an individual or a group. Where do they lie? That is one of the riddles the Sphinx asks journalists.

(Lacouture, 1989, p. 213)

These considerations are fundamental. Yet they cannot close the breech. There seems to be no way to get beyond this very stage of the riddle. If we try to extract a clear and final message from either one of these experts, all we find, especially in the works quoted above, are comments about uncertainty and a lack of clarity, against a backdrop of anguish that summons our respect. At a few pages' interval, they contradict themselves. After pleading vigorously in favour of telling all, they meditate deeply on what an error it would be for a journalist to lack discernment; then they beat their chests again for not having revealed everything. This is the struggle—a titanic one when a crisis heightens the ambiguities, risks, and contradictions involved—between committing a professional error by holding back, and indulging in the irresponsibility of a 'pharisee of total truth' (Lacouture, 1989, p. 179).

When decision makers drift back onto the rocks: the dangers of disillusioned surfing

We have now seen the delicate problems that journalists face, and it is important that decision makers are aware of them. However, it is equally important to draw the decision makers' attention to another strategic briar patch that they themselves may fall into. After the overview given here of the media issue, one response (which is in tune with the times) would be to follow these new demands without exercising the slightest critical sense. If the media are looking for circus tricks, send us into the ring! The briar patch emerges when political power succumbs to this game. Then everyone, including the decision makers, find themselves behind the camera, filming not the event and how it is handled, but rather the way it is staged.

Michel Rocard, French Prime Minister
Ceasing to work for information means working only for what makes a splash. Political figures sometimes find a guilty pleasure in doing this if it gives them a chance to get away from

their dusty case files without feeling a twinge of conscience. But the results are devastating.

The entire thrust in recruiting political staff is to find individuals who are skilled at communicating, rather than at commanding or managing.

With that, we can define the role of the politician in the age of omnipresent communication. It no longer has much to do, and sometimes has nothing to do, with managing or governing.

The price we pay is a profound undermining of the role of government. Yet our democracies continue to need to be governed. I even suspect that in these hard times, the first requirement for overcoming crisis is to improve the quality of service rendered by those in power to their nation.

(Rocard, 1987, pp. 138, 140, 171–2, 172)

The slipperiest medium: rumour

Movement is its life and it gains strength as it progresses. Humble and frightened at its birth, it soon takes to the air. Its feet are on the ground and its head in the clouds. At night, it stands between heaven and earth, in the shadow, strident; and never sweet sleep closes its lids. During the day, it keeps watch, seated on the stoop of houses or the towers of the palaces, and it frightens vast cities, this messenger as attached to lies and slander as to the truth.[53]

Crises are a choice moment and foundation for the proliferation of rumours, which Jean-Noël Kapferer (1987, p. 25) defines as 'the emergence and circulation in a society of information which either has not yet been confirmed publicly by official sources or has been denied by them'.

All the ingredients are brought together to produce this hard-to-grasp phenomenon. A trigger: the initiating event, whether real or assumed. An important problem. A situation rife with uncertainty, ambiguity, and unknowns. Worry, which generates an irrepressible need for information and opinions.

The reactions from official sources are generally fine additives that stimulate the development of the phenomenon: silence, denial without satisfactory supporting information, an authoritative tone expressly requesting people to listen only to the one official and therefore legitimate version, and suggesting that any other interpretation of the facts would be 'irrational', and so forth.

The way the crisis unfolds reinforces this process further. Much information circulates informally before receiving official confirmation; some information is denied only to be acknowledged later as being true. It then becomes legitimate to anticipate the official information and not to be dependent upon it. If an authority proves to be truly out of control, everyone concludes that it would even be irresponsible not to listen to other sources, especially if they contradict the official line. Also, out of selflessness or a desire to exorcise their own worries, or to gain the esteem of their peers, people make sure that they share their 'tips' with as many others as possible.

Trying to react against rumour may have no impact; or worse, it may simply aggravate the situation.[54]

Keeping quiet. In a crisis situation, it can be dangerous to wait for the process to wind down by itself. Keeping quiet can 'confirm' any rumour. It may provoke resentment in-house. It may even be read as a sign of spite, when a rumour actually signifies a failure to communicate.

Issuing denials. First of all, this is not a very powerful communications weapon. It does not create striking news, and it does not calm people's imaginations. Furthermore, it can create a boomerang effect. It makes everyone aware of the matter, which may not have been the case earlier. It makes people wonder about questions they had not asked before. Inattentive hearers (i.e. the majority in the case of television audiences) may confuse the matter and the denial made. It can also be hard to distribute 'true–false' statements about subjects characterized by complexity, uncertainty, the vital importance of the message's source (which may be more important than its content), as well as the irrational aspects of rumour. The closed stance of a denial does not stop the rumour's driving force described above; it is always rooted in insufficient communication. Finally, a denial is a negative gesture, which can reinforce the feeling that the individual or organization being targeted really feels very unsure.

The Procter & Gamble Case, 1981–1985
This is an example of a crisis based solely on a rumour. In the summer of 1981, this American producer of consumer goods became the target of an unusual attack. Its emblem, created in 1882, was said to contain several satanic symbols (the emblem represented a circle with the face of Jupiter and thirteen stars). It was accused of having a pact with the devil. With a little imagination, one could pick out three sixes in this emblem, which created a link with the number 666, designating Satan in

the Bible. Jupiter's stylized beard could also be interpreted as containing three more sixes—there could be no doubt. The first rumour suggested that the company paid 10 per cent of its profits to a satanic cult, in exchange for enormous financial gains. Then the rumour held that the firm was actually owned by a sect. The rumour spread fastest in the Bible-belt states, where religious organizations called for a boycott of Procter & Gamble products.

At first, the firm decided to keep a low profile. How could such a rumour be denied? How could one *prove* there was no pact with the devil? By the time Procter & Gamble realized it had a real crisis on its hands, the rumour was already widespread. There was no point in pursuing the matter in court.

The company chose instead to attempt to explain and inform in order to deny the accusations. When people called in, telephone operators explained the history and meaning of the company's emblem, and clarified just what the company did and how it was managed. The rumour died down, but flared up again in late 1981. This time, Procter & Gamble was supposed to be possessed by the devil. Floods of phone calls came in, some 15 000 between December 1981 and June 1982.

The group then focused its action on 67 religious leaders and sent an organizational dossier to 48 000 religious associations across the country. One year after the crisis began, the rumours persisted, so the company turned to the media. Journalists were invited to visit the firm. Toll-free telephone lines were installed. Six persons were eventually brought before the courts: two of them had nothing to do with religious groups; instead, they worked for competitors.

Still the rumours would not die. In 1985, the group made the decision to drop the emblem that had caused so much trouble, even though it had represented the company for a century.

Procter & Gamble was easy prey for this kind of crisis. The company had always been secretive about its activities. It did not communicate with outside publics because it feared that would help its competitors, who would then be able to analyse its products and marketing techniques. This general image of secrecy and non-communicativeness were just the foundations on which rumour could thrive.

(Based on Kapferer, 1987, pp. 265–9; ten Berge, pp. 124–6)

Facing the victims: the risk of paralysis and spite

The crisis will become a terrible ordeal if it happens to involve more than just financial damage—if it affects human beings, their health, their bodies, and their lives. This is the most overwhelming challenge for someone in a position of authority: the direct confrontation with people who are suffering, with deaths, and possibly with a veritable hecatomb.

Such a situation calls to mind the words of Warren Anderson, the Chairman of Union Carbide, following the Bhopal accident, when he stated that he would carry the disaster with him for the rest of his life.

This section will adopt an approach focusing on individuals. The question of dealing with entire populations affected by a large-scale catastrophe will be handled in the following section. The people in charge encounter difficult problems on both levels, but facing individuals is certainly the most disturbing.

Chief executives, between disarray and flight

This is a matter of suffering, live and in colour. The issue is no longer one of general organization or management strategy; it is no longer possible to hide behind systems and hierarchies. The top executives can no longer hold up the very convenient argument that their place is in the crisis room, not on the front lines. Here one individual, whose job description places him or her in a position of responsibility, must face the pain and horror of other individuals.

There is a strong tendency to assume that if the paramedics and the fire department do their work, 'those people' have been taken care of.

Very often, the situation is tinged with guilt: 'How could I let such a thing happen?' This is not conducive to the most open attitude towards 'those people' and their misfortune.

Executives are just as susceptible as everyone else to a basic law of human nature: people run away from misfortune and trouble, because they are disturbed and frightened by them. No doubt such situations conjure up a sort of superstitiousness: if you brush too closely with misfortune, it may rub off on you. In addition, the situation contains the silent and anxiety-producing image of one's own death, and of past wounds that return like deep psychological threats (remember Robert Kennedy's comments during the Cuban

Missile Crisis, on seeing his brother wrestle with a terrible decision). The decision maker becomes defensive: Did the victims really do nothing to get themselves into this situation? Couldn't it be just a little bit their fault? And in fact, the guilt that every victim feels serves to reinforce the decision maker's tentative thoughts. The victim feels a certain shame at his or her misery, and this simply stimulates the decision maker's urge to flee responsibility.

Everything lends itself naturally to this flight. The people in charge become caught up in other things, including solving the crisis, dealing with the media, making speeches, and—the icing on the cake— organizing official ceremonies in honour of the victims.

This pattern is reinforced by legal worries, which may be played up by the departments involved: these actors may suggest that any humane gesture will automatically be taken as an acknowledgement of responsibility, and making any contact will be stepping into a trap, as 'the victims will tear us to shreds'.

And yet the top executive does indeed have a responsibility with regard to these people and their families. The goal here is to show that these leaders must be willing to recognize the difficulties encountered in this field, in order better to deal with them and fulfil their duties. These issues often seem to create barriers, so we shall attempt here to create some margin for manoeuvre.

First of all, the person in charge is not the only one who has to live through such difficulties. It is often noted that doctors protect themselves by considering their patients as cases rather than as human beings. The victims want the manager to give up his or her protective armour and stop being a mere representative, just as they sometimes expect their doctors to stop taking refuge inside their white coats.

So let us step across this barrier which creates both protection and paralysis. The ideas offered below for reflection are taken from accounts by Françoise Rudetzki, Claude Peyrat and Colette Bonnivard, all victims of terrorist attacks, and from that of Karine Robak, a victim of a technological accident. Françoise Rudetzki[55] has created the SOS-Attentats (SOS-Terrorist Attacks) association, and Karine Robak founded an association for the defence of victims of dioxins and furans.[56]

Individuals feeling rejected and abandoned

Aggression

Françoise Rudetzki: The terrorist attack
First of all, the individual has been violently assaulted by the
event. He or she will have been cared for and taken to the hospital
by competent emergency services. Often you are very grateful
to these initial rescuers, who make humane gestures and to
whom you may even owe your life. But of course however
remarkable the work they do, the shock of the event remains,
and it produces life-long effects.

Yet it is important to emphasize that very often, the victim does
not receive any immediate psychological attention. And waiting
on that issue increases the probability that troubles more difficult
to resolve will emerge in the near or distant future.

In fact, the psychological aspects of such a trial are generally
very badly managed. In the case of the DC-10 that exploded in
flight on September 19, 1989 because of a terrorist attack, the
families had to wait in complete anguish at Roissy Airport. It
would have been useful to have psychologists on site (as there
are several ways to announce such news). People got uptight.
One manager threatened to throw all the families out of the area
where they were waiting. When the decision makers start losing
their cool in front of the people who have every reason to do so,
that's serious. They should learn to control themselves in front
of the families of the victims.

If you are hospitalized, make sure to have a first medical certificate
made out with great care. Without it, victims undergo endless
hassles with their insurance companies and the agencies providing
compensation.

Karine Robak: The technological accident
In our case, the sequence was the following: a violent explosion
that shook the building; a power outage that plunged us into
darkness (at 7.40 pm in January); thick smoke and soot that
infiltrated everywhere (garbage chutes, air shafts, apartment
doors opened bruskly). We were suffocating, so we took to the
balconies, where some of us had to wait one or two hours, in
−20°C temperatures; a fire broke out in the basement but was
quickly brought under control; the firemen finally rescued us
and made us breathe some oxygen before taking us to the hospital
for a routine check-up. At the end of the evening, we came back
home. The apartments were completely covered in greasy soot.
What a horrible sight!

A first observation: the victim is strongly destabilized by this
brutal loss of his or her habitat. You feel deeply depressed, you
feel things are unjust. All the first reaction is to erase the traces of
the aggression. Everyone is seized by a frenzy of cleaning and

putting in order. This is an animal reflex: you remake your nest. No time to ask yourself questions—you go to it with mop and bucket! And then there are the exhausting steps to take: discussions with the tenants' association, with cleaning companies, with the insurance and their experts—not to mention the difficulties in camping out at home or living with friends.[. . .]

My second observation: it isn't easy, in fact it's almost impossible, to convince victims that they have to deal seriously with the situation. Everyone wants to be left alone to clean in peace. And if you insist, the reaction is of the type, 'If there was a risk, the people in charge would say so.'

The void, the obstacle course
The victim immediately feels tremendous anxiety, which arouses a desire to feel connected to other people and to institutions. Instead, he or she feels abandoned, and a sort of void quickly forms around the victim.

The families: not informed, not visited

Françoise Rudetzki: The terrorist attack
My husband and I were both taken to the hospital. No one stopped to wonder whether we might have a child alone at home. The social workers should visit the families: the resources exist in France to do so.

But all energies are apparently turned first of all to dealing with the material belongings that were destroyed, and the victims' fate is secondary. People are amazingly efficient at promptly erasing all physical traces of the event: when an attack was made on a major department store (December 7, 1985), 120 persons worked all weekend long to remove any material trace by Monday morning. The restaurant where I was had insurance against physical damage. The City and the State helped rebuild the place. But bodily harm was not covered by the insurance policy [. . .].
When [the arrested terrorist] Anis Naccache was released from prison (July 27, 1990), the victims and their families were not informed. Of course declaring a pardon is a prerogative of power. But the official communications department did not fulfill its role, because the victims and their families learned of the release of their persecutor via the media.

Distressingly tactless behaviour: brushing off the victims

Françoise Rudetzki: The terrorist attack
The manager of the restaurant never gave any sign of life. I've always said that I might never have undertaken this battle if the Taittinger group, which owned the restaurant, had sent me a bouquet of flowers or a case of champagne. In light of the

silence and spite displayed by everyone, I wanted to fight for the rest of us.

The public authorities arrived within fifteen minutes after the event (since there were television crews). The deputy minister of security visited the site of the attack; he promised that the truth would be uncovered. Neither he nor his department ever contacted me. And their investigation led nowhere. After the Orly incident (July 15, 1983) and the 1986 terrorist attacks, key figures visited the hospitals and sent baskets of fruit. When people are in intensive care or a post-operative unit, even the most exotic fruits are pointless. These people find themselves in the hospital in the blink of an eye, and they need soap, towels, and pyjamas; they need somebody to be there more than they need a basket of fruit.

And what can I say about the visits when an official, surrounded by a horde of journalists, cameramen, and photographers, happily makes the rounds in the media eye. People take this very badly, because when the victims see the journalists, they realize the official is turning this visit to his own advantage.

There has never been a terrorist attack in France after which the victims received a letter of condolance in the name of the nation.

Karine Robak: The technological accident
. . .the victim rapidly is placed in the position of a suspect, guilty of being impudent enough to stand up against public policy and the State's prerogative.[. . .] No one forgives victims for wanting to understand, for standing up as citizens, for refusing to submit and to grovel for a little charitable compensation.

Victims have to put up with errors, contradictions, unpleasant attitudes, outright provocation, calumny, and insinuations about their private and professional lives. What's more, their friends avoid them, people won't shake their hands for fear of being contaminated, and in their eyes you can see them wondering just how much the victims are making off the case.

We were looking for a comforting word or a kind gesture.

Those responsible for the problem never offered their apologies; they didn't answer when a little girl wrote to express her suffering. There was, however, a little dubious humor in the company that was at the source of the accident: employees offered a bottle of Chateau Magdeleine to their superior when he was transferred [the accident occurred in the rue Magdeleine].

. . . the victim no longer sees a way out of the problem. Was I going crazy? People suggested I was. [. . .]

Our only real source of support was Jacqueline Denis-Lempereur of *Science et Vie* [magazine].

Abandoned by everyone

Françoise Rudetzki: The terrorist attack
A victim is someone in a state of shock, who needs to be
informed and to communicate. A victim who is unfortunate
enough not to have family or close friends during this period
will have the impression to have been abandoned once he gets
back home. Nobody asks for his phone number or address.
Nobody writes him, no one at all. He has nobody to cling to,
nobody to telephone and talk with about his anxiety.

A victim may also want information about what has happened to
him. He rarely gets any. Too often in terrorist cases, the State's
prerogative is held up as an excuse to cover up the truth.

There are financial problems: you may lose your job. You feel
totally abandoned. If you suffer from post-traumatic neurosis,
your entourage—neighbors, friends, husband or wife—may
brush you off as well. The family unit threatens to disintegrate.

Such victims could get in touch with associations, but without
enough information, they do so very late in the day, when the
psychological problems have already taken root. They have
already tried desperately to manage alone. Before they finally
get some help, they have to run a veritable obstacle course, and
they wear themselves out in a maze of problems and
misinformation.

When I started this battle, a leading national journalist invited
me to his radio show. This was in the Fall of 1985. He also
invited the Minister of Justice to come debate with me about the
legal void with which victims of terrorism were faced. Half an
hour before the broadcast, the Minister of Justice sent word that
no one would come to represent his ministry. I talked by myself
for a full half-hour. I would have preferred a discussion. The
same thing happened again a little later at a conference organized
by a group of lawyers. No one came to represent the Ministry of
Justice, though once again, an invitation had been issued. I was
there alone.

We had some success by taking advantage of the 1986 electoral
campaign: we asked questions to the different parties, specifying
that their answers would be published.

Karine Robak: The technological accident
Against the company . . . you run into a wall. . . . But there were
other fronts. No one wanted to stand up after the accident and
cast doubts on the official story, or muddy the waters. People
worry about their respectability, about the dangers in sticking
their necks out for such an uncertain matter. . . . In this type of
matter, you rapidly discover a network of people who don't
want to have problems. Politicians as well as civil servants (who
can always hide behind the absence of legislation, something

frequent in crisis situations), to professional organizations, experts, insurers, businesses. Everyone closes ranks! So for us, we rapidly felt we were working in a void. There was no one in charge, just slippery officials. . . .

What's more, other networks contributed to reinforce this paralysis. Many of the officials were prominent members of groups like Rotary Club, a political party, or the campaign staff for a local politician. In short, everywhere we ran into walls. No way out. The only ones who at least listened to us were Environment in Paris and in Châlons, the regional capital. But they have so little power. . . .

You need the devil's own energy or rashness to pull through. You also have to resist attitudes of disdain—disdain for someone who 'causes problems', disdain for women who ask too many questions, especially technical or scientific ones. ('A woman isn't meant for that.') In fact, everyone was waiting for us to crack.

The media issue: taken by storm with pictures, ignored without them

Françoise Rudetzki: The terrorist attack
In favorable cases, the media play a very positive role: they conveniently alert the public, they warn those in charge of cases not handled, they help get assistance for victims. But when the event is spectacular, then sensationalism takes over. Television stations show blood-covered victims, and that does no good. We had to plead with photographers not to walk on the wounded, for example, in order to get a great photo. [. . .]

Then there are the pictures that keep coming back, reprinted for all occasions. In the case of the department store attack, for instance, it's always the same image of Colette [Bonnivard]. That's hard to live with. The whole recovery process for a victim, both physically and psychologically, involves erasing the event and trying to integrate it into your life. Seeing that picture interrupts the recovery process. Simply seeing the place where I was when the bomb went off is very painful. You feel a little as if a prying eye were watching you all evening long. The way the media stage an event gives the impression that it was even worse than what you went through. These images are very destabilizing.

In fact, every word counts here, for the victims and their families. Word comes through that there are 'only' slightly wounded individuals. That doesn't mean 'slightly wounded' people—they are handicapped for life. The expression is supposed to be reassuring, but people take it badly. Behind each casualty there is a human being, a life that has been altered, a life pattern that has been torn apart.

Karine Robak: The technological accident
Except for Jacqueline Denis-Lempereur, who gave us the
impression that she took things seriously, the other journalists
were difficult to work with. First, it isn't easy to contact them,
either. You get rebuffed, brushed off. They're hard to convince,
because you also have to explain to them what's happening—and
they generally don't have scientific background. Furthermore,
they're also susceptible to the assurances they receive that there
is no risk.

So you have to educate them, but above all, give them pictures.
That's the key: pictures and headlines. Victims asking themselves
questions and talking about complicated issues don't give many
pictures, so they don't capture an audience. A victim's only
chance of being heard by the press is to appear on TV. You
have to realize that we live in a snapshot society: as long as
something is only probable, as long as there aren't 200 corpses
on the ground, there's nothing serious. You are accepted as a
victim once you create a picture. When the furniture was being
taken out of our apartments, at one point a woman was hugging
the wall. That's a very powerful picture, and they took it.

Journalists aren't easy allies. One subject drives out another, so
they're not very faithful. You have to motivate them endlessly,
interest them in the problem and prove that it can get them
something. These people aren't working out of pure generosity
toward the victims. We may not get sick for some time, so we
don't interest anyone. You need dead bodies on the ground to
catch people's attention.

Cumbersome institutions

Françoise Rudetzki: The terrorist attack
The hostages in Kuwait: When the decision was made to provide
for the families through the Anti-terrorism Guarantee Fund, the
crisis unit at the French Ministry of Foreign Affairs had only the
telephone numbers of the families. It would have been so simple
to ask them for their addresses from the very beginning, as
numerous phone contacts had already taken place between the
unit and these families. It took three months for the information
to get around.

During the wave of terrorist attacks in 1986, I was overwhelmed
with calls from people from all over France who wanted information. So I called the City of Paris to ask them to do something.
They offered to install extra phone lines in my home. I suggested
they could set up an information center—and they eventually did so.

Karine Robak: The technological accident
While I was quickly gathering documents and technical opinions,
Mrs. Botella telephoned everywhere, including to city hall, the
municipal laboratory, the sub-prefecture, and the prefecture. Every

single one said, 'It's a private matter, go see Electricité de France.'
Every single one received our May 31, 1985 letter which explained
the situation and requested their help. No one answered. They
were all waiting for the polluter's reaction. They all clung to one
idea: the State's prerogative. The idea of public service got lost.
Always the same refrain: 'It's a private matter.' We had to wait
three months before the Ministry of the Environment pushed the
prefecture to order the mayor to have the building closed up.

Victims' reactions

Françoise Rudetzki: The terrorist attack
Some people want to fight and have the will to do so. Often the
victims are fighting for their rights; but when a child has died,
this struggle expresses a desire to keep alive the memory of the
lost child. It gives the parents a reason to live. For them, it's the
only way they can survive and be faithful to the memory of their
child. For example, when an explosion destroyed a building in
Toulon on February 15, 1989 (13 dead), the victims immediately
set up an association.

But with post-traumatic neurosis, very often a feeling of guilt
develops which wipes out any desire to fight.

And you can't criticize those who don't fight. Some people feel
that they have no right to make claims or to come begging,
especially in terrorist cases, when the government's liability is at
issue.

Some victims struggle for the just acknowledgement of their
rights, some simply wait because that's the way they are. You
have to respect each individual and know how to help those
who don't have the ability or the strength to fight for themselves.

Karine Robak: The technological accident
There is one central lesson: without exceptional circumstances
(e.g. extreme gaffes on the part of officials in charge, or an
unusual effort by damage victims to combine their strengths),
there is little hope that victims will be able to stand up to events.
To see why, just look at the obstacle course you encounter in
trying to mobilize people who've just been affected by an accident:

1 You have to pull them out of the depression and feverish
activity that leaves them no energy or time to think.
2 You have to inform them with simple words, and it's hard to
convince them when the danger is invisible.
3 Victims are profoundly persuaded that 'if there were something serious, the authorities would have taken steps.'
4 If you get past all that, you still run into defeatism: 'We can't
fight a major company.' The idea that the battle is already lost
is part of the mentality of a victim. In fact, there are a lot of
born victims.

All the company has to do then is to be forthcoming and help the people re-establish a familiar way of life. People won't ask any questions. If in our case the game had been played this way ('Listen, we caused you harm; we'll repair everything quickly; you'll be able to go back home; things will be like before'), I don't think anyone would have followed me. [. . .]

I really don't know what they can do; I don't know what advice to give. . . In fact, I wouldn't give any, but I'd say, 'You have before you institutions, companies, experts, a whole bunch of people. But all these people have are the authority and influence you are ready to grant them.' That's what we did at Reims. We always showed them behavior that told them, 'We don't give you the power.' We hammered in our messages: 'We won't admit that you have the knowledge you pretend to have, even though we know you aren't stupid; you confirm this and that, but on this particular point, you're lying to us.' This approach brings them down off their high horses. All they had left were the trappings of their authority. Naturally, that generates enormous aggressiveness. [. . .]

But above all, I learned that, quite naturally, our primary difficulty was the passiveness maintained by the victims. That's what's most serious. Taking action is exhausting. And what's more worrying, even if you manage to win (after all, we have made progress in our case and in the legislation as a whole), many victims still regard the whole thing as a failure ('What does it change?'). That's an underlying attitude. Some prefer to believe that it isn't worth the effort, otherwise they would have to recognize some serious things: a citizen can't place blind trust in institutions; you have to take responsibility yourself.

It would be so easy for large companies to hire social psychologists and carry on business as usual. . . All the odds are in their favor.

But it only takes a spark. . .

Mrs Misseri, tyre fire at Hagersville, Canada[57]
As in many other cases, the plaintiffs have grouped together in a committee, and they will not accept just any statement intended to calm them down: Mrs. Misseri states that the committee will pursue its activities long after the site has been cleaned up. 'There can be no question of anyone telling us that we have nothing more to fear and that they expect us to settle down,' she emphasized.

What is expected of those in charge

A bond, human reactions
Françoise Rudetzki: The terrorist attack
The main thing is not to lose touch with the victims, not to abandon them. When somebody visits a hospital—which is a good

gesture—it should be done without journalists, photographers, and not just for publicity's sake, but for the people being visited. The message from the person in charge should be, 'We're here; here is how to reach us, a direct phone number. Don't hesitate to contact us if necessary.' Offering a business card is a way of making a bond. What's more, when you have received a card with an official's name and address, you feel acknowledged and better equipped if you have problems later on with social or administrative services. A visit that occurs only for propaganda reasons is a visit that shouldn't take place. Simply holding out your hand is a humanitarian gesture. Unfortunately, decision makers feel too often that it suggests an acknowledgement of liability.

As soon as the principle of dialogue, information, and on-going contact has been accepted, tremendous progress can be made. The victim has a means of recourse, someone to turn to. In fact, the company can probably even prevent the victims from attacking it. If management could simply learn to listen, that would mark great progress. But those in charge are always busy being *representatives*. They should try to remember that they're human beings, too.

They always suppose that we're going to ask them to provide an immediate response. I think they're mistaken—but that's why they're afraid. We understand that they can't solve all our problems.

If an executive arrived in a television studio and said, 'I'm not familiar with the case, I'm here to listen to you and to take notes, we'll meet again in a week or a month' depending on the problem, that would already be a great step forward. But will the people in charge ever be able to adopt such an attitude? It would be extraordinary. Unfortunately, I've never heard such a response. Yet such behavior is probably the only way to get an answer suited to the need.

Claude Peyrat: The terrorist attack
I've been able to go on living because people have reached out to me, especially in my company and in the association. They've been great. That's why I couldn't give up the struggle. The bond you make with a victim is a lifeline.

Colette Bonnivard: The terrorist attack
[A civil defence representative who helped Colette in the midst of this tragedy looks back:]

She had eyes that were calling out with incredible force. She was thirsting for help and seemed to wonder where in the world she was. She didn't say a word, but her face expressed so precisely everything she could have said. I looked at her evacuation card. She was number 12.

[Colette also recalls:]

He speaks to me with a calm, soft, peaceful, comforting voice, and this feeling of deep intimacy between us helps me summon up what strength I have left each time I'm about to go under. I'm at death's door and he is all that keeps me attached to life.

[This is an exemplary model of fundamental psychological help offered by someone who is present at the scene of the incident, dealing with the victim. Later at the hospital, Colette added:]

When I feel discouraged and wish this endless effort were over with, when I'm ready to throw in the towel, to give up, to drift away, I feel all these hands that hold me back and bring me back to life with an irresistible force. People's looks prohibit me from dying. Many times, I was tempted to try and comfort those who loved me.

(See Bonnivard, 1987, pp. 25, 28, 38, 40, 177)

Karine Robak: The technological accident
Alone with their anxiety, victims are afraid:

- afraid to know that they have toxic chemicals in their cells and that no one can tell them what their future holds;
- afraid when they read the contradictory opinions of scientists;
- afraid when they realize that people are only interested in the universally-observed effects. Does this mean that something which only a few experts have observed does not exist?

Victims have lost everything, and they feel as though they've lost their past as well. They aren't sure whether they have a future.

Feeling completely lost, they are waiting for a word, a gesture, some psychological help, or a little compassion.

They find themselves thinking, 'My skin won't itch so much once I've received some compensation.'

Competent responses

Françoise Rudetzki: The terrorist attack
In offering a response, a representative of the company could have a psychologist assist him and invite someone close to the victim to come and see him.

Managers should be capable of guiding victims toward agencies adapted to their needs, especially associations. But they have to know of such agencies, find them, and evaluate their competence in order to avoid giving bad advice. Offices for victims' assistance have been set up all over France, but the private associations must maintain their independence *vis-à-vis* the authorities.

In addition, it's important not to forget that there are people who were not harmed physically but who were there when a catastrophe occurred, who are in shock and should be taken care of immediately. After a commuter train crashed in a Paris train station, many commuters who took that train every day should have received psychological help to allow them to overcome these visions of horror.

Similarly, those who go back to work at the site of a terrorist attack should, if at all possible, be granted special schedules, because going back to that place every day can be an unbearable ordeal.

In short, no matter what type of disaster occurs, mobile interdisciplinary teams should be sent in immediately with the emergency and security teams to set up help for the victims, their families, and the people who have lived through the crisis situation. Each team could include a doctor, a psychologist, a technician specialized in the area in question, and members of appropriate associations. The job of this team would be to listen, to inform, to accompany people as they dealt with various social and administrative services, and to provide psychological follow-up.

Karine Robak: The technological accident
Throughout this case, all we encountered were people who were incapable of making consistent decisions. 'It isn't our domain,' was their favorite refrain.

They had decided there was no problem; consequently, there was no reason to ask any questions. All their efforts were devoted to proving their theory and to shifting the blame elsewhere; everyone worked together to maintain silence about the matter. Some hid behind the legislation without stopping to analyze the facts and the events, and without investigating. Others declared they were experts, but the experts' advice was only used to silence the victims rather than to uncover the truth. We were dealing with people completely caught up in their systems, the kind who end up saying, 'We were only following orders.'

Some day, the people in charge will have to realize that victims cannot accept this official doubletalk, or arguments founded solely on their authority, or inconsistency and the lack of openness.

Finally, to complete these vital issues of acknowledging the human aspects and all that can be done in that area, it is important to touch on the issue of victims' compensation.[58]

Before 1985 in France, victims of violent incidents were compensated under restrictive conditions, according to complex legal procedures, and a ceiling of 250 000 French francs [about $50 000] was placed on the sums they received. Late in 1985, victims of terrorist activity banded together in the SOS-Attentats association and undertook a battle to receive full compensation for all physical harm suffered (the 9 September 1986 law). Since then, a guarantee fund financed by a national solidarity tax provides coverage for victims of attacks committed after 1 January 1985. Preliminary payments are made in less than a month. This agency determines the amount of compensation on the basis of an expert report. This agency and Social Security are the only authorities with whom the victim must deal, and the victim has direct contact with them. When an incident is undoubtedly of terrorist origin, the agencies take action without the victims having to contact them first. Property damage is covered by insurance.

When victims have suffered physical harm and the perpetrator of the crime is unknown and cannot be discovered, the sums are set by a compensation commission that works with the French high courts. Since 1 January 1991 (law of 6 July 1990), full compensation is offered. The courts set the amount, which is paid by the guarantee fund for victims of terrorism and other crimes.

The victims of technological accidents are usually required to under-take court proceedings in order to obtain a preliminary payment from their insurance companies for physical harm and property damage suffered, while they await the results of the technical invest-igations that will determine liability. Final compensation may only be paid years after the accident. The value of property lost, especially real estate, is often underestimated, and it is often impossible to find new housing. International conventions on the subject do exist. They provide for compensatory measures in the event of disasters. But as Christian Huglo (1990, p. 75) notes, the appropriate legislation depends on the type of catastrophe, whereas victims don't care whether it was radiation or toxic gas that wounded or killed them. Generally speaking, there are significant disparities in the way payment is made: in the case of Sandoz, things went very quickly; in a case like Bhopal, the matter and its complications dragged on.[59]

As for natural catastrophes, the property damage they cause is covered by insurance, but compensation is subject to the difficulties inherent in evaluating the damage (13 July 1982 law). No law yet covers physical harm incurred in such cases.

Numerous corporate actors

In-house: unions and the organization's internal structures

Especially when a technical failure forms the basis of a crisis, the incident has profound repercussions on the organizations directly involved. The victims may include members of their personnel; human error may become an issue; or the organization's future may be endangered.

The head of the company or agency in question will immediately be confronted with the need for in-house information and dialogue. Many other organizations—unions, in-house communication services such as the workers' committee, or the company committee within a large corporate group, personnel representatives, and employee health and safety committees—will all feel obliged to be involved.

What difficulties can arise in this area? They are as diverse as the situations creating them, but some basic guidelines for reflection do exist.[60]

The major risk: implosion
As has been shown earlier, the slightest lack of internal information can cause the crisis to implode. As in the outside world, rumours will arise to fill in the gaps, at an incredible speed.

The risk in cutting off the information: they'll go elsewhere
Unions and members of the personnel may have crucial information on what has happened. If the top executive does not open up communications channels, then not only will a good source of information be lost, but those who are cut off may be tempted to turn to the outside to be heard.

No crisis communication without prior communications
The way in which a crisis is tackled and perceived in-house will depend heavily on the quality of employee-employer relations before the event. How much dialogue and acknowledgement existed beforehand? Were there possibilities for discussion?

Human error: an issue with a high potential for added aggravation
Much depends here on how the issue of the human factor was handled before the incident.

- If the concept of human *error* still reigns, there is every chance that the unions will immediately take a hard line, fearing to see blame placed on one of their members.

- If analytical tools using more modern concepts based on the human *factor* or the organizational *factor* have been implemented, this will allow unions to cooperate in attempting to understand clearly and quickly the underlying reasons for the failure that has occurred.

Highly variable situations

In some corporations, the pre-existing climate makes it possible to start handling the crisis without running the risk of complicating the situation further. The climate can even have a positive influence, especially as it is in the interest of the personnel and unions to save their enterprise. The management may even discover that those who are its most virulent adversaries under normal conditions are more than eager to join forces. (This may, however, imply renegotiating other issues after the crisis.)

In other, more archaic enterprises, unions or personnel who are generally ignored may resent attempts to make an overture when the crisis hits. The same tense confrontation that was generally present will persist on both sides.

The quality of personnel relations: a yardstick for external relations

As union activist Jacques Fournier notes, 'Generally speaking, the quality of personnel relations within a company is also largely indicative of the broader quality of relations which the company has established with its environment. If internal relations are not good, external ones won't be either. On the whole, the whole corporate culture is what governs the capacity for communication, whether internal or external.'[61]

Audiences: tenacious and dangerous myths

It is important here to take note of two major references in the area of crisis management which are part of the shared cultural baggage—and which must be taken with a considerable grain of salt. The core of this cultural perception is the conviction that the first problem to be dealt with in a crisis is panic.

The work of the Disaster Research Center (Quarantelli, 1982, 1986) has provided more specific evidence on the preconceived ideas that immediately come to mind as soon as the word 'catastrophe' is pronounced:

> In a catastrophe, the victims are supposed to be in a state of shock, completely haggard, unable to do anything. It is assumed

people will panic: they will loot and display anti-social behaviour. Terrified by the situation, middle-level managers will abandon their positions to seek shelter, look after their families, and so forth. Only outside organizations will be of any assistance. It is assumed to be pointless, or even dangerous to count on the victims and key interested figures.

Theories also exist to support such convictions. Jean-Pierre Dupuy (1990, p. 11) has revealed the contrast in tone between a so-called French school which prefers to emphasize the danger of panic, and an 'American' school that denounces this approach with equal energy.

The French school is part of a pure tradition of crowd psychology, to use the title of the famous work by Gustave Le Bon. This mental state of panic (Crocq and Douteau, 1988) is characterized by the decay of individual consciousness as it merges into a larger whole, which Le Bon refers to as the collective soul of the crowd. This merging brings about a loss of all critical sense, a breakdown of the capacity for judgement, reasoning, and decision making, and the disappearance of sentimental influences (e.g. sympathy, solidarity, or love). According to the well-known clinical tableau established by mass psychology, these individual regressions are founded (this is important) not so much on panic itself as on the overall presence of the crowd, which produces gregariousness, infantilism, irresponsible anonymity, a propensity for violence, or a sense of unlimited power (Crocq and Douteau, 1988).

It is useful to be aware of these factors in the event that panic does actually arise. But according to the Disaster Research Center (DRC), and on the basis of hundreds of studies performed world wide, panic is first of all a myth, both a tenacious and a dangerous one. Panic only develops extremely rarely. A closer look reveals another reality which represents the general rule.

- Contrary to what the authorities fear, panic and looting are not obligatory curses against which measures must be taken as quickly as possible. Instead, these phenomena only appear in very specific— and rare—situations: when overwhelming disaster strikes; when the major systems of social order vanish completely; when tension and violence existed before the catastrophe, so that post-accident looting is merely the continuation of business as usual, but on another scale. Studies actually tend to show that security is generally better in a post-accident setting.
- On the whole, individuals react well in major catastrophe situations.

The first people affected are often the ones to take the first positive steps. Post-disaster intervention should be planned to make better use of their involvement and increase their effectiveness, instead of assuming that they are highly suspicious actors. Here again, studies have shown that many post-disaster problems are caused by the agencies mobilized to help, because they are unable to coordinate their activities, use the resources available, and avoid overlap. In other words, action should be planned on the basis of trust rather than mistrust.

- Along the same lines, many studies demonstrate that the people called upon to intervene, whatever their level, do not 'abandon ship'. They stay at their posts and perform their duties. Of course they may suffer terrible stress because of a conflicting sense of duty, but, in general, they continue to do their jobs. There is some absenteeism, as Enrico Quarantelli[62] notes, but mainly on the part of those for whom it was already a habit. The opposite tends to happen: people who are absent from their posts at the time the crisis hits do everything to return to work—except for those who know that their presence would be useless and that they would simply add to the confusion in the office.

Quarantelli also emphasizes the importance of verifying reports received on this subject. When reaching the scene of a disaster, an analyst will usually be submerged by stories of looting and panic. It is important to check the details. These are often interpretations that do not hold up to a factual examination. For instance, running away may not be panic behaviour; it may be the most logical thing to do, and taking goods from a damaged store may simply be a way to survive rather than an example of looting, especially if it happens with the authorization of store managers (though this may not be mentioned when the images are shown on television).

Of course, no series of studies can definitively reassure a manager, who is always confronted with a unique situation. These examples are simply given to point out that there is a tendency to become locked into preconceptions which are often (indeed always, according to DRC) false.

What is the result of these preconceptions?

- The alert is not given in due time, and no one is informed, because management is afraid of triggering panic.
- At a time when resources are strained to the limit, significant efforts are devoted to maintaining order, although this isn't really

a problem. Excessive numbers or levels of security personnel may be sent in, e.g. armed soldiers when the police would be sufficient.

- The victims are brushed off, the towns affected are invaded by outside help, people are displaced, avalanches of useless material donations are sent, and basic social structures are disturbed. In short, a second disaster is superimposed on the first.

As DRC points out, it is very difficult to combat the myths behind such errors. The media fall into the trap without thinking. For instance, when 30 000 persons were evacuated from the town of Nantes, the front page headlines in the newspaper *France-Soir* read, 'Scenes of looting in Nantes,' and its page 2 was titled, 'Armed soldiers on patrol'. Yet on site, security had never been so good—as was the case in Mississauga, another example discussed earlier. Even more insidious, other studies have shown that the victims who actually lived through these situations tended after the fact to exaggerate the negative aspects when describing events.

Of course, observations of some cases reveal that these principles do not always apply, especially when the area involved has been severely marked before the event by serious conflict.[63] It could also be argued—since good crisis management requires maintaining an open mind—that the American studies have not dealt with highly deadly catastrophes such as severe radioactive or biological contamination. Then, individuals find themselves without the means to understand and act directly on the situation; rumours that are impossible to confirm, and therefore very dangerous, begin to circulate; the people involved feel claustrophobic, even within an entire city, and this is propitious for panic. Yet here again, our North American colleagues insist that this will not produce general social disorder. At the very least, the idea to retain is that it is wrong to believe these myths outright: if they do seem valid for a set of circumstances that escape from the norm, they should still be regarded with great caution.

That much said, Quarantelli also analyses the political savvy applied: the panic-and-looting myths are very powerful, and they will be stirred up by the press and even by people who did not panic and who saw no signs of looting. Indeed, people will invent stories of looting to comply with expectations aroused by the situation. Therefore, it is in the interest of the authorities to behave as if this were the case and to respond at least symbolically. For instance, small groups of policemen will be sent to highly visible locations, and this move will be heavily publicized as one taken in case disorder were to break out. This type of intervention, when carefully handled, is reassuring to citizens and can eventually facilitate evacuation operations. Its disadvantage, though, is that it then reinforces the conviction that catastrophes engender panic behaviour.[64]

The observations of an active witness to the terrible earthquake that hit Mexico City on 19 September 1985 provide an interesting illustration for this discussion. Gustavo Esteva worked to encourage the victims to organize themselves. His comments should also reinforce the humility of officials, if that were necessary, and relieve their anxiety: in fact, those in charge are not the only ones who can 'do something'.

Gustavo Esteva: A major earthquake in Mexico City[65]
What impressed us most at the time was not so much the heroics or the solidarity, but rather the extraordinary demonstration of how these people were capable of organizing themselves. It wasn't a horde or a panicking crowd, it was an organized society. [. . .] People tend to think, and this had been our feeling too, that in a city of that size and with its particular characteristics, people have become totally dependent on institutions. [. . .] The earthquake proved that this wasn't true, that in this city a capacity still existed for conviviality, solidarity, and amazingly lively self-organization. [. . .]

At the start, we felt hopeless when we saw how limited we were. But very quickly, we found other ways to be useful, by organizing the damnificados, the victims (for problems of constructing shelters, getting food, and so on). By the fourth day, some of us had begun to share information about groups that had already worked with peasants or social dropouts and who were now trying to work in an organized way with the quake victims. That was when the idea emerged of setting up what we called a coordination. [. . .]

The San Juanico experience [a catastrophic natural gas explosion on 19 October 1984] had demonstrated one fact: [. . .] there was no point in waiting for someone from the outside to come take charge of the problems. This realization was certainly engraved in collective memory, and the earthquake served to awaken this memory. Yes, the population was capable of doing something—contrary to what it had been indoctrinated with for decades, i.e. that the people are fundamentally incapable of doing anything under such circumstances. [. . .]

This episode was a spectacular demonstration of ability and the capacity of the governed to organize themselves. It suggests that the authorities should design their policies in such a way as to reinforce what the people can do. The key idea is to be complementary, not to substitute. The second lesson casts a small shadow on the first: left to themselves, people can't do everything. Under harsh conditions marked by numerous stresses inherent in the post-accident period, people need outside allies. But those on the outside must respect their independence and at the same time support their initiatives.

Associations and emerging groups

Associations offer the affected populations possible intermediaries. Here is an outline of the types of difficulties they create for those in positions of authority.

As a general rule, all the reproaches accumulated in peace-time will resurface during a crisis, framed in terms of 'we told you so,' and 'if you had only listened'. The atmosphere of the crisis is immediately full of recriminations and, in consequence, the associations seem to have common sense and morality on their side. They are faultless: for years they sounded the alarm unsuccessfully until the inevitable finally happened.

The decision maker, already feeling shaken and guilty because of the event, will suffer further from these attacks, which often take on a personal tone. The first reaction will be to respond with intransigence, but this will only render the attacks still more virulent.

Distinguishing among groups

Especially when a crisis is geographically circumscribed, two types of association can quickly be distinguished.

Local groups. They are directly affected by the crisis and seek to resolve an immediate, local problem. Their references are a specific factory, waste dump, or other facility.

They find themselves in conflict with those in charge, but at least they acknowledge the officials' role, by summoning them to solve the problem. This type of confrontation is harsh and very personal, along the lines of: 'We're the ones directly affected, not you. You claim there is no problem. But would you live here with your family? Well, then, here are the keys to my apartment.'[66]

Outside groups. For them, the crisis itself is a sort of victory, a great day, an opportunity. 'We told you so' is the basis of their discourse.

They speak of factories in general, of waste in the country, or of industrial society as a whole.

Their conflict with those in charge is more ideologically tinged. Their message takes the form of: 'Give me more information. But in any case, I don't believe you, and after what has happened, you have no line of defence; we don't acknowledge that you can participate in the solution.'

Groups that may come into conflict. Very quickly, conflicts may arise between local and outside groups. The latter are perceived as attempting to take advantage of the situation and using it to create an exemplary impasse. After all, solving the problem necessitates finding a compromise, and larger external groups tend to reject this option. For the local groups, what counts is the value of people's homes, the cost of land, or the decision to close a plant in severe cases. This dichotomy was clear in the case of Three Mile Island.[67]

Differences that may change over time. The local groups may be easier to deal with at first, because what counts for them is finding immediate solutions. The nationwide groups seek above all to create an example.

But beyond a certain point, the roles may be reversed. The nationwide organization will become involved with other issues and its attention will waiver. In contrast, at the local level, people's wills tend to be strengthened: they want to clarify problems like the loss of a home or a piece of land as quickly as possible.

Contradictions within groups. Internal tension is to be expected as well. Every watchdog group contains both partisans of compromise and members in favour of radical struggle.

Difficult dialogue
These groups will make heavy use of symbols. They may be very well informed, and they will not hesitate to use their imaginations. Above all, they will be hard to satisfy and to convince.

Radical approaches. The first set of demands is usually aimed at eliminating *the* cause of the crisis: 'After the serious failure that has occurred, we can no longer trust you to manage the slightest risk. Therefore, we want total safety, and in light of the way you've made these people suffer, you should spare no expense.' This can be an effective means of pressure. Demanding such a high level of compensation provides an absurd demonstration of how fragile the system is and how ridiculous the option was which triggered the crisis.

A second tack deals directly with the emergency intervention policy.

Pressure groups may call for the application of standards even more exigent than those normally adopted (rather than accepting temporarily flexible standards in light of the short duration of the episode—provided it actually is short). This creates an impasse and adds fuel to the fires of the critical association, who can then argue more firmly that the original standards really were ridiculous.

Discussions will take place in such simplistic terms: all or nothing, black or white, 'you must be for us or against us, you side with the criminals or with the victims'.

Positions easier to defend than those of the people in charge. Some watchdog associations may claim to be groups without much power, but would like to have more influence. Yet they may not give themselves the means to achieve their ends, which are considered dubious. They may also be tempted to play the role of the martyrs on every issue. This allows them to brandish the argument of: 'We are powerless!' This argument is unbeatable, because the person who wields it always looks weaker than an authority figure who is assigned a specific responsibility.

These groups tend to highlight everything that is wrong with a given system. All they need is to find the exception. In contrast, the person in charge is preoccupied with making the system function as a whole. No matter what efforts are made, it will never offer total satisfaction, from either a technical or an organizational point of view.

By playing directly on emotions and using simple arguments, these groups of critics offer a message that comes across better on television. While the decision maker is struggling to explain why the latest calculations seem to indicate that in all probability there is no reason to worry, the opposition is virtually leaping out of the television set as it plays on all the registers of emotion. Often too, they have a whole string of anecdotes about how they were treated by the official services and how unresponsive the authorities were. They may even cite blatantly unacceptable statements made by various officials or tasteless rumours started to discredit the critics—and which end up boomeranging back on those in charge.

In their role as representatives of the victims, managing a story ideal for media consumption, they may often be better treated by the media than the authorities are.

Some of these groups may take a more feminine approach than the official agencies involved; their language will be more personal. This unsettles decision makers accustomed to moving in masculine circles which are (even in the 1990s) very distant from family problems. The officials may then put up a wall of refusal to these critics. (This is what happened in Reims, where they had to deal with women in the roles of minister, journalist, medical doctor, labour inspector and president of a victims' defence organization, chemist, and others. Despite their differences, these women were no doubt perceived as forming a sort of diabolical conspiracy.[68])

All these opposition forces need to do is denounce the existence of unknown and therefore grave risks (e.g. 'Can you guarantee that at no time in the last 30 years, anyone has dumped even a spoonful of dangerous waste in this 20-acre garbage dump?'). As for the decision makers, they soon find themselves obliged to demonstrate the total absence of any risk, especially if they have been intransigent and highly self-assured. This will be an impossible task.

The key issue: quality of dialogue before the crisis
As for all the other actors, the quality of relations established before the crisis will be the decisive factor in dealings between authorities and special interest groups when the crisis strikes. Relations that were strained before the event will become untenable during the crisis; even better cultivated relations will be tense during this period.

In general, some countries seem to have greater difficulty than others in assuring good rapport between authorities and citizens. This cultural backdrop necessarily comes into play during a crisis. The rule of thumb is, if you tell lies often enough, in the end no one will believe anything you say. Thereafter, it is very hard to regain people's trust.

It is interesting to consider the words of Alexis de Tocqueville (and it is amusing to note that they were quoted in an unpublished 1976 report by the French government on 'The participation of the French in improving their living environment').

> What characterizes the Administration in France is the violent hate it develops without distinction towards all those, whether noble or bourgeois, who wish to take care of public affairs outside its sphere. The slightest independent body that seems to want to constitute itself without the Administration's aid frightens it; the tiniest free association, no matter what its goals, disturbs it; all it allows to subsist are those agencies which it has composed arbitrarily and over which it presides. (Alexis de Tocqueville, *L'Ancien Régime et la Révolution*—an unofficial translation).

Elected officials and political authorities

Many crisis managers are confronted with the problem of the massive arrival of political representatives. These figures naturally play a major symbolic role, and high authorities are often the only ones who can cut through impossible amounts of red tape. Nonetheless, their presence also has its disadvantages. Here are a few of the most typical ones:

- Some elected officials come to gather information but have no wish to become implicated in the crisis, as it could be dangerous for their image. It is difficult to count on them if they are needed.
- Some are primarily looking for media exposure. They will annoy those who are actually at work and who have accepted taking risks.
- Some officials, as well as the media, will divert resources that are already thinly stretched in order to visit the site and be shown around.
- The crisis room may be invaded.
- These people may unwittingly interfere with crisis management. A top official may make unwise statements, for instance, by promising an evacuated group that they will be able to return to their homes that evening. And there may be unpleasant mix-ups that everyone could do without.

> *President Lyndon B. Johnson visits New Orleans in 1965 after Hurricane Betsy*[69]
> The President was invited to visit a shelter set up by the Red Cross. But due to an error no one could explain he was taken, not to the official center set up by the Red Cross, but to a make-shift shelter across the street. This building lacked the most basic facilities. The President went on to make unflattering statements to the effect that these agencies were not capable of taking decent care of people who had lost everything.

> *President Carter visits Three Mile Island (1 April 1979)*[70]
> This presidential visit, which included the First Lady and the couple's daughter, was appropriate for its symbolic value. However, it left some bad impressions: at the press conference, White House journalists received the best seats, and the local press was consigned to the back of the room.

The site itself may present both physical dangers and risks of media confusion.

> *Port Edouard Herriot in Lyon (May 1987)*
> Listeners to a major French radio station could hear the follow-

ing report shortly before 7 pm, abruptly cut off, on the Port Edouard Herriot fire: 'The Minister of the Environment is on site, and the blaze seems to be under control . . . but I see explosions! The port authorities are starting to run, the minister is running . . . over to you in the studio!'

Accident on a branch of highway A3 in Lyon, 10 April 1985[71]
As was explained earlier, a gas truck overturned and a cloud of gas formed. There was apparently an elected official who unfortunately arrived in his car, not thinking twice about pushing past the safety roadblock. The problem here was that this inopportune 'official' intervention directly increased the risks involved.

In fact, this event presents a fairly interesting case study:

- a press helicopter refused to observe the ban on flying over the area;
- an elected official ignored safety provisions;
- a public service vehicle set out to ensure that the highway had been blocked off above and below the site, and to the dismay of the firefighters, simply drove right through the gas cloud.

This may represent a problem with protocols: an official vehicle considers that it has priority to go where it wants. But what holds true in terms of rules and directives poses a physical problem: the gas cloud does not distinguish between official and non-official vehicles. Furthermore, another official vehicle could not start its engine in order to leave a parking lot that was being evacuated. The explanation was simple: the atmosphere was too rich with gas.

Burgeoning numbers of actors appearing out of nowhere

On this front, those in charge must expect the unexpected. Perhaps a miracle man will appear, claiming to know everything about the problem and, above all, to be able to solve it with a snap of the fingers, provided he is granted total control over operations.

Perhaps in a surprising twist on the well-known scapegoat phenomenon, a self-designated scapegoat will appear and will rave about the sufferings inflicted upon him or her by the authorities.

Religious or cultural groups may take action that is completely unexpected. Or an issue arising in another country may suddenly become implicated in the problem.

Surprising coincidences may also arise. A faulty missile may have the unfortunate idea of landing in the prime minister's yard; the daughter of the attorney general turns out to be a friend of the most vigilant journalist on the beat; or the mayor of the tiny town affected happens to be a world famous celebrity known for an ability to use the media.

In short, anything is possible: remember the earlier example of a major industrial group that received 15 000 calls in six months when it became a target of religious fanatics who accused the group of having made a pact with the devil (and of competitors who knew how to use the information).

One often neglected actor: the courts

A decision maker must deal with the avalanche of problems that has been outlined here. The decision maker may tend to forget one actor—the courts—but that actor won't neglect the decision maker. Once again, there should be no shortage of surprises and problems, especially if victims have suffered physical harm. Seals may be placed on the facilities involved, in which case the manager no longer has access to the site. This will hinder investigations or efforts to revitalize activity. And the paralysis may last some time: the Port Edouard Herriot facilities which burned in June 1987[72] are still sealed to date. It is easy to imagine the problems this situation poses for the media battle: being cut off from one's sources of information is a key to immediate defeat.

The next step is a court-ordered investigation which can take years and which will go over everything written and done by the business with a fine-toothed comb. Indeed, the very life of the organization will be examined, from procedures to training practices to the distribution of responsibilities. Analysing the data may prove extraordinarily complicated if the system's elements are already closely intertwined in normal circumstances (e.g. various legal entities operating on the same site, poorly defined attribution of liabilities, shared personnel, subcontractors). The court's investigation will run into some of the problems defined above, due in particular to the gap that may exist between theoretical knowledge, of an expert chemist for example, and the specific knowledge required to run an industrial facility.

Then comes the issue of the charges. The prosecution may choose to file broad charges in order to bring as much information to light as possible. This is very disturbing for the people involved, because they find themselves engaged in proceedings that target individuals, when the real problem is usually with the organization in general. And, of course, the charges give rise to a media campaign in which, no matter how careful the journalists may be, the accusations come to be equated with convictions. The trial only takes place much later, when the case no longer interests the media.

This is a clash between worlds with very distinct cultures: industry, law, and the media. On the one hand is an approach characterized by the notion of specific and deliberate individual fault; on the other is a concept more in tune with the world of complex technologies and organizations, where mere error is more common than fault, and where failures can be attributed less to isolated individuals than to whole systems. Contrast the media verdict—which is immediate and whose consequences, if any, are not subject to appeal—with the court's verdict, more respectable, but which arrives too late to be relevant for the social perception and the battle for images.

This is in fact an area which scholars and professionals are beginning to explore, and it cannot help but pose problems for every crisis manager.[73]

In actual practice, situations like the following may arise (the example is not imaginary): in the aftermath of an accident, the technology developed by a firm is accused by the press; representatives from the firm are prohibited by court order from having access to the accident site; to complicate things further, the site is located in a foreign country; furthermore, the firm's competitors know they have everything to gain from the paralysis that has struck the firm, and the firm's chairman is charged with liability for the accident.

Summary

Difficulties to be expected

- The crisis: off to a difficult start
  - The initial shock
  - Warning systems that fail to function
  - Getting organized: a laborious process
- Back to the past
  - Protection systems that are less effective than planned
  - Insufficient emergency systems
  - Organizations that don't know one another
  - A basis of mistrust

- Vulnerable individuals
  - Destabilized by the event
  - Worn by stress
  - Unpredictable reactions
  - Peaks and troughs in their performance over time
- Small groups: caught between two ills
  - Dissipation, confusion, conflict
  - A flight into unanimity which leads to a fiasco
- Organizations on the razor's edge
  - In-house: gaps, confusion, biases, paralysis, conflict
  - Between organizations: the danger of burning bridges
- Major systems: complexity and dissipation
  - Huge, unwieldy machines
  - General dynamics characterized by risk and randomness
  - Arrival of new actors
  - Fragmentation of the usual systems
- Expert advice and the experts: more problems
  - Advice that arrives too late to be taken into account
  - Highly unreliable opinions
  - Quarrels between experts
  - The limited usefulness of compartmented knowledge
  - A need to integrate a range of scattered information
  - The temptation to turn the expert into a decision maker
- The media: the diabolical trap
  - A series of confrontations
  - The risks of doing what not to do, and the media fiasco
- The victims: destabilizing those in charge
  - The flight reflex
  - Messages to victims that they are abandoned and despised
- The merry-go-round of actors
  - Unions and other intermediaries: the risks of a standoff
  - Populations: the dangers of well-established myths
  - Emerging groups: new conflicts
  - Elected officials, political authorities: the risks of interference
  - The arrival of hordes of unexpected actors
  - The courts: additional contradictions

Notes

1. Interview with Marc Becam in Lagadec, 1990, pp. 45–6.
2. This was the equivalent of one-sixth of the energy released by the Hiroshima bomb. See Joseph Scanlon, 1990*a*.

3. Interview with Geneviève Decrop and Marie Pierre Touron.
4. Interview with Philippe Vesseron in Lagadec, 1990, pp. 94–6.
5. Jules Beliveau, 'Catastrophe en Ontario: 13 millions de pneus brûlent', *La Presse*, 13 February 1990.
6. Jean-Claude Leclerc: 'La Montagne qui brûle: quand le gouvernement met en jeu la sécurité publique', *Le Devoir*, 22 February 1990.
7. P. Eddy, E. Potter, and B. Page, 'Destination Disaster', *The Sunday Times*, 1976.
8. 'Survival clothing "secrecy" attacked', *The Times*, 9 July 1988, p. 2.
9. These ideas were provided by Joseph Scanlon in an interview.
10. This was the problem faced by the director of rescue activities in Gander. This did not reduce his effectiveness, but it did generate an understandably high level of stress. (Taken from an interview with Joseph Scanlon.)
11. Ole Holsti, 1971, p. 62, quoted by Smart and Vertinsky, 1977, p. 642.
12. This attempt to overthrow the Castro regime was launched on 17 April 1961, with massive backing from the United States government. It was a resounding failure. John F. Kennedy, who had just arrived in the White House, apparently felt it was either inopportune or impossible to call off this project, which was prepared by the previous administration.
13. This is why the Dow Chemical group has developed new organizational structures for dealing with this type of difficulty. These will be discussed later.
14. Interview with Philippe Vesseron in Lagadec, 1990, p. 100.
15. The tensions in Cyprus between the Greek and Turkish communities flared up in July 1974. Faced with endless conspiracies backed by the ruling junta in Athens, Archbishop Makarios decided to meet force with force. On 2 July he asked the government in Athens to recall all Greek officers stationed in Cyprus and demanded that it put a stop to subversive activity directed from Greece. The Greek dictators responded on 15 July by a *coup d'état* that overthrew Makarios. The Archbishop managed to escape and left the island. He was replaced by a notorious terrorist who was a fanatical partisan of unification with Greece. Ankara began to worry about the fate of the Turkish community, fearing that the island would be proclaimed a part of Greece. Turkish forces disembarked on 20 July. The cease-fire requested by the Security Council of the United Nations took effect on 22 July, after Turkish forces had occupied a significant part of the northern half of the island. On 24 July, the military regime in Greece collapsed. (Based on Ali Kazancigil, 'La question chypriote', *Encyclopaedia Universalis*, Corpus 5, p. 785.)
16. Gallup poll published in *L'Express*, 24 October 1986.
17. Interviews with Dr William Dab, Philippe Vesseron, Joseph Scanlon, Professor Lucien Abenhaim of McGill University, Montreal, and Monique and Raymond Sené of the Collège de France-GSIEN, Paris.
18. Interview with Enrico Quarantelli. The name of the dam was never revealed by DRC, for reasons related to the media issues that will be discussed later.
19. The same type of assessment could be made of highly-specialized experts as Philippe Legorjus makes about international-level athletes

asked to join a crisis intervention group: 'A large percentage of top-notch athletes have a major flaw: they are individualists, unable to live in a group. Many of the candidates for the unit have a background in track and field or martial arts. These are superb athletes, which is to say narcissists. They often tend to be egocentric and pay little attention to others.' (Legorjus, 1990, p. 176.)

20. Peter Sandman, 'Explaining environmental risk: some notes on environmental risk communication', Rutgers, NJ, Environmental Communication Research Program, Rutgers University, cited in Quarantelli, 1990, p. 19.

21. Interview with Monique Sené, President of GSIEN (scientists for information on nuclear power) and researcher at Collège de France, and Raymond Sené, researcher at Collège de France.

22. All the points discussed here are taken (1) from testimony collected during training seminars, especially the think tank sessions on previous encounters with the media, and (2) from many discussions with Philippe Dessaint, who has been part of our training seminar team for many years. Obviously the ideas developed here and in the following chapters on the subject of crisis communications are focused primarily on 'civilian' crises.

23. Interview with Joseph Scanlon. See also Scanlon, 1987.

24. Interview with Philippe Dessaint.

25. Robert V. Andrews (one of six J&J press officials), quoted in ten Berge, 1990, p. 24.

26. Sandman, P. and Paden, M. 1979, 'At Three Mile Island', *Columbia Journalism Review*, 18 (7–8), quoted in Scanlon and Alldred, 1982, pp. 43–58.

27. Generally speaking, everyone is always a generalist in relation to certain specialists, and a specialist in relation to a great many people. If you turn to someone for a diagnosis of a question, you are usually a generalist in relation to that person.

28. Interview with Raymond Sené.

29. Interview with the firm's spokesperson.

30. The teleprompter is a device used to scroll a script above the camera the speaker is supposed to watch. This is another tool that gives the journalist a considerable edge: no more worrying about finding the right word or maintaining a train of thought. This gives the impression that the journalist is improvising, thereby reinforcing an image of sincerity. After all, the key to the message often lies in appearances.

31. This is an example of the groupthink phenomenon.

32. Interview with Philippe Dessaint, describing an experience as a consultant.

33. This section follows the model developed by Scanlon and Alldred (1982, pp. 13–19). We have enhanced the model with studies from the Disaster Research Center (Wenger and Quarantelli, 1989; Quarantelli and Wenger, 1990) and with interviews, in particular with Philippe Dessaint, Joseph Scanlon, and Péter-J. Hargitay.

34. Philip Revzin, 'A reporter looks at media role on terror threats', *Wall Street Journal*, 14 March 1977, quoted in Scanlon, 1981, p. 142.

35. Quoted in Scanlon, 1981, p. 154.

36. Earnest Volkman, 'How they brought the news from Harrisburg to the world', *Media People*, November 1979, p. 80, quoted in Scanlon and Alldred, 1982, pp. 13–19.
37. Interview with Joseph Scanlon.
38. Interview with Philippe Dessaint.
39. Interview with Philippe Dessaint.
40. Richard A. Kerr, 'Earthquake—or earthquack?', *Research News*, 26 October 1990, p. 511.
41. Interview with Philippe Dessaint.
42. The author notes that better cooperation is being achieved in kidnapping cases. Yet they wonder why this has not yet occurred in the field of terrorism. Scanlon, 1981, p. 154.
43. P.J. Troustine, 'We interrupt this program', *More*, p. 15, quoted in Scanlon, 1989*b*, p. 117.
44. Frank Boltz, quoted in Scanlon, 1989*b*, p. 129.
45. On this point it is interesting to study the work of Veron (1981) on how the media operated during the Three Mile Island incident.
46. Interview with Enrico Quarantelli.
47. As with any model, this view is somewhat rigid, and Quarantelli himself remarks that there are scientists who work like journalists and vice versa. This model does have the merit of opening up the discussion, however.
48. Peter Sandman, 'Explaining environmental risk: some notes on environmental risk communication', Rutgers, NJ, Environmental Communication Research Program, Rutgers University; quoted in Quarantelli, 1990, p. 11.
49. Alvin Toffler, 'Powershift as excerpted', *Newsweek*, 116, 15 October 1990, p. 92; quoted in Quarantelli, 1990, pp. 17–18.
50. *Le Temps*, 30 November 1987, quoted in Greilsamer, 1990, p. 104.
51. Press conference by Hubert Beuve-Méry, 30 November 1969, cited in *L'Echo de la Presse*, 22 December 1969, quoted in Greilsamer, 1990, p. 563.
52. Interview between Hubert Beuve-Méry and Pierre Desgraupes, published in *Le Point*, 25 February 1974, quoted in Greilsamer, 1990, p. 563.
53. Virgil, *Aeneid*, pp. 173–88, quoted in Robert, *Les Stratégies anti-rumeurs*, Francom, 1989.
54. According to Bertrand Robert, *Les Stratégies anti-rumeurs*, Francom, 1989; see also Kapferer, 1987, pp. 272–86.
55. All quotations made under the heading 'Françoise Rudetzki: The terrorist attack' are drawn from an interview with the president of SOS-Attentats. Françoise Rudetzki was a victim of terrorist action committed on 23 December 1985 in a Paris restaurant. The obstacles she encountered thereafter, especially in the legal arena, led her to organize this association, which has helped make great legislative progress for victims of terrorism in the area of compensation. This section also draws from an interview with Claude Peyrat, whose wife was killed in Paris on 17 September 1986 by a terrorist attack on a department store; his daughter was injured. The third source is the book by Colette Bonnivard (1987).
56. All quotations made under the heading 'Karine Robak: The technologi-

cal accident' are drawn from interviews with Patrick Lagadec, published in Lagadec (1990) and from an additional contribution made in December 1990 for the purposes of this work. Karine Robak was the owner of an apartment located in a building in Reims which was contaminated when an askarel transformer exploded in the basement. With Arlette Botella, another homeowner, she founded the victims' defence association mentioned above, of which she is the president.

57. 'Les effets sur la santé de leurs enfants inquiètent les résidents d'Hagersville', *La Presse*, 3 March 1990.
58. We would like to thank Françoise Rudetzki for a statement summarizing this issue.
59. For more complete information on this point, see Huglo, 1990; Smets, 1985; Rocard and Smets, 1990; Kiss, 1989; Rémond-Gouilloud, 1989, pp. 169 ff.
60. This section is notably based on an interview with Jacques Fournier, CFDT union representative on the French High Council of Classified Industrial Sites.
61. Interview with Jacques Fournier, CFDT union representative on the French High Council of Classified Industrial Sites.
62. Interview with Enrico Quarantelli in Lagadec, 1990, p. 226.
63. Enrico Quarantelli is currently preparing a study on one case in which substantial looting occurred, following the passage of hurricane Hugo across Sainte-Croix island in the Virgin Islands in September 1989. In this case, all the criteria that could trigger panic and looting were present: 90 per cent of the buildings were destroyed, the entire social structure collapsed, and in terms of law and order, the social situation was very strained before the event.
64. Interview with Enrico Quarantelli.
65. Interview with Gustavo Esteva in Lagadec, 1990, pp. 214–21.
66. See Karine Robak in Lagadec, 1990.
67. Interview with Enrico Quarantelli.
68. See Karine Robak in Lagadec, 1990.
69. Interview with Enrico Quarantelli.
70. Interview with Enrico Quarantelli.
71. Based on a personal investigation performed in Lyon shortly after the event and various more recent interviews.
72. See Gilbert Carrère in Lagadec, 1990.
73. A working group headed by M. Grollier-Baron is studying the issue of the human factor and liability at the Institut Européen de Cindyniques.

Chapter 6

Disarray at the top: what levers do we pull, what do we decide?

Whether all at once or inexorably one after another, all the difficulties identified earlier come crashing down on the person in charge. All the plans that had been made, all the documents drafted, and everyone's declarations had assured the manager that in a crisis situation, clear and definite powers would be given. Now the manager discovers that it just isn't so: the decision-making processes are severely impaired, and it is no longer possible to make the system respond.

Worse yet, the manager is not even sure what decision he or she would make if permitted, or what he or she should be trying to do.

Severely affected and insufficient decision-making mechanisms

Ideally, you would like to be able to count on much stronger resources than are ordinarily available, but this simply is not the case: as was demonstrated earlier, both individuals and groups perform much less effectively in crisis situations.[1]

It would be natural to assume that the specialized crisis units set up can easily overcome such difficulties. At present, though, prudence remains the rule: these groups do not always have the abilities that are spontaneously attributed to them, no matter how prestigious they may be.

> *Crisis Management at the National Security Council*
> According to Richard Beal (1984), former director of crisis management systems and planning at the White House, a great many present and former members of the National Security Council feel that much of the information available during a crisis is either useless or wrong, that decision makers have little, if any, experience in the crisis management field, and that planning in this area is inadequate.

Beal is also quoted as saying that the expression 'crisis management' is a very flattering way of describing American practices
in the field. For Beal, what actually takes place is more a matter
of adapting to a crisis situation and simply muddling through.

A system that does not respond

Even under normal conditions, the idea that orders are given and
obeyed is largely misleading: negotiation is often what keeps things
ticking. Nonetheless, the hypothesis remains that should an ordeal
develop, a more 'military' order will somehow be implemented. This
is far from certain, as such periods of high risks are in fact times
when every individual and each organization feels it has a great deal
on the line. This tends to reinforce already existing defensiveness
and inertia considerably.

The first conflicts will emerge between the manager and that person's
inner circle. What President Roosevelt experienced surely represents a basic rule for any large organization:

> *Franklin D. Roosevelt*
> Half of a President's suggestions, which theoretically carry the
> weight of orders, can be safely forgotten by a Cabinet member.
> And if the President asks about a suggestion a second time, he
> can be told that it is being investigated. If he asks a third time, a
> wise Cabinet officer will give him at least part of what he sug-
> gests. But only occasionally, except about the most important
> matters, do Presidents ever get around to asking three times.[2]

Trying to rouse the major departments of a corporation is even more
difficult. The following example shows that the task is a harsh one,
even for those who supposedly have full power. Heads of local government or of businesses certainly encounter similar problems.

> *Franklin D. Roosevelt*
> The Treasury is so large and far-flung and ingrained in its
> practices that I find it almost impossible to get the action and
> results I want [. . .]. But the Treasury is not to be compared with
> the State Department. You should go through the experience of
> trying to get any changes in the thinking, policy, and action of
> career diplomats and then you'd know what a real problem was.
> But the Treasury and the State Department put together are
> nothing compared with the Na-a-vy. The admirals are really
> something to cope with—and I should know. To change anything
> in the Na-a-vy is like punching a feather bed. You punch it with
> your right and you punch it with your left until you are finally

exhausted, and then you find the damn bed just as it was before
you started punching.

(Neustadt, 1980, p. 33)

Yet the conventional response to crisis is always to affirm the
principle of designating a single authority. The idea is certainly
appealing, at least on paper: one goal, one leader, one strategy, and
the means they require. It sounds like a sensible argument: to deal
with complexity, you need a little order and discipline; bring the
stragglers into line. In the background hovers the military image of
an army marching in step to crush the enemy.

Certain situations can only strengthen the leader's desire to do away
with resistance from any quarter. Resistance during a crisis is
intolerable—not only with regard to what is written in the plans, but
especially for the nerves of those in charge. On this point, the
political scientist Richard Neustadt of Harvard University cleverly
points out that though we always speak about the *separation* of
powers, the model actually functions differently: the institutions are
separate, but they *share* powers. This results in endless conflicts and
resistance—including, indeed especially, in times of crisis.

> A few examples: During the Amoco Cadiz oil spill, a member of
> civil defence requested outboard motorboats for the northern
> coast of Britanny. He was told it was impossible to send the
> boats up there: 'If a second oil slick occurs, and if it hits the
> south of the region, it would be disastrous not to have the boats
> down here.'
>
> In another case, which called for extremely rapid action, the
> guardian stubbornly refused to open the door of a laboratory
> that was indispensable to performing a vital post-accident
> analysis. It did not matter that the order came from the top
> executives. The leader of the crisis management unit had to
> negotiate for ages, deploying all his diplomatic skills, before the
> door could be opened. On one telephone line he had the
> guardian who refused to give up the key, and on the other, top
> leaders of the country who were struggling on site with a
> situation that could become grave.

Of course it is necessary in a crisis to demonstrate authority in the
narrowest sense of the word, and that may sometimes yield the
desired results. Of course it is indispensable to clarify the distribution
of responsibilities in order to stabilize a system that might otherwise
begin to tremble if it has neither clear architecture nor keystone—
and this, too, may help.

But it is important to realize that on the whole, in a complex crisis involving numerous organizations, the mechanical order model is not what is most pertinent. A crisis generally brings a great many power centres into play, both within and without an organization, and each jealously guards its independence.

Outside your own organization, you will rarely be able to give orders. The more you attempt to impose an operating system based on strict obedience and a single leader, the more resistance you will arouse. Very quickly, each actor will respond with a list of technicalities to explain why the person in charge has no control over a given field.

> Can the head of local government forbid the head of regional government from speaking out on television? If a major industrial group decides to destroy its products in order to protect its image, can it be denied the right on the grounds that this will feed the fires of rumour? Can a minister of one country stop a counterpart in another country from making a declaration? How does the fire chief give orders to the head of the paramedics, or vice-versa? How can a major public agency order an independent laboratory not to publish the results of tests performed? Can the agency prevent foreign scientists from entering the country?

These are clearly no longer situations in which a well-oiled machine reacts at a snap of the fingers. When a great many organizations must be mobilized, especially if there is no clear hierarchy governing their relations, the only way they can succeed is by cooperating.

The same is true in-house: each organization can be said to comprise a patchwork of organizations. The system functions because strategic balances are constantly being negotiated. Cooperation is undoubtedly the most efficient method.

In some situations, forcing your ideas through may be the only option, but that method should only be adopted when it is impossible to do anything more appropriate. And you can expect that this strategy will bring about considerable squandering of energy, including the conscientiously distorted application of the most stupid orders (stupid because they are poorly understood). In fact, the central team will have great difficulty in drafting clear orders: the information and knowledge necessary to dictate a clear approach will be unavailable.

In the face of such difficulties, those involved often wish that the military model could be applied—at last, once and for all, a strict chain of command, strict orders, implementations that don't slip up, and 'troops' not bothered by sentiment. In short, bring those civilians into line and the crisis will be in a stranglehold. Unfortunately, the best military leaders realize, and try to make their admirers understand, that the military realm is not as close as that to paradise. Studies have actually demonstrated that as soon as a system becomes complex—take a modern aircraft carrier, for example[3]—the ancestral hierarchical system must give way to much more elaborate organizational configurations. Orders no longer descend directly and unaltered from the commanders to the operational levels: at each stage, there is a subtle play of negotiation:

> Our team noted with some surprise the adaptability and flexibility of what is, after all, a military organization [. . .]. On paper, the ship is formally organized in a steep hierarchy by rank with clear chains of command and means to enforce authority far beyond that of any civilian organization. We supposed it to be run by the book, with a constant series of formal orders, salutes, and yes-sirs. Often it is, but flight operations are not conducted that way. [. . .]. Events on the flight deck, for example, can happen too quickly to allow for appeals through a chain of command. Even the lowest rating on the deck has not only the authority, but the obligation to suspend flight operations immediately, under the proper circumstances and without first clearing it with superiors. [. . .]
>
> Coordinated planning for the next day's air operations requires a series of involved trade-offs between mission requirements and the demands of training, flight time, maintenance, ordnance, and aircraft handling. It is largely done by a process of ongoing and continuing argument and negotiation among personnel from many units, in person and via phone, which tend to be resolved by direct order only when the rare impasse develops that requires an appeal to higher authority. [. . .]
>
> The remarkable degree of personal and organizational flexibility we have observed is essential for performing operational tasks that continue to increase in complexity as technology advances.
>
> (Rochlin et al., 1987, pp. 83–4, 87)

Finally, in addition, the person in charge must not forget, even when conflicts have been smoothed over, to count on the monumental gaffes that everyone involved will make. Nothing can be taken for granted when trying to manage an organizational dinosaur moving at top speed. Distressing errors wear down the system. More seriously, in light of the context discussed above, they fan the fears that are always present and which suggest that some people have Machiavellian plans or that conspiracies are being planned in the wings. This in turn stimulates other perverse processes . . .

Henry Kissinger: The Cienfuegos, Cuba Crisis (1970) and the gaffe by the Defense Department
I convened a restricted meeting of the WSAG[4] in the situation room on September 24 (. . .) The discussion dealt entirely with press guidance should the construction in Cienfuegos become public while the President was in Europe. It was decided that if the issue came up, Defense would put out the bare-bones facts but offer no comment; State would express the view that the introduction of offensive weapons would be regarded with concern; and the White House would confine itself to stating that the President had been informed and was following events. The departmental press officers were given a detailed factual description; it was intended for their background guidance, not for use in briefings. We were on the way to implementing the President's decision when it was made irrelevant by a bureaucratic mix-up of monumental proportions.(. . .)

By the time I returned to my office chaos had erupted. The morning had started with a column (. . .) in the *New York Times*, which warned of a possible Soviet submarine base in Cienfuegos. Contrary to our carefully planned press guidance, the spokesman of the Defense Department had filled in every detail when asked a question at his morning briefing. (. . .) The Pentagon briefer had seen the contingency guidance but did not understand that he was to use it only in an extremity and was not to refer to the background material at all. He therefore volunteered everything he knew, giving a detailed account of Soviet construction and naval movements of the past few months. (. . .) It was inconceivable that the President could leave the country two days later without some White House statement on the new 'crisis'. Though [the secretary of Defense] called to apologize for the inadvertent Pentagon briefing, the fat was in the fire.

(Kissinger, 1979, Vol. 1, pp. 643–4)

In short, in a crisis, decision makers are often likely to find themselves face to face with mechanisms that no longer reply. This produces the feeling of powerlessness and extreme danger that the manager feels: intervening in any way, however slight, on such a sensitive system in which everything is interrelated, can have drastic and unexpected results. When the decision makers decide to act, they no longer know which levers they are pulling.

And do they even know which ones they *want* to pull?

The leader's hardest trial: the black hole

High expectations

The major task facing those in charge is to make a decision, to choose which option should be taken—yet they have only very limited information and a foggy vision of where they should be heading.

Though everyone may be poised to resist, at the same time they turn towards the people in charge, eager to have them make sense out of the whole business and give directions and instructions. This may well result in general cacophony which prevents anyone from getting anywhere.

> *Henry Kissinger: the EC-121 shot down by North Korea and the failure of the decision-making system*
> The EC-121 incident was not primarily significant for the decision to do nothing—it was a close call, which probably should have gone the other way, but one on which reasonable men could differ. But it did show major flaws in our decision-making. We made no strategic assessment; instead, we bandied technical expedients about. There was no strong White House leadership.(. . .) To manage crises effectively, the agencies and departments involved have to know what the President intends. They must be closely monitored to make certain that diplomatic and military moves dovetail. In this case we lacked both machinery and conception. (. . .) Coordination was poor; the President never really made up his mind.
> (Kissinger, 1979, Vol. 1, p. 321)

Because of the complexity involved, operational guidelines may quickly vanish. It would be ideal then to be able to take some distance, wait, and declare that the crisis manager is not in a position to provide the answers being called for. But this is an emergency, whether real or artificially generated (by public opinion, the media, other actors, or various interest groups).

The difficulty is further exacerbated by two factors: because communications resources offer such high performance, the crisis manager can, if he or she so chooses, be in direct contact with the 'front' (the White House, for instance, could be virtually in contact with a fighter pilot sent to carry out a critical mission). Secondly, the manager knows that, like it or not, the technical resources that are selected will convey a political message, because of what they can do. Consequently, the manager is pushed ever closer to the front lines, losing the distance necessary for reflection.

Disarray when facing the unknowns

The decision maker's fundamental difficulty has been luminously described by Yehezk el Dror, a professor at both American and Israeli universities. The decision maker is confronted with what could be called *fateful* decisions. In the etymological sense of the word, these are decisions that determine fate.

The problematic of fateful decisions, according to Dror, is illustrated by a saying of Sun Tzu: 'Yang Chu, weeping at the crossroads, said, "Isn't it here that you take a half step wrong and wake up a thousand miles astray?" ' (Dror, 1990, p. 1).

The thoughts of Karl Jaspers, who was working with the problem posed by the atom bomb, are enlightening here, even taken outside their original field. In borderline situations, explains Jaspers, everything is at stake rather than just one element in the system. For this reason, compartmentalized thinking is no longer effective; 'common sense', too, can lead to defeat, as the main rules of reference are no longer applicable. Realists, specialists, and scrupulous users of jurisprudence will all be caught off guard by the event. Large-scale organizations, which are fond of order and consistency, tend to stumble over borderline situations, which are unusual by definition. In borderline situations, politicians should not imagine they must return to the previous balance: some situations create true breaks with the past (Jaspers, 1963).

According to Dror, these decisions, which directly influence destiny, seem much more isolated than everyday decisions (which fit into complex chains). This means the decision maker is directly, personally involved.

Yet as the responsibility becomes more direct, the difficulty becomes incomparably greater than what everyday situations require.

What we are confronting here is the unknown. The full impact of this statement should be taken into account: the issue is not 'I do not know', as is usually the case, but rather 'I know that we cannot know' (Dror, 1990, p. 5). The problem is not one of insufficient forecasting, which could be remedied by better quantitative approximations; the difficulty we run into here is that of establishing even qualitative outlines of a future which we are going to mould to a large extent. A true turning point is marked by the fact that you cannot see what lies beyond it.

This future comprises three factors: necessity, chance, and choice. The mix of these three elements is a matter of circumstance.[5]

Dror (1990. p. 7) adds:

> On a more fundamental level, the recognition that outcomes of fateful decisions depend significantly, and often largely, on quasi-chance factors corrodes the feeling that human societies are in charge of their future. The resulting feeling of insecurity may motivate decision makers to seek mystic supports for their decisions, such as astrology; and may undermine the naturalistic cosmology on which Western culture in general and humanistic democracy in particular are, in part, based.

The decision maker may then be tempted to take refuge in headlong flight into the future: why not play Russian roulette? The opposite option is simply to wait and see—or merely to treat symptoms, in the hope of avoiding any major slip-up. The goal then is to do the minimum necessary: when driving in dense fog on an icy road that seems to transform itself as you move forward, above all don't make the situation worse. Don't touch anything. There is a great temptation to drop any disciplined management, based on scientific models and sophisticated tools which seem hopelessly useless. To maintain a façade, there is the danger that those in charge will be reduced to mere symbolic gestures.

The underlying premise of this book is that it is possible to provide at least a few guidelines in response to decision makers' problems so that they can manage an unknown situation as well as possible. Not all situations are as extreme as those presented here—and, in any case, it is best not to make them worse by applying inadequate measures. If you really are standing at the edge of the abyss, it helps to have thought about the issues beforehand, so as to make the most of the crumbs of luck that are left.

Summary

Decision makers in disarray

- Severely affected decision-making mechanisms
  - Insufficient and biased search for information

- Misperceiving the absolute urgency and constraints involved
- Getting locked into models from the past
- Making incomplete evaluations of goals
- An inability to look for variations
- The frantic search for a 'solution'
- Getting trapped in the justification for this solution
- Failing to look at the risks that the chosen option entails
- Setting off in an irreversible direction
- A system that no longer responds
  - Inertia; lack of cooperation
  - Negotiations necessary at every level, for every detail
  - Monumental gaffes committed by one's own group
- Which way to go? The black hole
  - Face to face with the unknown
  - Decisions with incalculable consequences

Notes

1. A summary at the end of this chapter states the various factors that have a negative impact on decision-making processes in crisis situations.
2. Quoted in Neustadt, 1980, p. 32. Along the same lines, it is most interesting to read the humourous and insightful works written by two former high-level British civil servants about ministerial powers: Jonathan Lynn and Antony Jay, *Yes Minister* and *Yes Prime Minister*, BBC Books, 1989.
3. Interview with Enrico Quarantelli.
4. Washington Special Actions Group, an interdepartmental crisis unit set up after an American plane had been shot down by North Korea in 1969. Its purpose was to endow the Executive with a real crisis team.
5. Dror is referring here to Gerd Gigerenzer *et al.*, *The Empire of Chance: How Probability Changes Science and Everyday Life*, Cambridge, Cambridge University Press, 1989.

Part 2
Taking strategic action

Travelling the hard road to action

The purpose of this second part is to provide decision makers with a control panel from which they can develop and undertake their strategic action. Remember that the goal is to obtain tools for thought, not turnkey solutions. The elements that will be presented here are neither exhaustive nor perfectly adapted to each individual case. (It is important, for instance, to distinguish between fast-moving crises and those that are slower to develop.)

Here again, teamwork is essential. The many tasks that must be performed cannot be executed by a single leader; this is why it is useful to prepare for crisis as a network, and to meet the challenge in the same way.

It is also important to remember that every form of presentation has its limits, especially when the subject at hand is the crisis phenomenon. The three chapters in this section present a succession of points organized sequentially. It should be obvious that in reality, events are much less likely to unfold this way: the order of sequence may be completely upset, every element may play off every other element, and so on. Furthermore, while the first stage identified here is clearly the beginning of the crisis, the other two stages are to be handled simultaneously to a large extent, and they will interact with each other.

For the purposes of this presentation, there are two key phases:

- The **reflex** phase, at the beginning of the crisis. This is crucial, because it can lead those in charge to discredit themselves immediately. This is the classic emergency phase, but it is complicated by the fact that the context is that of crisis, which is infinitely more confused and unstable than the usual background of a limited incident.

- The **strategy construction and implementation** stage comprises two aspects: that of reflection from a distance, too often neglected by leaders who hastily jump into action and become swamped by it; and the actual management aspect, which requires specific choices and general supervision of the system for which the manager is responsible.

This last point is a touchy one: the issue is not merely to separate prior reflection from action. Of course the thinking must take place before resources can be engaged. This is especially true with the crisis phenomenon which, like a cloud, can be neither grasped nor circumvented nor attacked head on. Throughout the management of the event, you must work to maintain your critical distance, to open up your reasoning and to mobilize your networks. Otherwise, you constantly run the risk of losing sight of the strategic landmarks that are essential for consistent action.

Chapter 7

Avoiding being discredited immediately

The first danger for those in charge when managing a crisis is to find themselves almost immediately discredited.

This is often what happens when they make a poor entrance onto the scene of the crisis. To avoid being condemned to such a cameo role, you must quickly perform a number of acts. This chapter describes just what they are.

The risk of losing a large part, if not all, of your capabilities and margin for manoeuvre right off the bat is considerable. In a few hours or a few days, it only takes one slip-up, one absence, one sign of inability, one move made too slowly or too quickly, or one particularly untimely statement, and you may be discredited. Then no amount of effort can compensate your loss. The opening moments of a crisis are often marked by the collapse of several actors as their images become tarnished; this remains a handicap throughout the rest of the crisis. How many decision makers have been promptly and enduringly knocked out of the race because they were perceived as 'lying from day one', 'completely overwhelmed', or 'stabbing around in the dark'?

To avoid being dealt out of the game so early on, you must determine a few minimum requirements to be respected and the major mistakes not to commit at the outset. In fact, as a general rule, it is more important when handling a crisis to know what briar patches to avoid than to know the 'right' approach to take.

Special attention must be paid to all the points that will be examined here successively. But the bottom line remains that a solid preparation should take place before the crisis comes.

High-quality prior planning

As a prerequisite to these observations, it is absolutely necessary that both systems and people have a solid preparation behind them: this is a leitmotiv that will return in the following chapters. When the crisis breaks out, it will of course be too late to start developing the capacities you wish you had.

As illustrations, here are two cases from fields in which such preparations have been developed:

> *Claude Frantzen and Laurent du Boullay: Air traffic safety*
> The way you manage a crisis is intensely tied up in what you've done before the crisis, in terms of studying and certifying the equipment and the procedures. We have the equivalent of 200 full-time experts and technicians looking after aircraft safety in France, not to mention the air traffic controllers. At the top of the chain, we certify equipment, we survey maintenance, we examine what airlines are doing, we oversee how workshops are organized. So even when there is no crisis, there is a pre-existing information network, which of course has its imperfections, but when the crisis hits, we can work from it to plan and to try to link the crisis with the pre-existing scenario. With that kind of base to stand on, we can hone in on whatever sector seems most heavily implicated in the problem. If we had to start from scratch, as seems to be the case for certain technological hazards, it would be a different problem! That's when you see officials start creating committees during a catastrophe—it's all hot air. They've got nothing to stand on. And our system holds up to international comparison: the same intellectual guidelines, the same approaches. Our system is never cut off from the outside. What's more, we're constantly training on mini-crises that are happening all the time. The architecture is being tested every day. We see hundreds of regulations every year involving machine inspections. That's more than one per working day. So we have living concepts and experience that we can really fall back on when a super-crisis arises.[1]

> *A safe water supply*
> In the event pollution occurs, the response will obviously be very prompt, as the major drinking water distribution centres have already identified the types of products stored upstream from where they draw their water. If a sudden and serious event occurs, it is easier to react if you have the means to gauge immediately the most likely causes of the problem and locate them. If these data have already been collected and computerized, many incidents can be scaled down before they become actual crises. (See Dutang et al., 1983; see also Lagadec, 1986a)

These preparations concern technical and organizational aspects. The same approach should be taken to information, especially with regard to priority publics. In France, for example, very important work has been done in accordance with the Seveso directive concerning information for inhabitants living near high-risk sites. Information campaigns are often instigated by the DRIRs (regional administrations for industry and research) working together with industries, fire departments, and elected officials. The programmes already carried out or currently under way in various regions provide an invaluable foundation should a future crisis occur.

Bearing these points in mind, we can continue to follow the chronology faced by an actor confronting an event (or 'non-event') that can generate a crisis.

Realizing, warning, taking charge

The first requirement is simple: do not be the last one to discover the existence of a disturbing event and to start dealing with the crisis. Of course some delay is often tolerable. But beyond certain limits, especially when the issue is potentially very worrying, waiting too long may trigger or accelerate your being discredited.

The question, then, is: How should you sound the warning and mobilize your resources as efficiently as possible?

As is often the case in the field of crisis, three types of ability are called for: technical resources; organizational capacity; and a broader aptitude that can be briefly summed up as 'cultural' skills. This goes for any type of crisis. However, a crisis without a clear trigger poses additional problems; as it is not easy to grasp, the entire system described below may remain inactive. Consequently, this particular case of the insidious crisis will be examined in a separate section.

Three aptitudes: technical, organizational, cultural

Technical means for warning
In this area, modern technology can give a decisive edge. The following types of tools are available[2]:

Liaison systems are very worth while, such as Eurosignal, Operator TDF, or radiotelephones (from which users often expect greater capacity, reliability, and ease of use). Some case studies, such as the San Francisco earthquake (17 October 1989), have shown that only satellite systems can provide greatly improved (though not total) reliability (Scott and Freibaum, 1990, p. 5). This is even more true for organizations that must develop a network of relations with areas with which contact can be difficult (e.g. the many areas with which an airline company would have to be in contact following a disaster).

Automated warning systems can also be highly useful: one example is a push-button system connected to a central computer server.[3]

> From any appropriately equipped site, all you have to do is hit the button. (Several units can be installed in a plant, or may be placed in company cars and trucks.) This sends specific emergency information (for example, one button may mean 'chlorine gas alert') and instantly triggers a carefully targeted response via a central computer. Dozens of telephone calls are made simultaneously by the computer to locate and bring together key personnel, who have already given the computer their office, home, and car phone numbers as well as a contact for when they are travelling. Very quickly, almost a dozen members of management can hold a telephone conference. This automatic system saves considerable time and energy. Furthermore, because the computer is located far from the affected site, there is less risk that it will be affected by overloaded local telephone networks. (This risk cannot be reduced to zero[4]; manual control should be possible in the event the computer goes down.) This type of set-up is especially useful for organizations whose physical plant or personnel is very spread out. The most difficult case is caused by transportation, which always raises acute problems in terms of warnings. Firefighters regularly regret that they must wait too long to reach executives or experts on the move whom they need to contact.

Other tools include audio-visual screens, which can be used to broadcast pre-recorded messages to large groups (especially in-house), turbo-faxes, and turbo-phones.[5] The latter two systems operate in parallel mode, as the sequential mode of conventional equipment causes delays that become unacceptable under crisis management conditions.

Organizational devices for mobilization

These approaches satisfy three critical principles: they are simple, fast, and reliable. As for more specific measures, these can be developed for each case. The following examples will serve as illustrations.

- Alert flowcharts should be defined ahead of time and should be familiar to everyone, so that the key actors can move into action immediately. For instance, in-house this means the technical managers directly involved, the security managers, and the communications managers; with the outside, such actors include fire and rescue services, the police, and city hall. This requires that a system of being on call already exists, and it should include the communication and general management divisions.

- A central 24-hour switchboard should be set up with a single telephone number to receive warning calls. The warning receivers record the message and trigger the essential steps for mobilization.

- Preformatted messages should be used. Experience has shown that the first statements are hard to formulate for those caught up in an emergency situation. To avoid leaving out information or creating confusion, a basic guide is to be supplied to the personnel. All they have to do is fill in the blanks to produce a high-quality declaration. This tool can be integrated into the organization's computer system (but it should include a special protection: if the appropriate blanks are not correctly filled in, the computer refuses the message and indicates it has done so). As an example, the following preformatted message has been developed by the Rhône-Poulenc group:

This tool is part of a general emergency plan developed in 1987. It is used by all the group's facilities throughout the world. It is based on the principle that any event which could concern Rhône-Poulenc directly or indirectly (especially an accident occurring on a Rhône-Poulenc site that could have external implications), wherever it may happen, must be handled by communication from headquarters and immediate information to the authorities and the media.

Two guides have been prepared. They set down the major points of the message to be sent to the guard post at headquarters and the press release to be issued by the local Rhône-Poulenc representative.

Message to the guard post
The keyword 'emergency information' establishes a link between the broadcasting unit and the security department. The message must be delivered in the following order:

A Time at which message is broadcast.
B Specific identification of person sending information (e.g. name, position).
C Time at which the event occurred.

D Description of the type of event (e.g. accident involving people, fire, explosion, toxic emission, pollution, terrorist threat, natural disaster, transportation accident).
E Location of the event (e.g. place, number or name of facility).
F First assessment of consequences:
  – persons injured: number and apparent type of injuries
  – physical damage
  – potential dangers, etc.
G Specific situation at the time of the call:
  – fire under control, still burning, etc.
  – injured persons taken to hospital, etc.
H Whether to implement the emergency in-house plan.
I Likelihood of implementing specific intervention plan.
J If appropriate, specify whether the media have already reacted.
K End by indicating the phone number at which the caller can be reached (enter number twice).

As soon as the message is concluded, the security department acknowledges receipt.

Message to the media
On the initiative of the facility or the local Rhône-Poulenc representative, and in any case whenever the emergency plan or the in-house plan is implemented, a press release is to be sent immediately to the local media. It is to include specific information, limited to the facts.

It is essential for those who know the facts to provide this information very rapidly, in order to prevent rumours from developing. The information should be updated regularly until the crisis is over.

The first point in the press release identifies the issuer: 'Rhône-Poulenc, from its site at . . ., announces: . . .'

The contents of the press release comprises paragraphs B, C, D, and E of the in-house message (above).

The press release closes with the following sentence: 'We shall issue additional information as soon as new developments occur. For further information, please contact . . . (telephone number).'[6]

Corporations are not the only ones who can use such tools, as is demonstrated by the declarations of a high-level civil servant in a large French city:

The municipal services (e.g. roads, water and sewage treatment, garbage collection, heating, gas, transportation) all have long-standing practices of keeping technicians on call. But it should be noted that this 'cultural' practice is oriented more towards incidents or accidents than towards major events. It isn't enough to have immediately operational technicians: for large-scale events, you have to be able to count on the presence of high-ranking officials. Two years ago, the security managers began arranging to have an engineer and two high-level officials (with a rank equivalent to that of deputy secretary general) on call each weekend (as well as during the week). The strength of this system is that the high-ranking people all know each other, and because of their past experience in emergency departments, they understand the problem of a crisis situation.[7]

Greater aptitudes for taking charge

This logistical arsenal and plans for emergency organization are, however, only frameworks to allow those in charge to clarify the situation and vanquish confusion. In addition to monitoring the reliability of these systems (ensuring that they provide good technical responses and effective organizational interfaces), the general problem that remains is to make sure that the personnel follow these frameworks and to ask probing questions about how the whole organization actually works under disruptive circumstances.

To provide support, therefore, it is necessary beforehand to develop a strong sense of responsibility at every level in the organization, with smooth communication channels, flexibility, and a sense of initiative. None of these may be taken for granted. It is imperative that the people involved be able to take charge of problems. The first person to receive the warning message may not be the least bit responsible for taking the measures that need to be taken: nonetheless, it is that person's duty to take full charge until someone else assumes responsibility for the problem.

This means that people must be ready to move spontaneously to the forefront and to ensure that the necessary steps are carried out. To reach this stage, a corporate culture must be developed that encourages people to stand up, that calls on its leaders to state what is expected in difficult and uncertain situations, that values risk-taking (rather than viewing it as something suspicious to be punished), and that sanctions those who refuse to take risks. This calls for people and systems that are open to the idea that crises do happen, i.e. that events can overstep carefully defined territorial boundaries.

For any information distributed, it is important to follow up and make sure that the messages are actually circulating and are reaching their destinations (i.e. the persons for whom they are intended and not just the reception desk of the organization or department). It is also good to check whether these people are responding and whether the systems are actually getting in gear. Remember, important messages can get lost even though the warning systems are solid. An agency may be alerted according to procedure, but the message may never reach its destination. This shows why it is important to think about just what it means to inform someone. The process can become severely distorted, even in-house: for example, an individual is supposed to inform headquarters if a problem arises; but because his or her immediate superior cannot be reached, the individual waits instead of going over the boss's head.

This is the basis for the following rule, which must underly all prior preparations: don't work from standard plans; ask instead, 'How are people going to work? What are the corporate cultural, rather than technical, distortions that may affect the organization as it goes into action?' In short, it takes more than defining procedures and buying equipment to be able to mobilize an organization.

Finally, it is important to emphasize the individual dimension. A basic requirement for everybody, beginning with the leadership, is: manage your stress so it doesn't manage you. In other words, 'Begin with yourself: To meet the external crisis effectively, you must restore confidence in yourself' (Bensahel, 1980, p. 24). Having the support of trusted individuals, whether inside or outside your organization, is often very helpful. These people are vital when the crisis becomes long, serious, and highly destabilizing. Everyone in a leadership position should think about who can be called upon, outside the corporation or administration, to find support and strength in a grave situation. These should be persons with whom a leader can discuss anxiety and uncertainty as well as the technical and ethical problems that are sure to arise. Here again, this support will only be effective if it doesn't have to be improvised.

Additional demands for crises with slow fuses

The systems discussed above are even slower to get into gear when the situation is fuzzy, ambiguous, and slow-moving, rather than starting off with a thunderclap. The most classic trap is the episode whose destabilizing force comes more from the way it is presented than from the 'objective' reality. This is typically the case with a non-event, which is recognized as such by the experts—and by them alone.

In this type of crisis, the persons and systems involved must have even greater resources of attention, openness, and initiative. If this basic prerequisite is fulfilled (at least partially, because there is always room for improvement), then you can become immediately operational by attempting to answer two key questions.

How does an organization know it faces a potential crisis situation?
You should become doubly vigilant as soon as you begin to notice any of the following elements surrounding an issue:

* A strange drift: it seems decidedly impossible to analyse certain questions within existing frameworks; something doesn't fit, but no one can say why.
* There is a degree of uncertainty and ambiguity that causes unusual uneasiness.
* The people you would expect to take action remain absent from the scene.
* There is no common measure between the events and the explicit or implicit values that seem to govern how the matter is being handled.
* Resistance within the organization to considering a given problem is stronger than the obvious elements of the case would lead you to expect. This is a way of detecting a crisis through its effects (i.e. the vague fear it arouses even before it is diagnosed) rather than by its causes, which may only become apparent later.
* Gaps keep getting wider, and they threaten to merge into yawning voids.
* A symbolic problem takes on great importance, even when the original event is minor. (For instance, a lack of vigilance with no consequences, but which occurs in a field of activity that is supposed to be beyond reproach in security terms.)
* A strange and somewhat strained unanimity reigns.
* Bizarre expressions, that run counter to general thinking, emerge through 'safe' channels such as laughter, jokes, or caricatures.

Henry Kissinger: A failure; Watergate
There was, hindsight makes plain, something that should have alerted me early in 1973. It was the behavior of Nixon himself. I found it difficult to get Nixon to focus on foreign policy, to a degree that should have disquieted me. In the past, even in calm periods, he had immersed himself in foreign policy to enliven the job of managing the government, which ultimately bored him. Now it was difficult to get him to address memoranda. They came back without the plethora of marginal comments that indicated they had been carefully read.
(Kissinger, 1982, Vol. 2, p. 77)

A subtle perception: the report by an American General in
Berlin just before the 1948 crisis
Within the last few weeks, I have felt a subtle change in the
Soviet attitude which I cannot define but which now gives me a
feeling that it [war] may come with dramatic suddenness. I
cannot support this change in my own way of thinking with any
data or outward evidence in relationships other than to describe
it as a feeling of a new tenseness in every Soviet individual with
whom we have official relations. I am unable to submit any
official report in the absence of supporting data but my feeling
is real. You may advise the Chief of Staff [General Bradley] of
this for whatever it may be worth if you feel it advisable.[8]

A success: the Tylenol case
On 30 September 1982, the director of public relations for the
Johnson & Johnson group was informed by a member of his
department of a strange phone call from a *Chicago Tribune*
journalist. The journalist had asked basic questions about
Tylenol, Johnson & Johnson, and its subsidiary McNeil Consumer
Products Company. The conversation left the employee with an
uneasy feeling. The director called back the reporter and asked
what was going on. He was told the reporter was investigating a
suspicion of the Chicago medical examiner that there was a link
between Tylenol and a recent death.

The public relations director called his boss, the corporate vice-
president for public relations, who in turn immediately called his
superior, the chairman of the board. The vice-president's first
thought was that there had been some kind of mix-up at a plant,
and he hoped it was all a mistake.

The chairman summoned these executives together. The
incident seemed to be escalating rapidly. But all this handful of
executives knew was that a rumour going around in Chicago
was linking a Johnson & Johnson product with death.

Death . . . when health was what Johnson & Johnson was all
about! The leadership was disoriented. The chairman lost no
time: he told the vice-president of the executive committee and
the public relations director that a helicopter was waiting to fly
them immediately to McNeil headquarters in Pennsylvania, not
far from Johnson & Johnson headquarters in New Jersey.

The chairman turned to his vice-president; not a man to waste
words, he said, 'Take charge.' Ninety minutes later the two men
were doing just that.

(Drawn from Fink, 1986, pp. 204–6)

Such abilities for listening and perceptiveness can be backed up by
structured organizational measures. It is impossible to count solely
on the sort of sixth sense displayed in the Tylenol affair, though this
is an indispensable skill.

What measures to ensure a better reaction to uncertain crises?
The basic issue is being able to detect low-intensity signals, when every organization has a naturally high level of background noise. The solution is to have fine sensors and flexible processing mechanisms that can identify unusual signals and take charge of analysing and monitoring them—without necessarily throwing the system into premature general alert.

Different types of concepts, tools, and measures have been developed. They can provide a good working basis or solid support. They are focused around ideas of active watch and gradual escalation. In other words, don't wait until things explode to start asking questions, but don't set up an all-or-nothing, calm-or-crisis system either; this could very quickly either become inoperative or paralyse operations.

Prior identification. In a fuzzy environment with low levels of contrast, the only messages you can uncode are the ones that have already been inventoried in one form or another, or whose existence is at least suspected. This is one reason why a number of corporations have implemented mechanisms to monitor accidents, of course, but also alleged incidents and the risks surrounding certain issues. Some corporations keep a constant watch on several dozen subjects that could give rise to a public opinion crisis, and these issues are sometimes monitored worldwide.[9] One major corporation[10] organizes bimonthly meetings at which actual or potential crisis case studies are systematically examined.

A collective memory. Having access to previously analysed cases can be of great help in finding a few initial landmarks. One international corporation has developed a reference 'library' on computer. Information may be entered or consulted from several points all over the globe. Queries may be made on-line, and the procedure for entering and recording requires less than 20 minutes.

Groups of experts ready to form crisis units. Potential problems are monitored by expert committees that can go into action if a problem turns into a crisis.

Monitoring 'foreign' crises. Another good tool to have available is a system for continuously monitoring crises that don't involve the organization directly, but which present aspects worth thinking about.

The possibility of mobilizing hybrid groups. This is a very open way of monitoring problems. The choice is sometimes made to use outside observers.[11]

Gradual escalation. Interesting progress has been made by defining the concept of pre-alert and incorporating it into crisis flowcharts. This means a certain number of high-level executives can be placed on active watch, while others at a lower level continue doing what is necessary at that point to treat the problem. This gets preparations started, but without triggering an out-of-scale mobilization. As the situation is analysed and developments take place, this state of pre-alert can be lifted (if the episode was not too disturbing), maintained, or upgraded to a higher stage in the escalation. The advantage is that no level is abruptly plunged into the problem.[12]

> One illustration is the flowchart adopted in France by the mass market foodstuff industry. It includes three levels of mobilization:
>
> * Active watch, in the event a potential problem is detected. This involves intensive information exchanges in order to assess the situation in detail.
> * Serious alert, if the risk becomes more specific. This triggers a series of preparations: developing a history of the problem at hand, reviewing ethical rules, developing a set of arguments, obtaining outside validation of these arguments, reinforcing security measures, and making the professions both upline and downline aware.
> * Grave and imminent risk. If a political decision is made (by the general managers, and not just the technical experts committee), this leads to a meeting of the crisis committee which undertakes to consider various strategic options, such as withdrawing or modifying a product.

This whole set of measures enables a corporation to become more sensitive to its environment and more flexible in the way it reacts. It also offers greater security to both the organization and the individuals involved. The shift from routine operations to full-blown crisis is not made abruptly, and management knows that the systems are working and that the problems will rise smoothly to the top. (This means they are less likely to find themselves saying, 'Someone's been hiding something from me again!')

Obviously the organizations that have implemented such monitoring mechanisms as part of their everyday operations, and are accustomed to tracking abnormal events, will be the first ones ready to act. In his analysis of the Nîmes flooding crisis, Claude Gilbert has shown that the major national networks (electricity, telecommunications) were already taking action at both local and national levels before many other actors had even realized that what was happening in Nîmes on 3 October 1988 was a veritable catastrophe and not just exceptionally heavy rains (Gilbert and Zuanon, 1990).

Triggering protective measures and relevant emergency actions

Within the crisis phenomenon, there are areas in which the conventional rules governing emergencies can and should be applied; a certain number of reflex reactions should be made to limit the effects of the event that starts the crisis. The appropriate emergency intervention mechanisms must be triggered: this obviously includes fire and rescue operations in the event of catastrophes, but it has broader applications. Every field of activity (e.g. business, finance, computers) has its security measures and must be able to implement them. In a major event, any hesitancy on the part of the emergency services is quickly branded unacceptable: if those in charge are so unable to deal with the situation, people will ask, they clearly made the wrong choices—how can they be allowed to continue holding their positions? Indeed, some crises seem to have been created solely because those in charge were unable to react, or because the emergency services fumbled the ball—they are no more immune to error than anyone else.[13]

In some cases, immediate action can even block the crisis process and nip it in the bud (though managing crises by treating the symptoms and ignoring the underlying problems may simply generate more serious crises over the long term).

At the very least, an effort should be made to circumscribe the event as quickly as possible and to prevent it from spreading. For example, do not ship more products through a network in which serious contamination has occurred; do not allow free access to a building that is suspected of being contaminated; do not continue to send bus loads of tourists into a valley that is already overflowing because of a truckers' strike, and so on.

When an event threatens to extend its impact beyond a facility, the population should be alerted quickly and skilfully. To do so, four requirements must be met:

1 An alert can only be understood if:
 • the problem
 • what to do
 • exactly who is involved
 are all specified.[14]
2 The alert message must be repeated.
3 The response to the alert will only be appropriate if it occurs in a favourable context: credibility and prior information (which must include more than just passing out pamphlets) are mandatory. This assumes that some very serious work has been done on raising awareness and preparing people. For instance, if an incident occurred at the nuclear power plant on the banks of Fundy Bay (New Brunswick) in Canada, the biggest problem would be warning the fishermen.[15] A study demonstrated that information could be very effectively dispatched via the marine radio, which the fishermen listen to. This is not the kind of problem you want to discover when the situation is already critical.
4 When drastic civil defence measures such as confinement must be taken, it is probably best in most cases to avoid abruptly announcing the prohibition. For instance, if it is announced that residents are forbidden to leave the area, the measure will be perceived as an unacceptable quarantine; people will feel trapped, as if they are being sacrificed to save those on the outside. In such cases, it is much better to convince and obtain voluntary participation than it is to coerce. Strong recommendations should therefore be preferred to an outright ban.

But in complex crises, the emergency is not always the only aspect of the problem to be dealt with. Consider the following:

• Even the emergency activity may prove to be ambiguous. As was indicated above, you will be dealing with a highly complex phenomenon, and the crisis may throw you off balance on many points. This is why it is necessary to weigh the options carefully before taking action. Even fire and rescue departments must be able to keep a critical distance.

This is the fundamental issue in disaster medicine, for example, which must itself be revised in certain circumstances.[16] As the case of Edmonton (Chapter 2) demonstrated, the conventional scenarios of disaster medicine assume that the site is well controlled; this is necessary to be able to regulate the general movement of injured towards the hospitals. If the site cannot be controlled and the victims arrive by their own means, in large numbers, at the hospitals of their own choosing, the very concept of *triage* loses its meaning.

- Situations in which there is apparently nothing to be done can also be destabilizing—for instance, when a serious threat requires a capacity for emergency epidemiological action and the conventional emergency services cannot help. Here again, it will be too late to develop regional or national resources of this type when the problem arises.

An episode of adulterated cooking oil in Madrid (May–August 1981)[17]
The most urgent task was to identify the cause of the epidemic of pulmonary disease, and specifically, to determine whether the cause was infectious or toxic. The Spanish epidemiologists concluded fairly quickly that the source was probably food poisoning, but the results were only considered credible after the intervention of American epidemiologists. Only then were appropriate response mechanisms set up. And by that time, some 12 000 persons had been hospitalized, and more than 300 were dead.

- Very frequently, those in charge discover that they have lost the resources that were designated for use in such cases. In such cases, the natural reaction is to wait until all these logistical resources and all one's forces are once again available—in the hope of going ahead and implementing the planned responses. But these situations call for a different approach: putting together a minimum capacity for action, by patching together odds and ends if necessary.[18] These problems highlight what will prove to be a frequent requirement: you must deploy treasures of initiative, adaptability, and creativity—and some of the tasks to be accomplished will seem virtually heroic.

An example of what not to do: prudently respecting actual or supposed standards
This was the case with a group of employees of a company who had to take action urgently on a given site. They avoided taking the tollroads to get there, as they weren't sure they would be reimbursed for the tolls.

Stand up and fight: Péter-J. Hargitay and Bhopal
As soon as he learned that he would have to take charge of communications for Union Carbide Europe, Hargitay knew he would need to establish highly efficient communications

between his Zurich offices and the chemical corporation's Geneva headquarters. He therefore demanded that the Swiss telecommunications authority install a direct line between the two offices, within half an hour. His request naturally stunned telecom employees not accustomed to handling crises, so he backed it up with a warning that he would call a press conference immediately at which he would denounce their sluggishness at satisfying a demand made in such exceptionally dire circumstances if the line wasn't installed right away. 'Crisis drives you to do unheard of things: you must be daring, and you must have courage.'[19]

Total mobilization: Henry Kissinger roused from sleep—90 minutes to a Middle East War
At 6.15 A.M. on Saturday, October 6, 1973, I was sound asleep in my suite at the Waldorf Towers in New York City (. . .). Suddenly Joseph J. Sisco, the energetic Assistant Secretary of State for Near Eastern and South Asian Affairs, barged into my bedroom. As I forced myself awake, I heard Sisco's gravelly voice all but shouting that Israel and two Arab countries, Egypt and Syria, were about to go to war.(. . .) When Sisco awakened me there were only ninety minutes of peace left for the Middle East. (. . .) I therefore plunged into a frenetic period of intense diplomacy to head off a clash. (. . .)

At 6.40 A.M. I called the Soviet Ambassador, Anatoly Dobrynin, at his Embassy in Washington. Roused from bed, he was sleepy and confused (or pretended to be). (. . .)

At 6.55 A.M. I called Mordechai Shalev, the chargé d'affaires at the Israeli Embassy .(. . .)

At 7.00 A.M. I telephoned Egyptian Foreign Minister Mohamed el Zayyat, who was attending the UN General Assembly in New York.

(Kissinger, 1982, Vol. 2, pp. 450-3)

Johnson & Johnson and the Tylenol case
Most Johnson & Johnson executives believe that their comeback would not have been possible if the corporation had not reacted rapidly and taken a series of critical measures to maintain public confidence.

At the time, J&J did not have a crisis plan. Nor had the group ever imagined such a crisis due to malevolent action could develop. Yet in an hour and a half, the company managed to:

• detect the crisis
• give the alert
• mobilize, and involve the chairman himself in the crisis.

The chairman was able to:

• name a top executive who took charge of the crisis

- instruct the executive to visit the sites of the crisis
- instruct a public relations professional to accompany the crisis manager
- request that he himself be kept informed.

J&J took a series of immediate measures to:

- alert the public via the media
- alert the medical community
- take the product off the shelves in the Chicago area
- concert with government agencies
- pull all advertising for the product
- offer a reward of $100 000 for information on the perpetrators of the contamination
- bring together a crisis team of seven members working on two key questions: 'How do we protect consumers?' and 'How can we save our product?'
- inspect millions of capsules in Johnson & Johnson offices and in regional offices of government agencies
- withdraw the product completely after the capsule's vulnerability was discovered (along with two additional bottles that had been tampered with in Chicago stores)
- start publicity to distribute this information and announce that the capsules could be exchanged for tablets, another form of the same product
- destroy all their stocks, to avoid any further risks
- establish a toll-free number to respond to the public's worries
- train employees to handle the phone calls (30 000 were received within the next month).

    (See Johnson & Johnson, 1982; ten Berge, 1990, pp. 25–6; Fink, 1986, pp. 203–18.)

Looking for information

A crisis is by definition a crisis of information. Nothing is known about the problem; the elements needed to understand it are missing; or, on the contrary, there is an overwhelming amount of insignificant, useless, or simply unprocessed data.

Consequently, one step to take very rapidly is to collect the relevant information. Preferably you should be able to use pre-established systems for seeking out and analysing these data, but if necessary, set up the means to do so.

This research effort must become structured very quickly. It should be based on the idea that the event itself is not a crisis: what you are trying to understand are the overall dynamics that are developing, rather than any one form they may take. This task of systematically collecting information recurs at later stages in crisis management. But for the time being, you must at least gather a few details on the event taking place.

> This was the situation in which the chairman of Johnson & Johnson found himself when he learned that people were dead, and others perhaps dying, in Chicago or elsewhere, and that the cause was reputed to be Tylenol. The first urgency was to get some information. He dispatched a team on site.

If it proves impossible to pinpoint where the problem lies, then adopt a negative approach: attempt to determine what has not been affected by the phenomenon. If a problem has been reported at one point in the network, then ask, 'Is this an isolated incident?' and start the necessary verifications to find out. This allows you to establish protective measures that can prevent or delay the spread of the crisis and avoid giving the impression that the crisis is already out of control in all potentially affected domains (a source of confusion, demoralization, and error).

Setting up a log book

Events are going to pick up speed. It is important to set down quickly in writing the elements of information received, the procedures undertaken, and the steps already decided upon. This must be done rapidly throughout the entire organization, but above all it requires an individual reflex: everyone has to write down what he or she is doing and where he or she stands.

This may seem like a secondary issue. It is not.

- If the log book is not kept up to date, within a few hours no one will be able to know what is going on, how the procedures have been implemented, who said what, who did what, and so on. Writing things down makes it possible to undertake consistent action over the long haul. Philippe Vesseron adds:

  > Events that take such a convulsive turn often develop slowly. If you don't force yourself to record the facts, the information, the decisions made, very quickly you lose all means of re-evaluating the situation when the crisis becomes drawn out. You have to be able to go back to the real facts behind the interpretations that are made at any given moment. But nobody thinks spontaneously of establishing this verifiable chronology of events from the start.[20]

- Writing is also a very good discipline: it forces you to try to see clearly through the mental fog in which you may be operating (Fink, 1986, p. 146). It also forces you to put some distance between yourself and what you are doing, and this is the breathing room in which you will be able to develop critical reflection.
- In addition, writing is a form of action that creates stability in stressful situations, because it forces the writer to become objective about events (Parry, 1990).
- A log book can be used to share information among individuals or teams. And in a crisis that drags on, it will be necessary to use relief teams. Without a log book, it is very difficult to provide for a smooth transfer from one team to another.

This brings up an important detail: by definition, there will be a certain delay before the crisis management becomes mobilized and the log book is opened. Consequently, one of the first steps must be making the effort to recall everything that has happened or been done during the crisis up to the point at which you start writing.

It should also be noted that starting this written trace is not enough. Philippe Vesseron's comment above that people are not motivated to start a log book can be taken one step further: you will also encounter resistance to maintaining the book.

- The task may be considered to be secondary—what is at stake is saving lives, not scribbling notes.
- The job may also be considered unworthy—once again, people reject the image of 'pushing paper'.
- Everyone probably prefers to be in the heat of the action rather than behind a writing desk.
- At a deeper level, being able to write means clearly stating all the difficulties. At the outset, this merely serves to increase everyone's stress levels.
- Writing and clarifying issues creates the possibility of formulating a response. This may not actually be what people want. By staying vague and keeping an intellectual distance from events, actors find it easier to escape their duty to find answers: they make it effectively impossible to manage anything whatsoever. (The classic model is the person who never takes notes at a meeting—and who will never be asked to write the minutes.)

This explains the *natural* refusal to write things down. To fight against it, one solution is to designate ahead of time a 'historian' in a crisis unit. (In the Prussian army, this was a task entrusted to a high-ranking officer, sometimes even a colonel.[21]) To motivate the historian, it should also be emphasized that this record will be very useful after the crisis, when it becomes necessary to place a given action in its context, provide explanations, or justify decisions. If, for instance, follow-up information is distributed, it is easier to locate all those with whom the team was in contact during the crisis. Finally, and perhaps most importantly, the log book is a useful training tool; without it, any review of the experience can only be based on approximation.

Developing a team, separating crisis management

As quickly as possible, a core group must be brought together that can hold the fort until the planned structures are set up.

Furthermore, organizing this team helps avoid tumbling into a typical briar patch to which special attention must be paid. There is a natural tendency for everyone to join in the general commotion around a poorly defined problem. You must absolutely avoid having 'everybody' try to help manage the crisis. Otherwise, several serious disadvantages appear:

- The excessive number of people makes it impossible for the crisis unit to work effectively.
- Many people feel useless, and this simply frustrates and demoralizes them.
- Those who are present on the site of the problem or at operational headquarters are not doing their regular jobs and are leaving the areas as yet unaffected by the crisis without resources or leadership. This, in turn, creates marvellous openings for the crisis to spread and intensify its strength. Sometimes, because everyone is paying exclusive attention to the crisis, failures happen at other points, generating new crises in turn. These are much more difficult to handle: the reaction is 'You told us everything else was under control, and now another accident has occurred!'[22]
- If they know that the organization is not overrun by chaos in every other sector, the crisis team will feel that much less stress. Those who are working on the crisis will know that their usual jobs are being efficiently covered by someone else and that they can devote themselves fully to the crisis.

Everyone should be well aware of who belongs to the crisis team. By deduction, this makes it clear who is not a member. This is the type of mechanism that works more smoothly if it is set up and tested in advance. Most of those involved should have been designated ahead of time.

In short, it is crucial to ensure that everything does not begin to drift and get caught up in the wake of the crisis.

Avoiding irritating gestures

The issue of aggravation is a problem that deserves a special note. This is a problem we create for ourselves, and it threatens every decision maker. Practise differentiating between things that cannot wait and things that really do not call for absolute emergency action. Remember that everything works to narrow the time frame of actors involved in a crisis, and this creates unnecessary irritation as to the urgency of things. But there are other traps.

Decision makers who are not careful find themselves *naturally* led to act, to take large-scale measures. They think more about the absolute urgency than about the relevance of their actions, for several reasons:

- It often seems like a good idea, indeed like common sense, to stop an entire system.
- Action has the advantage of doing away with the ambiguity of the situation, which is what is hardest to bear about a crisis.
- This creates an impression of doing something, which is a relief to everyone, beginning with the person in charge.
- Action lets you use the resources that are available, which is always very tempting, even if they are inadequate (e.g. 'We'll evacuate everyone because we have the means to do so').
- Taking action builds stronger team spirit and avoids or camouflages conflict.
- It is a great way to win popularity.
- The ethical appeal of this strategy is non-negligible, especially in the case of technological hazards: Who would want to make the innocent population run additional risks? Who has anything to gain in so doing? If the action costs a lot of money, then maybe the people responsible for the problem will think more about prevention next time around!

But action for action's sake can be disastrous in many cases, as its unexpected side effects slowly emerge. Consider the following examples:

All-out evacuations
A local population risks being exposed to a theoretically carcinogenic substance for a few minutes. But it is more dangerous than vital to evacuate them in the middle of the night under emergency conditions, as the carcinogenicity has been studied on the substance when ingested during several months. (In public health cases, an essential distinction must be made between acute effects and chronic exposure.)

'Everyone off to the hospital!'
This type of reaction only overwhelms the hospital with people who have no real problems. Tests are run which in any case will yield no useful results, as the necessary protocols have not been defined. Instead, a whole range of pre-existing conditions, totally unrelated to the crisis, will be discovered, and these must be treated urgently. It will become impossible to treat the truly urgent problems that arise, because the resources for action will be completely monopolized.[23]

Turning off a water supply system without a specific diagnosis
The decision sounds courageous—at last, an official who assumes some responsibilities. Then the difficulties start to appear: for instance, the drinking water supply was cut off, but so were the fire hydrants. People are supplied by a replacement system that would horrify the health authorities if it were analysed. And when the system is turned back on (based on unclear criteria), an analysis reveals that this water is unsafe, possibly less safe than the water that was cut off in the first place.

Massive recall of a product
After Johnson & Johnson recalled 31 million bottles of Tylenol in 1982, other companies tried unsuccessfully to imitate their example. Withdrawing a product and reintroducing it with no changes can be catastrophic. Johnson & Johnson completely altered the protective packaging of its bottles before bringing them back on the market. A Canadian beer brewer tried the same approach, with less attention to detail: after the recall, it turned out there was no serious problem, and the product was brought back unchanged. The public reaction was, 'If they withdrew the product, there must have been some danger. If they are bringing it back unchanged, they must be criminals.' The company went bankrupt.[24]

A non-crisis managed so that it becomes a real crisis
This example sounds like a caricature, and it illustrates an aberration to be avoided. The case took place a few years ago in Canada. An individual (who was never identified) wrote to a

journalist, threatening to put poison in South African apples. The envelope was misaddressed, and by the time it reached its destination, the fateful deadline indicated by its author had passed. Since nothing had apparently happened, the reporter took the letter for what it was—a bad joke. All the same, he turned it over to the police, noting that he believed the threat was unfounded: 'I don't believe it, but I thought you should be informed.' The police, too, assumed the letter was a bad joke. They showed it to the health minister for information, stating, 'We don't believe it, but we thought you should be kept informed.' The health department informed the distributor's association, adding once again that they believed it was a joke. The wholesalers informed the supermarkets. Then a Quebec supermarket chain decided that as a precaution, it would be good to withdraw all South African apples from its shelves.

This simple gesture was the tripwire: the media gave broad coverage to the case, which suddenly became a real crisis.[25]

Unfortunately, not all cases are this simple. It should simply be borne in mind that it is best to maintain a certain reserve and to avoid forging straight ahead with a decision that hasn't been thought out.

In any case, the message accompanying the steps taken is important. Stopping a system 'because a risk exists', with no other specifics, will in all likelihood lead to an impasse. This initial message suggests that the system will be started up again 'when the risk no longer exists'. But while it is easy not to rule out the existence of a risk, it is very difficult, if not impossible, to prove that there is no risk, or no further risk (this is reminiscent of the debate over minimum harmful doses). A system should never be turned off without stating why the step was taken (there is a great difference between doing so for psychological reasons and doing it to avoid a danger), and the conditions under which it will be turned back on.

Saint-Basile-le-Grand, 10 September, 1988[26]

One problem arose when it was time to return to the evacuated area, 18 days after the fire. The scientific committee had just stated that the area could be considered free from any risks justifying prolonged evacuation. At the same time, the Ministry of Agriculture announced that crops in the region would be destroyed because of the risks of contamination—in complete contradiction to what the scientific and medical experts claimed. The experts were threatened with losing some of their credibility over the case. When they protested directly to the Ministry, they were informed that the measure had been taken on psycho-economic grounds: the danger was that Ontario

would refuse all produce from a much larger area, so the
Ministry was trying to stay ahead of the game. But because none
of this had been stated in the message, what people understood
was that the area was still at risk, contrary to the declarations of
the scientific committee.

Nor should ambiguity be done away with by systematically refusing
to take large-scale emergency action. Once again, a technical
dilemma may be complicated by the weight of things that no one
wants to discuss: a desire not to underscore a touchy issue, the fear
of committing expenditures or arousing conflict (especially when
there is no absolute proof),[27] or the simple conviction that there is
no real problem. Yet a refusal to act in an emergency, and if
necessary to take large-scale, drastic measures when the danger is in
fact imminent, can create other worrisome situations and possible
over-reactions as well.

The case of the Montchanin waste dump (France)[28]
For a long time, public affirmations that there was no problem
created a conflict between the official line and what people
thought. This finally led the Minister of the Interior to close this
industrial waste dump completely—when in fact, it would seem
that with a few improvements, the facility could have continued
operating without any danger. Then, thanks to an
epidemiological study performed by the Grenoble team of Dr
Zmirou, it was revealed that the health situation was far from
being as satisfactory as the public powers claimed.

Between a catastrophic wait-and-see attitude and irritating gestures,
the more complex a crisis is, the more important it is to incorporate
critical distance into the reflex desire to act. Break free of simple
rules.

As was indicated at the beginning of this book, everything generally
comes down to a question of judgement. It is easy to over-react
when a great risk threatens a small number of people (for example,
to send two helicopters to save one human life if that's the only
demand on those resources). The situation is more problematic
when an uncertain danger could affect a million people.

This point will be treated again later. What must be retained here is
that you should not systematically opt for the most radical and far-
reaching measures. No decision is without risk, and few actions can
be adopted without striking a balance between various dangers. This
is what people tend to forget in crisis management—instead, merely
deciding and taking action are spontaneously believed to be good.

Trying to 'stay ahead of the game' in a crisis can result in turning the game into a crisis of vast proportions.

Getting a foothold on the communication landscape

The problems involved in giving the alert have already been discussed. Here we shall examine another issue: communicating with priority publics that are not in danger (at least not imminent danger) in the aftermath of an accident. This section will deal primarily with public communication, which seems to pose the most difficulties. But it should not be forgotten that rapid in-house communication is also vital, if you want to prevent your own organization from imploding. This is too often neglected, especially in an age when so much attention is paid to the media.

Of course, crisis management requires that you deploy a considerable communications effort, and not everything can be done immediately. The following are the steps to be taken as you first attempt to come to grips with the crisis.

Informing families of victims

It is natural that the families should be informed before the media. This is not always easy to do, especially if journalists are the first to get hold of the news. This approach actually encompasses a more fundamental requirement: the victims need to be acknowledged as human beings; more than anyone else, they need information, assistance, and respect.

Here again, this cannot be improvised. If procedures have not been defined, and if no preparations are made within the organization, those in charge run a high risk once the situation arrives of running into technical, organizational, and above all cultural barriers. The only response is flight, and this becomes degrading for those inside the organization and unbearable for those on the outside.

No matter what the intentions are, the difference between decency and indecency, humanity and spite is summarized here by the choice of speaking up or remaining silent, being present or absent, reaching out or turning a blind eye.

Look again at the words of the victims in Part 1: they speak up for their right to be informed, demand basic respect, and expect that some bond of emotional and physical support will be offered in a period in which they feel totally lost and abandoned.

Communicating with all the audiences, beginning in-house

Attention should be paid to ensuring that essential information is disseminated throughout the structure. It is important to start thinking about what initiatives need to be taken to make sure that the concertation measures provided for will actually work.

Beyond this, various publics will have an immense and pressing need for information. If this need is not met, the system may well explode.

Dieudonnée ten Berge (1990, pp. 50–2) introduces an interesting concept of four types of publics: enabling publics (administrations, shareholders, boards of directors, various authorities); functional publics (employees, unions, suppliers, customers); normative publics, with more general ties to the organization in question (trade unions, scientific societies); and diffused publics (the media, environmentalists, residents, minorities).

Holding your own on the media scene

As was seen above, the first reflex is to remain silent. Yet there can be no doubt: communication is the fruit of a wilful counter-reaction—a difficult but indispensable reaction. Everything will push you to remain silent:

- 'Common sense': The idea that reasonable people must have sure, specific data that have been checked and cannot be contradicted, before they make any pronouncements; the more serious the situation is, the more sure of yourself you would like to be before saying anything.
- The manager's sense of responsibility: You don't gamble lightly with the reputation of your organization; you only speak when you have a mandate to do so, on the basis of a document approved by the executive committee, the legal department, the communications department, and all the rest.
- It is never pleasant to have to announce a serious or potentially serious problem.
- Describing a potentially grave problem can heighten your own sense of disorientation: when you explain the danger in public, it becomes much more real and worrisome for you personally.

- Making an announcement always worries the speaker, haunted by the panic myth—so you think, 'Why not wait until we're sure before we get everyone upset?'
- When someone speaks out, that person becomes one highly exposed individual, whereas if everyone remains silent, the failure can be blamed on the structure.
- And there is always the hope that no one on the outside will notice that anything is amiss.

So you wait. You wait to know everything before speaking up; you wait for permission before giving even a few facts on the event. In order to be sure not to take too many risks, you can even ask for impossible instructions: the 'model manager' can always come away with the feeling of having fulfilled his or her duty towards all the requirements of the situation.

Yet in every case, it is vital to communicate without waiting. The reasons are already familiar.

- Other actors will fill any information vacuum; these actors may not be in the best position to give correct information. Above all, they may be promoting their own interests.
- A filter immediately falls into place to determine the trust placed in your communications. If they are insufficient at the outset, you will suffer for it throughout the crisis. Those who remain silent are automatically assumed to be guilty of the worst.

'One thing is certain,' Edgar Fasel, communications director at Sandoz, states unequivocally, 'the stage is set in the first hours, the first 48 hours. This is the stage on which the coming weeks and months will be played out—it will be almost impossible to modify.'[29]

It could even be added, in contrast to the 'common sense' motives listed above, that the more serious things are, the more people crave information. Silence will be covered by any available means, and foremost by the wildest rumours. (Some suspicions even point to a subtle tactic on the part of those who feel vulnerable and deprived of information: 'Let's spread the worst possible rumours; that will goad them out of their silence. From what they admit and what they deny, we'll be able to piece together what's going on.')

Then again, the issue of remaining silent or announcing the news is often a moot point: the information has already reached the press and has become public knowledge while the decision makers are wondering if they aren't better off keeping quiet.

Begin, then, by laying down the following rule: take the communications initiative immediately, because it is one of the keys to the survival of the organization in a crisis situation.[30] In other words, tell it and tell it fast.

This rule may send chills down your spine. What should you say? Above all, remember that not knowing is not an evil in itself; it is a normal condition in a crisis. What no one can accept is absence, a refusal to comment, an apparent (read: 'flagrant') lack of interest, or the incapacity to react, not only technically but also in civic and human terms.

Three messages should underly the initial communications effort:

1 We are aware of the problem, and we have taken charge of all its aspects, including the technological, organizational, human, and social ones.
2 Many unknowns remain, but everything is being done to acquire additional information and to handle the situation: the emergency plans are being enacted, and here is how they work . . .
3 More information will be provided as soon as it is available.

All this naturally requires some skill, especially in the area of warning, mobilizing, and taking charge, examined above. To have any impact in public communications, you have to be one of the best sources of information. This means having the ability, before going public, to collect high-quality information. Performing magic illusions for the public will not work: both private individuals and the media are quick to cross-check information and decide which actors are trustworthy. Judgements are quickly formulated here, on a scale with the level of shock or anxiety.

What this requires—and what is most difficult to obtain—is a corporate culture based on openness, even in the most difficult times.

It is important to avoid the litany of automatic assurances that is so tempting in such situations:

• 'Nothing is wrong, everything is under control', when in fact no one is really sure and the situation is evolving constantly.
• 'These systems were supposed to be fail-proof, everything was done correctly,' when in fact no system is ever perfect. At the same time, it is constantly repeated that 'it is impossible to exclude all

risk'—thereby confirming what the accident has shown: that the system has its weaknesses.

- 'We have the best system in the world—just look at our record,' when dozens of deaths have been announced.
- 'There are no deaths, only injuries.' This is taken as proof by the injured in question, whose very lives have been shaken by the event, that those in charge are monsters.
- 'Everything will be back in order by tomorrow evening,' when the actual duration of the episode is emerging as a major question mark.

By the same token, avoid boisterous declarations that quickly back you into a corner.

In a case like the Seveso dioxin drums, for instance, the French minister of the environment was careful not to set out on the warpath against all waste imports. Such a reaction would have calmed people's fears, but the decision to stop imports would have had other significant consequences.

More generally on this subject, it should be emphasized that communicating does not mean saying just anything. This is worth remembering. Often, when decision makers abandon all cultural references (in this case, keeping silent), they run the risk of demonstrating, almost out of spite, that the new standards to which they are being subjected are by definition absurd and dangerous. This risk is especially high among those who have no preparation for the openness they are called on to practise in a highly turbulent situation.[31]

Finally, there are a few fundamental aspects of crisis communications that are often missing from the discussion.

In these situations, everyone begins by weighing the words that are used. Yet communication is more than a verbal exercise: it also comprises gestures, underlying attitudes, and physical presence. In what are often dramatic circumstances, the psychological disturbance drives the person in charge to take refuge in well-defined frameworks, such as technical jargon or legal restrictions. The crisis manager voids statements of any personal sensibility toward the event, when in fact (often[32]) this very heightened sensitivity is what lies behind the withdrawn and intransigent attitude. This reflex defensive posture is perceived on the outside as a provocation, especially by the victims. It leads to bitterness, which in turn produces additional uneasiness, thereby making the decision maker act even more intransigently.

In the same register, the leadership should never let the idea take root that the victims are mainly a source of trouble that must be dealt with—though for appearance's sake, these feelings are hidden from the outside. In such cases, the truth quickly shines through: you cannot trick victims, and any trickery (for instance, the neat little speech made after training before a movie camera) is devastating for those who try to carry it off, and it strips them of all dignity. In those circumstances, what was merely a crisis can turn into all-out war.

Yet to avoid sounding excessively naive or tilting suspiciously towards communication for communication's sake, we should make one reservation about these pleas for openness. In the event of difficulties that have caused no damage and pose no imminent threats, the most urgent task is clearly to remedy the situation, and not to undertake a massive media campaign. Do not confuse prompt post-accident communications with systematic public self-flagellation. Many decision makers wisely note the importance of this point: if nothing is happening, prepare to communicate just in case—but don't go rushing into the limelight.

Yet the ambiguity of this issue cannot be dismissed lightly. The same decision makers rightly emphasize that things often go better if the eventuality of a problem has been raised beforehand. They sometimes regret not having insisted more on a detail made public but not played up sufficiently by the press. A few months later, the issue resurfaces and is presented as a shameless cover-up! There is no easy way to dispense with these complications once and for all. The contradictions and ambiguity that mark the terrain of crisis resist all defences—including the natural one of naivety. In a crisis—however it may unfold—nothing can replace a capacity for evaluation and good judgement.

Finally, it cannot be ruled out that in the case of certain threats (not imminent risks), especially terrorism, immediate communication can have negative consequences. There are also cases of disturbances which are clearly analysed as false alerts intended to disrupt a system. The following guidelines seem helpful for handling these delicate issues.

- Silence is a communications strategy: the decision not to inform must derive from a specific analysis of the risks run and those avoided, rather than from a classic reflex to cover up.
- The decision not to inform must be perceived as an exception to the basic rule which can be justified by overriding motivations.
- It should be understood that this wilful lack of communication may become public knowledge at any moment. You must therefore be in a position to offer convincing explanations about opting to remain silent, on both technical and moral grounds.

Undertaking an integrated approach: a plan for action

Throughout a crisis, two approaches are necessary: specific action and comprehensive management.

At the end of the first phase of minimum action, a number of things need to be verified. Everyone should prepare specific checklists for the potential crisis situations that are likely to be encountered. Key data should be prepared: names, phone numbers, assignments, and so on. On this basis, it is possible to determine whether each aspect of immediate action has been taken in hand:

- The fundamental alerts have been given, emergency procedures are implemented.
- Rescue operations are started.
- Information is being actively sought out.
- The log book has been opened.
- The crisis, or at least its management, has been separated.
- No grandiose, all-or-nothing decisions have been made.
- Active communication has been undertaken, aimed at the victims, the personnel, and the media.

But, as has just been pointed out, in addition to specific actions, you must also begin working, from the very outset, on another type of activity: summarizing and coordinating these actions. Even if it is too early to establish a general plan to treat the crisis, already at this stage you can begin thinking about a first outline for getting organized.

Start thinking about who should do what, with whom, and in what order; how to use your resources; whom to ask for what, and so forth.

Philippe Legorjus: A plan of action
[As commanding officer of the GIGN [French SWAT unit], he
has just arrived on the site of a hostage-taking. He surveys the
area and notes the general commotion and confusion. Before
taking any action, he undertakes the mental exercise of
formulating a general plan.]

As I head back out of the prison, I start setting up an
organizational plan in my head. Before anything else, the
command must be brought together: several officials, numerous
ranking officers are there, in addition to firemen, journalists and
others. [. . .] We'll have to get all these folks sorted out.

(Legorjus, 1990, p. 87)

*Péter-J. Hargitay: Working with Union Carbide in Europe during
the Bhopal catastrophe*
The first hours were crucial: naming spokespersons, structuring
the crisis center and implementing the basic communications
policy, informing the media, providing in-house information.

One of the immediate decisions was to name four spokesmen.
Why four? There was both a language problem and a
knowledge problem. You have to realize that there are twenty
nations in Europe, and twenty languages. So we named two
generalists: one vice-president, who spoke fluent English and
French, and myself for the other languages (I speak seven). For
technical questions, there were two top-notch expert chemists
who knew how MIC (the compound involved in the catastrophe)
was produced.

By 8 am the next morning, we had already chosen our crisis
room, a central room in the Geneva headquarters (to shorten the
coming and going). There a blackboard was set up, on which I
began by writing the rules that we were to observe scrupulously
in responding to all questioners:

1 No contradiction among spokesmen.
2 No questions without answers: if we don't have all the
  elements, we promise to find the information and to call the
  person back—and we do it.
3 Generalist spokesmen never answer a technical question.
4 Mandatory politeness and maximum patience in all contacts.

[. . .] The first step we took with regard to the outside world
was to send a telex to some 800 European media, informing
them that we were at their disposal, that the doors were open—
that we couldn't answer all their questions, but that we hoped to
satisfy their requests for information. This first step was very
well received.

In terms of in-house communication, even though we didn't yet
have any details about the accident, our first concern was
informing Union Carbide's employees. Twice a day we sent

them an 'internal information report'. We posted information in
company cafeterias about how events were developing. This is a
vital lesson: your priority is not the press, it is your own
employees. Otherwise, you run the risk of things simply
imploding.

To accompany information to the outside, with the first telex we
set up a log book in which we made a record of each telephone
call, each request and each interview, minute by minute. We
named two people—a chemist and an executive secretary—who
did nothing but write down information about all the calls
received in this log book: when the call arrived, caller's phone
number, contents of the reply, and so on. In the long run, this
300-page document proved to be exceptionally useful. In it we
had the names of all the interested media organs, whether
critical or positive. We were able to pursue our information
effort for two years without a break—in fact, at the end, the
journalists were even asking us to stop this flow of information
(this might look like a cynical tactic of over-informing, but that
wasn't our intention). In the short term, the log allowed us to
evaluate, day by day, the mistakes we made, the list of people
whom we hadn't yet called, those whom we hadn't been able to
call back, and the points on which we lacked information.
Creating this log book drove us to advise Danbury [Union
Carbide world headquarters] several times a day of the subjects
about which we needed more information.[33]

*Henry Kissinger: War in the Middle East in 90 Minutes—the first
steps in getting organized*
My next task was to give [chief of staff Brent] Scowcroft
instructions for the WSAG [Washington Special Actions Group]
meeting. [. . .] From New York I asked Scowcroft to obtain by
noon, first, a plan to move the US Sixth Fleet—at the moment
scattered among ports in Spain and Greece—into the eastern
Mediterranean; and second, plans to reinforce our
Mediterranean naval units if necessary. No troop movements
should take place, but the readiness of our forces should be
enhanced. Departments should do no briefing on their own.
When anything was to be said, [presidential advisor Alexander]
Haig or I would clear it. The President or Haig should decide
whether the White House or some other agency would do the
briefing.

(Kissinger, 1982, Vol. 2, p. 455)

Do not create an unmanageable landscape

The question of initial action is often posed in the following terms:
given that at the start of a crisis you are working on an undefined
issue (due to a lack of information) which is largely impossible to

define (as the crisis has not yet decided what path it will take), and given that the first actors do not have all the desired resources at their disposal, what should you do, and what should you not do?

Answer: At the very least, do not create a landscape that will be unmanageable later on—hospitals filled to overflowing, an operational site so choked with people and confusion that it takes considerable time to organize action, or seriously compromised credibility.

> **Example:** In a case like the askarel affair in Reims, no one could be expected to have in-depth knowledge of the risks or absence of risk involved in this type of situation. But the problems would have been infinitely less complex for the specialists if they were called in early enough to have only to examine a dozen people— instead of some 400, including the building's inhabitants and everyone who had visited the site.

The following illustration is taken from another field. Philippe Legorjus makes the same reflections on dealing with a hostage-taking.

> *Philippe Legorjus: Avoid generating madness and general confusion*
> It is just 7.30 pm when we arrive in Saint-Maur [. . .]. The cars of journalists, radio and television stations are parked all over the place. A roadblock has been set up on the road near the power plant, but the photographers get around it by crossing through the fields. There is a lot of commotion around the prison; official vehicles are blocking the road, and uniforms are running all over the place [. . .].
>
> The situation is completely mad. There is total confusion in this corner of the Britanny countryside, and the little information provided to me upon my arrival is not reassuring. Not all the neighbors have been evacuated. The gendarmes do not have full control over the zone; instead of spreading themselves out, they are all right around the farm. Last but not least, to top things off, I learn that my men won't be there for another half hour [. . .] We have to put things on hold until they arrive. We decide to observe the site attentively. [. . .]
>
> What has always struck me about arriving on the site of a hostage-taking is the way authority is diluted, the lack of an overall approach to the problem, the making-it-up-as-we-go-along. And yet there are crisis plans for this type of situation. But they are linear, based on procedures, and the chaos orchestrated by the adversary makes them useless. So my first attitude is not to worry directly about the hostage-taking, but about how to handle it. You have to gather the authorities together in one place, protected from the clamor, you have to

have communication and information tools available, and above all, you have to assign priority so that the real decision makers have access to them.

Here, the GIGN was called in too late, when the situation had already turned into trench warfare. No one should have waited until there were two civilians and five policemen injured before calling on us! And yet for the past ten years, every year, we've been bringing together future commanding officers on the local level to explain to them the role they have to play whenever the GIGN is called in. We ask first of all that they establish a buffer zone; this means evacuating all the inhabitants located in the proximity of Fort Chabrol. Next, we want preventive measures taken to avoid any sudden rise in the tension, and we want permanent observation of the site organized. Last, the officers must have total control over any decision to open fire.

(Legorjus, 1990, pp. 85–6, 87, 155, 160)

In dealing with a crisis, wisdom is better than frantic energy. The first goal is to avoid the grave errors that such disturbing circumstances naturally seem to inspire. As Jane Bensahel (1980, p. 25) notes: 'Take only the most urgent first steps. Despite your best efforts to define the crisis, [. . .] it is not the best atmosphere for longer-range planning.'

This does not necessarily mean sitting back and waiting. Sometimes a lack of action can also create an impasse.

Kissinger and the beginning of the Cienfuegos, Cuba Crisis (1970)
I strongly favored facing the challenge immediately lest the Soviets misunderstand our permissiveness and escalate their involvement to a point where only a major crisis could remove the base. I opposed time-wasting moves such as waiting for a Gromyko–Rogers conversation in a month's time. The Soviets knew that we were photographing Cienfuegos almost daily; if we did nothing they had to assume that we were acquiescing. If we then suddenly confronted them, they might have run out of manœuvring room; the consequent crisis might well be sharpened by their belief that they had been set up for humiliation. Moreover, we were expecting an imminent reply to our suggestion of a summit. If the Soviets' answer was positive, we would face additional obstacles in confronting them, and if we did so, we would have to do it abruptly and at a level that would stake the prestige of the top leaders on both sides, making it even more difficult to contain the crisis.

(Kissinger, 1979, Vol. 1, p. 641)

This whole first reflex phase has made it possible to set up a certain number of minimal barriers and to buy some time. Now the next step is to start developing a real strategic action plan—developing, not jumping into operation. This is precisely the major goal of the second phase: deploying all possible means of reflection in order to think, prepare, and pursue this action in depth.

Summary

Avoiding being immediately discredited

- Recognize that a problem exists
- Give the warning, mobilize the organization
- Trigger protective measures and emergency actions
- Look for information
- Set up a log book
- Develop a team, separate crisis management from other activities
- Avoid making irritating gestures
- Get a foothold on the communication landscape
- Start thinking about a plan for action

Don't work on an unmanageable landscape

Notes

1. Interview with Claude Frantzen and Laurent du Boullay in Lagadec, 1990, pp 138–9.
2. This branch is evolving constantly. The Francom group recently prepared an update on the range of emergency systems available: 'Suivi des systèmes de communication pour les temps de crise' (Follow-up of communications systems for crisis periods), a document that is regularly updated.
3. This system is produced by TIS and has been adopted by ICI France and EDF.
4. The case of the emergency systems located in Chicago for use in a San Francisco crisis should give pause when considering the most appealing models of modernity.
5. A trademark of Framacom-Turbocommunication.
6. *Source*: Rhône-Poulenc, group communications division: 'Consignes pour la permanence du plan d'information d'urgence', 19 August 1987. For a more complete description, see Lagadec, 1990.
7. Interview with the secretary general (who requested that no further details be given about the very interesting advances made by his city).
8. General Clay, 5 March 1948 (the crisis lasted from 20 March 1948 until May 1949). Cited by J.E. Smith, *The Defense of Berlin*, Baltimore, Maryland, Johns Hopkins University Press, 1963, pp. 101–2, and used by Jonathan Roberts, 1988, p. 51.

9. This is the case in the agro-business.
10. In the field of mass distribution.
11. For example, at EDF, the Sandoz group, and elsewhere.
12. EDF, for instance, uses this type of approach at its nuclear power plants.
13. It is interesting here to consider the discussions surrounding the *Amoco Cadiz* and *Exxon Valdez* accidents. See also the Vincendon and Henry case (involving mountain rescue) in Claude Dech, 1983, 'La Tragédie Vincendon et Henry', *La Montagne*, No. 133, 3, pp. 141–51.
14. We would like to thank Joseph Scanlon for formulating this point.
15. This illustrates the primary importance of efforts made to distribute information around high-risk sites in compliance with the Seveso directive. On this subject, see the work about Berre Lake by Lalo, 1990.
16. Interview with Joseph Scanlon, who has done considerable work on the limitations of conventional scenarios surrounding mass behaviour (e.g. automobile races, a papal visit).
17. Interview with Dr William Dab.
18. See Gilbert and Lagadec, 1989, and Claude Gilbert's analysis of the Nîmes flooding crisis, in which some services managed to work effectively with the bits and pieces available and return speedily to operating capacity; in the meantime, others that were more concerned with recovering their usual resources never caught up with events (Gilbert and Zuanon, 1990; Gilbert, 1991).
19. Interview with Péter-J. Hargitay.
20. Interview with Philippe Vesseron in Lagadec, 1990, p. 98.
21. Interview with Rolf Kaiser.
22. Péter-J. Hargitay illustrates this point, which he considers essential, with the story of the accident in Institute, West Virginia, at the sister plant of Union Carbide's Bhopal facility. In August 1985, an accident occurred in which toxic gas was released from the plant. Everyone was so busy thinking about India . . .
23. Interview with Dr Lucien Abenhaim and Dr William Dab.
24. Interview with Joseph Scanlon.
25. We would like to thank Joseph Scanlon and Enrico Quarantelli for this example.
26. Interview with Dr Lucien Abenhaim (member of the international scientific committee)
27. Imagine the conflicts that would be caused by declaring a health quarantine on turkey farms just before Christmas!
28. Interview with Dr Dab.
29. Interview with Edgar Fasel in Lagadec, 1990, p. 88.
30. Interviews with Péter-J. Hargitay and Joseph Scanlon.
31. This calls to mind a simulation exercise led by the author and Philippe Dessaint. The first manager adopted the traditional closed attitude: 'There is no danger: let's not panic.' This information policy led to a fiasco, and when the second manager's turn came, he adopted the opposite approach: 'Nobody is in control of the situation. But things are worse than that: nothing is working, and everything should be turned off, all the major systems and not just the one that broke down today. I would go so far as to add . . .

32. This is the author's experience; other consultants have a less positive view.
33. Interview with Péter-J. Hargitay in Lagadec, 1990, pp. 76–7.

Chapter 8

Attitudes and capacities for getting a grip on events

The 'emergency' level on the crisis has been dealt with. The situation has been stabilized and contained as far as possible. So, can you now go on the offensive?

First of all, you must arm yourself with the means to carry out in-depth analysis and intervention. You must also make sure you have some way of maintaining a critical distance. You will constantly have to remind yourself of this distance throughout the whole crisis.

Without these preparations and this permanent critical follow-up, you will not have the slightest chance of making your intervention 'bite'. A crisis is a slippery creature, and superficial attacks on it will be like water off a duck's back.

1 Arm yourself with an autonomous information-gathering capability.
2 Start thinking: distance yourself and ask questions.
3 Set up networks, lay the groundwork.
4 Prepare the ground for a decision-making and organizational capability.
5 Form a critical intelligence group to provide general support.
6 Try to draw up logical patterns of action.

Great care has been taken to deal with the extreme emergency, without making the situation worse through useless arm waving. Once again, the temptation is to act first and think later. Everything, in fact, is conducive to that line of action, from the distress of unbearable inactivity to the availability of resources that you are tempted to send to the scene of the disaster.

And yet, before entering the complicated maze of the crisis, you must pause for a moment, in order to gauge the size of the problem facing you. You must tackle the crisis in depth, not just its most obvious symptoms, and think through your response properly, instead of using your forces in a muddled fashion. Indeed, on a more general level, this critical distancing must become a permanent feature of your crisis management, until the entire episode is finally over.

If you attempt to avoid this preparation time and continuous process of critical distancing, you run the risk of never being able to grasp this inherently elusive and changeable problem fully. There will be a constant discrepancy between events and your interpretation of them; you will systematically lag behind the dynamic process of the crisis and you will be unable to identify the fundamental issues at stake. If you are consumed with impatience, just remember the words of Sun Tzu. Though he was talking about war, his words are just as relevant to a crisis: 'One who is good at martial arts overcomes other's forces without battle, conquers other's cities without siege . . .' (Sun Tzu, 1991, p. 19).

The problem with crises is that they may never offer battle at all, or they may present you with false battlefields. You must therefore bring some intellectual reflection to bear and summon up every available capability, if you want to attack the true heart of the crisis, what Sun Tzu (1991, p. 112) called 'the enemy strategy' when referring to warfare.

Here, it is not so much a case of implementing ready-made responses as formulating pertinent questions. It is not so much a case of finding the single decision maker and expert, as rapidly creating a series of 'backdrops' that will help you overcome the problems facing you. There is a realm of uncertainty in a crisis. There is no point in tiring yourself out trying to remedy one or another of its localized symptoms when, at the end of the day, this will have very little to do with the overall dynamics.

It goes without saying that you must spend as much time on this in-depth preparation as is warranted by the seriousness of the crisis. The more serious, complex and profound the crisis, the more time and energy you should devote to this temporary pause.

Developing independent information-gathering capacities

Faced with the unknown, the first thing you must do is find some means of systematically gathering information. As the Americans say, with matchless concision, 'Knowledge is power'.

We have already seen how important it is to pay attention to information-gathering from the very outset, in order to atone for the dearth of facts. Now this activity must be given a proper structure, to face not the initial event but the dynamics of a fully fledged crisis. As Yves Stourdzé (1979, pp. 126–30) writes, 'a catastrophic crisis manifests itself as a fantastic growth in the amount of information which is generated and drastically slows down the speed at which this information is broadcast and disseminated'. It is easy to see why very considerable abilities are needed in order to take up such a challenge.

Several types of information need to be gathered.

- Additional facts about the initial event: in particular, you need to find out if other hazards exist or whether the crisis is limited to the point that is directly posing problems (this is where we isolate the crisis).
- Facts about the effects of the events and the way they are changing.
- Facts about available reaction capabilities.
- Facts about the dynamic process of the crisis overall: the way it is being portrayed and the types of reactions it is triggering.
- The rumours being circulated (you must have this information in order to manage communications effectively).
- Information which, while not necessarily directly useful to leaders when they are taking decisions of a technical nature, may help them meet the needs of the media, whose needs differ from the needs of those directly involved.

This last point deserves to be emphasized,[1] as there will be a tendency to neglect these 'useless' details, even though they are vital if information is to be handled properly. Accordingly, the information-gathering team should not just comprise operational specialists, but should also include people who are familiar with the media and their needs.

You should take the precaution of gathering information from a variety of sources, including unofficial channels, which are often far swifter, as well as being more prompt to seize on variables lying outside the classic terms of reference. In particular, it can be useful to cultivate the media and 'independent' groups and networks, which are often very rapidly fed with information and rumours, thanks to the witnesses or correspondents ready to pick up on every anomaly. These correspondents, who often have very poor links with official sources, are more likely to inform the media (they are more likely to call the hotline of a major radio or television station than the prefecture or police) or groups known for their independent action. Once again, this approach is very much out of the ordinary, and this sort of suggestion, in context, can be seen as an aberration, nothing short of provocation ('Ask your enemy for information?'). Yet again, it is all a question of judgement. When you are running an organization, you have to make sure you do not become a prisoner of the besieged fortress model.

A point of method needs to be underlined at this stage. It is vital that this information-gathering capability be clearly distinguished from the decision-making function proper. Otherwise, information which seems too difficult to act on may well be rapidly swept aside. In other words, the task of the information-gathering team is to provide the best possible information, not to decide how to react to this information. Nor is its role to assess this information. It is not required to make value judgements or carry out any specific appraisal. Its job is to tell the decision-maker what is happening, what is being done and said and, most of all, which rumours are circulating.

Note too that if an information-gathering team is to do its work properly, it must be completely familiar with the issues worrying the decision-maker. There must never be any weaknesses in the link between in-depth thinking about the crisis and the search for information.[2]

Lastly, let us look at a question that it would be cowardly to ignore— namely, the ethical problems that can arise when looking for information in crises where there is conflict. Just how far can you go in the sort of methods you use to find out the strategies of the other actors? This confronts us with a general problem, as this ethical question concerns many levels of crisis management. With this in mind, note that there are two radically opposed ideas on how to deal with crises: 'A crisis is not a war'[3]; and the strictly opposite opinion, whether expressed or not, that is held by many people involved in crisis management. At the very least, we must all adopt our own values and be ready to defend them.[4] I say at the very least, because it is not at all certain that companies and, more generally, democratic societies can do without some form of collective thinking on this subject.

Opening the thought process: asking questions, getting distance

Although everything encourages you to look for rapid solutions, you must sit down and start to think—perhaps we should say, force yourself to think.

> *Philippe Legorjus: How to think in the heat of an operation*
> As for me, my main task is to calm people down, all the while trying to decide which decision maker will be able to provide concrete help later on—in negotiations, for instance. The most important thing of all to remember is that *crisis management is first and foremost about finding ways to think through the situation, even in the heat of the action.*
> (Legorjus, 1990, p. 91—our emphasis)

> *Henry Kissinger: Failure through not asking questions (war in the Middle East, 6 October 1973)*
> At the latest on October 5, as we learned of the Soviets' evacuation of their dependents from the Middle East, we should have known that big events were impending. We uncritically accepted the Israeli assessment that the reason was either a crisis in relations with Egypt and Syria or the result of a Soviet assessment that hostilities may break out in the Middle East. But the only danger of hostilities foreseen lay in the 'action-reaction cycle': each side's fear that its adversary was about to attack. There were questions crying to be asked that would have rapidly reached the heart of the matter. That they occurred to no one, including me, seems inexplicable in retrospect. What crisis could possibly occur in Soviet-Arab relations that involved *both* Egypt and Syria simultaneously? Why would the Soviets evacuate dependents but not the advisers if there was a political crisis? Why would they undertake an emergency airlift if they were not working against a deadline? And what could the deadline be other than the opening of hostilities? The Israeli view that the Soviets might fear the outbreak of war should have given us pause. For if we had reflected, it would have been clear that Soviets could not be fearing an *Israeli* attack. Had they done so they would have made urgent representations in Washington to get us to dissuade Israel, and perhaps added public threats. If the Soviets evacuated dependents because they feared a war, they must have had a very good idea that it would be started by the Arabs. Policymakers cannot hide behind their analysts if they miss the essence of an issue. They can never know all the facts, but they have the duty to ask the right questions. That was the real failure on the eve of the Mideast war. We had become too complacent about our own assumptions. We knew everything but understood too little. And

for that the highest officials—including me—must assume
responsibility.

(Kissinger, 1982, Vol. 2, p. 466)

Yet asking questions is the last thing the person in charge will want
to do when absorbed in the action. The uncertainties and the
complexities involved, the danger and the urgency of the situation
all encourage that person to close his or her mind. Yet nothing
pertinent can be done in a crisis without an understanding of the
deep-seated forces behind the dynamics of the events. Questions
need to be asked about the true nature of the crisis and the surprises
it may have in store. What are the successive ground swells that may
come crashing against our defences? Which phenomena may
suddenly surface and strengthen the dynamic process of this crisis?
What traps might we fall into? Up which blind alleys are we likely to
find ourselves?

There is something tragic about this need to ask questions. Why
can't we just go by appearances? Why can't we allow ourselves to be
reassured or swept along by events without constantly and endlessly
having to ask painful questions?

> *As the confrontation starts to go badly for Israel (9 October*
> *1973) Henry Kissinger is dumbfounded*
> By the end of the third day of the war we went to bed expecting
> a repeat of the Six Day War of 1967. But the gods are offended
> by hubris. They resent the presumption that great events can be
> taken for granted. Historic changes such as we sought cannot
> be brought off by virtuoso performances; they must reflect an
> underlying reality. And that reality caught up with us in the
> middle of that night.
>
> [Israeli Ambassador to the United States] Dinitz phoned me at
> 1.45 a.m., shortly after I had gone to sleep, waking me with a
> puzzling question. What could we do about resupply? I was
> baffled. By this prognosis of only a few hours earlier, the battle
> should be turning at about this time toward a decisive victory.
> What then was the problem? I told Dinitz that we would talk first
> thing in the morning, and I went to bed.
>
> At 3.00 a.m., Dinitz called again with essentially the same urgent
> message. Unless he wanted to prove to the cabinet that he could
> get me out of bed at will, something was wrong.
>
> (Kissinger, 1982, Vol. 2, p. 491)

Crises and fundamental breeches in the system cannot be remedied
by conjuring tricks. At most, superficial tactical action can circumvent
them. If pressing reasons force you not to deal with the problem but
merely to sidestep it, questions must have been asked beforehand.

The guiding principle is this: it is not a question of being able to foresee everything, but of being able to set up sensors and criteria for analysis capable of adapting in a big way to the unexpected.

You must look at several lines of action.

Grasping the immediate context

Our first question concerns the capabilities you have at your disposal for short- and medium-term resistance as you face the ordeal. What preparation have the organizations directly responsible made to cope with emergencies and crises? How good are existing emergency plans? Have organizations developed any procedures for working together in this field? Have relations based on trust been developed with the outside world? Are the opposition journalists, experts, leaders or public opinion, political leaders and civil servants already known to the organizations involved or will most of them only make their appearance once the crisis has hit?

A second line of thought consists in drawing up a strategic map showing the exact context of the crisis. At the very least, you must ask yourself the following three questions, based on Allison's models:

1 What are the prime objectives of the main actors involved?
2 How are the major bodies likely to be affected by the crisis, in terms of their procedures, capabilities, limits and interrelations?
3 What roles are the leaders going to play in the crisis? Leaders may include people in charge of giving orders in the various bodies involved in the crisis; outside personalities, experts, potential scapegoats, self-designated scapegoats.

You must not restrict your thinking to these frameworks, however. After all, you may be confronted by actors who are totally foreign to the classic sphere of reference (e.g. an expert from the other side of the world, a major charismatic figure) or a leaderless social movement. Clearly, each organization must examine these questions in some considerable depth beforehand.

Breaking out of immediate representations

As a reaction to the event and the void it creates, those in charge are immediately inundated with answers, meanings and explanations.

This is done precisely to fill these voids at all costs, as they lead to individual anxiety and destabilize organizations.

People need to lighten the psychological burden the crisis has thrust upon them. The best way of doing this is to convince themselves that, when all is said and done, 'it's not as bad as that': 'it's just given everyone a good fright', or 'we got into a state over nothing'.

Organizations are afraid of voids, but more than anything, they cannot bear to see landmarks, such as borders, attributions, powers, functions and objectives, suddenly vanish. When it attacks these landmarks, the crisis attacks the very basis of their identity. Organizations will do everything they can to mask these unbearable threats.

From that moment onwards, individuals and organizations alike will come up with a great many optimistic interpretations and pieces of information. These may be motivated chiefly by the desire to avoid any questioning of existing balances, interests and ways of thinking.

At this point, the people in charge must display boldness and stubborn vigilance. They must turn their backs on these very tempting reflections and 'proofs' that would be so very convenient to them and to all their partners and would reassure the system. They must make people understand that they will refuse to accept certain facts that seem to suit everyone too well.

'Anything convenient is suspicious', could be a key motto here.

If, following a second analysis, these favourable facts are confirmed, the refusal made on principle could be changed into a simple vigilance. This is the central message of the head of emergency services during the Mississauga catastrophe.

> Chief Burrows, Mississauga (10 November 1979)
> . . . one thing you should never do is make assumptions. For example, if I had believed the people who said the chlorine tanker wasn't in the derailed portion of the train, a real disaster could have resulted. When you arrive on a scene, never assume what you are being told is accurate. Always check the facts as much as you possibly can, then make your own decision.[5]

One important point must be added, however. While efforts must be made to treat events as they actually are (and not as seen through rose-coloured spectacles), this must be done without destroying one's organization. Asking questions incessantly can become almost unbearable. Systematically keeping a critical distance can represent a trial far beyond the strength of any of us. Péter-J. Hargitay gave this clear message[6]:

> It is impossible to measure the frenzy with which those who are immersed in a crisis and who receive a constant stream of vague and depressing news clutch at the slightest straw . . . You devour every crumb of reassuring news—these crumbs become your survival rations. You would die to hear some good news. From a psychological point of view, you need to believe in it. You are in an ocean of negativity. You have a vital need for good news. Whence the true danger of being blinded by it.

It is therefore important to bear in mind that in the event of a major disruption, the person in charge will be under considerable pressure to use supposedly indisputable facts to reassure the system as a whole at all costs. The person in charge must therefore look upon this natural tendency as one of the pitfalls of the crisis and avoid falling into its trap. That person will be spared nothing:

- biased, or at the very least, insufficiently verified information coming from the scene of the disaster;
- convenient and ready-made interpretation models based on past experiences;

> Increases in set (rigid expectations)—which are likely in a crisis—decrease the probability of adaptive solutions through the overemphasis of similarities between the present and past situations . . . Be skeptical of 'solutions' transferred from other situations exclusively for the reason that they 'worked' in prior cases. Be careful of 'facts' in the present situation which seem to suggest that the previous situation is exactly like the present one. If there are no basic similarities, screen out the reference.
> (Milburn, 1972, p. 274)

- words of apparently good sense difficult to call into question;
- the pernicious idea, as we have seen with Janis, that anybody questioning this 'good sense' no longer deserves to belong to a team which must display a positive spirit and a determination to win.

One vital question that must not be forgotten in an emergency concerns time in a crisis, together with the deadlines—real or imagined—that crisis imposes. To find an answer to this, you will often have to begin by questioning your perception of the minimum deadlines available. We have already seen that everything conspires to shorten perceived time. You must therefore think very carefully about whether an intervention should take place within the hour, during the day or during the month. Very often, you will have to show that you have a whole day to take a decision, not just two hours, or a week rather than just one day.

If the leader is to pose all these questions, then that person must display a considerable personal capacity for leadership.[7] At the very least, leaders must take note of any information the group cannot make explicit and act accordingly. For example, while asking for information to be cross-checked, to make it more reliable, the leader will enthuse the teams by showing them just how far they have already come, fixing intermediate goals and chalking up their partial victories over the crisis.[8]

In addition, as we shall see in the final point of this chapter, the leader can draw support from an intelligence group or think tank whose job is precisely to pose non-stop questions that are too difficult for those directly involved in the incident.

Wondering about the background and the general context

In highly complex crises especially, think about the type of things that may surface during this episode—what may suddenly come to light?

Many questions need to be asked about the sector itself, especially its past, and the person in charge must not be the last to identify them.

1 What justification is there for the choices that have been made in that particular sector? What are the major references and images associated with it?
2 What are the precedents, the speeches given in the past on the subject, the guarantees that may have been given about safety in this field? Any assertion that there is no risk whatsoever will be a time bomb that can be expected to blow up quite rapidly, inflicting a dramatic loss of credibility on those in charge.
3 What abilities, both positive and negative, have been displayed in the past for dealing with episodes of this sort?

As for the general context, it is a good idea to look for every fault line, both close and distant. As we have already seen, every crisis tends to feed on them, so it is important to identify them.

In other words, it is important to start asking questions that are not just limited to the simple technical and logistical aspects of the intervention but take the overall universe of the crisis into account.

Anticipating

The leader must ceaselessly ask himself: What else can happen? What can happen tomorrow, the day after tomorrow, next week, next month?

Yet, this is not a natural process. As Thomas Milburn (1972, p. 274) reminds us:

> The more severe the crisis, the more foreshortened become the decision makers' perceptions of time . . . Attempt to look beyond the crisis. Anticipate future relations and long-term consequences. Avoid contractions of time perspective and over-emphasis on those things likely to occur in the immediate future.

As we have seen, several things conspire to prevent you from extending your reference framework.

- Urgent problems cloud your ability to think straight.
- The group or groups at work prefer not to think about possible developments, as the tendency is to seek reassurance rather than to play at being prophets of doom (we find the same leitmotivs as those listed above concerning the transmission of optimistic information).
- Everyone is used to dealing with accidents rather than crises. It is the long run that is important here, not immediate and visible difficulties.

Anticipating the nature and framework of the commitments that will have to be made is one of the essential strategic tasks. Otherwise, there is a risk of only ever tackling the shadow and the effects of the crisis. People often observe that, during a crisis, only the problems of the previous day are actually tackled, as they only become apparent the following day.

Here are some illustrations of this difficulty in anticipating, and the questions that need to be asked—in spite of everything.

> The shipwreck of the Mont-Louis (25 August 1985)
> The boat sank off the coast of Ostende, carrying drums containing uranium hexafluoride. The question asked in anticipation was, 'Wouldn't it be wise to approach the Belgian authorities quickly?' The reflex reaction from the crisis team was, 'We have enough problems already with French

organizations.' As a result, a few hours later, the Belgian Minister of the Environment made a statement on French-language radio to the effect that the drums surely contained nuclear materials, that as usual the French authorities had told him nothing, but that he was certain there was no danger. These are the same types of reflexes: 'I don't know what's going on, but don't worry, it's nothing serious.'

(Lagadec, 1990, pp. 30-2)

The case of the waste drums of Seveso (1982-1983)[9]
What would people do once the Seveso drums had been found, wherever they were? When the drums were still lost and everyone was hunting madly for them, the question seemed irrelevant: yet it was vital, and it required an answer urgently . . . some individuals were thinking, though not too seriously, of secretly recovering the drums in order to spirit them off to a secret site. This is exactly the type of behaviour that must be avoided at all costs. Nobody needs secrecy in a matter that is only kept alive by secrecy, which feeds rumours and fantasy. What is needed, to the contrary, are perfectly open procedures that can deflate rumours and stabilize a sorely tried system. The waste drums had to be recovered by the manufacturer, under government control.

The problem of the drum of lindane, lost in the English Channel on 13 March 1989, following the sinking of the Pérentis
A question raised during the frantic search for the drum: 'And what line do we take if we can't find it?'

Building a groundwork for the system

In order to lay the basis for future assessment—particularly the assessment of variations from the norm—it is often good to get a clear idea from the start of the way the system was before everything started to change. It is important, for instance, to recall that in the case of the *Amoco-Cadiz* oil slick, scientists bitterly regretted the absence of the information they needed to establish diagnoses. Naturally, it is a bit late, once the crisis is in full swing, to be laying these foundations. However, if no foundations already exist, information immediately available can still be sought and, if the crisis does not unfold too rapidly, investigations which fit into the prevailing deadlines can still be launched.

Joseph Scanlon emphasizes in particular just how important it is to have foundations relating to the state of public opinion and to conduct rapid studies during the crisis. The reasoning is as follows: it is vital for the people in charge not to depend solely on the media's presentation of public opinion. Decision makers must have their own measurement instruments. If studies were undertaken before the events took place, the major discrepancies—i.e. the important ones—can be pinpointed within 24 hours by using a tiny sample. Within 48 hours, a more accurate view of the way people's perceptions are changing can be obtained. This is an indispensable weapon when it becomes necessary to reject exaggerated comments on the trauma supposedly caused by the event. This presupposes preliminary work with a specialized institute, prepared samples, questionnaires that have already been used, and so forth.

> *Johnson & Johnson, the Tylenol case*
> Johnson & Johnson's executives did not rely on instinct alone for their decisions. From the very first day, surveys were taken to obtain concrete, expedient feedback on company actions and to track the awareness and depth of public attitudes towards the product. Johnson & Johnson hired independent research organizations to conduct daily polls, particularly aimed at learning what the consumers were thinking. [Questionnaires] were initially intended to assess the magnitude of the problem. Later they were used to estimate the willingness of the public to once again use Tylenol capsules in a safer package.
>
> These data on public opinion were analysed every day. It quickly became apparent that most people had confidence in both the company and the product.
>
> (ten Berge, 1990, pp. 25-6)

Opening the networks: creating a backdrop

Faced with the initial shock, your natural instinct will be to withdraw into yourself. Yet you must follow exactly the opposite path. You must build up wider reaction capabilities, and do so before it becomes an absolute emergency from which there is no escape. In crisis management, therefore, one of your priorities must be to open up communication channels as soon as possible.

> *Crash of an Airbus A-320 at Habsheim (Sunday 26 June 1988)*[10]
> The author was able to observe closely the reactions of one of the heads of the civil aviation division (DGAC) who belongs to its crisis unit. Before leaving home, he had already mobilized the personnel whose job it was to help in aviation emergencies. As soon as he arrived at the DGAC, he began to open up communication channels, while carrying out other crisis management tasks at the same time. He called up pilot trade unions, along with the heads of the other European and

American aviation services (this is where a first-class
knowledge of the network is precious, as it means being able to
contact one's American counterpart on a Sunday at his home).

The theme of the conversation was on these lines: 'We don't
have much information to go on yet, but here is what we know.
Naturally, we don't want to influence your reactions, we just
want to be able to reach you in a hurry. We will keep you
informed as soon as there is something new, so please tell us
how we can stay in contact with you over the hours and days to
come (today we have an accident, tomorrow we may have a
crisis). This is how you can reach me if you need to.' Once he
had called up several contacts, the director could be sure of one
thing at least: 'I now have my basis, on which I will be able to
work if the situation demands it.'

It must be remembered that setting up a network is not a natural
attitude. At that particular instant, it is more comfortable to sit back
and wait for certainties and reassuring news, before putting people
in the picture and making oneself more vulnerable. And yet the
action described above represents the positive attitude.

This field contains a number of classic pitfalls.

- You hesitate to call on high-ranking leaders. The reflex not to
  make that call is often a very strong one, along the lines of: 'a
  lieutenant does not wake a general'. Where necessary, and above
  all when you are dealing with an unfamiliar organization, do not
  hesitate to check the role of your contact and to turn to his or her
  superiors instead, if necessary.

  *Philippe Vesseron: Mistakes in handling the case of the waste
  drums of Seveso*
  The first [mistake] was to keep our original contact at Hoffmann-
  La Roche, without wondering about his position within the
  company. Large corporations, like large bureaucracies, are by
  definition complex systems, with their own internal problems.
  Things would certainly have evolved differently if we had
  pushed for the implication of Hoffmann-La Roche's president as
  early as December 1982.[11]

- On the other hand, people often assume that a structure is
  mobilized because they have talked with its leaders, or that things
  will get sorted out afterwards. Allison's organizational model must
  not be forgotten: organizations have a complex life of their own,
  and this type of assurance may well turn out to be unfounded.
  Worse still: wanting to do it via the people at the top can give rise
  to immediate crises from which it is difficult to extricate oneself.

As a general rule, networks comprising all the essential actors must be set up in order to handle the situation and all its possible developments—without forgetting victims, trades unions, journalists, and so on, and with a determination to establish these communication channels before being forced to do so.

Naturally, this can pose tremendous selection problems. The lesson is clear: all those who are likely to make a valuable contribution in these circumstances must have been tracked down and included in some kind of network beforehand. Once the crisis has arisen, all that will be needed will be an effort of imagination to think of additional actors, and even a few wild cards, whom it is important to include in the basic group.

As we have already seen in the above example, the purpose of this procedure is not to take control of these networks, but to become a partner in the situation. This is the only base from which you will be able to open up a negotiating space and create systems of dialogue and exchange of information.

If it is undertaken without delay, this initiative will considerably enhance the quality of the relations between the actors and will strengthen trust and the desire to work together. In the worst scenario, it will at least hold out a slender hope of dialogue. While the natural tendency in a crisis is to become suspicious of other people, close links must be established as soon as possible in order to prevent this happening, as it may well undermine all future action.

Lastly, one must not forget the diametrically opposed problem that always arises in a crisis situation, namely, the massive influx of people wanting to help and the avalanche of offers of advice, suggestions and 'good ideas'. When dealing with ideas, it is very important to sift through them. They can not all be rejected *en masse*, and they may contain judicious suggestions.[12] This sifting must be carried out with sensitivity, in order to avoid unnecessary ill feeling. As to the integration of people and networks into the crisis management units and systems, you will once more need all your powers of judgement. The basic rule is to avoid at all costs turning decision-making and assessment structures—which must remain effective (presupposing a small number of participants)—into discussion forums, which contribute nothing to the handling of the crisis. On this point, D. K. Burrows is absolutely adamant.

Chief D. K. Burrows refuses to throw open crisis unit membership
If we learned one thing [in Mississauga], it was that in such a large scale operation, you must separate those with responsibility and expertise from those without. Everyone wants to be in the think-tank sessions, but that simply isn't possible, because it slows down the decision-making process. [. . .] You don't want people converging on the scene just to get their names in the papers.

The next point is to assign people to deal with those who are not in the think-tank, and especially with the media. You should have a place set aside for them, where they may be informed but kept apart from the people in the think-tank.

The same goes for politicians without responsibilities. The politicians are naturally in a difficult position, as the media always descend on them, trying to get whatever information they can out of them. A police officer should look after them, like the media, but not allow them to have access to the think-tank unless it was clear they had some responsibility or expertise. In most large-scale disasters, you're going to have a great many people arriving whom you're not prepared to receive. You don't have time to be bothered with people who are there just to see or be seen. You must have people assigned to look after them and give them as much information as you can. You can't have people walking in and out of think-tank sessions and then speaking to the media, because information that reaches the media this way can be inaccurate and cause panic.[13]

Hence, once more, you must be ready to make one or two relevant adjustments. It can be vitally important to open up decision-making channels to outside figures or organizations, including victims and opponents, especially if the main problem you encounter hinges on the credibility of your diagnosis and the acceptability of the measures you have adopted. Naturally, however, as we have just mentioned, this opening-up must not get out of hand. This type of special integration can also take place within an advisory group, as is proposed in a later section of this chapter.

Laying the groundwork for decision making

Two things are required here: first, of course, an authoritative framework, providing one can be defined; secondly, and more problematically, a system operating on the basis of support and cooperation.

Setting the framework for authority to curtail confusion

It will often be useful to strengthen certain systems, by clarifying the duties and lines of authority that could provide the framework for a large system of intervention.

> *Marc Becam, Amoco Cadiz, 24 March 1978*
> In order to overcome a definite inertia, Marc Becam, Secretary of State for Local Authorities, in charge of civil protection, sent all the 20 organizations involved the following telex, which represented a first in France: 'The Prime Minister has made me responsible for directing all the emergency operations carried out under the Polmar Plan (to combat accidental water pollution). I am therefore entrusting the operational management of the plan to the national civil protection board. Stop. In my absence, all orders from the head of Civil Protection, Monsieur Gérondeau, and his deputy, Monsieur di Chiara, are to be regarded as my own personal orders and carried out immediately. Signed: Marc Becam.'[14]

Building a system for cooperation, dynamics for belonging

Strict hierarchies and lines of authority cannot always guarantee a real capacity for action. In many cases, nothing can be imposed when the resistance of the services is too strong or when you are working alongside actors who have nothing to do with normal systems of authority, such as independent groups and foreigners. The correct strategy here is to build up a system of cooperation as quickly as possible and to weave close links between the various decision-making centres involved. The notion of order and authority must be replaced by that of mobilization for a common cause.

The change is a major one. The various headquarters must share not only their optimism but also their doubts. They must ask questions about the crisis and look together at preventive measures to devise, initiatives to take and mistakes to avoid.

Both trust and a willingness to cooperate between decision makers are vital, if proper crisis management is to be commenced and continued throughout the episode.

You will find it easier to make people accept this vision of cooperation if you distance yourself from the notion that exercise of authority is simply about 'giving orders'. In a crisis situation, the decision-making function must be firmly rooted in the capability to gather and redistribute:

- information
- intelligence
- power
- resources.

It is the capacity to redistribute these essential commodities that makes it possible to be recognized as having authority and to exert it effectively. This is the process that can stimulate what a crisis calls for most—namely, support.

Here, once more, those involved must be prepared beforehand, both intellectually and culturally. It is no easy matter to slip into a multipolar universe which presupposes the genuine ability to assume varying types of responsibility. Where there is no impetus whatsoever, anyone involved may well drop out very quickly, with the excuse that the system lacks clarity and that only the good old reference models, the fruit of strict hierarchy and absolute obedience, can possibly improve the situation.

Those in charge must also be thoroughly prepared. It will no longer be enough to remind each person of his or her duty to obey and note any shortcoming in this respect, if orders on paper have not been carried out.

Basic support: the critical watchdog group

A contradiction will gradually emerge. In order to handle a crisis, the decision makers not only need a spirit of decision, faith in their analyses and confidence in their chances of success; they must also bring an element of doubt and a certain amount of critical wisdom.

In the most difficult cases, the mission is impossible and the outlook dangerous. There is a risk of turning the decision makers, who have to be people of action, into nitpicking analysts. At this point, it is therefore a good idea to separate these two roles. This means adding a system of critical analysis to the response system to act as a backup to the central management function. This does not mean replacing the decision makers with a commission. The jobs of the former remain intact. No one can replace them: their job is to take decisions and to take responsibility for any ambiguity. They are also the people who, as the main actors, will probably have the truest overview of the situation. However, they can be helped significantly if a particular group is given the task of assuming most of the work of critical intelligence.

Throughout the crisis, it is vital to have intelligence capabilities at your disposal, which can define the true nature of the situation and its risks and continuously ask questions about events and the way they are being handled. Questions need to be asked about the following in particular:

- the stated diagnoses
- the solutions put forward
- the major positions adopted in the face of the breakdown (the way the risk is assessed, the way responsibilities are assumed, the assurance given, and so on)
- the possible ways of developing the procedures that have been put in motion (regarding both the current dynamics of the event and the memories it stirs of past experiences)
- the initiatives already taken and needing to be taken
- mistakes both past and future
- the actors and networks that will play a part either immediately or later
- the possible outcome of the crisis
- the precedents that may be established during the handling of the crisis
- the worst possible scenarios imaginable: they will probably not happen but the exercise will be good preparation for less serious situations that will arise, and assurance in the event of misfortune.

In short, you must maintain a critical distance the whole time, vis-à-vis information received and given, decisions taken and actual intervention. This will enable you to avoid pitfalls due to a narrow and static reading of the problem posed or the action launched to deal with it.

Besides this additional analysis, a capability such as this (a localized team or a network that is easy to mobilize) can provide the reassurance that those directly involved badly need. When they venture forth into uncharted territory, they know that a broadly-based group of competent people will be covering them intellectually, so to speak.

We have stressed from the very outset that there is no question of depriving the decision maker of any prerogatives. Equally, care must also be taken to distinguish clearly the intelligence capability from the actual decision-making role. The job of the intelligence team is to help those in charge take decisions and not to take them itself. If this is not the case, it, too, will confront the same two handicaps as the information-gathering teams. First, any information that seems too difficult to act upon may get swept aside. Secondly, its critical function may lose some of its vigour. In other words, the mandate of the critical intelligence team must be to ask the best questions, not to find the most comforting answers and assurances.

How should this group or network be set up?

One possibility is to select a few people from the crisis group that has already been set up and to give them this task of critical reflection. Another, more ambitious, method is to set up a proper team. This would ideally boast a variety of skills, experience and cultures, so instead of choosing the heads of each division or office (to avoid offending anyone's susceptibilities and respect orders of precedence), you would choose those people who were the most valuable in this type of situation: the chairperson would therefore be a brilliant head of public relations with a good knowledge of the social context; there might be a legal expert who was accustomed to dealing with crisis problems; and someone who 'knew everything' about the subject (e.g. a computer whizzkid in the case of an information systems crisis, boasting the important combination of knowledge and cleverness). A good place to find the right people would doubtless be a group in charge of strategic planning (if such a thing exists in-house). This is because its members are used to thinking about issues in an uncertain and multi-faceted environment. In addition, as they are known to the structure, the exchange of information between the critical intelligence group and the rest of the organization will be far easier.

Two other criteria which need to be taken into account (and which are met by top-quality planning groups) are those of legitimacy and familiarity. The group must have a firm grasp on events and enjoy long-standing links with the organization. If it does not receive any recognition and if no one is in the habit of feeding it with information, it will remain isolated during the crisis and will rapidly become a millstone around the system's neck and a complete waste of time.

The intelligence group we advocate can be built up around this core. Care must be taken to bring new people into this analysis group. It is precisely here that it will be possible to bring in key actors who do not directly belong to the system. These will preferably be people from outside, who already know the institution in question but who are sufficiently independent from it to retain an entirely free and critical mind.

In certain crises, it will be possible to include victims and opponents, providing they do not display a deliberate desire for radical opposition. This initiative is not, of course, entirely without danger (nothing ever is in crisis management). Actors from outside may attempt to block the system, and they may publicly declaim against the cynical reasons for including them ('You're only bringing us in to muzzle us for the future'). However, situations do not always end in stalemate, and not all overtures are motivated by cynicism. This question is already familiar with regard to information: providing too much information for journalists to handle and populations to absorb can also be a deliberate strategy and could be denounced as a cynical move, but it does not mean to say that the information should necessarily be rejected out of hand. Each actor needs to display good judgement and a sense of civic responsibility.

In a democracy, and providing the crisis is not a virtual military operation ('A military operation involves deception', according to Sun Tzu [1991], p. 6), the idea of including people from outside in assessment groups can be seen as something positive.

In any event, a certain degree of exteriority is a necessity if one is to avoid the 'in-house' mentality that is especially acute in a crisis situation (cf. the arguments put forward by Janis which were discussed here earlier). Moreover, Yves Stourdzé has successfully pinpointed the difficulty of only using 'in-house' analysts:

> The classic systems of interpretation which have avoided being swept away by the information technology shock wave try to pile up information in order to prove the validity of their subsequent strategies. The field of information takes on a most unusual configuration, becoming a huge, confused and fragmented mass. The classic instruments of information processing continue to operate mechanically, in accordance with the lines of interpretation which appear the most favourable to their own defence.
>
> (Stourdzé, 1979, p. 128)

On this subject, Péter-J. Hargitay recalls the action of Union Carbide following Bhopal: 'They brought together a team comprising the best people in the world. I have rarely seen such a remarkable gathering of minds.'[15]

This group of people will immediately have to consider which major landmarks can best be used as a framework for strategic action. It is important for them to carry out some preliminary work in groups and practice seminars.

Here, it is useful reiterate the remark made by Yehezel Dror on the principles that should guide the activities of high-level political analysis groups and groups of experts. These bodies need a great deal of freedom of thought if they are to pose problems differently, question conventional paradigms, distance themselves from accepted dogma and rituals and devise and assess innovative options. In addition, they must have continual and direct access to the decision maker (Dror, 1988, pp. 282, 285).

Finding the patterns for action

One difficulty encountered during a crisis is the continual build-up of attacks and developments which, like a battering ram, can eventually wear down the fortitude and foresight of those in charge. There is a major risk of the entire response system becoming one huge echo chamber. Everyone will try to keep abreast of events, even though they have lost sight of their basic landmarks (a classic example of this is when people only act on what is being said or will be said in the press). The result is simply even greater chaos and confusion, as the crisis gains the upper hand.

In order to counter this risk, you must choose a certain number of essential landmarks, which will enable you to remain on course during the storm.

One lesson drawn from experience is 'it's important to have a logic, a guiding idea, flexible but solid enough to resist the ups and downs'.[16] The important thing is to draw up a set of basic rules governing the decision-making process, especially in situations marked with extreme uncertainty, constant change and general disarray.

Maurice Grimaud, Chief of Police on Paris in May 1968
When I saw the way events were going and realized that, henceforth, anything could happen, I adopted a guideline for myself that was of great help to me in getting through the weeks that followed. I knew that we had to get out of this chaos without faltering. I hadn't wanted to become chief of police, but since I had the job, there was no way I would abandon affairs of state to the street, i.e. to the mob. There, I took a firm and solid line that reassured me because it became so evident as soon as I had formulated it. The other term of my problem was to avoid letting

the disorder lead to an incident of bloodshed. It was reason as much as sentiment that dictated this language to me, because I knew that if one evening we had to comb the streets littered with burned-out cars and fallen trees to pick up the bodies of dozens of people killed in a shootout, that could very well signal the beginning of an adventure whose outcome no one could predict. I held the two ends of the chain firmly, and my behavior was fully inspired by this double conviction. Though it did not protect me fully from anxiety, it did give me a precious serenity in facing the minor twists and turns of this episode.

(Grimaud, 1977, pp. 135–6)

*Philippe Vesseron: The case of the waste drums of Seveso
(1982–1983)*
One of the guiding ideas was 'to remember that an industry leader is first and foremost responsible for evaluating the decisions made, for controlling their execution, and for reacting if something goes wrong'.[17]

Those in charge must devise these patterns for action case by case. The critical intelligence group, whose creation was advocated above, can play a vital supporting role here, especially if the search for suitable landmarks begins well before the crisis occurs. It must set to work rapidly, not to decide on basic options prematurely, but instead to pinpoint the various alternatives and to sketch a few basic outlines for the decision maker to work on.

The fundamental patterns in question concern the different types of rules needed in crisis management. These include rules on policy, on cooperation between the various actors, on the behaviour of an institution, on the handling of the crisis and on the way decisions are taken.

Political rules: values and references

The question posed by crisis management goes far beyond the classic problem of decision making. It is no longer a matter of making a system work as well as possible and of making the most of things within a framework of given policies. Nor is it any longer a matter of classic problem solving, which can be based on given rules, standards and objectives.

It is no longer a matter either of simply establishing goals, aims or objectives, as is generally said in order to distinguish between the roles of management and decision making. Instead, in a crisis situation, meaning must be reinjected, values and references defined, and standards and frameworks for appraisal established. These are the tasks that await the person in charge. Crisis management becomes crisis policy making.[18] It is this vital process of establishing regulatory factors that will enable the system to keep going through the crisis, holding a steady and consistent course.

This work is directly linked, of course, to the way you analyse the situation and what is really at stake. This is a tricky business, as it requires creativity in the delicate area of values. It means sifting through the jumble of nascent values to find those on which judgements can safely be based.

You will encounter yet another difficulty here, as values never emerge with perfect clarity. You will be faced with ambiguity and contradiction, for even though values come and go, you cannot lightly dismiss those that people see as fundamental. There is bound to be conflict, as not everyone recognizes the same values at the same time.

You will need to display discernment and decisiveness. Some people may prefer to fail in their handling of a crisis rather than espouse values they find unacceptable. Some people may decide that it is definitely not the right time to embark on this sort of discussion and that these fundamental questions are best left to one side. Some may choose to do everything possible to find a new set of values, while others may refuse to open the discussion on values that have always served well.

With every innovative option, you will always have to decide whether the challenge is justified and whether it can be sustained. How will you know if the chosen option is not or is no longer appropriate, judicious or acceptable?

A radical turning point will make it almost impossible to define these new reference values clearly. You can at least attempt to list a few negative commands, however, such as 'don't risk the future of mankind in order to save your country', or 'don't place your country in jeopardy in order to save your company or organization'. For the gravest of decisions, these could take the form of categorical imperatives such as: 'don't do anything that could reduce mankind's ability to survive'. Different imperatives could apply to less global levels. Indeed, this is what certain companies have attempted to do in drawing up their so-called basic charters. Sceptics will express doubts as to the seriousness of these references. Others will, on the contrary, see them as genuine attempts to establish a moral code to govern their actions.

Provided they are the fruit of collective research and discussions, these attempts will be interesting, if nothing else. For no one is the guardian of these values. Their development can only be a social process requiring plenty of time, as they are not deposited anywhere in a safe or a book ready for use when needed.

There is, of course, a contradiction between this necessarily social process of producing values and the relatively solitary and rapid action of the decision maker in a crisis situation. The least unsatisfactory response probably consists in carrying out preliminary work and holding meetings, in emergency situations, between varied groups of people trained to take on this sort of task. In this way, horizons are extended beyond the sensitivities and desires of a specific individual—even if that individual does happen to be the most senior person in charge.

Whatever the case, as soon as the crisis begins, a group with the job of providing greater insight into the situation, such as the one proposed earlier, will have to draw up working hypotheses on this level of crisis management. Its job will be to analyse the situation as broadly as possible, thereby ensuring that decisions are as enlightened as possible.

Rules for operating among actors

A large number of actors will intervene during the crisis. Even in situations that are not purely and simply about conflict, you will have to deal with clashes and handle relations between different groups. This is why patterns of behaviour also need to be drawn up.

Moderation, clarity, and communication in conflict

The following major principles (see Bell, 1978, pp. 53–5; Neuhold, 1978, pp. 4–18; Milburn, 1972, pp. 259–77) are lessons common to several international crises. They are doubtless of general value.

- Stick to a step-by-step involvement in the conflict: one of the lessons drawn from experience is that it is very easy to become sucked into an escalating conflict. Try to find anything that may add flexibility and prolong deadlines. Take particular care to avoid making irreversible commitments. This means keeping a very careful watch over the tools for intervention at your disposal.

- Take great care not to humiliate the opposing party; there should always be a safety valve (for crises involving conflict, a recognized principle is to be moderate in seeking gains).
- Keep channels of communication open with the opposing party: in a crisis situation, communication with your adversary (and more generally with your partners) must be maintained and even increased as the crisis deepens. As a general rule, communication between parties must be as unambiguous as possible (even if there are instances where deliberate ambiguity can turn out to be useful). So make sure you always express yourself with great restraint. Experience has shown that it is very difficult to maintain communications when the amount of in-house information to be handled never stops increasing. Hence the need for partners to envisage additional, specific means of communication. You should also take into account problems of mutual understanding due to different cultural backgrounds.
- Look for as wide a support base as possible. You must have both operational and moral support from other actors. This principle can run counter to the need for swift action. Interplay with the press and public opinion is also delicate, because of the time scales on which they operate and the interplay of the opposing party with this same domestic or international public opinion.

Breaking down barriers, validating partners

In order to resist the temptation of oversimplifying and of trying to concentrate all the powers on yourself, devise a plan involving every useful actor, despite the fact that 'in time of crisis, the natural tendency is to handle only what's most pressing'.[19] It is particularly important to bring in actors who may seem to be peripheral but whose involvement can improve the handling of the crisis. Give them specific roles. One actor often forgotten in the early days of a crisis is the judicial system.

> *Philippe Vesseron: The case of the waste drums of Seveso*
> In this business, the courts were only brought to the forefront after those tumultuous articles had appeared. They remained somewhat bitter about having been poorly informed from the start. Nothing is harder than rebuilding confidence when cooperation didn't exist before the crisis.[20]

On the other hand, in certain circumstances a decision maker may consider that while many actors should be offered openings, a different group, judged to hold extremist views, should be firmly excluded. This occurs especially in cases where such actors are of completely bad faith and have goals that have very little in common with the people fighting the crisis. Such groups can only be made partners to deal with the worst case scenarios. This is why it can be deemed totally unreasonable to offer them openings.

Rules for managing institutions

In every case, you will have to manoeuvre between two opposing lines of management.

Making the ordinary systems function

In a crisis situation, there is no question of getting rid of planned measures or of bypassing all the usual departments. On the contrary: existing institutions must be activated or reactivated, otherwise you will end up with a precarious pile of new measures and *ad hoc* committees added on at the last moment. In order to gain necessary recognition, these will have to embark on intestine and media wars, which will do nothing to improve the sturdiness of the structure as a whole.

If you choose this line of management, try to ensure that decision-making and management processes take place at the lowest possible level of the hierarchy. There is a natural tendency for crisis systems to become centralized immediately, losing all their intermediate levels in the process. This suddenly exposes the most senior ranks of management, leads to the loss of many skills and gives every incident repercussions that are not necessarily warranted.[21] Another disadvantage of immediate centralization is that it demobilizes those who are theoretically in charge of managing the system involved. This inevitably makes them feel bitter.

Hélène Denis: The fire at Saint-Basile-le-Grand, 23 August 1988
Even though the town council had not asked for a state of emergency to be decreed, it was very quickly deprived of its decision-making powers, so to speak, because of the intervention of political leaders and civil servants of all grades (the latter were sometimes known as 'the gang of savers'). [. . .] Some of the local people involved became somewhat disillusioned, even though they realized that they needed help from the provincial authorities. As they put it, 'You work your guts out to get something done, and as soon as you've succeeded, someone else comes along, gets all the medals and tells you to keep your mouth shut'.

(Denis, 1989, p. 23)

Do not hesitate to take firm initiatives with institutions

The opposite option can be defended just as stoutly: crises are often dramatized, according to this view, by the fact that the people whose job it is to tackle emergencies show themselves to be incapable of facing up to the situation. The leaders therefore have to take over the problems in a mad rush, at a time when the crisis is already beginning to look like a rout. Structures which have long shown a lack of initiative, imagination and flexibility, and which are already discredited before the episode because they have handled a previous crisis in what was perceived at least as a disastrous fashion, cannot be made to work.

Here once more, therefore, initiative and imagination will be required. *Ad hoc* institutions set up to deal with this type of situation must be activated, new entities must be set up and responsibility must be given to an outside organization to take charge of the crisis in desperate cases.

Let us now look at two different illustrations of this. Make sure you keep up a suitable critical distance, as these are not examples to follow but experiences that can teach us a number of lessons.

> *Three Mile Island: the setting up of a presidential commission of inquiry*
> The idea behind the setting up of this commission was that the group would reflect American civilian society as a whole. This explains the presence of a housewife, for example.
> (Kemeny et al., 1979, pp. 157–63)

> *The fire at Saint-Basile-le-Grand, 23 August 1988: the setting up of an international scientific committee*
> The uncertainty over the risks linked to the explosion and the population's distrust of the government led the authorities to set up an international committee of experts. This was probably a world first, as it was both a mechanism designed to fix new standards, and a democratic mechanism, including as it did experts selected by ordinary citizens. This was precisely what enabled such citizens to have confidence in the decision to return to their homes, confidence which had largely been eroded during the crisis, particularly by the (frequently contradictory) information they received. However, it did call into question the power of the in-house experts. If the expert committee represented a force, it was because of the consensus which arose from its deliberations. Caution is needed before repeating the experiment, as this type of mechanism needs a consensus of opinion [above all], which is difficult to achieve among experts, especially when they have been mandated by

different groups. In this particular case, the experts mandated by the citizens were known and respected by the other members of the committee.

(Denis, 1989, pp. 18–19)

The boycott of infant formula milk (Nestlé case 1973–84): the setting up of an independent high-level group
This is the well-known case of the boycott of Nestlé products, following a huge campaign over 'the milk which kills babies' and the harm caused by powdered milk in poor countries. It took Nestlé some time to shed its classic reaction to events such as these, namely caution and retreat behind its reputation. The crisis only got worse—in spite of court victories.

At last, the group adopted an innovation: it set up an external unit in Washington with considerable freedom in its actions (the Nestlé Coordination Center for Nutrition—NCCN) and followed a broad policy characterized by greater openness, the acknowledgement of its detractors, dialogue and initiatives. An independent group of experts was set up. It included several opponents and was placed under the presidency of a prestigious figure—Edmund Muskie, a former American Secretary of State.

Once moderate groups at least had recognized the legitimacy and worthiness of the partners brought in from the outside, Nestlé was able to gain the upper hand in the boycott, at least to a fair extent.

Let us now continue our study of various aspects of this institutional innovation by looking at the comments first of Edmund Muskie, then of Raphael Pagan, the NCCN chairman.[22]

Edmund Muskie

At a loss when facing controversy
Corporations know how to handle controversy arising in the legal field. They are basically at a loss when the issues are political and social. Their credibility and motivations may be questioned, yet they have no forum that provides them with procedures and assurances as to how their case will be examined: they cannot be sure that the objective truth will emerge or that the controversy can be resolved in an equitable manner. The powdered baby formula case developed outside the legal arena: there was no judge to interpret the law, no police to enforce it, and no lawmakers to amend it. Nestlé chose unilaterally to apply World Health Organization recommendations and invited a group of eminent figures to form a commission that would determine whether the Swiss corporation's practices complied with what it was saying in public.

Creating an independent commission

The commission was set up after intense negotiations between Nestlé and the individuals chosen to belong to it. The key to these negotiations was finding a way to ensure the commission's independence. This was done by making written assurances, by establishing various procedures (e.g. offering access to all the corporation's files and to its personnel, allowing the commission to bring in specialists, letting it perform on-site investigations, and allowing the reports to be published), by providing sufficient resources to the commission without strings attached by Nestlé, and by appointing respected and independent members. The first nominations negotiated by Nestlé involved high-profile figures from the fields of medicine, religion, and ethics who were experienced in dealing with public controversy. Additional members were brought in later by the commission itself, in consultation with Nestlé.

The commission was ignored at first by the groups supporting the boycott, and they refused to submit their grievances to it. During its first three months of activity, the organization established its rules of conduct: it studied WHO's recommendations and the medical, social, and legal issues related to its task; it developed constructive relations with WHO, UNICEF and other groups; opened lines of communication with the groups supporting the boycott; and negotiated with Nestlé to have it change the marketing instructions it issued, in order to ensure better conformity with WHO recommendations. The first contacts between the commission and some militant groups and the media were marked by conflict, as it was often suggested that a commission financed by Nestlé could not be independent. Nonetheless, the commission remained accessible to these groups and made sure not to do anything that could be interpreted as lacking of objectivity. Gradually, it earned understanding, acceptance, and even respect.

The roles the commission played
- It performed a public audit. This was useful to Nestlé, which had been unable to convince the outside that the group was complying with WHO rules.
- It provided advice. This helped assuage scientific uncertainty and the ambiguous points in the WHO reference recommendations.
- It applied pressure on Nestlé personnel, who were spread around 140 countries and were hardly inclined spontaneously to give up tried and proved marketing practices that were still used by the competition.

This work resulted in the publication of quarterly reports that highlighted the extent, for each grievance, to which Nestlé had or had not observed the WHO rules—rules that often had to be interpreted because they were vague or irrelevant.

The commission also investigated heavily in Third-World countries. In June 1983, it organized a conference open to the public. At this event, experts from both sides could be heard.

This work allowed the commission to establish its credibility, to strengthen Nestlé's position on several of the issues, to elucidate the complexity of the problems in light of the clichés and simplistic arguments being wielded, and to create an atmosphere in which Nestlé could dialogue with its detractors. The commission carefully remained within the expert role, staying above the fray. It was able to soothe the concerns of well-intentioned individuals, though it had less success with the radical critics.

Factors behind the commission's success
- *Independence*: this was the most important factor. The commission could not deny that it had been created at Nestlé's instigation or that the corporation was the source of its finances. But it had the will and the means to be autonomous, and it managed to be judged on its results rather than its origins.
- *The company's commitment:* Nestlé's top management was involved in the process. This gave meaning to the commission's efforts.
- *The members selected*: another important factor was the balanced mix of skills and personalities, characterized by a concern for independence, integrity, objectivity, and commitment to the issues.
- *Leadership*: the commission was given free rein. This meant it did not need to adopt a defensive posture that would have placed it at the mercy of various actors, including those who wanted to see it fail. Similarly, it had to take intiative with Nestlé in order to persuade the company to make the changes that were called for.
- *A reference document*: whatever criticisms could be made of the WHO recommendations, the document provided an international reference base.

A few lessons
- The corporation must seize the initiative, and it must do so early on. This doesn't require a spectacular gesture, but it should anticipate large-scale controversy and prepare for it.
- The corporation must not simply counter its opponents; it must also consider whether their concerns are legitimate. Paying attention early to legitimate problems can avoid the horror stories used by critics to exaggerate the issues and win otherwise moderate individuals.
- The corporation must try to understand the different aspects of the problem and to provide information to the public before the case becomes acute and the company is perceived in a very negative light by the public.

- The response made must be adapted on a case-by-case basis. Nestlé and its commission may not always be a model to follow.

The dangers
Turning to an independent commission raises one serious potential danger. The commission may disagree with the company, or it may adopt recommendations that put the company in a difficult position with regard to its competitors. The commission may also lack sufficient authority to win the respect of the public and official organizations. The corporation cannot dismiss the findings of its commission, yet opponents may criticize the commission for being a corporate pawn.

Conclusion
A corporation must be sure of its decision to adopt the commission process. It must be certain that its position in the controversy is defendable or that it is willing to comply with the commission's views. Both it and the public, which also wants an independent judgement, must be sure of the objectivity of this independent body. This means the company must be involved in setting up the independent group, rather than letting its membership be dictated by outside groups, especially hostile forces.[23]

Raphael Pagan
Four factors that arise frequently threaten to produce a failure during a public opinion crisis.

- The most powerful among them is the conviction of legal counsel—that being open involves too much risk.
- The second is the conviction of marketing managers—that being open threatens to reveal trade secrets to the competition.
- The third is the conviction of financial managers—that openness creates a risk of generating useless expenditures.
- The fourth factor is the conviction that the members of the corporation are all so naive and innocent that they may be betrayed or misused.

(Pagan, 1986, p. 18)

Use the emerging forms of institutions

This is the situation in which those in charge can no longer do the job of crisis management on their own and where other forces begin to emerge. It can be a good idea not to isolate yourself from them. But once more, each case needs to be examined on its own merits.

Hélène Denis: The fire at Saint-Basile-le-Grand, 23 August 1988
The citizens developed a directly democratic *ad hoc* mechanism, known as the citizens' committee. Actions such as this can undermine the municipal authority vested in the mayor by

citizens. However, the mayors realized that confidence in every level of government had already been undermined to such an extent that the citizens' committee had become the only means of reassuring the population over the decisions to have people return home. For this reason, most of them agreed to play the game, acting as liaisons between government and citizens affected by the catastrophe. The provincial deputy, who in actual fact had himself been evacuated, also had a role to play in these committees. He defined this role as a link between the citizens and the government, dissociating himself to some extent from the latter, in order to restore the citizens' confidence in the machinery of government.

(Denis, 1989, pp. 23–4)

Rules for crisis management

A certain number of different intervention methods are generally advocated for a given action. Here, once again, those in charge, along with the critical intelligence group, must prepare a series of suitable landmarks and different possible scenarios.

Question, anticipate, take initiatives (even symbolic ones)

This involves going beyond the established framework by questioning the facts, anticipating how the crisis will develop, and taking initiatives that will make it possible to influence the current dynamic process.

In a constantly changing situation, where all meaning has collapsed, subjective perceptions become very important objective factors. You must therefore pay particular attention to all the symbolic aspects of the crisis and the way it is handled. Yet it can be dangerous to get rid of all 'objective' references one by one. Managing psychodrama is no easy task.

When it comes to initiatives, a classic question needs to be asked: should you or should you not go to the scene of the crisis?[24]

Warren Anderson, the chairman of Union Carbide, was frequently criticized for going to India after Bhopal, or more accurately, for going in the way he did. Exxon's chairman was criticized just as severely for not going to Alaska (or rather not going in a high-profile way) during the *Exxon Valdez* case. In each case, counter-criticisms were expressed: the very fact that Warren Anderson had the courage to go to India made it far easier to handle the crisis over the public opinion; on the other hand, Exxon's chairman stayed put and managed affairs from his headquarters. The chairman of Exxon-USA travelled to the scene and that was judged to be sufficient. Everything is in fact a question of judgement, and also, doubtless, of luck. It is easier to make assessments after the event, though these may be just as uncertain. Although they may help you to think the matter through, they will not necessarily tell you exactly what you ought to have done.

Hence these rather abrupt appraisals of Warren Anderson's journey (Fink, 1986, p. 170):

- He did not have enough information to justify going.
- He did not know if he would be allowed to visit the scene of the disaster.
- He had no guarantee that he would be able to do anything at all if he did go to the scene.
- Communications with Bhopal were so bad that he would not have been able to give his headquarters any instructions.
- He did not take into account the risk of being arrested, even though this had already happened to those in charge of Union Carbide India. He was in fact arrested, on charges of negligence and liability. This reduced still further his ability to play a part in the handling of the crisis. It was impossible to get through to him for several days.
- Lastly, if he was not already in a position to take wise decisions, in his comfortable and sheltered Danbury offices, how could he hope to cope better by travelling to the front line, where he would be brutally confronted with the image of the disaster caused by his company?

A number of lessons can be drawn from this point.

- If the fact of staying put is seen as indifference or scorn, this may permanently taint the whole affair (even billions of dollars will not change this situation, as everything will henceforth be seen in this negative light).
- Once again, it is a question of weighing up the pros and cons. In certain cases, at least, failure to go to the scene of the disaster is not necessarily seen as scorn, provided other initiatives are taken, such as meetings with those involved. Going to the scene can be a means of triggering the event that will finally end the crisis, by showing that no one intends to leave the matter unresolved. However, it can also be the opportunity for hostile demonstrations and ill-advised commitments likely to complicate the situation still further. As time goes by, perceptions can change.

In the case of the Roumazères landfill dump (1983), for example, Madame Bouchardeau, the then French Minister for the Environment, initially met those involved in Paris, only travelling to the scene when there was a possibility of observing the progress that had been made and concluding a consensus.[25]

Remember that if you suddenly set off for a location posing problems, you must ensure that you leave behind you an organization that can still operate properly. You must leave a list of criteria that would signal the need for your immediate return. In short, you must not confuse initiative and sheer impulsiveness.

The following imaginery scenario (based on simulation experiments) is an illustration of this.

> A major alert occurs on an industrial site. The manager immediately leaves his office. Why? Because it's part of the emergency plan. He sets off without leaving any instructions for his assistants, who find themselves all alone at the front line, and for some time to come. He is in his car, on a long journey (nobody thinks of using a helicopter until they realize how long the journey is). Once he arrives, he notes several regrettable absences—in particular, there are no firemen, and that's the final straw. He stirs up a huge fuss. The firemen arrive some hours later, furious at not having been told, and what is more, at finding themselves the butt of recriminations. The truth eventually dawns on everyone: you cannot deal with a crisis from an advanced, but ill-equipped command post so far away from every base. The decision is then taken to stray from the plan, and a better-equipped command post is used instead. They can now get on with managing the crisis. Twelve hours have been lost. The cleverest participants consider that the rest of the exercise in fact serves no purpose: in their haste, the group members have forgotten to take into account the fact that the advanced command post used in the morning had been directly affected by the cloud of toxic gas and that the players should all be in intensive care.

The lesson is not to 'do nothing' (crises are often caused by the total absence of any reaction, when people simply sit and wait), but to keep on building a critical pattern in what you do, so as to avoid becoming a prisoner of your initiatives or lack of initiatives. In this line of conduct, moreover, you must make sure that you do not become locked in a rigid doctrine when it comes to locating command posts. In the above example, it was ill advised to choose a location so close to the source of the hazard. On the other hand, in a case such as the *Amoco Cadiz*, it was right to set up an advanced command post on the coast just next to Ploumaldézeau where the ship ran aground, rather than in the prefecture of police in Quimper. Proximity to the disaster scene is often vital. As the scholar Chia Lin said when interpreting Sun Tzu: 'There is no greater calamity than orders emanating from a sovereign sitting in his court' (Sun Tzu, 1972, p. 117).

Avoid radical responses and magic tricks

It is often very tempting to use a spectacular gimmick to settle a crisis, especially one involving public opinion. These may include the nationalization of all companies posing a risk—or the very opposite extreme, drastic reductions of existing systems or wide-ranging administrative measures that are known to be ineffective and impossible to enforce.

Responses such as these are often irresponsible. They open the floodgates for future dangers and are not without risks in the immediate crisis. And if they do not work, there is a strong risk that yet more of your credit will have been used up.

> *Philippe Vesseron*
> You certainly have to know how to react to events and understand the consequences. But our fellow citizens are not stupid. [. . .] I think the basic rule is, you should be able to explain and justify the decisions you make. Exorcism is a pretty feeble answer, and it shows disdain for the public opinion it seeks to appease. If you yourself choose to stand on irrational grounds, you're taking a risk that will very likely provoke further destabilization. When you're already in a crisis, playing with fire isn't necessarily the smartest thing to do.[26]

It is best to avoid going over the top and promising the impossible, especially since no one is really looking for that.

> *Philippe Vesseron*
> Oddly enough, even though the country is pretty aware that there's no such thing as 'no risk', and even though the model of arrogant and omnipresent government is no longer accepted by anyone, administrations often feel obliged to prove that their task is to guarantee absolute safety. By trying to prove too much, they give themselves an impossible mission and actually contribute to creating instability. Whereas the primary goal of an administration, like a business, is to create management capacity, to show that it is credible, and to ensure that it won't be shaken if an incident or accident does actually happen.'[27]

Nevertheless, managers are frequently heard boasting that they were able to get out of a sticky situation by a mere sleight of hand, without even risking the future. They are backed up by these reasonings: 'I order an evacuation, even if it is not absolutely necessary. Even if it causes five deaths, nobody will level any accusations at me, as everyone will see that I was being "cautious". If, on the other hand, I don't order people to evacuate and if there are five deaths, I am a criminal. If I cut off the water, I'm re-elected; if I don't cut the water off, they'll start wondering whether they can trust me.'

Some people stick to a more rigid version of this strategy, consisting of the following basic principle: in a crisis situation, there is no question of skimping. Do not take the slightest risk. Indeed, it is the only possible way forward, given the lack of trust people have in those in charge.

Yet these positions are not really irreconcilable. If you do not refine your arguments sufficiently, you will yet again find yourself obliged to weigh the various risks involved, including both 'objective' and symbolic risks. It is on this basis that you must make your final decision. If you are to avoid any initial simplism, you must acknowledge that there are no obvious precepts. You must not only avoid any refusal to act that is only motivated by the concern not to incur any expense or bad publicity, but also bear in mind that spending money does have its consequences. Causing a firm or an economy to totter (the theme of an exercise in the United States in December 1990) has fairly direct consequences, some on the lives of many people.

During a crisis, never forget the post-crisis period

When you are in the midst of dealing with the crisis, remember that you will have to live with the consequences of the decisions you take to resolve it. There is no point in taking just *any* decision which, though it may be useful in the short term, will turn out to have consequences that are impossible to live with in the longer term. Similarly, you cannot ignore the fact that this crisis will doubtless not be the last. The method you have chosen to deal with this crisis must not make a subsequent crisis impossible to handle. This is the 'precedent' effect. In other words, a crisis cannot be treated as an isolated incident. You must constantly think of the aftermath of the crisis and the way this determines the method you use to handle and resolve the present crisis.

Philippe Vesseron
You just have to remember that history is never written in a single chapter. It's fine to handle the case of the waste from Seveso, but it would be illusory to think that it will be the last

industrial waste problem. It's fine to handle the consequences of a fire involving a PCB transformer, but you mustn't forget that there will be others. If you begin to promise magic in order to get rid of one difficulty, a new event can arrive very quickly and poke holes in the scenario you've constructed. This is a frightful vicious circle that makes each successive problem harder to solve. To the contrary, I think that from each event you should try to draw all possible lessons that will improve your ability to anticipate. [. . .] What seems indispensable to me is not responding to crises like the drums with purely short-term pre-occupations, as though they were just a media distraction that would be played out more or less well. Each episode of this type generates powerful images that will progressively mark our risk culture. In this respect, even false crises are important—they carry us forwards or backwards, depending on what we do and say.[28]

The other side to this argument you need to consider is that constant questions about the long term can also reduce your energy and drive. Yet you need to ask these questions as you are attempting to ride the rapids of the crisis.

However, at least for the most serious cases, one imperative that certainly needs to be respected is that something must remain possible after the crisis. Having recourse to certain methods immediately makes it impossible to conduct any relations after the crisis not only with one's immediate adversaries (in the case of a conflict), but also with a great many of one's current allies. Partial successes achieved through these methods can, in fact, signal a general rout.

Seize opportunities offered by the crisis

The important thing is, of course, to gain the upper hand in a very serious situation. Often, however, a crisis also opens up a new potential. In order to make the most of it, you must be on the look-out for these openings. You must have thought up various modes of action well before the crisis, thereby making it possible to act positively in the event of a major disturbance. You must also have given thought to the positive results you might gain from a given crisis (it is difficult to find positive ways out at the height of a storm). In fact, there are some similarities between crisis management and innovative management.

Rules for decision making

In a crisis, a great many decisions may well have to be taken extremely rapidly. There is a grave danger of rapidly becoming lax and inconsistent. To make sure that the decision-making system does not fall into a state of crisis, a list of requirements can be drawn up—and respected. In this area, the 'critical intelligence group' can once more provide a very valuable backup.

A firm decision-making process

The sequence proposed by Janis (1982, p. 136), designed to counter the risk of groupthink, is invaluable for many other reasons. Forget it at your peril:

1 Carry out an in-depth study of a wide range of alternatives.
2 Study the objectives and values at stake.
3 Weigh carefully not only the positive consequences but also the costs, the disadvantages and the subtler risks of negative consequences, which might result from what seemed at the outset the most advantageous line of action.
4 Be constantly on the outlook for information that could be useful in assessing all the various alternatives.
5 Take into careful consideration the views of the experts who are shown these alternatives, even when you receive new information or opinions that do not condone the line of action you preferred at the outset.
6 Before taking the final decision, re-examine the positive and negative consequences of the main alternatives, including those you initially regarded as undesirable.
7 Prepare the implementation of the chosen option very carefully. Pay special attention to the emergency plans, which could become necessary if the various risks linked to this option come to pass.

In specific circumstances (relatively simple crisis, the moment when the emergency gathers momentum), the decision makers may find this type of safety net too much of an encumbrance. They must, however, at least be conscious of the major risks posed by their own styles of handling a crisis.

As a rider, we could also lay down general 'rules' governing major directions of policy. The following are often considered to be the most important, though in certain cases you may find it necessary to leave them to one side.

Keep as many options open as possible

In a crisis situation, your difficulties may well increase dramatically if you restrict your room for manoeuvre. This can happen spontaneously, by mistake, or less innocently. Having your back against the wall may be more bearable in some respects, as there is less uncertainty and ambiguity.

You must therefore give preference to decisions that leave as much room for manoeuvre in subsequent episodes as possible. In a more positive way, deliberate efforts must be made to increase the number of alternatives under review. As Henry Kissinger stresses: 'The edge of a precipice leaves scope for only one imperative: to obtain some manoeuvering room.' (Kissinger, 1982, Vol. 2, p. 126). You must observe the greatest circumspection when faced with very serious options.

That much said, you may judge this approach to be ill-suited to situations of extreme conflict, where the only way of resolving the crisis is to show your adversaries that there is no longer any room for manoeuvre, and that they must therefore either submit or go to extremes. This is notably the thesis developed by T. Schelling in his famous work, *The Strategy of Conflict*:

> . . . the power to constrain an adversary may depend on the power to bind oneself; [that], in bargaining weakness is often strength, freedom may be freedom to capitulate, and to burn bridges behind one may suffice to undo an opponent.'[29]

It was with a similar coup that Pierre Mendès France tackled the crisis in Indochina as soon as he took office.

> *Pierre Mendès France's speech of 17 June 1954*
> [As soon as he took office, the new prime minister informed his adversary that he was only there for one month. If peace wasn't achieved during that time, another government would take on the job. He warned that another team arriving on the scene would massively increase the potential for military action and would enter into a strategic alliance with the United States. There would then be nothing to prevent the war from taking on international proportions. (see Lacouture, 1981, p. 13) How could he convince his adversaries? Precisely by applying the Schelling model. This was the first speech by Pierre Mendès France to the French Parliament.]

> 'The ceasefire must therefore be rapidly put into place. The government I form will give itself—and its adversaries—four weeks to achieve this. Today is June 17th. I will come before you once more before July 20th and I will tell you exactly how much we achieved. If we fail to arrive at a satisfactory solution by then, you will be released from the contract binding us both and my government will tender its resignation to the President of the Republic.'
>
> (Lacouture, 1981, p. 13; *Journal officiel*, 18 June 1954)

Avoid decisions that cannot be implemented or enforced

Although this sort of seemingly spectacular and highly tempting dictate may afford some temporary relief, you must avoid taking decisions which rapidly expose the ineffectualness of those in charge, the hollowness of their projects and the weakness of their resolution. Decisions must be enforceable and enjoy the support of those who will have to implement them.

Work on many, contrasting scenarios

In order to thwart yet again a tendency to simplify reference hypotheses, you will have to think constantly of a great many possibly contradictory scenarios. This broad approach will provide you with a greater chance of being able to deal with a rapidly changing situation with particularly unexpected developments. It is important to study even the most pessimistic of scenarios.

> *Henry Kissinger: The conflict in the Middle East (1973)*
> I did, however, ask for two contingency plans. The first was for the eventuality that Lebanon might get out of control. The second I outlined as follows: [. . .] the kinds of things the Egyptians might do, the various ways in which the Israelis might react and the diplomatic issues that might ensue. Short of actual Soviet intervention, it's hard to envisage any direct U.S. intervention. But we should consider what to do to keep the Soviets out, the ways in which we might use the crisis to get diplomatic movement, if that is what we want, or to return to the *status quo ante* if it is decided that is desirable.
> (Kissinger, 1982, Vol. 2, p. 462)

> *Henry Kissinger: The Jordanian crisis (1970)*
> The position of the security adviser when he disagrees with the President is extremely delicate. The President must have the assurance that his adviser will act as his extension and will see to it that his wishes are carried out by the departments. On the other hand, the President must be able to count on being warned if his orders are dangerous. This was especially important for Nixon, given his tendency toward impetuous declarations that he never expected to see implemented. In the Jordan crisis, I solved the problem by having two contingency plans prepared simultaneously: one embodying the President's preference for unilateral American action; the other reflecting the WSAG consensus for the United States to hold the ring against outside intervention. The President would then be able to choose when the moment for the decision arrived.
> (Kissinger, 1982, Vol. 2, p. 604)

On the other hand, decision makers in a sticky situation may consider that they cannot allow themselves to dissipate their energies in gratuitous exploration and risk undermining the morale of the organization.

Time your interventions: know when to rush and when to wait
These are two extremes which, in reality, are always slightly fuzzy.

The first—rapid, decisive action—has the advantage of allowing you to gain the upper hand before the crisis has a chance to contaminate the whole system, making it necessary then to have recourse to massive means of intervention.

The second—patient waiting—means leaving the situation to decant ('deteriorate' is the term the advocates of rapid action would use) sufficiently to ensure sure-footed intervention, if it is still needed. As the various threads will have been unravelled by that time, you will be able to have several strings to your bow. These will make your strategies more flexible and less costly.

> *Henry Kissinger appears to be a fierce advocate of the first type of action*
> In my view what seems 'balanced' and 'safe' in a crisis is often the most risky. Gradual escalation tempts the opponent to match every move; what is intended as a show of moderation may be interpreted as irresolution. [. . .] Passivity in a crisis leads to mounting impotence; one is forced to react on issues and in contexts contrived to one's maximum disadvantage. By contrast, the side that has the initiative can occupy its opponent's energies in analysis. And since the opponent will always assume the worst contingency, even relatively minor moves can have a major cautionary affect, unless they are so palpably bluffing as to encourage contempt. For maximum effectiveness one's actions must be sustained; they must appear relentless, inexorable; hesitation or gradualism invites an attempt to test one's resolution by matching the commitment.
> (Kissinger, 1982, Vol. 2, pp. 622, 604)

> *The case of askarel in Reims*
> The deliberate delay in taking any precautions (controlling access to the contaminated building) created a situation that was difficult to handle from the health point of view. The follow-up of a mere handful of people has nothing in common with the need to monitor the health of several dozens or even hundreds of people. Similarly, intervening once you have already lost a considerable amount of credibility can seriously damage your public image and exacerbate the problems of medical supervision. Everything becomes an object of suspicion and worsens not only people's stress but eventually even their 'objective' medical state (the difference between the objective

and subjective always being somewhat difficult to establish in the field of medicine).[30]

Remain circumspect about grave options

It is possible that, during the course of events, you may find yourself sliding into extremely serious scenarios. At that point, it is important to pause for thought before taking any decisive steps.

> *Henry Kissinger: The Jordanian crisis (1970)*
> Nixon called back. He had decided to approve Israeli ground action and dictated a thoughtful message to convey to Rabin. He said, 'I have decided it. Don't ask anybody else. Tell him [Rabin] "go".'
>
> I was not about to let the President run the risk of a major confrontation with the Soviet Union without consulting his senior advisers. An Israeli ground operation could produce a Mideast war. I owed it to Nixon to check with [Secretary of State] Rogers and [Secretary of Defense] Laird.
>
> (Kissinger, 1979, Vol. 1, p. 625)

This whole process of asking questions, providing new openings and bringing in intellectual, organizational and human resources, will help you to prepare and to gain support for the way you decide to fight the crisis. Now that we have explored this level, we shall move on to the second, more 'operational' one.

Summary

Getting a grip on the event

- Arm yourself with an autonomous information capability
  - Facts to help identify the current dynamic process
  - Facts to feed to the media
- Start thinking
  - Define the context
  - Locate and destroy every hasty consensus
  - Define the background
  - Anticipate
  - Fix a foundation for the system
- Set up networks
  - Create your 'backdrop'
  - Don't hesitate to mobilize the people at the top
  - Look on each other as partners
  - Find common issues

- Create a decision-making and organizational capability
  - Create a minimum framework of authority
  - Build up links between decision-making centres
  - Build up trust
  - Redistribute: information–intelligence–resources–power
- Set up a critical intelligence group
  - An autonomous group boasting many different cultures
  - Designed to ask questions and act as a strategic watchdog
- Try to draw up patterns for action
  - Rules on policy: values and references
  - Rules on cooperation between the various actors
  - Rules on the management of an institution
  - Rules on crisis management
  - Rules on decision making

Notes

1. Interview with Joseph Scanlon.
2. This warning comes from Joseph Scanlon, who has made a special study of these questions with Angela Prawzick in Canada.
3. A position stoutly defended by Dominique Coujard (secretary-general of the Collège de la prévention des risques majeurs), notably at the seminar organized by Claude Gilbert with the aid of the French national scientific research centre (CNRS), entitled 'Catastrophe and crisis management—the role of the State and local authorities', 7–8 December 1989, Château de Sassenage, Grenoble, France.
4. The testimony of Philippe Legorjus, contained in his book, La Morale et l'Action, is of exceptional interest to this topic (see Legorjus, 1990).
5. Interview with Douglas K. Burrows in Lagadec, 1990, p. 72.
6. Interview with Péter-J. Hargitay.
7. Interview with Péter-J. Hargitay.
8. See interview with Robert L. Dilenschneider in Lagadec, 1990, p. 190.
9. Interview with Philippe Vesseron in Lagadec, 1990, pp. 101–2.
10. This case, and the way it has since developed, clearly shows how extraordinarily difficult it is to gain the upper hand in a crisis. There is constantly a risk of forgetting an element which will later turn out to be vital, even though at the outset there were dozens of others that were equally important. It only takes one actor to be missing from the basic group (the justice department, in this case). It only needs one accidental omission in the plan (sending the black boxes back by the first available plane without any legal representatives) for difficulties to arise. It will not be long before a whole series of problems (real or imagined, current or accumulated) attach themselves to these cores and begin to snowball. [It is obviously not our intention to make a general diagnosis of the case, which has just been mentioned here because certain aspects give food for thought concerning crisis management.]

11. Interview with Philippe Vesseron in Lagadec, 1990, p. 98.
12. Interview with Péter-J. Hargitay.
13. Interview with Douglas K. Burrows in Lagadec, 1990, pp. 68–9.
14. Telegram from Marc Becam on 24 March 1978, from the Polmar de Ploudalmézeau advanced command post.
15. Interview with Péter-J. Hargitay. It should be noted that even first-class capabilities can be stymied by very difficult crises. All you can do is hope that good systems will at least make it possible to manage what still can be managed. There are, of course, no miracle recipes here.
16. Interview with Philippe Vesseron in Lagadec, 1990, p. 102.
17. Interview with Philippe Vesseron in Lagadec, 1990, p. 102.
18. We refer here to the work of Vickers, 1965.
19. Interview with Philippe Vesseron in Lagadec, 1990, p. 102.
20. Interview with Philippe Vesseron in Lagadec, 1990, p. 102.
21. Joseph Scanlon, in an interview, believes this principle to be of paramount importance in terrorist acts and the taking of hostages: 'Make a local police superintendent say a few words, on no account the minister.'
22. You will find a fuller description of the case in Dobbing, 1988.
23. The case study reported here has been taken from Muskie and Greenwald, 1986, pp. 19–23.
24. Please note, however, that not every crisis necessarily has a specific location, or rather that the scene of the accident is not the scene of the crisis. (Very often, in practice seminars, the participants express just one principle: 'I would immediately travel to the scene.' It never occurs to them that there might not actually be one, or else that there might instead by a great many of them. This is the kind of intellectual surprise that it's best to discover before the crisis occurs.)
25. Interview with Philippe Vesseron; see also interview with Philippe Vesseron in Lagadec, 1990, p. 104.
26. Interview with Philippe Vesseron in Lagadec, 1990, p. 106.
27. Interview with Philippe Vesseron in Lagadec, 1990, p. 106.
28. Interview with Philippe Vesseron in Lagadec, 1990, pp. 104–5 and 154–5.
29. Schelling, 1963, p. 22. (Quoted by Claude Henry: *Flexibilité et dissuasion: incompatibilité ou association*, Laboratory of Econometrics at the Ecole polytechnique, No. 345, October 1990, p. 1.)
30. See the interview with Professor Sylvain Dally in Lagadec, 1986*b*.

Chapter 9

Managing the crisis: making and implementing choices

You have managed to avoid being immediately discredited. Work has commenced on gathering intelligence on the current dynamic process, and various options have been drawn up. While continuing this process of critical analysis, you must now also get down to actually managing the crisis. The aim of this chapter is not merely to provide a suitable checklist of things you need to do. Rather, its purpose is to present a general control panel, together with a set of basic guidelines for each gauge on it.

Once you are actually in the midst of the crisis, you will merely have to carry out those adjustments, combinations, and choices you judge to be the most appropriate.

The foundation act: taking a position

This forms the true core of strategic action. The decision-making process has been defined and fully implemented. In particular, the critical intelligence group, to which you will have to refer throughout your management of the crisis, has been set up. The person in charge must now take a number of decisions. Naturally, these may include the decision not to take any decisions, the setting of a future date for such decisions or else the continuation of vague uncertainty, giving the crisis a chance to show its true colours.

As Henry Kissinger emphasizes, 'the most important role of a leader is to take on his shoulder the burden of ambiguity inherent in difficult choices. That accomplished, his subordinates have criteria and can turn to implementation' (Kissinger, 1982, Vol. 2, p. 531).

In this chapter, we shall concentrate on the most difficult cases. Luckily, crises do not always require reorganization on this scale, as it is not every day that we have to establish new geostrategic balances of power. In intermediate cases, you can stick to the idea that you must at least fight for the survival of your own organization. This provides us with plenty of landmarks, but does not necessarily eliminate all ambiguity. The following considerations, which unfortunately cannot be simplified, are therefore relevant to everyone. The leader is expected to take three types of action.

Facing an indeterminate situation: put a name on the crisis, or at least determine your room for manoeuvre

As is so often done in this area, we could recommend resolute, frank, determined action, carried out by a leader devoid of sentiment, sure of his troops and with the sort of confidence that will enable him to overcome the crisis in a trice. This may be an interesting idea, but it is woefully inadequate as far as the more difficult cases are concerned, and these are, after all, perhaps the most numerous. The valiant hero quickly finds himself in the shoes of Don Quixote, exhausted at shadow-boxing the crisis and quickly abandoned by his demoralized troops, defeated without a proper fight, while the crisis continues to mock from the shadows.

The crisis mocks simplistic leaders. It follows the principles of Sun Tzu (1972) to the letter, retranslating them to suit its own purposes: the supreme art of the crisis is to subdue its enemy without a fight. The first victory of the crisis is an intellectual one, for technical questions are of secondary importance: '. . . the consummation of an army is to arrive at formlessness.'[1]

Once initial skirmishes have been contained and the intelligence systems have been deployed, the person in charge must then try to answer the central question, namely, 'What is the real problem?' Or, put another way, 'What is the reality behind the crisis facing me?'

Crises can be interpreted in an infinite number of ways. They are fleeting phenomena which can be nowhere yet everywhere, a blinding flash when seen from one angle yet nothing but darkness when seen from a different angle. Having no definite outline, a crisis can take whichever form it wants. As the bearer of every potentiality, it will not allow itself to be overcome by any one specific course of action. If prevented from advancing on one front, it will immediately create ten other fronts, on even more difficult terrain. Every partial victory can represent a weakening at the level of overall operations, a weakness that will only gradually be discovered.

If you are to take appropriate action and embark on a suitable operation, you must first put a name on the crisis. This will help you pin down its uncertain nature and reduce its barbarous form to a knowable and therefore partially manageable reality. Where there is dialogue, treatment and compromise become possible.

This, then, is the first requirement, but it is also the first risk. This opening act is a veritable bid for power, and this gamble must be suitably tailored if the barbarous form is to allow itself to be captured. It is not hard to see why this task is so difficult. In fact, you have to pin down something that has not yet happened, something that is entirely new and does not yet exist.

You may have to wait before you can put a name on your crisis. But put a name on it you must!

At the very worst, naming the crisis at least represents an attempt to make your mark and bring intelligence to bear on a phenomenon that is beyond you.

Hiroshima: the most extreme case
[The diary kept by Doctor Hachiya, the director of one of the local hospitals, is a good example of the way people can appropriate phenomena by putting a name on them:]

'I had to revise my meaning of the word destruction or choose some other word to describe what I saw. Devastation may be a better word, but really, I know of no word or words to describe the view from my twisted iron bed in the fire-gutted ward of the Communications hospital. [. . .]

The day of the bombing quickly became the basis for recording events in popular speech. 'That day' would mean the day of the bombing; 'the next day', the day after; and so on.

Pikadon was accepted as a new word in our vocabulary, although some . . . who had been in the city at the time of the bombing, continued to say simply pika. Those who had been outside the city insisted on saying pikadon. The latter finally won out. (Doubtless because most of those who would have said pika soon died.) Pika means a glitter, sparkle, or bright flash of lightning. Don means a boom! or loud sound. Together, the words came to mean to the people of Hiroshima an explosion characterized by a flash and a boom. Hence: 'flash-boom!'. Those who remember the flash only speak of the 'pika'; those who were far enough from the hypocenter to experience speak of the 'pikadon'.

(Hachiya, 1955, pp. 31, 208, 37, 48).

Of course, the person in charge always runs the risk of talking a lot of hot air. There is a danger that that individual may decide on a name too soon, before the proper process of analysis suggested in the previous chapter has been carried out, and before it has been possible to get to the real heart of the problem.

You may, of course, become deluded and mistake the name for the thing. So make sure the name exactly fits the thing to which you give it. In any event, nobody can cling to illusions for long in a crisis situation.

Accordingly, you will often need to be patient and curb your ambitions. If the form in question cannot be named, in other words, if you cannot identify the heart of the crisis by answering the central question, 'What is the problem?', you can at least attempt in the meantime to define the horizons of the crisis and map out a field of operations within which work can begin. This field of operations can be determined in two different ways:

- If the phenomenon's lack of shape and form means that there is a seemingly infinite choice of possible actions to take, you must define a field of reference. Decide what is most at stake for you, identify the people you most want to bring in and isolate the problems which you think must be tackled.
- Similarly, you must set yourself deadlines for thinking through problems and possible responses, with immediate, medium-term, long-term and very long-term goals. Separate deadlines must be set for specific constraints, questions, responses and contradictions. There will inevitably be some overlapping and a number of contradictions between these deadlines.

The nature of your response strategy will depend largely on the way you frame the problem.

Take the case of Bhopal. Was it a problem of how to get help to the victims or how to gain an understanding of the nature of the accident? Or, then again, was it primarily about the chemical risk, technology transfer or development models? It is clear that the responses differ according to the standpoint that is chosen.

In short, the important thing is to give a reply to the question 'What is the problem I choose to tackle?', which sufficiently respects reality but which reduces this reality to manageable proportions.

If you cannot give the desired reply immediately, you should at least begin to formulate it and attach the greatest possible importance to it through the crisis.

When many options are available: base your position on your fundamental focus

Once you have this tiger by the tail, you must define a consistent line of action (at least provisionally, and at least its major outlines, if the reconnaissance of the crisis has not yet been pursued as far as you would like).

The first necessity is to determine the new state of equilibrium you hope to attain at the end of the crisis. This calls for defining a world vision and focal goals.

This work, similar to what has been done earlier, draws upon creativity rooted in history, and on a good assessment of the constraints involved. It calls for daring, for persistence, for deadlines. Obviously it also calls for knowing what your values are.

The next step is to develop policies. This involves fundamental choices.

You should assume you will face one contradiction throughout the crisis: you must be able to hold to the focus you have set, or else you will become a pawn of the crisis; yet you must always be in a position to reconsider the understanding you have and the choices you have made, if this is clearly what the crisis requires.

Identifying values: Johnson & Johnson and the Tylenol case
[Johnson & Johnson could base itself on a very solid in-house charter which constituted a sort of anchor in the storm. This was the 'credo' laid down 40 years earlier by the son of the founder, who was chairman from 1938 to 1963. His ideas were very much ahead of his times:]

'Both public and private institutions exist only because people want them, believe in them, or at least agree to tolerate them. The time is past, if it ever existed, when economic activity was a private matter. In a capitalist economy, every business action has social consequences and can attract the public's attention. Each time a business rents, builds, buys, or sells, it acts for the public as well as for itself, and it must be ready to assume total responsibility.'

This group had always made great efforts to bring this creed to life. Meetings organized on the subject drew more than 4000 employees. The chairman himself chaired every meeting. In 1975, discussions were undertaken at the highest level to consider redrafting the creed. It was modified slightly.

The actions taken immediately after the onset of the crisis were made in reference to this creed: consumer safety and welfare were the first priorities, and everything else was secondary. The company's response figured in the first line of the charter: 'We believe that our first responsibility is to satisfy the doctors, nurses, patients, mothers, and all those who use our products and services.'

(Johnson & Johnson, 1982)

Johnson & Johnson strongly emphasizes the fact that this anchor was of great help to everyone when important decisions had to be taken in uncharted territory. It enabled them to see a faint light at the end of the tunnel and to legitimize their actions.

Facing an emergency: defining a strategy for response and implementing it

The most important questions requiring answers include: What is the global course of action we must take? Where must we intervene? When must we intervene? How can we handle the symbolic problems?

It is at this stage that you must make your mind up about the patterns of logic outlined previously, and for which various options will have been made ready.

A classic difficulty is that of overdoing or underdoing the response. An excessive response may create a secondary crisis which turns out to be even greater than the original crisis. An inadequate response may complicate the situation, especially when it comes to your credibility, and may result in the utter waste of precious resources.

Similarly, you must manage your time properly. This implies making difficult judgements in a situation full of contradictions. For example, should you take action without further delay, in order to maximize operational efficiency? Or, on the contrary, should you insist on legitimacy and acceptability, and only take action after a final legal judgement has been made and a proper communication campaign carried out? In the first instance, you risk rejection. In the second, you may arrive too late.

It should be emphasized once more that in an emergency, it is extremely difficult to make really thorough analyses, weigh all the pros and cons and make clear-headed judgements. Of course, the critical intelligence team suggested earlier can be of great assistance. However, the burden will be very much lighter if you have already given thought to a certain number of delicate circumstances and already have the makings of responses and a few tools to help you think and act. If the difficulties are too great, one possibility is to latch onto one or two negative principles, such as 'This is what we shall not allow ourselves to do in such-and-such a situation, as it would only deepen the crisis'. When it comes to specific operations, you might ask yourself the following question for each scenario: 'What are the three mistakes to avoid and the three initiatives to take within the next hour?'

You will have more time to think in later stages. The most important thing is to avoid immediately going up that absolute, but extremely tempting, blind alley. For example, what will you do and say if a manager is kidnapped, if a network is massively polluted, if disaster strikes a recently built aircraft without anyone's being able to understand why, or if an entire product line is rumoured to have caused serious health problems?

The following points may start you thinking, though they should be used as tools to help you ask questions, not as ready-made answers.[2]

- *Product defect*: Admit immediately that you are concerned, and act as quickly as possible. Even go so far as to help the consumer buy supplies elsewhere during the time it takes to get your products back on the shelves. When these products do return, carry out a hard-hitting campaign, highlighting your sense of responsibility during the crisis. If products are recalled, find out beforehand whether or not it will be possible to remedy their defects.
- *Kidnapping*: Announce immediately that the kidnapped director no longer represents anything. Bring in his replacement (chosen long ago) within the hour.
- *Crisis in public opinion*: If the criticism is judged to be well-founded, as in the case of a species such as the whale, threatened with extinction, be prepared to carry out fundamental changes. If you judge it to be ill-founded and unacceptable, as with the call to end all animal testing of medicines essential to mankind, be prepared instead to call up all your troops. If it is judged acceptable to a certain extent, be prepared to make compromises.
- *Intervention in a failure for which you are not responsible*: Act quickly, highlighting the fact that you consider it to be your social responsibility, even though you are not directly at fault.
- *Pollution with health risks*: Warn the people likely to be affected without delay, then eliminate the causes and deal with the effects.

• *Rumour of a public health problem*: Whatever your personal conviction may be, do not deny the possibility of a danger if you don't have rock solid arguments. While awaiting scientific arguments, you must look for a social consensus as to the interim measures to be taken. The greater the uncertainty surrounding the risk, the more explicit your policies must be.
 – Respond immediately to the concerns expressed, by setting up short-term studies that can provide efficient answers to the questions. [. . .]
 – Do not pretend that science can answer all the questions. [. . .]
 – Be wary of hastily prepared statistics.[3]

Johnson & Johnson faced with the Tylenol crisis (1982): resolute action on many fronts

The marketing dimension
• Bottles of Tylenol were back on the shelves in November in packaging with three tamper-resistant seals. This made the company the first to comply with the FDA's (Food and Drug Administration) new standards in this field.
• Discount coupons worth $2.50 were printed in the press and made available to callers via a toll-free telephone number from which coupons could be requested.
• Discounts of up to 25 per cent were offered to retailers in order to win back shelf space.
• A new advertising campaign was prepared for 1983.
• To back up the introduction of the new product, more than 2250 members of the total sales force (including Johnson & Johnson subsidiaries) were mobilized to make presentations to physicians and other members of the medical community (70 per cent of all users take Tylenol on the advice of a physician). One million such presentations were made before the end of 1982.

This programme to renew interest was founded on the fact that the intrinsic quality of the product was solidly recognized. The following positive factors came into play:

• Tylenol is a better product than its competitors; in particular, it is as effective as aspirin without the adverse effects.
• Tylenol continues to receive the support of the medical community: 50 per cent of all physicians continued to prescribe the product during the October 1982 crisis.
• Consumers understood that Johnson & Johnson was not responsible for what happened in Chicago. In a poll, 80 per

cent of those questioned understood that the Tylenol capsules had been poisoned after leaving the factory.
- The new packaging was highly appreciated by the public (77 per cent of those questioned said they would buy the product again 'without hesitation' or 'probably').

A large-scale communication programme
Large-scale is an understatement: 80 000 press clippings, 2000 telephone calls, hundreds of hours of radio and television reports. According to one editorial, this was the most widely covered issue since the Vietnam war. The company reacted vigorously to maintain its position in this market. The initiatives taken included:

- Establishing a direct phone line for consumers within the first week of the crisis. Some 136 000 calls were received within 11 days following the announcement that this service was available (at the 11 November press conference by the chairman). Specialized firms were used to process these calls; this freed Johnson & Johnson to pursue its other business.
- Full-page ads were taken out in major American newspapers on 12 October, offering to exchange bottles of capsules for tablets.
- Twice during October, letters were sent to employees and retired employees of the group to give them important information and thank them for their support. More specifically, the letters urged their readers to call for Tylenol to be returned to the shelves from which it had been removed.
- Sixty-second spots were aired in October and November in which the medical director announced that the bottles would soon be available again with a new packaging.
- More than 160 Congressmen were visited in Washington, D.C. and asked to call for new legislation, which would include making tampering with consumer products a crime. The FDA was also lobbied publicly to support tamper-proof packaging.
- The company's top executives made statements in the press and on the major television networks. Other executives were trained to give interviews.
- Four videos (three hours of film) were made about the crisis and Tylenol's comeback. These were distributed or shown to employees and former employees of the group.
- The quarterly report for October informed shareholders of the impact made by the withdrawal of the bottles.
- A four-minute video intended for television was prepared to show how the tamper-proof packaging was made.
- Every letter addressed to Johnson & Johnson received an answer. Some 3000 queries had been handled by the end of November.

(See Johnson & Johnson, 1982)

You must act with determination. Once you have chosen your lines of action, follow them. Furthermore, you must bear in mind yet again that events and their interpretation may well be turned on their heads, in which case you will have to change your strategy completely.

> *Henry Kissinger: A conflict in the Middle East requiring a fundamental re-examination of strategy (1973)*
> They explained that Israel's losses to date had been staggering and totally unexpected. [. . .] For what Dinitz [Israeli Ambassador to Washington] was reporting would require a fundamental reassessment of strategy. Our entire diplomacy and our resupply policy had been geared to a rapid Israeli victory. These assumptions were now overtaken.
> (Kissinger, 1982, Vol. 2, p. 492)

Overall management of the action plan

Here, we must place ourselves resolutely at the side of the person at the helm—whether it is the managing director or the person placed in charge of the crisis and to whom the managing director has entrusted the management of the system during the storm—or another of the actors, who is anxious to help the system face up to the ordeal as well as possible, even if that person has not received a specific mandate.

Here, once more, tactical principles are generally placed at the forefront: 'Don't hesitate, put someone in charge of the crisis, set up a crisis unit, take action.' Everything is useful, but must be incorporated into an overall strategy. Crisis management requires more than a set of tactical rules, however good they may be.

The director's overriding concern must be to ensure the coherence and cohesion of the system. The director's task will be made easier by the fact that the major positions to take have already been decided (as we have just seen). The director will also be able to draw on his or her knowledge of the best logic of action to adopt in a crisis situation (patterns of logic we have already attempted to isolate) and on the very wide-ranging investigation work carried out by the critical intelligence group—which must keep up its efforts.

The difficulty lies in keeping the entire system under control during the crisis. This means keeping abreast of overall developments and paying attention to the reaction of the system as a whole.

This work of vigilance and supervision at the highest level consists notably of the following stages.

- Ensure that the crisis is properly tackled. The natural tendency of very large systems is to grind to a halt when faced with a new challenge of this sort, which doesn't fit into any known framework. On the other hand, care must be taken to avoid the emergence of any Rambo-type attitudes towards the crisis.
- Encourage people to anticipate events. Most of the people involved will tend to become interested in the most recent difficulty, even though it will have ceased to represent a major problem by the time its main effects have begun to be felt. You must therefore constantly open up new horizons in your work and repeat the question: 'In what situation will the system find itself tomorrow, next week or next month?' If you do not look beyond the immediate situation, ask yourself 'What next?' and think of new scenarios incorporating possible changes to the system ('What if?'), the crisis will continue to lay down the law.
- Continually identify the major initiatives the system ought to take. Remember that the fundamental tendency, as we have seen, is to content oneself with reacting to difficulties as they arise. You must fight hard against this tempting line of thought, bearing in mind that the moments when you can intervene effectively and the useful initiatives you can take will be few and far between. It is therefore important not to neglect these fleeting opportunities.
- Rapidly identify gaps that can appear in roles and responsibilities despite the emergency plans you have drawn up. It is vital not to leave problems unanswered and contacts without a reply. In particular, it is a good idea to identify all the sections of the public with whom you will be working and communicating, otherwise you may well make the mistake of confining yourself to the undifferentiated public of the most powerful media.
- Constantly track down and pinpoint the mistakes made by the organization or the network of organizations involved, in order to correct them immediately. If this is not done, small cracks can rapidly turn into rifts that are impossible to bridge.
- Remind everyone that the crisis may be a lengthy one. Crises

always last longer than initially predicted. This reminder must be reiterated forcefully from time to time, as the sheer impact of the event tends to make people forget about the time dimension, even though it is vital if they are to gain an overall vision of the crisis, together with aspects of its technical management such as the handling of fatigue and the setting up of relief teams.

- Provide an intellectual backup for the network involved in the management of the problem. This means supplying landmarks to identify emergency situations and crisis dynamics. The same preconceived notions (the idea that there will be panic, that you must keep quiet about the risks, that you must start by mistrusting the press) and types of behaviour (withdrawal, conflict, retreat into fantasy world) always tend to crowd in and govern people's reactions. If senior management are able to get to grips with some of the problems raised by the crisis, they will be able to put these classic tendencies into context, thereby reducing the turmoil slightly.

- Constantly identify the system's weak points, both within the organization and in its relations with the environment. Which people and which services are the most exposed? What are the effects of a constantly worsening situation? What are the conflicts that loom? What do the latest rumours say? What are the manoeuvres waiting in the shadows, either real or utterly imaginary, that could upset everything? What are the risks of the action plan imploding or coming into conflict with the outside world?

- Acknowledge the system from time to time. As the crisis develops, the system and its actors will be faced with an avalanche of destabilizing news. Unexpected facts will appear to undermine the major principles that have been established. As time goes by, solidarity and support will wear away. The strong presence of major legitimizing figures will also be needed to cope with the symbolic dimension. The leader will therefore have to make his or her status and presence felt throughout the crisis, breathing conviction and courage into the system. As Philippe Vesseron stresses, 'when a crisis becomes drawn out, it is vital periodically to put the machine back on track'.[4]

- State and reiterate reference principles and values. More often than not, a crisis will be won or lost over the major positions you adopt and the reasons why you have adopted them. Both inside and outside the organization, the way these vital choices are perceived is of critical importance, as people often know little about them, understand them only poorly or interpret them the wrong way. There is a constant danger that the ongoing management of the crisis, with its highly visible technical aspects, will mask the existence of fundamental choices—choices which justify all manner of efforts and inconveniences. In addition, there is frequently a discrepancy between the implicit values conveyed by the management of the crisis and those values that the community considers to be important. This discrepancy, or risk of discrepancy, must constantly be analysed, and action must be taken if any widening of the gap is observed or feared. In particular, it is important to remember that people faced with an ordeal will not necessarily have the right reflex. When implicitly attacked over its values, an entity tends to justify itself by presenting new technical references, wrapped up in a jargon intended to prove its integrity and which gives it a feeling of being protected. This will only increase acrimony, as the most fundamental need is for answers to questions such as, 'why?', and 'in the name of what?' or 'who?', not 'how?'. In short, information about the facts alone is insufficient. A key point should be stressed here: you must not be the last person to address these fundamental questions. The person who first starts looking for basic landmarks is the one who has the best chance of imposing his or her own interpretation of the crisis.[5] This brings us back to a previous remark: power belongs to the person who can redistribute intelligence concerning the event, together with a set of basic guidelines. This holds true both within and outside the organization, for if your own organization no longer knows in what name its directors are acting, it may gradually just fall apart.

- Manage any contradictions that arise before they lead to rupture. It is particularly difficult to define major strategies, while the same time leaving one's colleagues a degree of initiative compatible with the need for overall cohesion on the one hand, and the need for them to feel at ease with the chosen line of action, on the other. If it is not the case, their messages may well have very little credibility, sounding like stiff official language. This is a difficulty which a multinational group is particularly likely to encounter. A policy adopted at headquarters may run counter to the ideas of the local manager. This requires careful, cool-headed thought and thoughtful drafting. Which basic values and directions need to be observed in the event of a crisis? For example, should industrial and commercial activities cease in (or with) a particular country if its régime is judged to be unacceptable by the general public?

- Make sure that people's sensibilities are not offended, especially when it comes to exposure in the media. The various departments are sometimes reluctant to communicate and have to be encouraged to speak out. But the person in charge must take steps to avoid conflicts arising from a disproportionate amount of media attention and limelight being given to one particular department (e.g. opposition between police and firefighters in the Mississauga affair), or to one particular level of responsibility (e.g. opposition between the municipal and provincial authorities in the affair of Saint-Basile-le-Grand).

Joseph Scanlon, Mississauga (10 November 1979)
The media emphasized the role of the police, which directed operations (as is standard procedure in Canada). This aroused some jealousy in the fire department. In response, the police had journalists escorted to the front lines, where they could interview the fire chief. The fire chief was also invited to participate in all major press conferences.

(Scanlon, 1989a, p. 315)

Direct management: general measures, crisis teams, and specific tools

Organizational capacities

To carry out consistent action, organizational guidelines specifically designed for a crisis must be defined.

Establish separations
The purpose of these separations is to reduce confusion.

- Separate things involved in the crisis from things not involved.
- Separate technical management from communication. (This offers some protection for those in charge of solving the technical problems, even if they are called upon to speak at specific points, e.g. during press conferences.)
- Separate the crisis team from general management. General management has a specific role to play which should not be confused with the immediate management of the accident. This should be entrusted to a crisis manager.[6]
- Separate the various roles within the communication team: set up a message-producing unit, a message distribution unit, and a unit to follow up information given to the media.[7]

Keep the in-house information process under control
There are two imperatives for handling the complexity of a crisis:

- Reduce the volume of exchanges necessary; otherwise your communication networks will become saturated.
- Reduce the pressure on the people on the front lines. (This is even more critical when several decision-making centres must be coordinated and the front lines are subjected to excessively pressing requests for information.)

Responses may also take the form of operating protocol and other tools:

- Set up a sort of press agency between the headquarters and the site of the incident. Communications that are not directly tactical go through filtering units to previously designated speakers. This system helps prevent an avalanche of requests.[8]
- Use telephone conferences and video transmission to strengthen the system's ability to undertake communications rapidly while limiting the demands made on network's resources.[9]

Provide support for the most exposed units
The idea here is to have emergency teams organized nationwide that can go to a site or area experiencing difficulty.[10] This requires technical preparations (e.g. preparation, keeping people on call, planning transportation, accommodations, and mobility) as well as a change in business culture: getting the exposed units to accept outside help can be a problem. A good preparation should demonstrate that the outside team is not here to replace the local officials in charge, but to help them as they require. It is vital for these support teams to have understood the importance of communication.[11] If necessary, a communication manager from headquarters may also be included in the support team sent to the site. And, of course, attention to detail should include planning for transportation to the site and entry pass.

Creating and managing crisis teams

Special attention must be paid to the intermediate level, at which small groups, in particular crisis teams, are set up. These will have a substantial degree of responsibility in managing operations. The term 'crisis team' often has almost magical implications—the simple announcement that a crisis team has been set up is supposed to solve all the problems. This idea must be transformed into a veritable tool, and the best possible use must be made of it.

Beyond gadgets: have the capacity to act

Steven Fink has clearly stated a number of measures to be taken and questions that should be asked:

> One of the first responsibilities of the basic crisis team is to draw up a list of specialists who can back it up, depending on the type of crisis. In addition to these names, a list of potential types of crisis must be made. With that, some general crisis plans can be made, without getting lost in the details—but remember to ask the right questions: How can the key people (in-house and on the outside) be reached outside business hours? Who is responsible for alerting the employees, the media, and local, state or federal government agencies? Who can fill in if these people back down? How is the switchboard (the first line of defence) set up? What instructions do operators have for dealing with journalists? Should the switchboard be staffed by multi-lingual personnel? Have special instructions been given for handling large numbers of typical calls (e.g. rumours about a product)? Does the organization have a toll-free number? If so, are enough operators available to staff it? How will they be kept up to date on developments in the situation? Is there someone explicitly in charge of keeping the emergency list of telephone numbers up to date?
>
> (Based on Fink, 1986, pp. 57–66)

Along the same lines, Rolf Kaiser[12] emphasizes that, above all, the crisis centre should not be thought of as a sort of shrine, hidden in the basement, filled with equipment that is never used (though it costs a fortune), and staffed by personnel that only step in during a crisis. To the contrary, a crisis unit should be in touch with technical, organizational and human reality; it should operate constantly and be capable of shifting into high gear the day the crisis comes. One crucial condition for its effectiveness is to validate the core team, which receives little consideration in large bureaucracies. In particular, this core team should be placed in charge of a regular duty when things are normal.

In large organizations, these crisis teams should practice step-by-step mobilization, as was discussed earlier. First, the crisis teams at the lowest level are activated, keeping in reserve an oversight team at a higher level, which can become a crisis team if circumstances require it.

These teams should be assembled with care. The major duties should be defined ahead of time, and the assistance of key figures such as a doctor, a social worker, or a psychologist should be included. These people can remain on the outside, but they should be in close contact with the team.

One recent innovation consists of incorporating observers into the team, i.e. guardians of the key values that could get lost in the heat of the action.[13] Along the same lines, outside observers can be used. Their job is to take some distance in providing opinions throughout the crisis.[14]

Have a sufficient physical vision: the centre, separations, and interfaces

You must allocate beforehand a specific area to house the crisis team. This area should preferably be somewhere central, near the offices of the management, and if possible also near the offices dealing with the day-to-day running of the organization (such as the operational headquarters run by certain airlines, for example). Nor should this crisis centre be too far from the press centre, though there should be a clear separation between them.

Experience has also taught us that this crisis centre should not group all its duties together on a single site. The implicit model of the crisis room generally consists of a place where everyone assembles around an impressive array of communication devices. The shortfalls of this model have been shown up during practice exercises. Almost immediately, you arrive at a state of general cacophony, which can be dangerously reassuring in some respects, with each person believing that this is how a crisis centre should operate. The layout of crisis centres should, in fact, be based on the idea of separation,[15] so that the reception area is separated from the place where information is processed, and the decision-making areas are separated from the rooms occupied by the experts. The idea of interface comes as a natural counterpoint to the idea of separation. Accordingly, you must have a number of small rooms next to the decision-making room where liaison teams can liaise between managers and their departments, via fax machines and direct-dial telephones. And do not forget to provide a central area, where summaries of the overall development of the crisis can be posted.

Details will vary according to each specific case, and in particular according to the size of the crisis. You may just plan to make pre-equipped rooms available, should the need arise, or else set up a full-scale crisis centre. The important thing is to refer back to these concepts of centre, separation, and interface.

Specific tools

You must pay attention to the following points: specific means of communication; the prior assignment of duties (without forgetting the communication dimension); blackboards; maps and paper boards to help visualize the current state of affairs; a log book on display, or possibly several log books, in order to distinguish between events and decisions taken; tools to follow media coverage, such as VCRs; fax machines for simultaneous dispatches; large numbers of the same piece of equipment, so that all the modules can work on the same basis (e.g. the possibility of direct monitoring from room to room, enabling people to hear what is going on in other units without having to ask for information); and various means enabling groups to function over long periods of time.

It is also important to display all the facts on maps and boards, as well as in the log book(s)—not only for reasons to do with follow-up which we already mentioned, but also because otherwise there is a considerable risk of everyone basing their work on recollections of the pre-crisis situation. Every effort must be made to prevent them from harking back constantly to their habitual references, as this could result in conflict and confusion.

Another advantage of displaying this information is that it can enable visitors such as senior managers and journalists to have an overview of what is going on while remaining behind a window on the crisis room, for example, thereby not disturbing anyone.

Guidance capacities: operating crisis teams

This is a point which, although often ignored, is vital all the same. We have already seen just how much difficulty groups can get into when they are faced with very turbulent situations. Throughout the crisis, from start to finish, you must fix all your attention on this question: 'How are we going to operate; how are we operating?' The general tendency is to rush into action and become submerged in general agitation and gesticulating. You then lose sight of the strategic side of crisis management and become entangled in group phenomena; you become less and less able to anticipate, sort out major problems or find simple tactical reactions to the latest turns taken by the crisis. If, however, you constantly ask the question 'What is happening; how are we reacting?', you will give yourself that vital distance that will prevent you from becoming entangled either in the crisis itself or in the complex strategies you adopt to deal with it.

Everyone must become involved in critical distancing, but it is a good idea to delegate this task to one person in particular, preferably someone who is not too directly involved in the affair. In an industrial group, this may be the manager of a division that is not directly affected by the crisis being tackled.

This is a vital point. We often come across groups made up of major figures who are unable to face the continual and multi-faceted pressures of a crisis, due to insufficient distancing. You must also enhance the role of the chronicler or historian, whose task is to keep the log book up to date. It can never be stressed enough just how important this capacity to analyse events within the crisis group really is. A recent experiment in a simulation situation proved that a group of competent people can lose all its capacity for action in the space of just ten minutes, simply because it has not questioned the way it operates and has merely reacted to the many manifestations of the crisis.[16]

Once you have acquired this critical distance, you will find it easier to respond to demands from the outside using carefully constructed strategies. You will also be able to take on a central function, weaving together an infinite number of actions and interventions so that each thread is tied to the next ('closing the loop'[17]).

It goes without saying that you must also tackle the problems arising from group phenomena.

In order to avoid being submerged in general cacophony, you must adopt a firm and sober style of leadership, in order to clarify who is to do what, with whom and within which deadline. You must also be sure to tell everyone to keep their comments as brief as possible, as time is a particularly precious commodity. If necessary, you should point out that group members have all been brought together to solve a crisis, not to be representatives for their own organizations.

In order to overcome the problems of groupthink (examined in the section on 'Small groups' in Chapter 5), Irving Janis (1982, pp. 262–309) puts forward a set of rules governing group management. It is most important to ensure that:

- the person in charge gives each group member the role of critical assessor and encourages the group to give priority to the expression of doubts and objections;
- the person in charge remains impartial, instead of displaying preferences and expectations from the very outset; this will enable the

group to explore a wide range of alternatives with complete openness;

- the procedures provide either for the setting-up of a number of independent analysis and assessment groups or else for the group to be split from time to time to allow separate study of the alternatives, with notes being compared later;
- each member of the strategic group can periodically discuss the deliberations of the crisis team with colleagues on a confidential basis and give an unbiased report of their reactions to the group;
- in-house or outside experts are invited to each meeting and encouraged to question the views of group members;
- during every meeting held to assess possible strategic options, at least one of the group members is given the role of devil's advocate;
- sufficient time is devoted to the study of signals coming from partners and adversaries;
- once a preliminary consensus is reached on the political alternative that seems the most suitable, the group holds a last-chance meeting, during which each member is asked to speak out about any lingering doubts that may be entertained, and to think the question through once more before making a final choice.

As with every aspect of crisis management, a sense of judgement is required here. Janis himself is aware of this: think carefully about the way you handle these phenomena of group dynamics. You may decide to do nothing at all, as precautionary measures of this sort can be extremely costly in terms of delays, the risk of leaks, loss of control by the leader and the considerable worsening of these very same difficulties if the remedies are applied too clumsily or too late. You must be aware of these possible briar patches, of the vigilance they require and of the means you have to remedy them.[18]

Dealing with the issue of expert opinion

As in every other area, these resources must be gathered before the crisis hits.[19] In particular, the experts who will be called in should already be identified; their skills and credibility should have been analysed; they should be organized into a network; suggestions about working methods should be given, including how hypotheses are to be verified, what analytical methods will be used, and how results are interpreted. A simulation of the expert's work in an emergency situation can be organized, and experts and decision makers should make sure each side understands how the other thinks and works.

This must all be taken for granted when a crisis hits. During the crisis, several guidelines can be established:

- By turning to a single expert, you can get an opinion quickly. But in a confusing and complex situation, it will immediately be necessary to turn to a network of experts. They will provide a broader range of knowledge and probably greater credibility. As a positive action, it is undeniably wise at this stage to open up your own network, in order not to be dependent on a single source. Indeed, be careful to avoid listening only to experts who think the way you do, or who act like 'house' or 'pet' experts. The problems of groupthink in this area are formidable. Decision makers should also realize that as soon as they turn to a network instead of an individual, the time required to obtain an opinion becomes significantly longer.
- Ask the following questions immediately of the experts you call in: 'How soon can you shed light on this, how reliable will your assessments be, and what type of information can you provide?' In this way, you will know right away what decisions must be made *without* the benefit of the expert's advice. This is crucial. There is an underlying idea that all actions can be based on the expert's evaluation, but this can be a trap. In the midst of the crisis, it can be very destabilizing to discover that you cannot wait for the experts to decide, or that precious time has been lost by insisting absolutely on following this inadequate strategy.
- Anticipate the possible results and study the various options that could be adopted according to the different scenarios.
- Look after the credibility of your expert network.
- Think about how these experts will speak to the public. It is helpful to have clear rules of conduct, for instance: 'We expect you to give an honest analysis that you can explain to the public; all we request is that you be ready to give us high-quality assessment.'
- Naturally, you must be careful not to fall into the briar patches identified earlier, e.g. placing constant pressure on the experts to deliver their results as soon as possible, or creating direct or indirect pressure on the experts to make up their minds.

Managing communication

Media communication

Having already ventured forth into the field of communications, you must now keep up this presence throughout the crisis.

Maintaining openness and competence

Your vigilance must not flag, even after getting through the initial shock caused by the announcement that the event has taken place. While organizations naturally enough experience considerable difficulty when reacting to the initial wave of media attention, it is the second wave that is the most dangerous. This unfurls just after the first has crashed down on the organization, when everyone is looking forward to a certain respite. The media return in force, this time armed with real questions—more specific, incisive and better documented—just when you are no longer expecting them, and when everyone is taking a rest after the initial ordeal. As Péter-J. Hargitay stresses: 'The accident after the accident is what kills the company, not the first accident.'[20]

At this point, it is important not to start automatically going against standard practice. To this end, a certain number of landmarks are often listed as references for use in crisis communication. In this field, at least, it would seem that a certain number of rules should be observed, except in very exceptional circumstances.

- Name a high-ranking spokesperson, both a technician and a decision maker, who has been fully prepared for communication with the media, rather than a communicator who has only rapidly been filled in on the technical questions.
- Make sure you are the first to supply information.
- Provide full and accurate information on a very regular basis, keeping close to developments in the crisis rather than just handing out the occasional press release.
- Give out this information from well-identified press centres, in order to pin down media demands.
- Take account of media deadlines. Treat different forms of media differently, as they all have their own specific needs.
- Use communication material prepared in advance. For yourself, this will comprise lists of correspondents and arguments prepared in advance in respect of a certain number of possible scenarios, while for the press, it will include outlines and reference data (e.g.

on the sector involved, the organization, or previous accidents or problems).

All this is in aid of just one thing, namely, to become the best source of information, or at least one of the most reliable sources and therefore rapidly the most credible and the one with the largest audience. If you follow these rules, you will keep a foothold in the competitive area of communication.

To these positive rules we must now add some negative principles.

- Never lie, for as soon as your lies are spotted you will be permanently discredited.
- Never just say 'no comment'. If you do not want to reply to a question because you judge that the information cannot be made public, you must give reasons (e.g. 'For obvious security reasons it would be irresponsible of me to tell you which strategy the intervention teams are going to follow in this hostage-taking.'; 'This concerns a secret manufacturing process and we can't go into in any further detail'; 'The police are carrying out an investigation and we are not allowed to give out any specific details'; or 'The families haven't yet been told, so you'll understand if, out of a sense of decency, I don't give you the victims' names').
- This does not mean you have to pour out wild speculations about the worst possible developments.

Organizations have often included these rules, a sort of crisis user's guide, in their reference documents, especially regarding crises resulting from accidents.

Hence these long-standing instructions at Dow Chemical Canada:

1 The public must be informed frequently and accurately through the media, from the outset. This must be done by one or two highly credible senior spokesmen who understand the situation and can explain it calmly and clearly in lay language. The first 24 hours of a crisis are critical.
2 If this is not done, a public information vacuum probably will develop rapidly—and be filled by rumours or alarms far worse than the real situation.
3 Silence in the midst of a crisis implies guilt, whether justified or not.
4 It is not enough merely to assure the public that everything is OK and there's no reason for alarm. To be credible, we must provide details of how that conclusion is drawn.
5 It is vital to realize that reporters face deadlines hour by hour.

> Information must always be correct, consistent, and current,
> even if all the answers aren't immediately available.
>
> (Stephenson, 1984, p. 3)

Fundamental skills to ensure better communication

We could give further details as to how to organize a press room, draw up a press release, prepare for an interview and structure communication duties. However, far more important than logistical improvements (which can always be carried out) are the fundamental conceptions that govern the whole area of crisis communication and structure reactions in a situation of shock.

First and foremost, you must regard the demand and the need for information on the part of all different publics as entirely justifiable. An organization does not only exist through its activities and technical results. It also lives through its relationship with its environment and through the richness of its in-house communication. You must take just as much care in responding to these publics as you would when dealing with the organization's other activities.

You will then find it easier to abandon the reflex of arrogance that always comes over people in charge when they come under attack both from the crisis and from all their publics, especially the media.

> *Péter-J. Hargitay*
> That is [. . .] a simple question of respect for others. The key is
> 'There are no stupid questions, there are only stupid answers.'
> More generally speaking, you have to realize that what causes
> fear is a lack of information. Therefore the first goal has to be to
> try and inform people. Let me specify, *not to calm them down,*
> *but to inform them.*[21]

Information and communication roles should therefore be given proper recognition within the organization. This means that the people in charge of communication should have access to the strategic echelons, even in crisis situations. The communication dimension must also be taken into consideration when major options are being decided on during the crisis.

> *Edgar Fasel*
> Develop a 'cybernetic perception' of public relations. This
> means not only getting messages from the company to the public,
> but also getting the organization to take into account expectations
> from the outside. Just as a banker won't allow any old decision
> to be made, the job of public relations is to indicate what won't
> be acceptable to the outside. This must go hand in hand with the
> appropriate status of external relations within the company. To

succeed, companies have a duty to think in 'peacetime' about their culture, their communications ethic, and their choice of communicators.[22]

In addition, the role of communication must be accepted by the organization as a whole. Those in charge of communication often encounter as many difficulties in obtaining information within their own organization, from the technical departments, as journalists have from the outside. Indeed, 'support' would be a more appropriate word to use than 'acceptance'.

This way, you will be able to give communication a higher profile.

Edgar Fasel
The company should say what it knows as quickly as possible. Don't wait to announce the bad news: in fact, the sooner you touch bottom, the less painful the process will be. Then you can always redistribute hope, instead of having to go on blackening the picture, which slowly deadens the capacity to react. Other rules: say everything you know, say only what you know, but be sure to specify, 'We don't know everything—be ready to receive other information'.[23]

Make sure you do not tackle communication in too fragmented a way. The goal is not to juggle with an avalanche of details and anecdotes to be unleashed without a thought. If people start chasing after insignificant details, it is mostly in order to make up for a lack of more essential news. When it comes to information, people do not want to follow all the turns the crisis takes. Instead, they want to know why you have chosen a particular approach and why a particular assessment has been made. They want to understand the general attitudes giving meaning and direction to the decision makers' responses. Once they have been satisfied, pressure will ease considerably, giving you more time to make your messages more relevant and show more consideration towards the publics concerned.

Philippe Vesseron
To show in a credible manner that there are guidelines, you have to avoid being simplistic. Don't try to cover up choices, arbitration, or strategies—to the contrary, bring them into broad daylight, use the least reductive images. This is the way to develop an openness that goes beyond short-term imperatives and that isn't limited to the necessarily anecdotal aspects of each new plot twist.[24]

Along the same lines, the idea is to gain greater freedom in the way you communicate. You will find this easier if you cease to believe that (1) the crisis is an incurable failure and the fault of those god-like figures at the top now about to be toppled from their pedestals; (2) the crisis can only be dealt with in a covert fashion.

You must never neglect safety, as there is no such thing as zero-risk; similarly, crisis management is essential if the situation is not to get any worse. To start with, instead of hiding themselves or the facts, the people in charge must shoulder their responsibilities and get down to managing the crisis. This shift in emphasis, from guilt and abdication to responsibility, will result in more fruitful responses showing greater respect for the facts and the actors involved.

With such a starting point, you will be able to anticipate problems and abandon a purely defensive stance. This is important, as failure in communication is still possible, not because of any hiding of the facts or an inability to respond, but because of a simple 'absence of initiative in the information field'.[25] For example, if you hand out a list of the products involved in a disaster without making it clear whether the list is exhaustive or not, you lay yourself open to future reproaches such as 'You didn't tell us everything!'.

The approach of taking the initiative therefore leads you to widen the scope of questions without being forced to.

Philippe Vesseron
To develop credibility, I think it's essential to know how to take risks. In particular, take the initiative of talking about an issue before it has been raised. Be wary of the fear of causing fear. If public opinion or the press is only interested in a narrow aspect of a risk, and a secondary one as well, in my experience you have to move quickly to re-establish priorities among issues.[26]

Lastly, it should be stressed that you will not be able to do anything in a time of crisis if you have not made thorough preparations beforehand, especially regarding structures. The views of Edgar Fasel, head of communications at Sandoz, on the experiences of his group during the episode of pollution in the Rhine in 1986, are most helpful in this respect.

Edgar Fasel
No business can equip itself on a permanent basis with a sufficient number of information professionals to handle a large-scale crisis. Therefore, you need a crisis plan. This should include lists of tasks to be performed and should set priorities. In quantitative terms, this crisis organization should provide for the rapid expansion of staff by co-workers 'borrowed' from other departments. These auxiliaries should have been designated and

informed about their tasks beforehand and should go through periodic training.[27]

For bordering situations beyond the basic principles: questions without answers

The basic rules we have suggested you should follow in order to maintain openness and authority constitute the body of doctrine that is generally accepted today by specialists. You must take good heed of these rules, but there are one or two problems which then need to be looked at. After all, it would be dangerous if these difficulties, which how-to books on crisis communication regularly neglect to mention, only became apparent to the decision maker once he or she was already embroiled in a high-risk situation. This is why we must complicate things by taking a second look at the principles underpinning the proposed set of rules.

- Never lie: this is clear, but what about the sin of omission, which conveniently gives rise to false interpretations? What about the people managing crises who choose not to correct false interpretations because they find them convenient though, of course, they have not lied in the strict sense of the word? Is it enough to say 'never lie', if you can still use every subterfuge in the book in order to obtain the same results?
- Always give reasons for not providing information in order to avoid having to say 'no comment': fair enough, but are these reasons always as acceptable as the precepts for good conduct suggest? For example, it is all very well for a manufacturing process to be secret, but if it involves huge risks which a rival process does not, the withholding of information cannot totally be justified. The argument that there may be a risk to security (malicious intent, terrorism) can sometimes be used in a rather dubious way.

We have no intention of getting involved in a moralistic quarrel. We simply want to point out the limitations, including operational ones, of the principles set out in all the how-to books. People are bound to question the supposedly good arguments you put forward. Take a closer look at the basic rules you have been given, and you will find all manner of tricky questions. The principles people normally put forward will not in themselves guarantee access to reliable information. These principles are first and foremost methods of avoiding the most common media catastrophes, not the be-all and end-all of this issue.

Conversely, the same applies to the principle of transparency. After years of excessive secrecy, which seriously eroded the credibility of a large number of official bodies, the watchword now has to be transparency. Operational effectiveness conveniently goes hand in hand with the ethical principles of access to information. Nevertheless, the policy of keeping nothing from the public can reach deadlock when it comes to contradictions that can exist in certain sensitive files (especially those exposed or linked to terrorism) and certain constraints that cannot be separated from the operations of any firm.

If we want to avoid falling into the briar patch pointed out by Pascal— 'he who wants to act like an angel will end up acting like a beast'— we must summon up our courage and point out a number of difficulties.

The most obvious case of all is terrorism, of course. There is a danger of using it as a convenient smokescreen and constantly hushing everything up. Indeed, the decision maker will frequently be advised to use public safety as a pretext to win the right to secrecy. Nevertheless, there can be cases in which absolute transparency is not necessarily a very responsible policy.

Imagine the following case—easy to do, as it is a real-life story: a popular television programme takes major risks as its theme. Everyone knows that no country is safe from terrorist attacks. What they do not know, however, is that a reply to these attacks has been found. Someone raises the question, but no one is going to admit that the vulnerability to terrorism has been overcome, as this might lead terrorists to direct their attention to chinks that still exist in the armour.

On the issue of terrorism again, victims involved in certain recent affairs have often deplored the printing of information in newspapers as this may have helped some terrorists escape justice.

Then there are the cases such as the one cited above (the American dam and the action of the police chief who, unable to help 80 000 in three minutes, decided to save his own ten men, thereby instantly earning himself a virtual lynching in the press[28]). Here the filtering of information by the media inevitably gives rise to widespread and harmful effects.

Nor should we forget that negotiations play a part in most crises, and that during these negotiations, some facts, gestures and movements cannot be disclosed immediately. Some people will object that no one should be left in the dark about anything, and that everyone should be kept fully informed. Yet others will take the opposite view, arguing that the problems thrown up by a crisis are so serious that it is especially important not to confuse empty noise with genuine attempts to find solutions.

> *Michel Rocard*
> I've seen many trade, financial, industrial and agricultural negotiations fail. The principal cause has often been the obligation to 'negotiate in public', which is in fact a contradiction in terms. Innumerable opportunities to improve the affairs of the planet through bold and imaginative agreements are lost in this way.
>
> (Rocard, 1987, pp. 133–4)

We shall end on a point which actually deserves an entire book to itself. This concerns some even more fundamental reasons why you should not sink into this fashionable dogma of transparency, with its occasional tinges of intellectual and sanctimonious terrorism. Philippe Roqueplo's analysis is well worth studying:

> No subject of interest to a large group of people can be totally imbued with transparency. Each actor has the right to his or her sphere of secrecy. Outlawing all secrets amounts to depriving a social group of the very possibility of asserting its identity. No group can exist if the spotlight is turned relentlessly and permanently on its identity, its deliberations, its uncertainties or simply its suspicions. Every gathering presupposes the possibility of having words in private, not intended for public consumption. The dogma of absolute transparency condemns a society to a generalized atomism. The democratic vote itself is indeed considered null and void if it does not respect guarantees of secrecy. It is therefore important to distinguish between, on the one hand, the need to publicize decisions and the reasons adduced for those decisions and, on the other, the entire set of considerations—possibly inexpressible—which have helped forge these decisions. When it comes to transparency, distinctions need to be made between different types of situation. If in order to exercise his responsibility, every individual needs to know about a particular piece of information which is being withheld, it is intolerable to withhold this information. If, however, the information being withheld does not affect the exercise of this responsibility or could even perturb it, the affair becomes less clear.[29]

As Philippe Roqueplo adds: 'Societies need a certain opaqueness.'

Television journalists themselves present a news programme, i.e. a construct, rather than the discussions that have led to the choice of subjects, the points they have chosen to leave to one side or the conflicts that have been caused by the chosen options. The flag of transparency needs to be waved because of past mistakes and new demands for information. However, this does not mean that all the problems linked to information in human societies, and which the crisis will probably exacerbate and complicate rather than simplify, can be made to vanish at the wave of the magic wand of transparency.

Crisis management is full of contradictions, and the aspect of transparency is no exception. All decision makers, and indeed all actors, would therefore do well to bear in mind comments made by Jean Lacouture, which were already quoted elsewhere:

> Nobody has the right to mark out frontiers between publishable and unspeakable truths for his own personal use. Yet you will come across these borders, when there is a question of the survival of a specific person or community. But where should they be located? This is one of the enigmas the Sphinx asks the journalist to solve.
>
> (Lacouture, 1989, p. 213)

Do not rush too eagerly into this breach! This enigma only applies to the most sensitive aspects of the most exceptional cases. In any other circumstances, this would be quite the wrong way of thinking and would lead to bitter failures.

So do not get these ideas wrong. The goal naturally is not to thwart a vital movement towards greater transparency. This combat is far from over—a source of great despair to the captains of industry, who deplore the appallingly long time that is needed to open up structures obsessed with secrecy. They find it difficult to explain that silence can also be a communication strategy—a fact that has never been grasped by their colleagues.

If we had to come up with a simple teaching principle for use by people finding it difficult to broach this complex and forbidden subject, it would go something like this: the credibility of officials today is almost non-existent and always subject to suspicion, and the risk of a confidential piece of information being broadcast by the media in the worst possible circumstances is so great, that it is almost always best for the decision maker to practise transparency, even aggressive transparency. Any other strategy, including that of half measures, presents considerable risks.

François Ailleret's message[30] is doubtless the most appropriate here. It fits in very neatly with those of Jean Lacouture and Philippe Roqueplo, in that it provides people with strong, but not dogmatic, basic principles upon which to base the exercise of their responsibilities.

François Ailleret
If we say what we know while respecting an ethic of both openness and what I call total good faith, it seems to me that we can earn full legitimacy for our explanations. If the people who know aren't talking, their attitude immediately lends legitimacy to other sources, with all the risk for error [that that implies].

Of course, some situations are extraordinarily tough. It's the responsibility of those directly in charge of the matter to keep an eye on their guidelines, but also to have a sense of the situation—and this may lead them to speak up earlier, thereby taking a risk, or to wait, thereby ensuring greater reliability. Or to let some other source speak out, provided they don't think it will contradict their strategy of openness. Or, on the contrary, they may choose to take the high ground right away, and even be firm and direct about it, if they think there is undue risk in letting non-legitimate sources be heard. My experience is limited, but every time bad information has got out, it was because we waited too long to say what we could have said early on. [. . .]

Then, if it comes down to a very confused and tough situation, I'd say everyone has to examine his own conscience and evaluate his responsibilities . . .[31]

Non-media communications

Constant attention must be paid to employees, customers, suppliers, administrations, elected representatives, victims and the families of victims, along with essential sections of the public (e.g. doctors, in the case of a pharmaceuticals company). If you are to handle communications successfully, you must have identified your many different publics and your most important publics beforehand.

In-house public
This is one of the most important publics, though it is easy to lose sight of that fact when under siege from the media. You must have prepared networks and thought out specific ways of contacting your in-house public both quickly and regularly. You must have prepared relays capable of providing summaries of the situation before or immediately after a press conference. You must also make full use of dialogue structures (their importance was noted in Chapter 5).

Edgar Fasel: The Basel affair (November 1986)
At Schweizerhalle, the physical and psychological pressures created by the hordes of journalists on our departments made us tend to forget other groups who were nonetheless essential in such circumstances: our personnel, the subsidiaries, shareholders, our colleagues, authorities not directly involved, certain

categories of consumers and prescribers, and so on. The worst is no doubt that we completely neglected our employees —they had to watch television, read the newspapers to know what was going on here, 'in our company, in-house', as they say. It is therefore imperative that the crisis organization ensure full service to all these target publics, independently of the actual press service, but coordinating with it.[32]

Péter-J. Hargitay and Bhopal
In terms of in-house communication, even though we didn't yet have any details about the accident, our first concern was informing Union Carbide's employees. Twice a day we sent them an 'internal information report'. We posted information in company cafeterias about how events were developing. This is a vital lesson: your priority is not the press, it is your own employees. Otherwise, you run the risk of things simply imploding.[33]

Johnson & Johnson: The Tylenol case
Our most valuable constituents are the employees. We realized that from day one. In all, we produced four different videotaped special reports on the Tylenol crisis. We had an internal video network for our 165 companies and divisions, and we sent them cassettes. The tapes, lasting more than three hours, covered all important aspects of the evolving story and treated at length the teleconferences and appearances of Jim Burke [the president] on the Donahue Show. The chairman and president cosigned a letter that went to every domestic employee, explaining the crisis, what the company was doing, and the steps we were going to take. The employee response was impressive. [. . .] The crisis knitted our employees together, and bonded them as never before in the company's history. Of course, you'd rather wish it hadn't happened at all. But because the company responded the way it did, the employees were very proud of the organization.[34]

Victims

At this point, we must remember everything that was said earlier about the very many mistakes that are made when communicating with the victims and their families. Follow these golden rules: provide information rapidly; maintain a tactful presence and ensure the family is not left out in the cold; offer help in overcoming the many difficulties likely to confront the victims, including the names and addresses of associations well-known for their expertise in the specific area of difficulty.

It is useful to repeat the point made by Philippe Dessaint previously regarding communication with victims in a television programme. As you will recall, there was very little preparation for the ordeal, while the basic message received by the so-called volunteer being sent to the front line was 'Be careful, it'll be dangerous!'.

Philippe Dessaint
You can't confront an ordeal of this sort without thoroughly preparing the organization beforehand. The colleague being sent to the programme to represent the company and dialogue with the victims should receive the following message from both his president and the rest of the organization: 'I know that you're about to do something extremely difficult. First of all, thank you! Don't forget that though the company may be running a risk, you at least are not. We think you will be our best advocate in this affair. We certainly won't shoot you down in flames if there's a problem. Just be yourself. Be human. Forget the technical notes, at least to start with. The important thing is to communicate, not to chuck tonnes of reports at everyone.'

Naturally, the whole thing would be more natural if there was some sort of contact with the victims before a meeting of this type. However, these contacts are often restricted to discussions between legal experts. The victims should be recognized as people, not just as costly legal problems.

The worst part about the whole thing is the fact that this initial meeting is taking place in a television studio, and not so much the issue of how you express yourself, or the words or postures you adopt in front of the camera.

If it was possible to make preparations, though this would be a bad thing psychologically, they would amount to getting those preparing for such a dialogue to recall previous crises they have experienced and to think about them in personal terms, rather than on a purely professional basis, as you would during a simulation exercise. They would then see for themselves the difference between a purely defensive message and one addressed to people who are suffering. This latter approach would be seen as quite indecent during the programme.[35]

Nor is it forbidden to go one step beyond simple common sense in this question of relations with victims. It is useful to look at the action the Norwegians take, especially when catastrophes have taken place far away and information is difficult to obtain.

Dr Lars Weisaeth: Taking charge of the victims, a Norwegian approach
In order to cope with the air disaster which took place on September 5th 1989 off the Danish coast, the authorities set up a reception and information centre for friends and relatives of the victims. The idea was to bring together in one place all the resources required to meet these people's needs. They could obtain information, as all the organizations involved had representatives at the centre (transporters, authorities, doctors, members of the Church) and could also get any psychological help they needed. Having everyone together in a group, with

each person living through the same experience, was seen to be a positive aspect. It was on that occasion that we realized that the circle of friends and relatives of each dead or missing person numbered around fifteen people. It was thanks to our information and help centre that we were able to meet the needs of these larger groups. In addition, the authorities sought to adapt their communication to suit the different members of the victims' families, on the basis that small children could only understand that they had just lost their mother or father if there was a very physical description of the accident, whereas 8–12 year-olds could understand a verbal message. Children of 12 to 14 could understand technical explanations, while teenagers were able to take part in more symbolic processes, such as religious services. The families were cared for using these new types of approach, which opened up fresh horizons. The same model was adopted a second time during a disaster at sea on April 7th 1990.[36]

Many publics with different needs

As a rule, it is important to understand that each public has its own specific need for different, and in some cases, contradictory types of information. For example, in the case of the death of cattle following the distribution of a faulty product, farmers first and foremost want to be reimbursed and have the carcasses removed. An association for the protection of animals, on the other hand, will want to know whether the animals suffered or not, while consumers will ask if there is any risk to their health.[37]

There are, of course, various ways of reaching these different publics without relying on the media, which have their own criteria and cannot therefore meet every need. These include advertising, public speeches, letters, meetings, toll-free calls, posters, and communication by telephone with some targets. These methods are especially useful when launching counterattacks against unfounded rumours. Conversely, some of these techniques can be used to gain a clearer idea of people's fears and needs for information without going through the media, which are not necessarily the best channels for gathering information.

This non-media communication must be based on rigour, initiative and openness.

As has already been said, you must carry out your own studies to gauge public opinion accurately, not just view things through the eyes of the media.

You must even check whether your messages have been properly received and passed on. This would have avoided many difficulties in France during an affair such as Chernobyl. Do not hesitate to show that you, too, are human, despite the fact that long-standing attitudes have artificially projected the idea that people only take heed of dehumanized economic constraints.

Péter-J. Hargitay and Bhopal
Mr. Zutty and I made a tour of Europe every two or three weeks. We visited the major capitals, disseminating the latest available information. On his part, this was what I call civic courage. A chemist, a CEO, he didn't know Europe. He had two options—either he trusted me or he didn't. He chose to trust me. We went everywhere, to talk with left-wing and right-wing journalists, without any filtration. In my opinion, that was the most positive part of the information strategy: the CEO himself took time to go talk to everyone. He was there in person, not to defend himself or make excuses, but to explain what had happened and to guarantee that the company had decided to take moral responsibility for this catastrophe. [. . .]

My conviction is that in such cases, we should develop our relations with our so-called adversaries, who present their serious concerns over the future of the western world. Even if there are differences of opinion, we have to take them seriously. And above all, we have to understand that communication is not always just a matter of technology and professionalism, but rather a question of culture.[38]

Handling rumours

You have already learned about the dangers of oversimplisitic strategies when faced with rumours—phenomena that are often deeply rooted in the social reality from which they emerge and spread. You can, of course, adopt guidelines such as these:

- It is possible, and sometimes appropriate, to remain silent, if the rumour only reaches the ears of publics that are of minor importance to the organization concerned. Take care that intervention on your part does not turn a very limited phenomenon into an extremely large-scale affair.
- A denial may be sufficient in cases where checking the truth of your assurances is a simple and straightforward affair.
- A strong and well-aimed counterattack can bear fruit, provided you have a sufficiently strong case.

More often than not, the crisis will involve uncertain realities. It will still be possible to say that there is only a very slight risk, but impossible to guarantee that there is no risk at all. Rumours will be fed by a substrate comprising general defiance and a very negative heritage. This substrate will be more important than the immediate facts, which will only serve as material for making predictions on both sides. In these conditions, it is essential that rumours be thoroughly and carefully dealt with by interdisciplinary teams producing expert analyses and a large number of intervention scenarios. Jean-Noël Kapferer has some useful suggestions for teams such as these. These include giving a rumour an identity which is unacceptable to it, thereby diminishing the status of the gossipmongers, and providing explanations for any rumours going around (Kapferer, 1987, pp. 287–302).

Make sure you do not get caught in the communication trap

If you are to avoid major disillusionment in the medium term, three rules must be spelled out:

- Communication during a crisis depends largely on prior communication. You cannot suddenly wheel out a totally artificial arsenal of weapons to wage a media war.
- Although communication is an important aspect of crisis management, it is not the only lever, and certainly not the most important. You must therefore make sure you do not become trapped in the increasing tendency to make communication the be-all and end-all of crisis management.
- Similarly, remember that crisis management is only possible if it represents part of a general effort to prevent risks and limit vulnerability. If this is not the case, communication will become almost impossible the day the crisis strikes.

Managing the crisis to the end

A crisis is a dynamic process. It usually begins with a peak, extends into a plateau phase (which may include several new developments), and ends abruptly or, as is more frequently the case, continues to be a drag on the life of the organization.

During the initial impact, the means for response are weakest. In the plateau phase, too many teams prevent the work from being done efficiently. In the terminal phase, weariness sets in, and the means for response are again weakened. It becomes necessary to react in a more orderly manner and to avoid making classic mistakes.

Do not stop until the crisis is truly resolved

No matter what type of crisis occurs, there is a great temptation to lower your guard before the crisis is over—or, indeed, as soon as a glimmer of hope indicates that the episode may soon be over. Yet it is important to continue your efforts to the very end, and to maintain a capacity to handle the violent reactions of the crisis in its final throes. This is the problem with forest fires or peat fires, which can flare up just when they seem to be extinguished and the fire trucks are leaving the scene. The same is true of crises involving a high degree of conflict.

> *The end of the crisis in Jordan, 1970, as seen by Henry Kissinger*
> To close a crisis, the problem lies in choosing the right pressure to be applied in order to incite the adversary as much as possible to seek a settlement, yet without giving him the impression that he has no way of avoiding conflict. Paradoxically, the most critical moment is when the other camp seems ready to negotiate. You are tempted to lower your guard, or even to make a gesture of good will to speed things up. And that's the mistake. The only time for making concessions is after the crisis has been resolved and a settlement or modus vivendi has been reached. Then and only then moderation becomes a gesture of generosity and good will. But if it is too apparent, it creates the risk of making everything fail by creating last-minute doubts: the adversary wonders if it is really necessary to pay the price of the settlement.
> (Kissinger, 1979, Vol. 1, pp. 651–2)

Do not confuse ending technical management with ending the crisis

There is a tendency to remove the crisis management mechanisms at the first encouraging sign, or at least as soon as the breakdown appears to have been vanquished technically. This is to forget that many other aspects besides technical ones are involved. Removing these measures is an important decision that must only be made at the appropriate level, after an in-depth examination.

> *The lessons from periods of electrical outages, according to François Ailleret*
> I think we tend to dismantle the crisis units and the specific pro-cedures for exceptional situations too early. The people in charge tend to check out when a problem is 95 per cent solved. The reaction is 'OK, tomorrow it will be 100 per cent solved'. This leads to a brutal letdown after the tension of the previous phase. And the people busy with the remaining 5 per cent are

forgotten. For them, the problem hasn't been solved: they need a contact person. Especially in the area of communication.

I've seen this clearly during power failures, for instance in January 1987 after the electricity strikes. We set up a crisis unit. When the strike was over and the network could be managed normally . . . we disbanded the crisis unit (besides, we were getting almost no more telephone calls). But we realized, looking back, that the measure had been lifted too soon. A number of regional managers still had local problems to handle, often of a different type, and they were hindered by the disappearance of the crisis unit. We should have checked with them whether we could close the crisis unit. When you've had a widespread incident on the network and 95 per cent of the customers have electricity again, the remaining 5 per cent feel even more handicapped. If at the very moment when the demands of those people become justifiably more pressing, you also take away their contacts, then you can only aggravate the situation pointlessly. The crisis unit should never be dissolved until the people it deals with, and who are its main reason for existing, feel it has nothing more to offer them.[39]

Mississauga: the worst problem isn't evacuating, but returning home
The phase that was the least well handled in this evacuation of 216 000 persons was bringing them home again. Insufficient attention has been paid to this aspect. People felt reassured, and there was a very natural letdown. This is when gigantic traffic jams developed, against a backdrop of confusion, because the various sectors had not been reopened simultaneously. But the people concerned could not have cared less about the explanations.

(Lagadec, 1983)

Do not keep measures in place longer than necessary

This is the opposite extreme: artificially prolonging the crisis because those involved hesitate to give up the exceptional atmosphere and all that goes with it, e.g. a sense of challenge and a greater freedom of action.

As Claude Frantzen warns, 'When you're pulling all the strings pretty much the way you want to, getting a whole network moving, mobilizing a huge number of ambassadors in the wee hours—it goes to your head.'[40]

Do not confuse the end of the crisis with the end of the problems to be solved

The spotlights of current events gradually focus on other matters. The problems, however, are far from being solved. This is when the work begins behind the scenes—while you wait for the media to come back for the first, second, and third anniversary of the event, *ad infinitum*.

Conducting the aftermath of the crisis

First of all comes the immediate aftermath of the crisis, which can give rise to some very destabilizing jolts. You must remain vigilant if you are to absorb these jolts.

> *Philippe Legorjus*
> Before the assault, I said to my NCOs, 'Take care. At the beginning, people will treat us like heroes, because the media are conditioned to make a big issue of the freeing of hostages. Later, though, they'll start examining exactly how we obtained the results we did and forget the results themselves. Don't forget that we'll be criticized whatever happens.' That's why I'd have liked a team of journalists authorized to follow operations, not to supervise them, just to witness them. I subsequently had considerable cause to regret that it had been not possible, when I read inaccurate accounts in the newspapers and listened to certain offhand commentaries on the way we had carried out the assault and on the determination of the Kanaks.
> (Legorjus, 1990, p. 277)

There is also the longer term, however. Every crisis is a difficult moment for individuals and organizations. You must reappropriate the ordeal and heal your wounds as best as possible. You must also do something about the inconvenience inevitably caused by the choices you will have had to make in an atmosphere of contradictions. You must also draw lessons from it and take care to rectify any misleading conclusions that have been drawn rather too hastily from the style of crisis management adopted on this particular occasion. Several things need to be taken into consideration at this point.

The will to forget vs well-planned debriefing

There is a great temptation to reassure oneself, alert after alert. For example, people in positions of responsibility repainted the picture very rapidly after Chernobyl, asserting that they had never been at all shaken by events. It is very natural to forget, but you must force yourself to go over recent events with a fine-toothed comb.

Philippe Legorjus: Debriefing the GIGN (French SWAT troops)
'Debriefing' does not have an exact translation in French. It means that each participant in an operation must painstakingly dissect his moves, his thoughts and the reasons for his behaviour. At the GIGN, debriefings are collective affairs, and underpin our whole profession. After each operation, we do an initial commentary at the scene, in the heat of the moment. We all try to remember our movements and the positions we adopted, and sometimes we even do replays of certain phases of the action. We all note our good points and our mistakes. We are free to criticize each other. The goal is to strip all our acts and initiatives down to the bare bones before ruthlessly analysing them. This can be direct, even brutal, but it is never harmful.

Few observers have been admitted to these sessions, but those who have had access have been amazed by the vigour and freedom of expression which prevail there. Our boss presides over the debate, but is never above criticism. The operational plan he chose is also placed under scrutiny and submitted to the comments of the NCOs.

Back at our base, a second debriefing is organized the following day or the day after that. It is opened up to include those who did not directly take part in the operation, roughly two-thirds of the personnel. We then try to draw lessons, with the help of hindsight, though we don't forget collective criticism. The operation is definitively analysed, dismantled and reassembled to the benefit of everyone.

(Legorjus, 1990, pp. 77, 132–3)

Comforting the troops

Every crisis leaves its mark. Individuals and organizations alike need to take a breath after this type of ordeal. There is often a need to talk. Here, yet again, forgetfulness, deriving from lassitude and above all guilt, is the most tempting reaction. This means that deep wounds are left which will never heal. These will have many sorts of harmful consequences in the future.

Philippe Legorjus: Thinking about the aftermath of the ordeal
I'm furious that nothing was prepared for the aftermath of the assault. After an ordeal like this, the men need to be cocooned and reassured, and they need help in sorting out their ideas. As far as I am aware, the French army has not found an answer to this problem, which concerns all modern armies, namely how to cope with the aftermath of an operation and the inevitable trauma it causes.

(Legorjus, 1990, pp. 278–9)

Reviewing the situation for more than the psychological aspect

Like Enrico Quarantelli,[41] we can get rid of some of the assumptions that so often restrict the way we approach the aftermath of the crisis. This approach is often marked by a psychoanalytical model, and therefore focuses on the individual and the trauma he or she may have suffered.

- The writing of reports does not have to be the only form of action following a crisis.
- The theory that people suffer considerable trauma after a crisis may not always hold good, even if emergency workers may suffer severe trauma, especially those who have seen dismembered bodies, in particular those of babies or children.
- The ordeal may not have been entirely negative. The people involved may have the feeling of having taken part in something big, of having shown their true worth in the crisis. For them, at least, the purpose of action taken after the catastrophe should not be to cure traumatic shock.
- The individual approach is not always the best. The unit under analysis should sometimes be the group, the way it operates and its standards (as in the case of the GIGN, described above by Philippe Legorjus).
- It is sometimes necessary to take management decisions that have nothing to do with the management of individual problems. This may involve the group's methods, the make-up of the teams, or the structures of the organization.

Avoid a triumphal backlash

A crisis is a painful ordeal. It is impossible to manage everything perfectly. Many problems will remain unsolved. A little modesty and humility are welcome, even if relief can lead to an overboard reaction coupled with unhealthy repression.

Maurice Grimaud and May 1968
Even in the heat of the action, my colleagues and I had never really feared the insurgents would take power. Once the danger was passed, I was more worried to see how much of a hurry the authorities were in to erase even the memory of these events, which had struck such terror into the hearts of rulers and citizens alike for a whole month. I felt we should remind these men with such short memories that we would not always be lucky enough to receive warnings from above.

And then, as May receded, I realized painfully that scorn and arrogance were replacing the vestiges of fear. [. . .] I would have preferred a more modest triumph, just as large a crowd, but a silent one, meditating on that strange moment when France's destiny was, as it has been more than once in its history, suspended between contradictory hopes. Order was returning, which was, of course, a good thing, but the voices which, for thirty days, had called for the birth of a more just and less oppressive world should not be stifled. The France of law and order should not cover its ears to the cries of its youth, otherwise events would repeat themselves one day . . .

(Grimaud, 1977, pp. 11, 322–3)

Henry Kissinger: The end of the war in the Middle East (1973)
In managing the conclusion of any crisis the problem is to calibrate pressures to produce the maximum incentive for settlement without giving the other side the impression that it has no way of avoiding a confrontation. Paradoxically, perhaps the most critical moment occurs when the opponent appears ready to settle; then it is the natural temptation to relax and perhaps to ease the process by a gesture of goodwill. This is almost always a mistake; the time for conciliation is after the crisis is surmounted and a settlement or modus vivendi has in fact been reached. Then moderation can be ascribed to generosity and goodwill; before it may abort the hopeful prospects by raising last-minute doubts as to whether the cost of settlement need in fact be paid.

(Kissinger, 1979, Vol. 1, p. 629)

Correct dangerous perceptions left by crisis management

This is where we can gauge the importance of thorough debriefings. In such-and-such an affair, it may have been preferable to follow a particular line of conduct, or then again a particular mistake may have been made. However, it would be dangerous to let the idea take hold that the path followed on that occasion was necessarily the best and only one possible and should be followed on every occasion. It is quite possible to correct the way the situation was interpreted, in order to draw lessons for the future, without condemning the people involved, whose actions can doubtless be explained by any number of reasons and constraints.

In this respect, it is important to free those in charge from the fear of criticism. They must learn that criticism inevitably follows a crisis and that a searching analysis can help everyone, including the leader, by sorting out the good from the indifferent.

> *E. Quarantelli: A very comforting analysis for the American Red Cross*
> One day, while visiting the American Red Cross, the head of the Disaster Research Center was asked by his despairing hosts why they had systematically been criticized during catastrophes in which they had been involved. The head of the Disaster Research Center was able to reassure them by saying that studies showed that the criticism had nothing to do with what they may or may not have done. Instead, it was linked to the fact that the Red Cross was the last visible actor to arrive at the disaster scene. As a result, the Red Cross was the only body to which recriminations could be addressed. A few years later, following a reorganization of the emergency aid systems, the FEMA became the last agency to appear on the scene . . . and the Red Cross ceased to be attacked, as the FEMA has taken on this unenviable role instead.[42]

Naturally, debriefing is most likely to lead to changes if it is conducted in a positive way. If the aim is to learn from one's experiences, less accent will be put on what did not work and more on improvements to be made for the future. Here, as always, the amount that can be achieved will depend largely on the general climate that prevailed before the crisis. A body that is practising considerable openness and is not on the defensive will find it far easier to conduct first-rate debriefing sessions.

After the crisis, take strong initiatives

Often, the episode will have left a bitter taste in people's mouths. Many leaders wonder how to tackle the numerous difficulties that remain. Sometimes, the main problem is one of image, as the impact of the happening was less damaging than was feared at the outset. Sometimes, on the other hand, the situation is extremely serious and there is no immediate solution. How, for instance, can every trace of widespread pollution or contamination be eliminated in Alaska or the Ukraine?

Some leaders then wonder whether to give money or publish a PR brochure. Whatever you do, you must respect two criteria: provide technical justification for the proposed action; inspire respect and attempt to be inspired by a sense of respect.

This brings us to the initiatives taken by the Sandoz group, following the accident of Schweizerhalle (November 1986), as part of the general effort to clean up the Rhine. These included the creation of a fund of 40 million FF to help research into reducing river pollution, a call for the submission of projects to be selected by a commission made up of independent experts, and the sponsoring of 34 research teams.[43]

This way out was very different from the one chosen by Amoco. With a major disaster such as *Exxon Valdez* or *Amoco Cadiz*, you could envisage not only taking charge of the effects of the drama in a responsible way,[44] but also taking major initiatives in other areas, in order to associate the company's image with something other than abomination. One example would be a huge operation to combat a different problem affecting the world, to make up for the one you caused.

Summary

Crisis management

- The foundation act: taking a position
  - Determine your room for manoeuvre
  - Decide on a fundamental focus
  - Define a strategy for response.
- Overall management of the action plan
  - Take the crisis in hand
  - Display options and essential values
  - Anticipate and take initiatives
  - Track down gaps, mistakes and weak points
  - Help the system to keep going throughout the crises
  - Restabilize the system from time to time: analyses, values, goals
  - Manage contradictions and avoid offending sensibilities
  - Bear in mind the aftermath of the crisis.
- Managing the system
  - Apply key concepts
    Separate functions in order to combat confusion
    Keep in-house information process under control
    Provide support for the most exposed units
  - Know how to operate crisis teams
    Preparation
    The center, separations, interfaces
    Critical vigilance on the operating mode.
- Dealing with the issue of expert opinion
  - Mobilize the network of experts set up beforehand
  - Immediately define their ambit
  - Anticipate possible results and options

- Make sure the experts are not disturbed
- Increase the credibility of this network
- Avoid confusion between the roles of experts and decision makers.
- Managing communication
  - Manage media communication
    Full, frequent and exact information
    Inform, rather than reassure
    Be the best source
    Make sure messages remain consistent throughout
    Don't tag behind the media: take inititatives
  - Use non-media information channels
    Define all your target publics: in-house, victims and others
    Define specific types of management
    Deal with rumours
  - Don't get caught in the communication trap.
- Managing the crisis to the very end
  - Don't dismantle your crisis organization too soon
  - Don't remain in crisis mode too long.
- Managing the aftermath of the crisis
  - Organize rigorous debriefings
  - Comfort the team
  - Comfort the general system
  - Correct dangerous perceptions left by crisis management
  - After the crisis, take strong initiatives.

Notes

1. Sun Tzu, 1972 (French edition: foreword by Liddel Hart, p. 7; preface by Samuel Griffith, p. 11; English edition: p. 47).
2. Interview with Joseph Scanlon.
3. Interview with Lucien Abenhaim in Lagadec, 1990, pp. 177–8.
4. Interview with Philippe Vesseron in Lagadec, 1990, p. 101.
5. Thus, in the Gulf Crisis, letting the other side broach the subject of regional balances of power gave it a precious advantage and an effect of surprise. It was more or less allowed to choose its theatre of representations.
6. EDF, France's electricity board, has done noteworthy work on this point.
7. This is another point on which EDF has done important studies.
8. This is done currently at Dow Chemical and was also practised at Orkem, another chemicals firm which no longer exists.
9. This system is used by EDF.

10. This process is used by companies such as Esso-Saf, EDF and France Télécom.
11. As has been done at Esso-Saf and EDF, among others.
12. Interview with Rolf Kaiser.
13. The Sandoz group, for example, has decided to include 'environmental' observers in its crisis team.
14. This has also been done by Sandoz.
15. We owe this concept to Dr Rolf Kaiser, who introduced it in an OECD study on the management of crises linked to technological risks.
16. Simulation exercise carried out in collaboration with Philippe Dessaint in a major organization.
17. Interview with Joseph Scanlon.
18. An in-depth study of this problem of groupthink is not within the ambit of this work. For further reading, we recommend the book by Janis, with its theoretical presentation and particularly illuminating case studies in the way group processes can lead to major fiascos or, on the other hand, consolidate decision-making processes. More recent work on this topic includes the thesis by Paul 'T Hart (1990).
19. Based on interviews with Dr William Dab, Philippe Vesseron, Joseph Scanlon, and Professor Lucien Abenhaim.
20. Interview with Péter-J. Hargitay.
21. See Péter-J. Hargitay, 'The Bhopal catastrophe', in Lagadec, 1990: *States of Emergency*, pp. 75–83 (pp. 76–71, Our emphasis).
22. Interview with Edgar Fasel in Lagadec, 1990, pp. 88–9.
23. Interview with Edgar Fasel in Lagadec, 1990, pp. 87–8.
24. Interview with Philippe Vesseron in Lagadec, 1990, p. 105.
25. Interview with Edgar Fasel in Lagadec, 1990, p. 86.
26. Interview with Philippe Vesseron in Lagadec, 1990, p. 105.
27. Interview with Edgar Fasel in Lagadec, 1990, p. 131.
28. See Chapter 5 (the question of the media).
29. Interview with Philippe Roqueplo, research director at CNRS, the French National Centre for Scientific Research.
30. François Ailleret is deputy chief executive of Electricité de France.
31. Interview with François Ailleret in Lagadec, 1990, pp. 198–9, 200.
32. Interview with Edgar Fasel in Lagadec, 1990, p. 88.
33. See Péter-J. Hargitay in Lagadec, 1990, p. 77.
34. Robert V. Andrews, quoted in ten Berge, 1990, p. 25.
35. Interview with Philippe Dessaint.
36. Taken from a speech given by Dr Weisaeth, OECD: 'Workshop on the Provision of Information to the Public and the Role of Workers in Accident Prevention and Response', Stockholm, 11–14 September 1989. Second session: 'Alert and Information of the Public after an Accident'. Completed by an interview with its author, who works in the Department of Catastrophe Psychiatry at the Institute of Psychiatry, Faculty of Medicine, University of Oslo (due to be published in the *European Handbook of Psychiatry and Mental Health*).
37. Interview with Patrick Magd, at the time head of communication at Rhône-Poulenc Santé.
38. Interview with Péter-J. Hargitay in Lagadec, 1990, pp. 79–80, 81.

39. Interview with François Ailleret in Lagadec, 1990, p. 200.
40. Interview with Claude Frantzen and L. du Boullay in Lagadec, 1990, p. 138.
41. Interview with Enrico Quarantelli.
42. Interview with Enrico Quarantelli.
43. Interview with Edgar Fasel. See also: *Sandoz s'engage pour un Rhin propre,* Sandoz, brochure, summer 1988.
44. See the epilogue of the book by Dieudonnée ten Berge for an analysis of the Exxon group's reaction to the *Exxon Valdez* affair (ten Berge, 1990, pp. 182–7).

Part 3

Learning about crisis

Learning how to handle a crisis today is obviously no small matter. Indeed, it requires a certain daring, as you will be forced to reshape the cultural bases of all the entities involved, set up new forms of organization and develop a new set of tools. Nothing will be achieved unless a special effort is made by every single member of the organization, beginning with its senior management.

This final part therefore sets out to explore ways and means of making progress in this field. We have based our ideas on a series of surveys conducted within major industrial groups both in France and elsewhere,[1] as well as on work carried out in a number of these organizations which actually wished to make their existing resources better able to prevent and deal with crisis situations.

However, there is no point in disguising the fact that many deep-seated reservations need to be overcome before the necessary work can be done. In general, only painful experience can make this wall of uncooperative silence crumble and give way to questioning. Indeed, we begin our exploration of the third aspect of our discussion with the observation that you can only learn if you seriously wish to.

Note

1. These surveys enabled us to collect a large number of different operational techniques, test out our theories and implement learning strategies. We extend grateful thanks to all those who agreed to take part in this fundamental investigation, including Gérard Brugères (communication manager) and Claude Nicaud (health–safety–environment co-ordinator) from the economic interest grouping ICI France; Jean-Pierre Chaussade ('crisis–environment–nuclear energy' technical consultant from the communication department of Electricité de France); Jean Desse (safety manager for the Orkem chemicals group); André de Marco (communication manager), Gérard Vuillard (quality and safety manager), Gilles Nobécourt (public affairs manager) at Rhône Poulenc; Edgar Fasel (outside relations and communication manager for the Sandoz SA

group); Jean-Pierre Jacobs (public affairs manager at Dow Chemical); Patrick Magd (communication manager) and Elizabeth Duchêne (head of the press division) at Gaz de France; Maurice Gauchrand (deputy production manager) and Gentiane Weil (adviser to the chief communication executive) at France-Télécom; Bertrand Robert (Francom group); Jean Verré (president), Jean Taillardat (secretary-general, communication and human resources manager), Jean-Pierre Huguet (head of communication department) and Alain Le Broussois (head of the development and communication department) at Esso-Saf; Jean Barrier (president of Esso-Rep).

Chapter 10

Solid refusal and a time to ask questions

There is often considerable reluctance to learn about crisis management. This frequently results in a refusal to consider the issue at all, or in measures that are too superficial to be truly relevant. The aim of this chapter is to gauge the level of this resistance. If this is not done, innovation strategies are doomed to failure.

Crisis? Crisis management? These issues often fail to arouse any reaction. They do not traditionally belong to the universe of management, whose goals are more likely to be excellence, optimization, and gradual change. Terms such as 'chaos' (Peters, 1989) and 'weak signals' (Ansoff and McDonnell, 1990) have only recently entered managerial vocabulary.

You must therefore not be surprised by the diagnosis that emerged during the first international conference on industrial crises and their management (New York, 1986) and which still holds good today: even though they recognize that major crises inevitably do arise, most companies and administrations are poorly prepared to deal with them (Shrivastava, 1987b, p. 3). There is good reason to regret:

- the serious lack of good case studies, which could bring effective practices in crisis management to light;
- the paucity of rigorous research and theoretical work in this all-important area;
- the extreme inadequacy of management tools and techniques, which could help organizations to prevent and deal with crises;
- the absence of publications providing managers, communities, and decision makers in the public sector with thorough and well-targeted information on industrial crises and their management.

Should people be forced to think about the subject? There is considerable reluctance to do so. Managers talk about common sense, and point out that 'crises still only happen very occasionally and then involve a very few organizations'. Accordingly, they decide that their time is best spent on other important issues. We can generally divide organizations into two different categories. The first, and by far the largest category comprises those that have not even broached the subject. The second comprises those that have established a considerable lead.

A number of interviews conducted recently with senior managers in both the public and private sectors in France and elsewhere, provide a good illustration of the current state of crisis management in the second, reticent group. They also highlight a great many truths that must be taken into account when learning about crisis management. So, over to the managers, now.

1 We can't embark on investigations like these. They'd immediately highlight organizational and individual aberrations, which certain people would like to forget about.

2 If something more serious than a simple accident occurred, it would no longer be our problem. It would be up to the authorities to handle the affair. We're a private company—go and talk to the minister.

3 You can't imagine how much trouble I've had within the corporation, trying to make people begin to take crises seriously, especially those affecting public opinion.

4 I can't imagine our current chairman sitting down to think seriously about how to deal with a possible crisis.

   Although they obviously have a crucial role to play in a crisis situation, especially regarding overall positioning, I'm sure they're still not really prepared for it. This perhaps accounts for the ambiguous attitude towards crisis units, as it would be dangerous if they made the supreme leaders feel too safe. There are several reasons for their reluctance to participate in crisis simulation exercises. To start with, they may think that, when the moment comes, they'll know which is the right decision to take. Then again, they may think that those who make them take part in these exercises ask them the wrong questions.

   As a result, the chairman's team must assume their chairman will hardly have prepared himself at all for the situation and will doubtless not have the best of reflexes. This is one more reason why they themselves must think about the question, talk to him about it, if possible, and be able to advise their president what line to take in the event of a problem. He will be delighted that not everybody has lost his head.

5 I haven't really any progress to report. Quite the opposite, in
   fact, as these last few years we seem to have gone into
   reverse. We have had accidents, even crises, but each time
   they proved too easy to deal with and I couldn't learn
   anything from them. We've always come out on top, not
   because we were well-prepared, but because the crises were
   easy to handle. We have several things going for us, such as
   undeniable technical prowess and an excellent network of
   international relations. However, these strengths derive from
   the general operational requirements of our field, not from a
   desire to manage crises properly.

   There are many explanations for the reluctance to begin
   learning about crisis management. In very large
   organizations, there is a tendency to cling to delicate in-house
   balances, which are inevitably upset, once people begin
   simulating crises or even just thinking about them. There is
   also opposition from politicians, who rely on two dangerous
   assertions. The first runs like this: 'there won't be a crisis
   while I'm in power', the second like this: 'if there is a crisis,
   with my vast experience and knowledge of the press, I'll
   know exactly what to do!'.

   This results in a total lack of preparation, and above all a lack
   of any psychological preparation, which proves to be a
   problem once a crisis starts to unfold. It is far more serious to
   approach a crisis with a false set of ideas than with
   inadequate preparation. The number-one priority is therefore
   to get rid of false ideas such as, 'there won't be a crisis', or,
   'if there is one, I'll know what to do, I'll muddle through'.

   First and foremost, therefore, the men at the top need to be
   made more aware of the problem, in order to stop them from
   burying their heads in the sand any longer.

6 The inability of executives to come to grips with this kind of
   problem has caused many crises to become bigger than they
   are. Generally most people try to figure out how to hide.
   They do not want to be blamed. The strong people in a crisis
   are the ones who emerge to say 'I'll take responsibility, and I
   will do something about this'. There are not too many who do
   that. Most try to get away from responsibility because they
   know their careers and families' security are on the line; their
   own reputations can be compromised. [. . .] Corporate
   officers are under such pressure to perform financially that
   they are often unwilling to invest the time and thought
   necessary for crisis preparation.[1]

7 Large private-sector groups operate like governments. In
   crisis situations, the leaders figuring in the organization chart
   are never the actual leaders. A great manager, who excels in

periods of calm, will often be completely at sea when his universe topples into what, for him, is something quite unimaginable. Moreover, what is needed are people who are prepared to expose themselves. Such people are not legion. It is easy to understand those who hesitate, as they have had to pursue a career, with all its attendant internal political battles, in order to reach the top of the pyramid, and are not especially keen to risk seeing this career disappear down the plughole in the space of a single instant. It is vital to be aware of this human factor. In general, a middle- or even a lower-ranking executive is forced to move up the front line, expose himself and deal with the situation, only to disappear once the crisis is over. Indeed, those who have handled crises often see themselves pushed to one side. Even if they have taken the right action, they remain tainted in some way, and the structure prefers to forget about them. This, in fact, explains why people who have already invested a great deal in their career may be reluctant to expose themselves. Moreover, the solving of the crisis is not really what matters. The only thing that counts is the company's financial survival. Its managers therefore come to resemble generals in a war, sacrificing their soldiers. It is like a game of chess, where only the queen really counts. In reality, crisis management is power management. Individuals and organizations alike will do anything to remain in a position of power. If a problem arises, they switch to a different brand, or give money to a charity (only a small amount is needed). In this light, people who solve crises become fodder to some extent, to be used then pushed to one side, into some honorary post if they have been successful. Besides, who can be sure that it really is possible to learn about crises? This is above all an area where you have to display exceptional leadership qualities, coupled with real gifts for communication, which you must have a liking for.

In addition, crisis management is also about gut feeling to a considerable extent. You can never be more than 50 per cent sure that you're right when you take a decision. And yet the decision has to be taken. Lastly, to be good at crisis management, you must do nothing but that . . .

I will only grant you one thing, namely that training can help people get rid of false ideas which their environment may have instilled in them. It can give them the necessary freedom of action and thought.

8 Getting a major organization to tackle a crisis is nothing short of impossible. It requires individuals with strong personalities to step forward, stray from the beaten path, take risks and no longer limit their thinking to their own particular field. This is

the opposite of normal practice in an organizational pyramid. Major companies continually push out strong personalities, or 'kick them upstairs' at best, and constantly reject innovations which are too drastic. They operate according to the well-known concept of cogs and wheels. A cog receives and transmits an impulse, but doesn't contribute anything itself. So how can you expect suddenly to find a whole reservoir of top managers ready to risk everything and leave the beaten path?

Nor can you ignore the severe conflicts which reign in the upper echelons of the pyramid, where the higher you get, the narrower these echelons become. How can you expect people, as if by magic, to back each other up, forget their rivalry and not even think about the end of the crisis, when fierce competition will resume?

These are indeed cogs, but cogs with sharp teeth . . .

These, then, are just some examples of reluctances and the reasons for this reluctance.

Yet accidents have happened, alerts have been worrying, examples of initiatives in other organizations have made people think. Over the last few years, companies have discovered that their emergency measures often need serious re-examination, especially when they are already at full stretch when everyday incidents occur, such as problems in information circuits and equipment, new constraints or mislaid telephone lists. They have had to face the fact that the skills they have for dealing with crises often amount to a sort of magic black bag which they never opened and which they have every reason to suspect may be ineffective.

Even more seriously, people have come to realize that crisis management can also become an additional area of conflict between firms: in some ways, a crisis is the continuation of competition on a different battlefield, using different weapons. Something you may have been competing for over many years may suddenly fall into your lap in the space of a few weeks, if your rivals become trapped in the methods they have chosen to manage their crises.

Here is a list of observations which hold good for the majority of organizations.

- There is considerable reluctance, even to think about possible disruptions.
- Those crises that are actually experienced are hardly ever studied in a thorough and systematic way. Only reports of an exclusively technical nature are ever drawn up. Accordingly, ordeals that

could provide valuable lessons for the future are more or less explicitly consigned to oblivion.

- There is consistently a great deal of hesitation about sounding the first alarm, and a long wait before any information emerges, yet the first few hours of a crisis are crucial.
- Later on, information continues to be difficult to obtain in a continuous, structured and accurate form. Yet it is vital to follow developments closely, in order to provide a technical response and to ensure a good supply of information.
- In-house communication is quickly beset by confusion. No one really knows who is in charge of what. Paralysis spreads throughout the system, with everyone phoning everyone else. At the same time, key decision makers strangely, and perhaps deliberately, disappear, only to spark fresh and particularly untimely in-house conflicts if anyone tries to get directly in touch with their departments without their knowledge.
- There are even more serious shortfalls when it comes to the crisis centre. To start with, no premises have been designated in advance and no crisis group has been set up beforehand. Meetings are held in the offices of the president or chief executive, who therefore can no longer use these offices for their own purposes. By the same token, there is no press room.
- In the general confusion, it is realized that there is no available information with which to analyse or tackle the situation or help along the initial communication process. The result is a treasure hunt which wastes precious time and is bad for everyone's nerves. Despairingly, you realize that you have come up against the same problem on countless previous occasions.

In short, this kind of observation leads people to ask, in the short term at least, how they could improve the resources available for tackling crisis situations.

The communication departments are often in the first line of fire when it comes to receiving criticism from outside. The people who work in them will often have been marked by many different backgrounds, thanks to their training and their types of jobs, and they are frequently the ones who start people thinking that something undoubtedly needs to be done when it comes to learning about and preparing for crises. After several difficult episodes, the management agrees to broach the matter and, more importantly, to make sure that the right course of action is taken.

What is the right course of action? Chapter 11 presents a few alternatives based on real-life experiences.

Notes

1. Interview with Robert L. Dilenschneider in Lagadec, 1990, p. 192.

Chapter 11

Undertaking and managing the learning process

Today, many organizations are seeking to reinforce their capacity for crisis management. The first question they face is discovering how to undertake and successfully pursue this learning process. This final chapter suggests some tried and proved strategies for action.

A growing number of both public- and private-sector organizations are becoming open today to the issue of crisis situations and how to handle them. After the time of refusal comes the time for learning.

Generally, the trigger for this desire is a concern with improving their ability to communicate in a highly disruptive situation. Deficiencies in this area are the easiest to spot, for the simple reason that communications are the way an organization enters most directly in contact with its environment. This is the area in which an organization's many weaknesses with regard to crisis management often become visible.

Their most frequent request, then, is 'How can we communicate better in crisis situations?' Obviously the first step in answering is to place this question in a broader context. The issue is not merely to communicate better: you have to have something to communicate, something well-founded that will be accepted by those to whom it is addressed. You must also be in a position to handle the other aspects of the crisis, starting with the in-depth treatment of the difficulties that created the situation.

It takes a certain boldness to pursue this openness. What strikes everyone who undertakes this work is the variety of registers in which you must play in order better to prevent, anticipate, and handle these highly turbulent situations. Here again, there are three familiar levels for reflection: technical resources, organizational measures, and the foundation of business culture.

This work ranges from setting up crisis rooms to reviewing the means and ends of training provided to management; from implementing new communications systems to organizing regular meetings devoted to anticipating potential crises; from training personnel at all levels to forming teams that can build bridges between various departments (often separated by different practices and traditions) or even bringing in outside observers; from acquiring new emergency equipment to developing a capacity for judgement on several levels. This is not, of course, an exhaustive list of the aspects to be dealt with.

By far the most difficult issue is integrating the world of crisis into corporate culture. It is not possible to handle the problem by simply acquiring new equipment, or even by reorganizing here and there. Priority must go to transforming the habits and the underlying references that determine the attitudes and actions adopted by those involved.

As the previous chapters have shown, the crisis forces you to work in a setting shaped by considerable complexity, uncertainty, an extraordinary number of actors involved, and a very destabilizing tendency to call everything into doubt.

Consequently, a special effort must be made in this 'cultural' area. That accomplished, it will be possible to add on logistical or structural modifications with some chance of success.

Several approaches have already been tested and have proved satisfactory. Before presenting them, it is important to emphasize the spirit behind them all: a systematic attempt is made to draw the most from the existing wealth of know-how and to implicate fully all the actors involved in the effort to make changes. The purpose of intervention is not to supply turnkey diagnoses or solutions, but rather to launch a learning process that takes into account the specific resources of an organization—including its corporate culture.

Changing business culture

Breaking with values: good citizenship and openness

A few examples should make the goals clear. One North American corporation has a past reputation for being especially inward-looking and prompt to set out on crusades (with all the connotations that term has for dubious tactics) against its critics—in particular against environmentalists. It has set rules for openness and good citizenship that represent a veritable cultural revolution.

This is a fairly general trend among all those who have grasped the problem, even if different institutions express it in varying ways. Sometimes the closed attitude was so blatant in the past that the situation cried out for change; sometimes a catastrophe or a serious alert triggered the process of change; sometimes, when previous behaviour patterns were not so clear cut, things could evolve more gradually. But on the whole, awareness is rising, as if to say: 'We just can't remain as closed and arrogant as we used to be.'

But this increased openness to the social environment cannot simply serve as a cover to give actors a clear conscience: it is vital today that words correspond to acts. A crisis is a moment of truth, and mere cosmetic treatments would surely prove to be counterproductive.

This type of change is also going on in all the other areas, be it in-house operating rules, communication with the outside, strategic options, or other aspects. Some actors have sought to demonstrate their solemn commitment to these new guidelines in the aftermath of an accident or alert: this was the case, for instance, with the environmental safety charter signed by the chairman of the Orkem chemical group in 1989. This document highlighted new requirements in terms of ethics and responsibility, openness, safety (which henceforth became an explicit criterion in evaluating executive performance), liability (with rules applying to subcontractors as well), training, concertation, and audits.

Making reference very early on during a crisis (within the first 24 hours) to the ethics of the enterprise involved has become an important concern.[1] Here again, this represents an attempt to confirm values; just a few years ago, it would have been enough to announce technical certainties and speak with an authority that was supposed to guarantee the enterprise's natural and flawless legitimacy.

Refocusing to take strong initiatives in-house

Once the principles and the basic sense of direction have been redefined, it is possible to undertake action that will bring about significant change in the corporate culture.

Commitment at the top
This means, for example, that when a simulation exercise is organ-

ized, those designing the exercise must no longer have the reflex attitude, 'The chairman is of course much too busy to take part in person.' Even the highest-ranking executives should participate in these operations, and not merely as observers and judges: they should be full participants in the game, taking the same risks as the other actors. By the same token, when a seminar is organized on the subject of crisis, they should make a point of being present, and their purpose is not to say a few encouraging words, but to demonstrate how much value they place on studying this field. Such gestures immediately have a strong impact in-house.[2]

Overall responsibility

Delegation of authority should increase; this goes hand in hand with an obligation to become more accountable and to take charge of problems as they arise, without wondering if they are part of the job description. Especially in situations marked by vagueness and ambiguity, the baton must be passed flawlessly if the relay is to keep running. One basic rule should be that no one drops a problem, even if it is outside his or her competence, until it is certain that someone else has taken full charge of it. In this type of unusual circumstance, it is vital to lose the reflex of thinking that 'someone else' is surely dealing with the problem, and that 'someone else' may even already have found a solution.

The duty to provide outside information

Until recently, the classic rule was that in the event of an accident occurring, ordinary employees were to refrain from giving any information to the outside, even straight facts. Only the official spokesperson had the right to speak. More recently, the contrary has become clear (for example, with Esso-Saf): the first person from the organization to reach the site has a *duty to provide information*. This means the facts: any commentary naturally remains the prerogative of the customary spokespeople. Clearly this points up the incredible need for training, as the first person at the scene will not necessarily be the executive who was on call.

Taking into account crisis and safety skills in career plans

As was indicated earlier, performance in terms of safety is becoming a criterion for evaluation. Dow Chemical has become aware of how important it is in a crisis situation to have personnel with strong capacities for judgement, and pays great attention, in defining the careers of its managers, to the variety of situations that future directors may have to face. In another sector (e.g. the agro-business), executives are regularly chosen among those who have opted for the track in their work that is most crisis-prone.

These new perspectives place individuals more squarely in the firing line. Every member of an organization has the job of resolving the problems that arise, rather than beginning by protecting their fields of competence. This type of approach is crucial when working in crisis units: these units must be teams first and foremost, and not—as is so often the case—a simple juxtaposition of various bureaucratic zones of influence where everyone is primarily concerned with not becoming 'excessively' vulnerable.

Fitting into a new environment

It has now been explicitly recognized that no one can manage a crisis situation without having previously ensured that he or she has credibility and legitimacy. This means first of all that these two qualities are not to be taken for granted—nor are they of secondary importance. By acknowledging this, it becomes possible to undertake the considerable efforts required for openness, through a series of initiatives:

- making a general information effort: brochures, open-houses, meetings with various publics
- building broad relations with journalists
- opening up exercises (especially in-house operation plans)[3] to firefighters, local government authorities, mayors, and journalists[4]; this type of initiative has much more impact than the traditional 'meet-the-press' luncheon
- establishing interprofessional agreements (that go beyond mere good-neighbourly behaviour); these should cover prevention, watchfulness, crisis management, ethics, and so on
- setting up more informal networks, for both pre-crisis and crisis times; these are proof of a desire to break down barriers.

These steps can be carried further when the crisis hits. Basic principles may be laid down: for instance, if an accident occurs, the plant manager's primary duty is to communicate with personnel, the authorities, and the media—technical questions will be handled by the manager's co-workers.[5]

In another enterprise operating in the aeronautics industry, individuals directly in contact with customers are immediately mobilized to respond to requests for information (and they are trained for this difficult task). This is in fact what the Johnson & Johnson group did, when it used its sales force to help deal with the Tylenol crisis.

These considerations lead people to assume responsibility spontaneously in a way that no one was accustomed to seeing. Let us consider a few examples. In one case, an enterprise became involved in a transportation accident even though it was not directly concerned, and despite the risks it ran in terms of media exposure (the company's logo appeared as its personnel participated in the support effort, but television viewers seeing the image could mistakenly assume that the logo identified those responsible for the accident). A system has been set up to help small businessses, which are generally less well equipped to handle crises than large groups. Safety practices are often extended to those upline and downline (suppliers and customers) of the company.

Strategies for change

Crisis simulation seminars

The goal here is to plunge those involved into situations presenting serious difficulties. These situations may be provided to them, or better yet, participants can imagine the situations themselves. The goal is to train individuals, and above all, to build strong, flexible, and creative teams. Experience has shown that after participating in such seminars, the managers involved are infinitely better prepared and receptive to doing further work. This means that simulations are the way to start the overall learning process.

Imagining oneself into these situations is a much more demanding exercise than the usual lectures scheduled into training programmes. It forces individuals—as members of a team—to live through uncomfortable experiences. Actual cases[6] are also reviewed during this type of training.

Media training can also be offered, in which a journalist makes the players react in a very realistic situation. This exercise has undeniable advantages: members can go through the ordeal of standing before the camera, and the difficulties of a situation often become much clearer when they must be explained to an outside public. Be careful, however, not to be fooled by the power of this tool: as was emphasized earlier, television communication is not the only key to crisis management. As Philippe Dessaint points out:

> So much attention has probably been paid to communication problems because this was the easiest aspect in terms of training. For outside actors, it is fairly easy for a television professional to offer media training (he can always offer criticism and make suggestions). For the organization and the individuals involved, doing nothing but media training can be very comforting by not forcing them to consider everything else—and that's the basic problem.[7]

As was mentioned above, these efforts are intended not only to develop one's personal capacities but, even more importantly, to strengthen the capacities of the team, which are often reduced to nothing by a crisis, and to make the organization's in-house culture evolve.

The thought of examining these issues used to be frightening until it was actually done, but the participants come to value these opportunities: in them they find an answer to underlying needs that could not even be discussed a few years ago. The tendency to reject the idea of crisis slowly changes into a will to take initiatives in the fields of training,[8] innovation, and behaviour patterns.

This makes clear the extent to which preparing for crisis calls for work on other aspects: breathing greater flexibility into an organization, opening it up to its environment, making it better prepared to seize the opportunities presented to it. By learning to confront the unknown and working on what makes individuals, teams, and entire institutions tick, aptitudes are developed which go far beyond mere crisis management and prevention.

It is interesting to note that the drive to bend or break old habits does not only come from the top down. Soon, strong demands begin to rise through the chain—for training, especially, and notably in the area of external communications, which is the newest and most surprising issue for those who were accustomed to the rule of silence. This is when corporate culture really begins to change.[9]

This type of training also creates openings towards the outside by bringing in actors who are not part of the enterprise.[10]

This point provides a good conclusion. Opening seminars to outsiders is crucial to strengthening the networks that are potentially involved. Living through a difficult experience together and sharing each other's doubts is certainly a key factor for success in managing any later crisis.

Some questions do remain, however:

- If undertaken too soon, opening up to the outside can considerably heighten anxiety levels and reinforce defence mechanisms. This is not conducive to the learning process.
- If undertaken too late, it may merely set in-house attitudes in concrete, leaving no room for manoeuvre to adjust to the other partners. At a deeper level, it confirms the idea that responses can be developed in-house alone, and that good communications will resolve any problems at the interface with the outside. This is dangerous nonsense: in a crisis, responses must be developed by multiple organizations working together, and this, too, is a skill to be acquired.

It should also be added that the seminar itself is not what is most important. Often, the previous phase teaches a great deal and offers a wealth of learning opportunities. Much anxiety and resistance will emerge during the indispensable preparation phase (deciding which scenarios to study, which ones to eliminate). The decisions about which agencies and organizations will be invited to participate—and which will not—draw an interesting map of the network into which the host organization fits. Equally crucial is the debriefing at the end of seminars, which is too often neglected or rushed. This is an opportunity for everyone, as individuals and as a group, to decide what the experience meant, to discuss the difficulties encountered, or to express desires for the future. As a general rule, as much time should be spent on the debriefing as on the game itself.

This is light years away from the conventional exercise whose more or less explicit objective is to reassure everyone that everything is as it should be.

One last point stands in the way of this type of seminar, and especially of opening it up to the outside—to mayors, journalists, associations, outside observers, and so forth. That is the 'revelation' factor, i.e. revealing the dangers of a given situation. On the one hand, involving a great many actors may appear to be a sign of confidence, and supposedly uninformed individuals are generally not unaware that major risks exist. On the other hand, it is impossible to neglect the possibility that suddenly revealing large-scale risks can trigger very strong reactions. Crisis scenarios are grave by definition, and they always presuppose a conjunction of misfortunes that can upset even the technicians who calculate the probability of such adventures occurring. Once again, this issue depends on the judgement of those in charge. But it should at least be clear that refusing to hold an open seminar because the risks are too serious is already an interesting indication of what would happen if there were a real crisis.

The situation becomes frankly worrisome when a seminar cannot even be organized within the circle of top executives, because there is too much concern or excessive tension between members. A crisis here will have a devastating immediate impact.

Looking back

The task here is to apply to crisis a practice that is already common in examining the technical aspects of accidents. These critical studies must be done very quickly after the event, before memories have time to fade. To complete this work, it is also possible to return to older cases that haunt the organization's collective memory. To ensure high-quality analysis, this is a good point at which to integrate outside analysts. As Enrico Quarantelli points out, too often the reports established after an event serve merely to defend or justify things that have been done, rather than allowing a frank, critical and straightforward look at the problems encountered or the errors made (Quarantelli, 1982, p. 7). Reviewing an experience is only truly useful to the learning process if it is done with the necessary thoroughness, in a spirit of questioning rather than close-mindedness or destructive criticism.

This exercise becomes even more valuable if it is opened to the outside. In one interesting case, a team of journalists sent to cover an accident were later invited by the company involved to give their point of view on how the event was managed.

One thing should be made clear: if a firm decision is not made to pursue this review process, and if no one in the team has been designated ahead of time to undertake these investigations immediately (and granted direct access, even during the crisis, to observe what is happening), it is impossible to obtain a high-quality review. The classic example is the organization that concludes after each incident that it would be a good idea to set up an analytical group—but never takes steps to implement the decision.[11]

Vulnerability audits

It is possible to determine the most important risks, establish procedures for reacting to them, and test these procedures. The starting point is undertaking a systematic analysis of the risks and vulnerability of the actors involved—which in turn assumes that the various actors are able to listen to one another's experience.

This has made it possible, at least in a few organizations,[12] to face the issue of crisis in its totality. This can lead to the discovery of unexpected areas of vulnerability, such as running out of stocks of a crucial medicine, having an old pollution issue resurface, or responding to a problem faced by a competitor.

Only by paying close attention to these questions can you get beyond the most superficial conclusions, and thereby begin building a real defence against crisis. The audit should be followed by the setting up of different batteries of tools, especially for use in prevention and communication.

But even more important is the process itself. By undertaking this work on thinking about potential vulnerability, the actors involved become aware of the situations that call for immediate action, thoughtful reflection, mobilization of teams, connecting with networks on the outside, and so forth. For this reason, an audit carried out entirely by an outside consultant, without strongly implicating the individuals, groups, and organizations involved within the structure, is of no real value.

Cross fertilization

Using cross fertilization to tackle crisis problems is not yet a widespread practice. One experiment was, however, undertaken in 1990 with the top management of a dozen major European corporations operating in very diverse sectors (e.g. agro-business, energy, air transportation, oil, chemicals, pharmaceuticals, telecommunications). This experiment demonstrated just how fruitful it can be to organize 'hybrid' encounters to exchange experiences.

There is, however, one absolute requirement for success: each participant must come to the exercise with a good dose of humility. No one is safe from crisis, and no one has all the right answers. The primary appeal of the above-mentioned meeting[13] was that it was organized to draw the participants out of their usual frames of reference (oil personnel dealing with oil personnel, transporters with transporters). The fact is that although actual responses must be specific, everyone really faces very similar questions. To their great astonishment and satisfaction, the participants discovered that they could talk in a non-defensive manner with one another about problems that are out of bounds within their organizations or at conventional interprofessional meetings.

Technical studies of logistics and organization

Once in-depth thinking has begun and the actors involved have become committed, it is possible to start studies on improvements to be made in the tools (e.g. liaison equipment, crisis rooms, basic documentation, emergency files), organizational flowcharts (e.g. watch, alert, mobilization, memorization), and specific preparations (especially the development of argumentation).

The briar patch to be avoided is to start with these logistical aspects and never get beyond this level of reflection, which does not make great demands on individual sensibilities. There is a considerable difference between investing in equipment and investing a personal and collective effort in exercises requiring more implication.

Broad crisis planning work

Throughout this exploration, one message has recurred continuously: prepare conditions favourable to handling a crisis before the ordeal strikes. The task is to take the many requirements that have been presented and integrate them into a consistent programme to anticipate crisis: identifying points of vulnerability, implementing sensors for abnormal events, developing alert and mobilization mechanisms, organizing in-house and outside communications for the crisis period, working on the organization's values, identifying the important publics according to various crisis scenarios, setting down these preparations in writing in the form of specific plans and checklists, carrying out specific tests and general exercises, and so forth.

Appointing a high-level official to support the process

To ensure the continuity of this progress and to maintain its dynamics, it may be necessary to place a high-level manager in charge of the project.[14] This person should be familiar with, and at home in, the organization and have a background in general management (to avoid the appearance of favouring one department over another). The manager should also have the ability to create openings towards the outside: having a foot in several corporate cultures is invaluable when it comes time to operate on the terrain of a crisis.

Looking at risk prevention again

One further observation will create a connection with another concern expressed at the beginning of this work: after pursuing the process described here, many major organizations state today that their point of view has been modified. They have become more open and more innovative about overall risk prevention. They emphasize that the reservations they may have had in the past about one aspect or another are now completely forgotten. The time has come for these firms to be much bolder in taking charge of risk prevention.

At a more general level, examining public policy

What goes for corporations is just as true for local government agencies and the public sector in general. Ongoing analytical work must be undertaken regarding the difficulties encountered, the major changes that may cause problems, or crisis case studies available at this more general level. Here again, investigations must be carried out in a spirit of learning, rather than negative criticism. The starting point of every exercise must be that crisis is a reality, and a very complex one, and that the crucial first step is better understanding; this in turn allows everyone—managers, observers, and others—to become better prepared.

It may be, for example, that at one point an agency preferred to make huge expenditures to deal with a problem that was not necessarily worth such an outlay. Perhaps the available expertise was weak, perhaps the agency's credibility was so low that it could not afford to look as though it was 'skimping' by limiting these expenditures. But this does not mean that spending as much as possible is always the right or indeed the only solution for that situation—especially as additional knowledge becomes available and it becomes possible better to circumscribe the risks involved.

The same goes for evacuating large sectors of the population. Perhaps it was a good idea in Nantes, for example, to do so. This demonstrated that the authorities were capable of taking large-scale measures and that the purpose of confinement was not to cut costs or cover up the existence of real and serious risks. But once this demonstration has been made, it can be useful to break out of a pattern that measures the courage of the local leadership by the number of people it decides to evacuate.

It would also be interesting to look back at the Tours water supply case (see Vidal-Naquet, 1990, pp. 268–81, among others). It may be that turning off the water supply was the least bad solution in that case (many managers and specialists have their doubts—though they remain discretely silent about them). In any case, it would be interesting to reconsider the experience in order to avoid leaving the impression in the public mind—and in the minds of decision makers—that a good manager is necessarily someone who takes this kind of step.

> *Jean-François David: The unexpected side effects of failing to evaluate crisis management*
> In dealing with the wide variety of accidents that can arise [. . .], the greatest risk lies almost as much in [. . .] the disorganization of the social fabric which can result from poorly analysed situations and thoughtless decisions as in the direct consequences of the accidents for the environment. [. . .] A succession of accidents or wilfully malevolent acts threatening the water supply of one or more French agglomerations would quickly create a technically unmanageable situation, even though no direct health consequences could be prepared for. The reactions and behaviour observed in some countries around the radioactivity released by the Chernobyl accident clearly showed the kinds of weaknesses that can emerge. The collective behaviour observed after the 'accidents' in Nantes and Tours demonstrate that the same type of 'useless vulnerability' is being developed in France. What seems most frightening is that this vulnerability has its roots in the behaviour of the public authorities, local government, and their advisers—more than in the actions of any irresponsible or undesirable pressure groups. [. . .]
> In order to change these ill-suited attitudes and decisions, it is necessary to improve the training of decision makers—members of local government, their closest advisers, elected officials and public service management. And in addition to enabling a re-evaluation of the chains of command, resources—networks of experts—should be set up to improve the quality of decisions and the ability to evaluate these decisions.[15]
> (David, 1990, pp. 108–10)

Evaluating public crisis management policy is an area that must be developed in the future.[16] This tack is more intelligent than allowing an implicit pursuit of new records to develop in the field (who will get the gold medal for evacuation?). What must be avoided above all is seesawing between different extremes: in one phase, only 'bad' decision makers will decide to evacuate; the next time around, the way to become a hero, and the only key to political survival, will be opting for evacuation—and back and forth. A little discipline is called for here, but it can never be attained if the standard for post-accident behaviour is to hide one's head in the sand in order to avoid any examination of events.

One problem that arises is the contradiction between the need to learn, which requires accessability and sharing of information, and any legal procedures that may be undertaken (for which secrecy is fundamental). The difficulty of striking a balance here cannot be underestimated.

This point is a constant source of dread—a dread that is sometimes acknowledged. After the Mississauga incident, for example, some interesting reflections were offered on the issue of how the evacuations—the largest ever undertaken in North America in peace time—were handled.

Joseph Scanlon, Mississauga (10 November 1979)
Why did the evacuation keep expanding? Was it because the threat became better understood? Was it because the threat kept growing worse? Was it a result of the increasing caution created by the growing lack of confidence in the 'expert' advice? Was it just the excitement that developed among the decision makers?

[. . .] Some of the evacuation decisions were made because of a clear and present danger. [. . .] Some were made to reduce real, future risk. [. . .] It also seems likely that some decisions were made because things went so well in the early stages that it did not seem all that difficult to continue; in addition, as resources grew, making a decision to expand became increasingly less threatening, a lower risk than leaving persons where they were. [. . .] If the police had to consider moving 217,000 persons immediately, they would have been awed by the challenge; however, doing it step by step made it almost easier as time passed.

[. . .] The initial decisions not only went well, they were perceived by the public and the media as having gone well. The authorities found themselves the center of positive attention. They were being portrayed as imaginative, daring and, above all, competent. Since the threat was unclear and since evacuation was becoming fairly easy, they were being pushed towards the safe solution, get everyone out, rather than the risky solution, trust the experts, the danger has passed. Moving more people out would gain additional plaudits, and lead to few risks. Keeping them in the area involved a risk, however small. Since there were few complaints from the public, playing it safe, especially when this led to plaudits from the media, seemed like the appropriate response.

(Scanlon, 1989a, pp. 320-2)

Yet the public authorities were taken to court by one actor on the grounds that they had evacuated too broad an area: it was discovered, at the end of the incident, that the chlorine railcar had spilled much of its contents in the first moments of the accident, and much of the toxic gas had been consumed when the propane cars started to burn. In this case, such a counterattack was surprising: the decision to evacuate had been made unanimously within the crisis unit. It took a very dubious sense of loyalty to argue after the fact, on the basis of discoveries made at the end of the crisis, that the authorities—whose decisions the plaintiff had supported—had acted irresponsibly and should be punished. The suit was thrown out of court.

Events seem to have taken a similarly absurd turn recently in the Nantes case. In an attempt to diminish his own liability, the operator whose warehouse was the cause of the accident accused the public authorities of mismanaging the event. This was rather brazen on the part of a company that had contributed so much to the gravity of the accident: its own prevention had been deplorable, and its management was remarkably unavailable throughout the crisis.

This is a good point at which to emphasize a basic guideline: if you do not obey the rules of prevention, if you demonstrate manifest incapacity during the event, then you do not have the right to make abusive use of the difficulties that are bound to arise in any crisis management effort.

Yet this highlights a real contradiction—just one more contradiction in the field of crisis situations and how they are managed. On the one hand, you do not want to take any risks, and you refuse to undertake any (serious) study—but that means no one learns anything, and the subject remains cloaked in ignorance, with all the consequences that implies for the long run. On the other hand, you have to take risks, but you begin slowly acquiring the knowledge necessary to avoid turning all crisis management into a game of Russian roulette. Once again, this is a matter of personal judgement made on the basis of general orientations.

Resources for emergency action: potential and limits

Finally, in an attempt to be directly operational during a crisis, you may choose to acquire new resources for action in crisis management. The idea is to develop networks of qualified and readily mobile people, covering an area the size of France, with connections extending to other regions or countries.

The goal is not to create groups of crisis management Rambos who believe that they can leap into action, without knowing anything about the terrain, and replace the local management. Following the model of what has been done in various industrial groups (EDF, Esso-Saf, and others), support teams should be set up that either are capable of long-distance action or can be dispatched to an area in order to work with those in charge—if the local team requests it. The types of situations encountered in an enterprise with specific activities may be very diverse; consequently, as a guideline, expert networks should be developed to include a range of competences, and this pre-existing pool can be dipped into case by case, according to the specific needs.

In order to avoid simply increasing the confusion, these actors should of course form a very professional team: each member should be well versed in crisis issues; the members should know each other, even though they come from different institutions; they should maintain relations with similar networks in other regions or countries, to avoid developing an obsolete and narrow vision of the potential problems; and they should work continuously to deepen their understanding of the subject.

Philippe Legorjus, a great emergency professional who has confronted a flagrant lack of public intelligence in several crises, gives added force to a message that rings true in many fields of activity:

> I felt the cruel gap between the extreme professionalism of which we were capable and the amateurism in which we were forced to flounder. Today, seven years after the fact, I still feel it. A unit worthy of the name must be capable of analysing information and processing it, using modern methods of research and analysis, in order to provide the political decision makers with a real decision-making tool in these serious situations. At the government level, nothing of the sort exists today. And as long as this is the case, the same causes may well go on producing the same effects.
>
> (Legorjus, 1990, p. 76)

Notes

1. Interview with Patrick Magd, communications director at Gaz de France.
2. A particularly good example may be found in the simulations carried out by the Esso-Saf group or Sandoz France.
3. These are the emergency plans implemented for accidents that do not reach beyond the walls of the plant.
4. This is the procedure followed at Esso-Saf.
5. This principle has been adopted by the Rhône-Poulenc group, among others.
6. This has been done several times by the Orkem group.
7. Interview with Philippe Dessaint.
8. Training in crisis management is now undertaken at Orkem and Esso-Saf, among others.
9. This was particularly notable in the author's experience at Esso-Saf and Orkem.
10. This has been done at Orkem, EDF, Esso-Saf, Sandoz, and elsewhere.
11. Natural gas accident at Chémery, France: initiative taken by the Gaz de France communications delegation.
12. Several studies of this type have recently been carried out by the Francom group.
13. This meeting was organized by the author with the help, in particular, of the chairman of Esso-Saf, as part of the study mentioned earlier.
14. This innovation has recently been introduced in two major French enterprises.
15. Jean-François David is an engineer for the rural waters and forests department. He was a former civil servant at the French Ministry of the Environment.
16. The report by Patrick Viveret (1989) is especially interesting in this respect.

Conclusion: facing unexpected crises

In the 'age of Damocles', to use Edgar Morin's expression (Morin, 1990*a*, pp. 1–2), crisis—and the threat of crisis—seems ever more present in the decision maker's daily world. There are innumerable examples that demonstrate the quantum leap that has been made in our level of vulnerability. An accident involving a train full of dangerous substances causes the evacuation of 220 000 persons for three to six days (Mississauga, Canada); a gas pipeline explosion kills 800 (Ural, 4 June 1989); a nuclear power plant brushes dangerously closely with disaster (Three Mile Island) and another (Chernobyl) has spread a shadow of death over the Ukraine for the indefinite future. One chemical accident generates tremendous anxiety (Seveso), while the worst-case scenario comes to life in another (Bhopal). In one country, the electricity grid goes down for a few days; in another, citizens realize how dependent they are on mainframes and vital data networks (Hindsale, Chicago, May 1988). One day the water supply is turned off in a small town; the next day, the measure is extended to the entire region. And these are just a few examples from the past. The systematic study of vulnerability would reveal potential cases that are considerably more distressing.

When faced with this type of potential—if not already actual—scenario, it becomes clear that our thinking and our capacities are in their infancy. Substantial investments must be made; they must be guided by teams with rich cultural backgrounds and a wide range of practical knowledge. These teams must have connections to a number of actors and be close to the decision-making process and the realities of crisis while being capable of taking critical distance. Their reflections must cover technical, organizational, ethical, and cultural concerns.

A first look at the question reveals just how important it is with such a subject to go beyond simplistic answers and to work continuously to develop better capacities for anticipating, judging, and taking action.

Other key words—discontinuity, complexity, fragmentation—must henceforth be integrated into our reference frameworks. The past is increasingly irrelevant to thinking about and handling current or incipient breakdowns (though it should never be forgotten, since inventions for the future are not spontaneously generated). But discontinuity is a driving force for innovation and creativity—especially in terms of reference values. In a crisis, you will run up against the general complexity and fragmentation of the theatre of operations. Images and understanding will be dismembered, then reconstituted in ephemeral and apparently random patterns, making a mockery of the best laid plans. Reality becomes something that cannot be planned, but must be negotiated with (see Morin, 1990b)—that is to say, if you know how to open and carry out these negotiations, and if this often slippery reality deigns to play the negotiating game. The outlook is clear: you must display endless inventiveness, rather than becoming trapped in references that are 'tried and true', or more precisely, ready-to-use.

This new state of the environment calls for veritable breaks with the past in the traditional organizational management structures. These systems were usually designed to function in relatively stable contexts, in which uncertainty was moderate and limited, and the consequences of a failure were of limited amplitude and gravity. Today, we find ourselves on another planet. The solution is not to be found in rigidly following obsolete models: centralization, uniformity, strict hierarchy, compartmentalization, or secrecy. Clearly these models offer the advantage of making it easy to place the blame when something goes wrong, as is assumed it inevitably must. Instead, work done on large complex systems, including the military (see Rochlin et al., 1987, pp. 159–76, and La Porte, 1975), highlights the contrary: responses to complexity must be sought in organizational differentiation and in coordination; rigidity and centralization must play an ever smaller part in the reply to uncertainty; uncertainty calls for flat structures, not pyramid models.

The operating systems and the responsibilities of each organization and suborganization must be rethought. Systems must develop a radically new flexibility. Because something exceptional can happen at any moment, everyone and each team must be ready for action in order to offer assistance at a weak or vulnerable point in the organization. This calls for models of responsibility that can change configuration as needed. Because crises are often announced by very low-intensity signals, everyone and each team must consider that they are vested with a duty to remain constantly vigilant. No longer is anyone safe in a foxhole, and reinforcing the walls will not help when the winds of crisis begin to blow over the neighbours. Because crises are realities both inside and outside—they even make the borders disappear between these two worlds—everyone and each team has a duty to develop a great number of relations with the environment. By sharing information and quality dialogue, this develops not only the organization's image, but, at a much deeper level, the social relevance of its action, its credibility, and its legitimacy.

The new tacks must be just as sharp when it comes to exercising authority. To manage systems in a structurally unstable world, it is less important to set specific goals than it is to adopt orientations; less important to define tactics than to generate a range of options; less important to memorize the authorized answers and the rules in force than to study the new issues and try to understand them. The goal is not to operate a series of separate entities, each jealously guarding its independence, caught up in territorial conflicts; it is to foster overlapping interdependence. This approach has the strength of creating a capacity to work together, based on emulation rather than internal warfare. Does this mean the issues of management and responsibility become any less important? Certainly not. Command structures are absolutely necessary to keep systems from imploding, fragmenting, or simply dissolving. But the framework in which these structures intervene must be rethought entirely. More than ever, decisions must be based on consultation, discussion, and negotiation. At a deeper level, they must be adjusted to the new context in which they are expected to operate—the context whose most surprising characteristics were outlined above.

Try to grasp the cultural revolution that these requirements imply for the most tradition-bound organizations: the conventional hierarchy that clings to external trappings of authority will be wiped out by the first slightly serious difficulty. In the age of crisis, authority can only be exercised if it demonstrates its relevance and its utility. Authority is now expected to inject a broader intelligence into the system in question, to provide meaning when ambiguity becomes too powerful, to ensure the availability of minimum resources, and to disentangle specific problems that can only be tackled using a higher degree of complexity (and not just greater power). Try to grasp what this assumes today in terms of reflection, in terms of new directions for both the initial and continuing education of decision makers: leaders must acquire creativity, openness to issues of values, a readiness to negotiate, and a capacity to operate and invent positively in an unstructured environment.

And, of course, an organization's survival depends on its ability to operate judiciously in times of crisis. Because crises on the scale of an enterprise are not frequent, this experience must be replaced by simulations and rigorous training. This is not just a matter of emergency drills such as how to evacuate the building. This is training for strategic management in an unstructured environment. It should instil in individuals, teams, and networks a capacity to react in highly disturbing circumstances. These efforts were once considered to be wasted time. Now they must be incorporated into the normal duties performed by any institution. They are a simple matter of survival because, more than ever, survival has become a matter of being able to deal with critical situations.

There are other, more general imperatives as well. Every actor must be aware of how extremely vulnerable our societies are to these major crises. It is relatively easy to trigger a crisis or keep it going, and this can be a source of temptation in itself (as a means, for instance, of pursuing a business, political, or labour confrontation by 'other means'). Everything that has been discussed up to this point has served to confirm how extraordinarily risky it is to play with these borderline situations (and especially to complicate them as much as anyone could wish through irresponsible declarations or initiatives). The concept of moderation came late to the theatre of warfare, but it should be incorporated quickly into the realm of crisis.

This requires reflection on the part of all the actors involved, and it raises sensitive issues. For instance: how do you practice indispensable critical watchfulness when you are a reporter, an opposition leader, or a watchdog group? The issue of crisis poses harsh questions about the uses of information, and about democracy in general. Here again, there should of course be no misunderstanding: the solution does not lie in an ignominious slide towards reducing access to information or ignoring democratic checks and balances—to the contrary. But you must give yourself the means to be inventive, while remaining responsible, along this new path.

Discipline should also be applied to more general systems management: vigilance must be maintained as these systems evolve and changes are made in them, and careful attention should be paid *before* changes are made to avoid incorporating new points of vulnerability. Many criteria contribute heavily to heightening the risk level: various risks accumulate, activities become more dense, management styles change, functions are streamlined—surprisingly, even the development of new security procedures may create additional risks. Once again, the very characteristic example supplied by Enrico Quarantelli comes to mind: the relays for the smoke detectors in San Francisco skyscrapers were located in Chicago (see Chapter 2); the detectors stopped working as soon as something went wrong, because the telephone connections at the site of the crisis were interrupted. The whole safety system collapsed. Nor should another frequent error be neglected: every industrial innovation that has not yet caused a serious accident is held to be infallible. As experience has already shown within some enterprises, thinking about crisis can lead to more general questioning about options and risk prevention. Such questions require high-quality information for all parties involved—this is a vital factor if the credibility and legitimacy of those in charge is to be maintained.

There is, however, a less dark side to this issue. The outburst of complexity, the weaknesses and breakdowns occurring on all sides, and the imperative need for action can also create precious opportunities. By liberating individuals, by enabling new means of organization and collective action, by splitting open the shells in which actors are paralysed, crises can offer fertile ground, at least to those who are ready for it. And when the moment comes, these are the actors who will be able to seize the luck without which no one can find a way out of a crisis. By creating an opening for creativity, the crisis can provide a useful—and sometimes indispensable—key to development in a world that can only progress through daring new tacks and innovations.

In any case, serious work remains to be undertaken. Without it, an iron-clad law will come into play: those who do not obstinately prepare to face crisis will soon be subjected to its reign.

Bibliography

Abenhaim, Lucien (1989) 'La décision. L'exemple du risque technologique', in G. Brücker and D. Fassin (eds) *Santé publique*, Paris, Ellipses, pp. 824–39.

Allison, Graham (1971) *Essence of Decision: Explaining the Cuban Missile Crisis*, Boston, Little, Brown & Co.

Amalric, Jacques (1990) 'Castro, Krouchtchev et l'apocalypse', *Le Monde*, 24 November, pp. 1–3.

Ansoff, Igor and McDonnell, Edward (1990) *Implanting Strategic Management*, London, Prentice Hall International.

Arbel, Avner and Kaff, Albert, E. (1989) *Crash. Ten days in October . . . Will it Strike Again?*, Longman Financial Services Publishing.

Beal, Richard (1984) 'Crisis management under strain', *Science*, Vol. 225, No. 4665, 31 August, pp. 907–9.

Béjin, André and Morin, Edgar (1976) 'Introduction', *Communications*, No. 25, pp. 1–3.

Bell, Coral M. (1978) 'Decision-making by governments in crisis situations', in D. Frei (ed.), pp. 50–8.

Bensahel, Jane G. (1980) 'How to stop a crisis from snowballing. The immediate action taken after a crisis often makes it worse than better', *International Management*, December, pp. 24–5.

ten Berge, Dieudonnée (1990) *The First 24 Hours. A Comprehensive Guide to Successful Crisis Communications*, Oxford, Basil Blackwell.

Bolzinger, A. (1982) 'Le concept clinique de crise', *Bulletin de psychologie*, Vol. XXXV, No. 355, pp. 475–80.

Bonnivard, Colette (1987) *La Vie explosée. Ce jour là rue de Rennes*, Paris, Filipacchi.

Bouquin, Nadège, Decrop, Geneviève, Gilbert, Claude and Touron, Marie-Pierre (avec la collaboration de Aline Cattan) (1990) *La Crue de la Loire du 21 septembre 1980, culture du risque et sécurité collective*, Groupe de recherches sur les risques majeurs, Université des sciences sociales de Grenoble.

Burckhardt, Jacob (1971) *Considérations sur l'histoire universelle*, Paris, Payot.

Camus, Albert (1948) *The Plague* (transl. by Stuart Gilbert), London, Penguin Books, pp. 43–6.

Clausewitz, Carl von (1965) *De la guerre*, Paris, Christian Bourgois, coll. '10/18', rééd. de la trad. fr. de Denise Naville, Editions de Minuit, 1955.

Colin, André (1978) *Rapport de la commission d'enquête du Sénat*, seconde session ordinaire 1977–1978, No. 486.

Crocq, Louis and Douteau, C. (1988) 'La psychologie des paniques', *La Revue du Praticien*, April.

David, Jean-François (1990) 'Risques technologiques et interventions publiques. Du mirage de la protection à l'accroissement de la vulnérabilité sociale', in Claude Gilbert (sous la direction de) *La Catastrophe, l'Elu et le Préfet*, Presses universitaires de Grenoble, pp. 103–10.

Delumeau, Jean and Lequin, Yves (1987) *Les Malheurs du temps. Histoire des fléaux et des calamités en France*, Paris, Larousse.

Denis, Hélène (1989) *La Gestion de catastrophe: le cas d'un incendie dans un entrepôt de BPC à Saint-Basile-le-Grand*, rapport commandité par le bureau de la Protection civile du Québec et présenté au comité de Protection civile provincial, Ecole polytechnique, Université de Montréal.

Denis, Hélène (1990) 'Gestion de crise: les faiblesses de la communication', *Préventique*, No. 36, November–December, pp. 29–39.

Dessaint, Philippe (1988) 'Communiquer en situation de crise', *Baril*, magazine d'information des sociétés du groupe Exxon, No. 26, pp. 4–8.

Dilenschneider, Robert and Forrestal, D.J. (1987) *Public Relations Handbook* (3rd edn), Chicago, The Darnell Corporation.

Dobbing, John (ed.) (1988) *Infant Feeding. Anatomy of a Controversy 1973–1984*, London, Springer-Verlag.

Draper, Norman (1986) 'Training managers to meet the press', *Training*, Vol. 23, No. 8, pp. 30–8.

Dror, Yehezel (1988) *Policymaking under Adversity*, New Brunswick and Oxford, Transaction Books.

Dror, Yehezel (1990) 'Fateful decisions as fuzzy gambles with history', *The Jerusalem Journal of International Relations*, Vol. 12, No. 3, pp. 1–12.

Drucker, Peter F. (1980) *Managing in Turbulent Times*, London, Heinemann.

Dupuy, Jean-Pierre (1990) *Approches cognitives du social. La Panique: du mythe au concept*, Centre de recherches en épistémologie appliquée, Ecole polytechnique (CREA), Report No. 9016A.

Dutang, M., Musquere P. and Retkowsky, Y. (1983) 'Stratégie opérationnelle de lutte contre les pollutions pour assurer la sécurité de l'alimentation en eau: solutions mises en œuvre dans la région parisienne', *Water Supply*, Vol. 2, Pergamon Press, pp. 71–82.

Eberwein, Wolf-Dieter (1978) 'Crisis research. The state of the art: a western view', in D. Frei (ed.), pp. 126–42.

Eddy, Paul, Potter, Elaine and Page, Bruce (1976) *Destination Disaster*, London, Hart-Davis, MacGibbon Ltd.

Elmquist, Soren (1989) *Public Information and Media Relations influencing Crisis Decision-making. The European Perspective*, Nato Civil Emergency Planning Symposium, Ottawa.

Fink, Steven (1986) *Crisis Management. Planning for the Inevitable*, Amacom, American Management Association.

Forester, Tom and Morrison, Perry (1990) 'Computer unreliability and social vulnerability', *Futures*, Butterworth-Heinemann, June, pp. 462–74.

Frei, D. (ed.) (1978) *International Crises and Crisis Management. An East–West Symposium*, New York, London, Sydney, Toronto, Praeger Publishers.

Freund, Julien (1976), 'Observations sur deux catégories de la dynamique polémogène; de la crise au conflit', *Communications*, No. 25, pp. 101–12.

Friedman, Sharon M. (1989) 'TMI: The Media Story', in Lynne Masel Walters, Lee Wilkins and Tim Walters (eds) *Bad Tidings. Communication and Catastrophes*, Hillsdale, New Jersey, Lawrence Erlbaum Associates Publishers, pp. 63–83.

Gallo, Giuliano (1987) 'Pompelui blu', *Cariere della Sera*, April 28.

Garthoff, Raymond L. (1988) 'Cuban Missile Crisis', *Foreign Policy*, No. 72, pp. 61–80.

Gilbert, Claude (1988) 'Situation de crise: objet d'étude. Le nuage toxique de Nantes, exemple d'une crise blanche', *Préventique*, No. 22, pp. 4–14.

Gilbert, Claude and Lagadec, Patrick (1989) 'Comment gérer les crises?', *La Recherche*, supplement to No. 212, July–August, pp. 29–34.

Gilbert, Claude and Zuanon, Jean-Paul (1990a) *Les Crues torrentielles de Nîmes (3 octobre 1988). Vers de nouvelles modalités de gestion des situ-*

ations de crise? Première analyse, Cerat, Institut d'études politiques de Grenoble.

Gilbert, Claude (1990*b*) (sous la direction de), *La Catastrophe, L'Elu et le Préfet*, Grenoble, Presses universitaires de Grenoble (actes du séminaire 'Catastrophe et gestion de crise, rôle de l'Etat et des collectivités locales', 7–8 December 1989, Château de Sassenage, Grenoble).

Gilbert, Claude (1991) *Le risque du pouvoir*, Paris, L'Harmattan.

Greilsamer, Laurent (1990) *Hubert Beuve-Méry*, Paris, Fayard.

Grimaud, Maurice (1977) *En mai, fais ce qu'il te plaît*, Paris, Stock.

Guillaumin, Jean (1979) 'Pour une méthodologie générale des recherches sur les crises', in Didier Anzieu and René Kaës (sous la direction de) *Crise, Rupture et Dépassement*, Paris, Dunod, pp. 220–54.

Hachiya, Nichihico (1955) *Hiroshima Diary*, Chapel Hill, The University of North Carolina Press, pp. 162.

Hart, Paul T (1990) *Groupthink in Government. A Study for small groups and policy failure*, University of Leiden, The Netherlands.

Hermann, Charles F. (1972) 'Some issues in the study of international crisis, in C.F. Hermann (ed.) *International Crises: Insights from Behavioral Research*, New York, The Free Press; London, Collier-Macmillan, pp. 3–17.

Holsti, Ole (1971) 'Crises, stress and decision-making', *International Social Science Journal*, No. 23, cited by Carolyne Smart and Ilan Vertinsky, Designs for Crisis Decision Units, *Administrative Science Quarterly*, December 1977, Vol. 22, pp. 640–57 (p. 642).

Huglo, Christian (1990) 'Les aspects internationaux de la prévention et du règlement des risques technologiques et naturels majeurs', *Revue français d'administration publique*, No. 53, January–March, pp. 69–77.

Irvine, Robert B. (1987) *When you are the Headline—Managing a Major News Story*, Hornewood, Illinois, Dow-Jones–Irwin.

Janis, Iriving L., (1982) *Groupthink—Psychological Studies of Policy Decisions and Fiascoes* (wnd edn), Boston, Houghton-Mifflin Company.

Jaspers, Karl (1963) *La Bombe atomique et l'Avenir de l'homme*, Paris, Buchet Chastel.

Johnson & Johnson (1982) *The Tylenol Comeback*, a publication of Johnson & Johnson Corporate Public Relations.

Kaës, René (1979) 'Introduction à l'analyse transitionelle', in Didier Anzieu and René Kaës (sous la direction de) *Crise, Rupture et Dépassement*, Paris, Dunod, pp. 1–81.

Kahn, Herman (1965) *On Escalation*, New York, Praeger.

Kahn, Jean-François (1989) *Esquisse d'une philosophie du mensonge*, Paris, Flammarion, rééd. Le Livre de Poche, No. 6839.

Kapferer, Jean-Noël (1987) *Rumeurs. Le plus vieux média du monde*, Paris, Le Seuil.

Kelly, Michael J. (1989) 'The seizure of the Turkish Embassy in Ottawa: managing terrorism and the media', in Uriel Rosenthal *et al.* (eds), pp. 117–38.

Kemeny, John *et al.* (1979) *Report of the President's Commission on the Accident at Three Mile Island*, New York, Pergamon Press.

Kennedy, Robert (1971) *Thirteen Days. A Memoir of the Cuban Missile Crisis*, New York, London, W.W. Norton & Company.

Kharbanda, O.P. and Stallworthy, E.A. (1987) *Company Rescue. How to manage a Business Turnaround*, London, Heinemann.

Kiss, Alexandre (1989) *Droit international de l'environnement*, Paris, Pédone.

Kissinger, Henry (1979) *White House Years*, Boston, Little, Brown & Company.

Kissinger, Henry (1982) *Years Of Upheaval*, Boston, Little, Brown & Company.

Kouzmin, Alexander and Jarman, Alan (1989) 'Crisis decision-making. Towards a contingent perspective decision path perspective', in Uriel Rosenthal *et al.* (eds), pp. 397–435.

Lacouture, Jean (1981) *Pierre Mendès France*, Paris, Le Seuil.

Lacouture, Jean (1989) *Enquête sur l'auteur*, Paris, Arléa.

Lagadec, Patrick (1979a), 'Faire face aux risques technologiques', *La Recherche*, Vol. 10, No. 105, pp. 1146–53.

Lagadec, Patrick (1979b), 'Le défi du risque technolgique majeur', *Futuribles*, No. 28, pp. 11–34.

Lagadec, Patrick (1981a) *Le Risque technologique majeur. Politique, risque et processus de développement*, Coll. 'Futuribles', Paris, Pergamon Press.

Lagadec, Patrick (1981b) *La Civilisation du risque. Catastrophes technologiques et responsabilité sociale*, Coll. 'Science ouverte', Paris, Le Seuil.

Lagadec, Patrick (1983) *L'Accident de Mississauga-Toronto (10–16 Novembre 1979)*, Laboratoire d'Econométrie de l'Ecole polytechnique, Ministère de l'Environnement, Service de l'environnement industriel.

Lagadec, Patrick (1984) 'Le Risque technologique et les situations de crise', *Annales des Mines*, August, pp. 41–53.

Lagadec, Patrick, in collaboration with Martine Maury (1986a) *Risques technologiques majeurs, gestion des situations de crise et vulnérabilité des grands systèmes urbains. Investigation sur le département du Val-de-Marne*, Laboratoire d'Econométrie de l'Ecole polytechnique, Groupe de prospective du ministère de l'Environnement (rapport de synthèse, rapport technique).

Lagadec, Patrick (1986*b*) *Stratégies de communication en situation de crise: l'affaire de l'explosion du transformateur au pyralène de Reims, le 14 janvier 1985*, Laboratoire d'Econométrie de l'Ecole polytechnique.

Lagadec, Patrick (1988) *Etats d'Urgence. Défaillances technologiques et déstabilisation sociale*, Coll. 'Science ouverte', Paris, Le Seuil.

Lagadec, Patrick (1990) *Prévention et conduite des situations de crise. Exploration d'initiatives récentes prises dans de grandes organisations*, Ministère chargé de l'Environnement, Laboratoire d'Econométrie de l'Ecole polytechnique.

Lalo, Anne (1988) *Information du public sur les risques technologiques majeurs*, IUT de l'université des sciences sociales de Grenoble, Ministère de l'Environnement, Rapport sur l'avant-campagne dans les Bouches-du-Rhône.

LaPorte, Todd (ed.) (1975) *Organized Social Complexity. Challenge to Politics and Policy*, Princeton, New Jersey, Princeton University Press.

Legorjus, Philippie (1990) *La Morale et l'action*, Paris, Fixot.

Neustadt, Richard E. (1980) *Presidential Power. The Politics of Leadership from FDR to Carter*, New York, John Wiley & Sons.

Meyers, Gerald C. and Holusha, John (1986) *Managing Crisis, a Positive Approach*, London, Unwin Paperback.

Milburn, Thomas (1972) 'The management of crises', in Charles F. Hermann (ed.) *International Crises: Insights from Behavioral Research*, New York, The Free Press, London, Collier-Macmillan, pp. 259–77.

Mitroff, Ian, Pauchant, Terry C. and Shrivastava, Paul (1988) 'Conceptual and empirical issues in the development for a general theory of crisis management', *Technological Forecasting and Social Change*, No. 33, pp. 83–107.

Mitroff, Ian and Kilmann, R.H. (1984) *Corporate Tragedies. Product Tampering, Sabotage and other Catastrophes*, New York, Praeger.

Morin, Edgar (1972) 'Le retour de l'événement', *Communications*, No. 18, pp. 6–20.

Morin, Edgar (1976) 'Pour une crisologie', *Communications*, No. 25, pp. 149–63.

Morin, Edgar (1990*a*) 'L'ère damocléenne', *Le Monde*, Saturday 22 September, pp. 1–2.

Morin, Edgar (1990*b*) *Introduction à la pensée complexe*, Coll. 'Communication et complexité', Paris, ESF.

Muller, Rainer (1985) 'Corporate crisis management', *Long Range Planning*, Vol. 18, pp. 38–48.

Muskie, Edmund S. and Greenwald, Daniel J. (1986) 'The Nestlé infant formula audit commission as a model', *Journal of Business Strategy*, Vol. 6, No. 4, pp. 19–23.

Négrier, François, (1979) 'L'assurance face aux risques catastrophiques', *L'Argus International*, No. 13, pp. 254–73.

Neuhold, Hanspeter (1978) 'Principles and implementation of crisis management. Lessons from the past', in D. Frei (ed.), pp. 4–18.

Neustadt, Richard and Allison, Graham (1971) 'Afterword' in Robert Kennedy, *Thirteen Days. A Memoir of the Cuban Missile Crisis*, New York, London, W.W. Norton & Company, pp. 107–50.

Nicolet, Jean-Louis, Carnino, Annick and Wanner, Jean-Claude (1989) *Catastrophes? Non merci! La prévention des risques technologiques et humains*, Paris, Masson.

Noto, René, Huguenard, Pierre and Larcan, Alain (1987) *Médecine de catastrophe*, Paris, Masson.

Pagan, Raphael D. Jr (1986) 'The Nestlé boycott: implications for strategic business planning', *Journal of Business Strategy*, Vol. 6, No. 4, pp. 12–18.

Parry, Glennys (1990) *Coping with Crises*, London, British Psychological Society and Routledge Ltd.

Pascal, Maurice (1979) *Le Droit nucléaire*, Coll. 'CEA', Paris, Eyrolles.

Pauchant, Thierry (1989) 'Le Management stratégique des crises, d'une mode éphémère à une nécessité stratégique', *Préventique*, No. 27, pp. 4–13.

Pauchant, Thierry, Mitroff, Ian and Ventolo, Gerald (1989) *Managing the Context of Information Technologies: Learning from the Hisdale Crisis*, Research Laboratory, Graduate School of Administrative Sciences, Laval University, Québec.

Perez, Yves (1988) *Prévision et gestion des crises. L'exemple américain*, Paris, Fondation pour les études de la Défense nationale.

Peters, Tom (1989) *Thriving on Chaos*, London, Pan Books.

Quarantelli, Enrico L. (1982) *Principles of Planning for Industrial and Business Disaster*, Disaster Research Center.

Quarantelli, Enrico L. (1986) *Research Findings on Organizational Behavior in Disasters and their Applicability in Developing Countries*, Ohio State University, Disaster Research Center.

Quarantelli, Enrico L. (1990) *A Preliminary Statement on the different Worlds of Science and Mass Communication: Implications for Information*

Flow between them, University of Delaware, Disaster Research Center.

Quarantelli, Enrico L. and Wenger, Dennis (1990) *A Cross-Societal Comparison of Disaster: News Reporting in Japan and the United States*, Preliminary Paper No. 146, University of Delaware, Disaster Research Center.

Regester, Michael (1989) *Crisis Management. What to Do when the Unthinkable Happens*, London, Hutchinson Business.

Rémond-Gouilloud, Martine (1989) *Du Droit de détruire*, Paris, PUF.

Revzin, Philip (1977) 'A reporter looks at media role on terror threats', *Wall Street Journal*, 14 March.

Ricoeur, Paul (1983) *Temps et Récit*, Vol. 1, Paris, Le Seuil.

Rivolier, Jean (1989) *L'Homme stressé*, Paris, PUF.

Roberts, Jonathan (1988) *Decision-Making during International Crises*, London, Macmillan Press.

Robinson, James A. (1968) 'Crisis', in D.L. Sills (ed.) *International Encyclopedia for Social Sciences*, Vol. 3, New York, Macmillan and The Free Press, pp. 510–14.

Rocard, Michel (1987) *Le Coeur à l'ouvrage*, Paris, Odile Jacob.

Rocard, Philippe and Smets, Henri (1990) 'Risque majeur et urbanisation. L'économie du risque', *Préventique*, No. 36, November–December, pp. 14–23.

Rochlin, Gene I., LaPorte, Todd and Roberts, Karlene H. (1987) 'The self-designing high-reliability organization: aircraft carrier flight operations at sea', *Naval War College Review*, Autumn, pp. 76–90.

Rocolle, Pierre (1968) *Pourquoi Dien Bien Phu?*, Paris, Flammarion.

Rosenthal, Uriel (1986) 'Crisis decision making in The Netherlands', *Netherlands' Journal of Sociology*, No. 22, pp. 103–29.

Rosenthal, Uriel, Charles, Michael T. and Hart, Paul 'T (eds) (1989) *Coping with Crises. The Management of Disasters, Riots and Terrorism*, Springfield, Illinois, Charles C. Thomas Publisher.

Scanlon, Joseph (1975) 'Crisis communications in Canada', in B.D. Singes (ed.) *Communications in Canadian Society*, Toronto.

Scanlon, Joseph (1979) 'Day One in Darwin. Once again the vital role of communications', in Joan Innes Reid (ed.) *Planning for People in Natural Disasters*, Townsville, Queensland, Australia, James Cook University of North Queensland, pp. 133–55.

Scanlon, Joseph (1981) 'Police et médias: problèmes et tactiques propres aux prises d'otages et actes de terrorisme', *Journal du Collège Canadien de la Police*, Vol. 5, No. 3, pp. 139–59.

Scanlon, Joseph (1982) *Crisis Communications: The Ever Present Gremlins*, Emergency Communication Unit, Reference to Comcon 82, Arnprior, Ontario, 26 May 1982.

Scanlon, Joseph (1982) *The Miramichi Earthquakes: The Media respond to an Invisible Emergency*, Emergency Communication Unit, ECRU field report 82/1, Ottawa, School of Journalism, Carleton University.

Scanlon, Joseph (1984) 'Prises d'otages et médias: le crime en direct', *Journal du Collège Canadien de la Police*, Vol. 8, No. 2, pp. 169–94.

Scanlon, Joseph (1987) *The Gander Air Crash, December 1985*, Emergency Communications Research Unit, Emergency Preparedness Canada, Ottawa.

Scanlon, Joseph (1989*a*) 'Toxic chemical and emergency management: the evacuation of Mississauga, Ontario, Canada', in Uriel Rosenthal *et al.* (eds), pp. 303–22.

Scanlon, Joseph (1989*b*) 'The hostage taker, the terrorist, the media: partners in public crime', in Lynne Masel Walters, Lee Wilkins and Tim Walters (eds) *Bad Tidings. Communication and Catastrophe*, Lawrence Erlbaum Associates Publishers, pp. 115–30.

Scanlon, Joseph (1990*a*) *EMS in Halifax after the December 6, 1917 Explosion: Testing Quarantelli's Theories with Historical Data*, Toronto, Carleton University.

Scanlon, Joseph (1990*b*) *Federalism and Canadian Emergency Response: Control, Cooperation and Conflict*, paper prepared for the Research Committee on Disasters, Madrid, International Sociological Association.

Scanlon, Joseph and Alldred, Suzanne (1982) 'Media coverage of disasters: the same old story', *Emergency Planning Digest*, No. 9, pp. 13–19.

Scanlon, Joseph, Colin, Daniel, Duffy, Andrew, Osborne, Gillian and Whitten, Jonathan (1984) *The Pemberton Valley Floods. BC's Tiniest Village Responds to a Major Emergency*, Ottawa, Emergency Communication Research Unit.

Scanlon, Joseph and Prawzick, Angela (1986) *Inter-Agency Communications Failure in Emergency Response: Planning is the Answer*, Paper presented at the World Congress of Sociology in New Delhi.

Scanlon, Joseph and Hiscott, Robert D. (1990) *Making the EMS System Fit the Plan: Individual Behavior and Organizational Response to the July 31st, 1987, Edmonton Tornado*, Paper prepared for the Research Committee on Disasters, Madrid, International Sociological Association.

Schelling, Thomas (1963) *The Strategy of Conflict*, Cambridge, Harvard University Press.

Scott, John C. and Freibaum, Jerry (1990) *A Review of the Effectiveness of Communications During and Shortly After the Loma Prieta California Earthquake*, Public Service Satellite Consortium.

Shrivastava, Paul (1987a) *Bhopal. Anatomy of a Crisis*, Cambridge, Mass., Balinger Publishing Co.

Shrivastava, Paul (1987b) 'Are we ready for another Three Mile Island, Bhopal, Tylenol?', *Industrial Crisis Quarterly*, Vol. 1, No. 1, pp. 2–4.

Smart, Carolyn and Vertinsky, Ilan (1977) 'Designs for crisis decision units', *Administrative Science Quarterly*, December, Vol. 22, pp. 640–57.

Smets, Henri (1985) 'La réparation des dommages à l'environnement causés par les catastrophes industrielles', colloque sur les risques naturels et technologiques majeurs, aspects juridiques, 14–16 October 1985, Toulouse, in *Droit et Ville*, No. 21.

Sorensen, Theodore C. (1963) *Decision-Making in the White House* (Foreword by John F. Kennedy), New York, Columbia University Press.

Spanier, J. Games (1984) *Nations Play*, New York, Holt, Rinehart & Winston.

Starn, Randolf (1976) 'Métamorphose d'une notion. Les historiens et la 'crise', *Communications*, No. 25, pp. 4–18.

Stephenson, D. (1984) 'Are you making the best of your crisis?', *Emergency Planning Digest*, October–December, pp. 2–4.

Stourdzé, Yves (1979) 'Hypothèses sur la relation catastrophe/réseau', *Futuribles*, No. 28, pp. 126–30.

Sun Tzu (1972) *L'Art de la Guerre*, Coll. de poche 'Champs', Paris, Flammarion.

Vermont, André (1988) 'Italy: alerte aux pamplemousses empoisonnées en provenance de Jaffa', *Liberation*, April.

Veron, Eliseo (1981) *Construire l'événement. Les Médias et l'accident de Three Mile Island*, Paris, Editions de Minuit.

Vickers, Sir Geoffrey (1965) *The Art of Judgment. A Study of Policy Making*, London, Harper & Row.

Vidal-Naquet, Pierre (1990) 'La crise de Tours', in Claude Gilbert (sous la direction de) *La Catastrophe, l'Elu et le Préfet*, Presses universitaires de Grenoble, pp. 268–81.

Viveret, Patrick (1989) *L'Evaluation des politiques et des actions publiques*, Coll. des Rapports officiels, Rapport au Premier ministre, La Documentation française.

Wenger, Dennis and Quarantelli, Enrico (1989) *Local Mass Media Operations, Problems and Products in Disasters*, report series No. 19, Disaster Research Center, University of Delaware.

Wiener, Antony J. and Kahn, Herman (1962) *Crisis and Arms Control*, Harmony-on-Hudson, N.Y., Hudson Institute.

Name Index

Case Index